# THE STONEHENGE PEOPLE

# THE
# STONEHENGE
# PEOPLE

*Aubrey Burl*

**J.M. Dent & Sons Ltd**
London  Melbourne

First published 1987
Text and line drawings © Aubrey Burl 1987

This book is set in 10½/12 Baskerville by
Input Typesetting Ltd, London SW19 8DR
Printed in Great Britain by
Mackays of Chatham Ltd for
J. M. Dent & Sons Ltd
Aldine House, 33 Welbeck Street, London W1M 8LX


British Library Cataloguing in Publication Data

Burl, Aubrey
  The Stonehenge people.
  1. Stonehenge (England)
  I. Title
  936.2'319    DA142

ISBN 0–460–04485–0

# Contents

# List of photographs

*To Margaret and Geoffrey*

The stones of Stonehenge are 'as prodigious
as any tales I ever heard of them, and worth
going this journey to see. God knows what
their use was!'

Samuel Pepys, *Diary*, June 11, 1668


'Tis of it self so singular, and receives so
little light from history, that almost every
one has advanc'd a new notion'.

William Camden, *Britannia*, 1695

# Preface

By the eighteenth century Stonehenge was a tourist attraction. The mystery of the great stones rearing out of Salisbury Plain lured visitors to count the tumbled pillars, to chip bits off them for souvenirs and to speculate about their origin. No one could understand the ruin. Daniel Defoe refused to guess: 'Tis indeed a reverend piece of antiquity, and 'tis a great loss that the true history of it is not known.'

When I first saw Stonehenge, years ago, in the empty sunshine of a Sunday morning, it was still a mystery. The place was quiet. Near the ring a custodian in his hut tore a ticket off a roll and one was free to wander peacefully amongst the stones, wondering what the circle was. Forty years later it is very different. In efforts to diminish the damage caused by hundreds of thousands of visitors each year the site has been gravelled, ungravelled, duckboarded and unboarded, a sprawling carpark has been built, a drab underpass like an unfinished fallout shelter has been constructed, the circle has been closed, opened, roped-off, mini-models have been displayed, taken away, mobile display boards have been arranged, re-arranged, new approaches have been proposed, but in all this turmoil Stonehenge has remained an enigma. Whether inside the ring or staring wistfully at the remote stones the puzzle persists.

> Pile of Stonehenge! So proud to hint yet keep
> Thy secrets. . . .
>
> William Wordsworth, *The Prelude*, XIII

The secrets endure because so few clues have been left for our enquiries, not because the ring has been ignored. To the contrary, there are hundreds of articles and learned papers, scores of books, a dozen excavations to be referred to. Antiquarians like William Stukeley have left records of features that no longer exist. Astronomers, Sir Norman Lockyer, 'Peter' Newham, Dr Gerald Hawkins, Professor Alexander Thom, have speculated on what sightlines were laid out by the builders. The researches of Stukeley, Stone, Thomas, Howard and, above all, of Atkinson have demonstrated the probable source of the stones, the methods of construction, the age of the monument.

Today, what is needed for the people who visit Stonehenge is an understanding of the people who built Stonehenge. It is from those people, their possessions, their way of life and the manner of their burials that a fuller picture of the stone circle may come. This book is about those long-dead men and women and their almost alien beliefs, and it has been written from excavation reports, from the objects in the delectable museums of Salisbury and Devizes and, most, from months of delightful fieldwork in the cool, fresh spaces of Salisbury Plain.

It is with gratitude that I acknowledge the help of colleagues and friends whose conversations about facts and theories contributed so much: Dr Douglas Heggie and Dr Clive Ruggles, as well as Professor Derek Simpson who not only offered opinions but was generous in the lending of equipment without which the surveying of the earthen long barrows around Stonehenge would have been very difficult. I am especially indebted to Professor Richard Atkinson not only for his deep understanding of Stonehenge problems but also for his information about the existence of an unsuspected Stukeley manuscript in Cardiff Public Library.

I also owe much to the kindness of others: Dr Peter Berridge who has re-examined Hawley's excavation notebooks and who freely discussed his conclusions with me; Tony Baker who sent me yellowing cuttings and photographs of Stonehenge; Ted Kipper and his dog while I was planning at Stonehenge; Major and Mrs Rasch who allowed me to see their lovely home at Heale House where Prince Charles hid in 1651 after the Battle of Worcester, overcoming his boredom by surreptitiously counting the stones at the nearby Stonehenge; Clare Conybeare of Salisbury Museum, Dr Paul Robinson of Devizes Museum, and the Bodleian Museum, Oxford, for the provision of photographs from their collections; and the former Department of the Environment who permitted me to tread once again inside the roped-off ring where, for the first time in decades, wild flowers grow. I must also acknowledge the kindness of John Wainwright and Macmillan London Ltd for permission to use the quotation at the beginning of Chapter Nine.

My thanks are particularly extended to the staff of Dent's both for their enthusiasm and care.

More than 800 years ago Henry, archdeacon of Huntingdon, wrote of Stonehenge, 'Nor can anyone conceive by what art such great stones have been so raised, or why they were there constructed'. It is my hope that this book will offer the reader some, if not all, the answers.

# Stonehenge: excavations, destruction and repair

| | |
|---|---|
| Pre-Roman | Stone 55 and lintel 156 had fallen. Roman sherds around but not underneath them. |
| Pre 1575 AD | Many lintels, including 104, missing. |
| 1620 | The Duke of Buckingham dug at the centre. |
| pre-1666 | Stone 59 had fallen. Many bluestones missing. |
| 1723 | Lord Pembroke and Stukeley dug near centre. Visitors chipping pieces off the stones. |
| c. 1723 | Thomas Hayward, the owner, introduced rabbits onto the site. |
| 1740 | Stones 14 and 48 leaning. Stones 8, 15, 19 and 26 damaged. |
| c. 1750 | Stone 14 fell. |
| 1771 | Rabbit burrows apparent under Slaughter Stone. Stone 48 leaning. |
| 1797 | Trilithon 57–58 fell on January 3. |
| 1798 | William Cunnington dug near the circle-stones. |
| 1802 | Cunnington dug at the centre on September 28. |
| 1810 | On April 24 Cunnington left a bottle of port under the Slaughter Stone. Found, spoiled, by Hawley in 1920. |
| c. 1839 | Captain Beamish dug at the centre. |
| By 1880 | Bluestones 35, 64, 65 and 66 were mere stumps. |
| 1900 | Stone 22 and its lintel fell on December 31. |
| 1901 | Gowland straightened Stone 56 and set it in concrete. In 1660 it had been leaning at 75°; in 1720, 70°; in 1870, 66°; and in 1901, 60½°. |
| 1919–26 | Hawley's excavations. South-east half of entire area stripped to bedrock. Aubrey Holes and Y & Z Holes located. |
| 1919–20 | Stones 6 and 7 straightened and set in concrete. |
| 1920 | Stones 1, 2, 29 and 30 straightened and set in concrete. |

| | |
|---|---|
| 1950 | Excavations by Atkinson, Piggott and Stone at Aubrey Holes 31 and 32. First C-14 date for Stonehenge obtained, 1848±275 bc. |
| 1953 | Excavations on the avenue. Carvings noticed on Stone 53. Others discovered on stones 3, 4, 5 and 57. |
| 1954 | Excavations on the ditch and bank. Q & R Holes defined. |
| 1956 | Further excavations within the circle. |
| 1958 | Trilithon 57–58 re-erected and set in concrete. Altar Stone partly excavated. |
| 1959 | Stones 4, 5 and 60 straightened and set in concrete |
| 1963 | Stone 23 fell in a gale. |
| 1964 | Stone 23 re-erected. It and Stones 28, 53 and 54 set in concrete. |
| 1978 | Excavation by Atkinson and Evans in ditch. Beaker burial found. |
| 1979–80 | Excavations by Pitts near Heel Stone. Second stonehole found there. |
| 1987 | Of the 160 or more original stones 68 are completely lost and 19 others are reduced to stumps. |

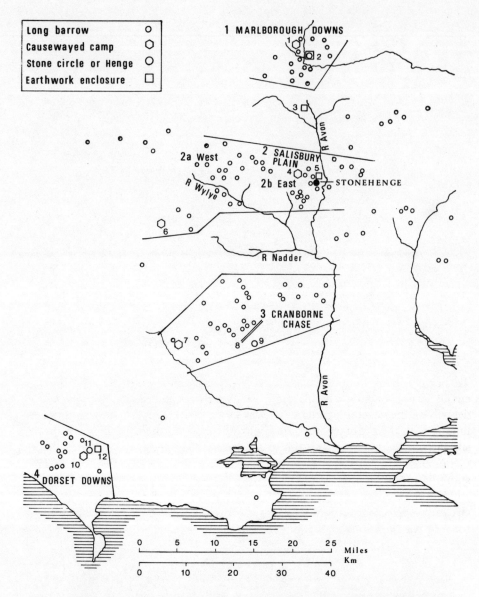

Fig. 1. The Five Great Regions of Neolithic Wessex. Sites: (1) Windmill
Hill; (2) Avebury; (3) Marden; (4) Robin Hood's Ball; (5)
Durrington Walls; (6) Whitesheet Hill; (7) Hambledon Hill; (8) the
Dorset Cursus; (9) Knowlton; (10) Maiden Castle; (11)
Maumbury Rings; (12) Mount Pleasant.

# Introduction

*I cannot but lament that so little is known of the authors of such a monument.*

William Camden, *Britannia*

To begin a book about Stonehenge by writing about other British stone circles is like starting a book about the Hanging Gardens of Babylon by describing the vegetable patches of prehistoric farmers. It is comparing the unique with the ordinary, the latest with the earliest, the complex with the simple and the massive with the small. Yet it is essential.

Stonehenge is a maverick. It is a megalithic oddity and for any understanding of it one must know something of the other, earlier rings which still stand, hundreds of them, on the stony uplands of Britain. These stone circles are referred to often in this book because they provide answers to some of the questions about Stonehenge:

(1)  Who built Stonehenge?
(2)  Was the latitude of Stonehenge deliberately chosen because it was astronomically important?
(3)  Why is the outlying pillar, the Heel Stone, *not* in line with the midsummer sunrise?
(4)  What was the Heel Stone intended for?
(5)  Was the number of the 56 Aubrey Holes significant?
(6)  Why was the Altar Stone different from the other bluestones?
(7)  Why did Stonehenge have a circle within a circle, unlike the majority of rings in the British Isles?
(8)  What was the purpose of the Four Stations rectangle?

*1*

(9)   Why was Stonehenge, the heaviest stone circle in the world, erected in a region where there was no good building stone?

(10)  Why did the final circle of sarsens have lintels on top of it?

(11)  Why are there five archways, the trilithons, in a horseshoe-shaped setting at the centre of Stonehenge?

(12)  Why do those archways rise in height towards the south-west?

The most important of these questions is the first. Who built Stonehenge? The men and women who constructed and used the circle lie buried in the countryside around it and to understand Stonehenge they must be understood. This book is concerned with the beliefs that caused Neolithic and Bronze Age communities to create a powerful monument in which the stones were arranged in circles and horseshoes whose shapes must have been significant but whose patterns have seldom been considered. No sensible study of the ring can overlook the clues that exist, crumbled and scattered in the pits, the settlements and the cemeteries on Salisbury Plain within a few miles of each other and barely an hour's walk from Stonehenge itself. It is not enough to examine Stonehenge and offer ingenious theories about its geometry and astronomy. If the theories conflict with what is known about the people who erected the stones, then the theories are wrong.

Very little information about its builders has come from Stonehenge itself: some tools, some broken pots, some burnt bone. It is as though the stones had been raised and then almost instantly abandoned to the winds blowing in across the empty plain. 'But what the Devil is it?' exclaimed Lord Byron in *Don Juan*, looking despairingly at the ring, and two hundred years later we are still puzzling over the ruin.

Stonehenge has been collapsing ever since it was put up. Men wrecked it. Pillars were smashed into fragments and carried away for footbridges and walls. Stones were chipped for souvenirs. But it was the wind blowing in from the south-west over the long, cold centuries that was the real destroyer. With it came the rains, trickling down the western faces of the stones, seeping into the chalkcut sockets, freezing in the winter, eroding the already unfirm stoneholes. Stones fell. Turf crawled over the crushed Altar Stone. Today, only flawed wreckage remains.

Antiquarians frequently described the destruction. Their observations and excavations show what has been damaged, what has been altered or removed. No one engaged in the study of Stonehenge could advance far without realising how much is owed to these early investigators, a distinguished gathering of Johns, Williams and Richards whose explorations discovered so much and whose reports, sadly, are often forgotten or disregarded.

The first was Inigo Jones (1573–1652), architect of the Banqueting House at Whitehall, who dug into Stonehenge in 1620 and, pleasingly, wrote down what had been found. John Aubrey (1626–97), 'never off horseback' in his search for antiquities, drew the first good plan of the circle in 1666 after detecting the faintest traces of some overgrown holes that are now named after him. The 'curious and credulous' fine fieldworker, William Stukeley (1687–1765), was Stonehenge's first great archivist, recognising the outlines of the Avenue and the cursus to its north, noting inconspicuous features in the stone circle, excavating barrows and drawing their sections before taking holy orders in 1729, becoming obsessed with druids and going quickly downhill as an archaeologist.

The architect John Wood (1704–54), having seen the plans of Inigo Jones, whimsically laid out the centre of Bath in imitation of Stonehenge so that to walk up Gay Street into the Circus is to follow the line of an imaginary avenue leading into the sarsen ring. Wood made the first accurate set of measurements for Stonehenge despite vile weather and two viler ruffians who eyed his horse and his fob-watch with equal greed. John Smith (*fl* 1770), an inoculator of the smallpox, rented Boscombe House, then used as a hospital for smallpox patients, in a village near Stonehenge. He was the first of a cavalcade of astronomers to develop the concept of Stonehenge as an observatory.

At the beginning of the 19th century Sir Richard Colt Hoare (1758–1838), a rich landowner living in his Palladian house at Stourhead, now visited by thousands each year, subsidised the extensive excavations of his colleague, William Cunnington (1754–1810), a wool merchant of Heytesbury, whose health was such that doctors told him 'I must ride out or die – I preferred the former'. Ride out he did with his pick-axed digger, John Parker, plunging into over 450 barrows and into parts of Stonehenge. Hoare conscientiously published the results of Cunnington's work in two sumptuous volumes, *Ancient Wiltshire*, 1812 and 1819.

Hoare and Cunnington were followed in their Wiltshire researches by John Thurnam (1810–73) of Yorkshire, who became Medical Superintendent of the Wiltshire County Asylum. Interested in the physiognomy of prehistoric skeletons, he dug into 94 barrows between 1849 and 1873, describing the skulls but often not bothering to give details of the burial mounds.

Another Stonehenge pioneer was Lt-Col. William Hawley (1851–1941), who steadfastly excavated at Stonehenge, almost single-handed, between 1919 and 1926. His methods have ever since been condemned. Much of the criticism has been unfair, but it has endured because Hawley published only a series of interim reports. Yet his notebooks reveal his systematic approach and his reputation deserves revision. He was so disregarded on his death that, despite all his work in Wiltshire, his local Society did not give him a proper obituary but merely quoted an excerpt from another archaeological journal.

Since his time there have been further research excavations at Stonehenge, as mentioned in Professor Richard Atkinson's *Stonehenge*. It is on such works that this book is partly based, reconsidering the accounts, revising out-of-date interpretations, examining the things that have been found and which are now in the museums of Devizes and Salisbury. Together with personal fieldwork, the reports, from Jones to Atkinson, and the objects compose a rich picture of life at the time of Stonehenge.

That time is now known. The scientific radiocarbon process of dating organic material such as charcoal and bone was producing 'dates' that were too young. By checking the results against a time-frame provided by the annual growth-rings of long-lived trees like the Californian bristlecone-pine, dendrochronologists were able to correct C–14 dates and compile accurate calibration tables for archaeologists to use. The first 'date' obtained for Stonehenge, 1848 ± 275 bc – meaning that there were two chances to one that the organic material had died between 2123 and 1573 bc – was updated to about 2300 BC, the capital letters indicating that this was a corrected date. At present the earliest date for the site is about 3200 BC, calibrated from 2460 ± 60 bc for an antler in the ditch, and the latest is about 975 BC, recalculated from an assay of 800 ± 100 bc from animal bones at the far end of the avenue. Even allowing for imprecisions, it can be assumed that Stonehenge remained in use for well over 2000 years, twice as long as any European cathedral.

The huge lintelled sarsens that most people think of as Stonehenge were, in fact, the last stones to be brought to a complicated structure that had undergone several changes. In its beginning the site was a simple, circular earthwork or 'henge', an open space bordered by a chalk bank and large enough to hold several hundred people. Outside the entrance stood a weather-roughened stone, the well-known Heel Stone. For a thousand years, forty or more unremembered generations, this earthwork continued to be the meeting-place of native farmers, unaltered except for the digging-out of a circle of pits, the Aubrey Holes, just within the bank.

Then, as late as 2200 BC, people brought some Welsh bluestones to the site, started to set them up in two circles, one inside the other, and constructed an avenue, undeviatingly straight, up the northern hillside towards the henge's entrance. Abruptly the work stopped. The bluestones were removed and in their place dozens of massive sarsens were dragged a score of heavy miles from the Marlborough Downs. A horseshoe-shaped setting of five archways, the trilithons, was erected. Around it, enclosing it in a ring of dark stone, the pillars of the outer circle were raised, lintels lifted and laid along their tops. It was labour that took years and yet even this monstrous effort was not enough. Later, the bluestones were restored, set up in a circle, dismantled, arranged differently, a process of change as ceaseless as the drifting waters of the River Avon to the east. The avenue was extended down to the river-banks, but only in part, one side finished, the other left undone as the work-gangs eventually gave up 2000 years after their ancestors had begun, abandoning the task in the rains of the Late Bronze Age.

Why Stonehenge was built, why it was rebuilt, why it was designed as it was, what its meaning was, these questions were asked by Richard Atkinson whose excellent book, *Stonehenge*, is the authoritative account of what is known archaeologically about the site. He answered his questions decisively: 'There is one short, simple and perfectly correct answer: we do not know, and we shall probably never know.'

This may be over-pessimistic. Stonehenge is still yielding information. It is not many years since carvings of a dagger and axes were noticed on its stones. Since then its age has been determined. Nor does it exist in isolation. Nearby are the worn-down banks of the Durrington Walls settlement. Against it is the site of Woodhenge. Half a mile to the west, just north of Stonehenge, is the outline of the mysterious Cursus that Stukeley thought was a race-course. North-west of it, desolate on War Department land, is the even earlier causewayed enclosure of Robin Hood's Ball. In the hills only a few miles away but 2000 years later, small farming settlements such as Thorny Down with fields and stockades and droveways and once with small thatched huts, storage pits and cooking hollows show how comfortably people were living at a time when Stonehenge was ancient.

Around, in the encircling landscape, are burial mounds, first the long barrows, later the round, a group to the north by the Cursus, a tree-covered line at the King Barrows to the north-east, the famous Normanton cemetery on the ridge to the south, even a fine grassy mound a mere hundred yards from the ring itself. These are the graves of the men and women who used Stonehenge.

Within three miles of the ring there are sixteen Neolithic long barrows, one of them a tree-darkened monster on the rising ground at Lake in sight of Stonehenge a long mile to the north. Over sixty such enormous mounds survive on Salisbury Plain within a few hours' walk of the stones and they cover the remains of men, women and children who lived on the Plain long before Stonehenge and whose traditions shaped the customs of the first builders. Their bones contain something of the story of their lives, their diet, the diseases and injuries they suffered, their early deaths, their beliefs. Their burials lie under the higher, wide end of the barrows, between NNE and SSE, hinting at some interest in astronomy.

Both buried bones and cremations provide details of the people's physique. Primitive surgery was apparent in a mound near the Cursus. A rounded piece of bone as big as a saucer had been scraped and scratched with a flint knife out of a young man's skull. The wound failed to heal and he died. Elsewhere, superstitions were evident. In one barrow Sir Richard Colt Hoare and William Cunnington found a man's skeleton. By it was a strange, kidney-shaped pebble, striped and 'spotted all over with very small white specks: and after dipping it in water, it assumes a sea-green colour'.[1] Almost two centuries before this John Aubrey owned another talisman from a barrow at Tidpit in Hampshire. Labourers levelling its top to make a base for a windmill dug up an urn, a bronze dagger and 'a Tusk of a Boare with a hole made in it, as if to putt a string in it. I had it but gave it to the . . . Royal Society'.[2] Colt Hoare commented of another find, 'The Britons seem to have attached particular qualities to certain stones; and this, probably, may have been suspended as an amulet from the neck'.[3]

Protective stones such as this, and fertility charms, remind us that if we can understand the beliefs and fears of those people we may have a better understanding of why Stonehenge was built. Stukeley noticed in a round barrow that he had dug into that 'the bones lay north and south, the head to the north'. Hoare and Cunnington remarked on the same phenomenon. One barrow at Winterbourne Stoke held 'two skeletons lying by the side of each other, with their heads to the north . . . one of them (from the size of the bones) was a tall and stout man: all their teeth very firm and remarkably even'.[4]

Care over the direction in which corpses should be laid suggest that the sun and moon were important to these distant societies. Skulls deliberately broken after death, excessively deep graves, mutilation of the body reveal that the dead were feared and that precautions were taken to prevent the return of their malicious ghosts.

Long before his excavations at Stonehenge William Hawley investigated a barrow near the present Bulford army barracks. In it, equally spaced apart, heads to the centre and lying on their left sides, were the skeletons of three men. They were doubled up as though their corpses had been tightly trussed. In every case, although all the other bones were in place, their forearms and hands were missing, ensuring that even in death they could commit no mischief.[5] From their possessions these men had lived when Stonehenge's bluestone circles were being erected, but whatever they had been in life their mourners made sure that they would lie powerless in their graves. They were not exceptional. Some other corpses were dismembered in this way. At Litton Cheney in Dorset a man under a similar barrow had had his dead hands amputated. They were thrown into his grave-pit before his corpse was buried above them.[6]

These are cameos of life at the time of Stonehenge. They give the impression of skilful, adaptable people with an intense awareness of the dead. This may be why the circle was built, why the sun and moon were linked to the stones, why there were carvings of charms and amulets, why burnt human bone lay in the pits that coiled like a chain around the ring.

Talismen against evil, astronomy, tools of stone and flint, weapons of bronze, jewellery of gold and amber, deep graves, brief lives, these clues have survived from the forgotten rituals that shift like shadows amongst the stones of Stonehenge. The questions remain to be answered. This book begins with the first of them, the people whose descendants were to build Stonehenge.

Fig. 2. (a) The Stones of Stonehenge
      (b) The Outlying Features of Stonehenge.

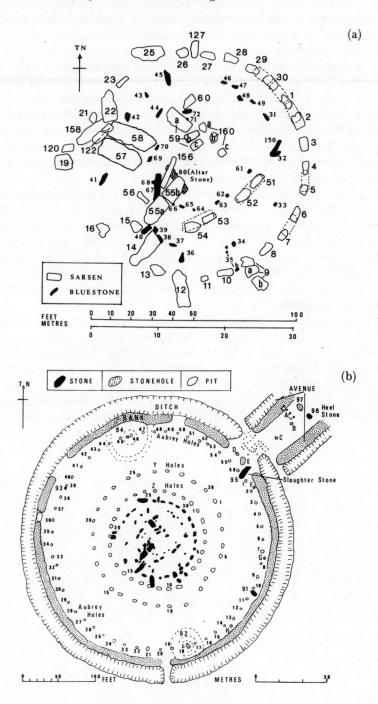

It is necessary to explain the numbering system used to identify the stones and other features at Stonehenge. Following the unsuccessful attempts of earlier workers, it was Flinders Petrie, later to win fame as an Egyptologist, who in 1877 proposed the system that has been used ever since.

He numbered the stones of the great circle clockwise from the north-east, starting with the outer sarsen ring and ending with the outlying stones. Numbers 1–30 were the upright sarsens in the circle, 31–49 the ruined bluestone circle inside them, 51–60 the uprights of the trilithons, 61–72 the inner horseshoe of bluestones, and 80 the Altar Stone. The rectangle of the Four Stations outside the circle, again starting at the north-east, became 91–94, 95 the Slaughter Stone lying by the entrance to the earthwork, and 96 the outlier of the Heel Stone. The stonehole discovered in 1979 by the Heel Stone logically became number 97.

Petrie identified each lintel by adding 100 to the higher-numbered of its supports. The lintel of the eastern trilithon, 51–52, became 152. The three lintels in position at the north-east of the sarsen circle, resting on the tops of stones 29, 30, 1 and 2 became numbers 130, 101 and 102. Prostrate fragments were lettered according to their stone so that the two pieces of the gigantic fallen trilithon pillar 55 became 55a and 55b, the latter lying on top of the fallen Altar Stone. It was an ingenious scheme and it has remained workable.

The 56 Aubrey Holes were first numbered by Hawley, their excavator, in 1921. They also run clockwise from the north-east entrance of the henge, first the excavated pits, 1–32, followed by 33–54 which have been located but not excavated, and, finally, numbers 55 and 56 which are the last, lying across the entrance just to the NNW of number 1.

The Y and Z Holes, now grassed over around the sarsen circle, were similarly numbered by Hawley, 1–30, clockwise from the north-east.

# 1

# Tombs in an empty land
# 4200 – 3500 BC

*As for their manner of living, the Britons were then a savage and barbarous People, knowing no use at all of Garments.*

Inigo Jones, *Stonehenge Restor'd*, 5

It was a dark land. Except for the higher slopes of the hills and the places where the oozing meanders of rivers choked and spread into swamps, the whole countryside was an unbroken forest. Animals moved in it, the wolf, the nervous deer, the sudden slithering of a snake like an illusion in the mottle of leaves, but it was a silent land and in it there were few human beings. It was a mild land of winter rains and warm summers in which droughts were rare. The soils were undisturbed and fertile, but everywhere they were overshadowed by the trees, birches and pines in the north, an oak wilderness in Ireland, expanses of woodland in Wales and Cornwall, and, on Salisbury Plain, the tall misty greens of alders alongside the streams and rivers. Beyond them spread patchy miles of scrub and grassland, with thickets of waving hazel fringing the darkness of the forest at the heart of the chalk upland.[1]

Occasional clearings of blackened, barkless trees showed where semi-nomadic natives had set fire to the forest, creating spaces of fresh vegetation to attract the deer. But this was a quiet, almost untravelled country with few trails to follow, an unexploited and enticing landscape to the first farmers of the British Isles when they crossed the sea from the European mainland over six thousand years ago.

To them the coastline may have appeared as forbidding as the shores of North America to the Pilgrim Fathers in 1621. As William Bradford, their leader, wrote: 'And for the season it was winter, and they that know the winters of that country know them to be sharp and violent, and subject to cruel and fierce storms, dangerous to travel to known places, much more to search an unknown coast. Besides, what could they see but a hideous and desolate wilderness, full of wild beasts and wild men?' The words might have been those of the pioneering Neolithic families, cramped in their leather-lined boats with bundles of possessions, flint tools, seed corn, tethered calves, as they searched the south coast for a river mouth and safety. Some groups passed the jagged landmark of the Needles and then came at last to the shelter of the River Avon that led inland to the rich chalk soils of Salisbury Plain.

Such an expedition may have had a score of boats, perhaps two hundred people linked by kinship and travelling together for protection before claiming their own territories when the journey ended where Salisbury now stands and where three rivers converged in an area of muddy wetland. The Plain was divided by them, the Avon flowing in from the north, the Nadder from the west and, between them, the twisting winding Wylye from the north-west, wriggling between the jumble of upland and valley before it merged with the Nadder near present-day Wilton.

Along these waters the people looked for a clearing where they could fell trees with flint axes and where they could plant wheat. Alongside the sowed patches they built sturdy timber houses. 'The habitations of the Britons were rude and incommodious, being little more than hovels', guessed Hutchinson in 1794,[2] but he was wrong. Remains of these early homes (Table 1) have shown them to be spacious rectangular cabins about the size of a modern through lounge and big enough for a family of a man, woman and children. With a framework of heavy, squared beams and with a pitched roof of thatch or turf, these were solidly constructed buildings with floors of compacted earth or clay. Their average size of 29 × 16 feet or 464 square feet (9 × 5 m or 45 s.m.) compared well with the 600 s.f. (56 s.m.) of the 19th century Hebridean blackhouses that were split into a living space for the family with one-third left for a cattle annexe. Indeed, a close comparison can be made with the Neolithic house at Ballyglass in Co. Mayo dated to about 3400 BC.[3] Discovered under a megalithic tomb during excavations in 1970, its foundations measured 42 × 20 feet (13 × 6 m), subdivided into three compartments of which one at the northern end may have been a stall for animals.

No certain evidence of any early Neolithic house has been found on Salisbury Plain, perhaps because the weathering of the chalk has eliminated all trace of these postholes and just as possibly because the remains are buried or destroyed under the foundations of today's villages and farms in the sheltered, well-watered hollows of the Plain. It can be assumed, however, that the settlement pattern was one of separate families farming the land in accepted land-holdings and set apart by a mile or two from their neighbours.

**TABLE 1. Dimensions of some early Neolithic houses**

| Site | Dimensions in Feet | Square Feet | Square Metres | Date from C–14 Assay in corrected years |
|------|------|------|------|------|
| Ballyglass, Co. Mayo | 42 × 20 | 840 | 78 | c. 3400 BC |
| Ballynagilly, Co. Tyrone | 29 × 21 | 609 | 57 | c. 4450 BC |
| Clegyr Boia, Dyfed | 24 × 12 | 288 | 27 | – |
| Fengate, Cambridgeshire | 28 × 23 | 644 | 60 | c. 3170 BC |
| Haldon, Devon | 25 × 16 | 400 | 37 | – |
| Hembury, Devon | 23 × 12 | 276 | 26 | – |
| Lismore Fields, Derbyshire | 49 × 16 | 784 | 73 | – |
| Lough Gur, Co. Limerick | 26 × 18 | 468 | 44 | – |
| Mount Pleasant, Glamorgan | 19 × 8 | 152 | 14 | – |
| Ronaldsway, Isle of Man | 24 × 16 | 384 | 36 | – |
| AVERAGE | 29 × 16 (=) | 464 (=) | 43 | |

It was an established and conservative way of life and it shaped their social and spiritual needs in a communal system with each family exchanging produce and goods with others in the region, meeting regularly, intermarrying, co-operating in tasks beyond the ability of a single group. On Salisbury Plain there were probably several areas of population in the vicinity of today's villages and towns – around Warminster in the west; by Grafton; at Tilshead and Amesbury in the central districts near the Avon.

What we know of the people themselves, people without literature, must come from the physical objects that have been preserved, usually incomplete or broken, often unrepresentative of more perishable possessions. Yet imperfect though it is, this material is very revealing about the first farmers of Salisbury Plain and their way of life.

Despite the many differences between them, these were, in general, a short, slight people, light-boned, more probably dark-haired than blonde, of Mediterranean appearance rather than Nordic. Tentative reconstructions of faces from skulls found in the long chambered tomb of Lanhill near Avebury suggest an almost American Indian likeness with high cheekbones, long narrow (dolichocephalic) heads and sharp noses.[4] Of their language we have no knowledge. It is just possible that a few words for natural features of the landscape have survived in a distorted form, *afn* or *afon* for river being an example, elementary numbers for *one, two* and *three* which are common to many European language, but of their oral traditions, the recited poems and ancestor-lists and myths nothing remains.

Their livelihood was mixed farming, with little hunting, simply the hard breaking of the soil with wooden and bone tools, coppicing the hazels for hurdling, sowing the fields, women making the coil-built, round-bottomed pots in brushwood kilns, scraping and slicing animal skins for clothing, the men driving the cattle to the uplands in spring, looking for nodules of surface flint that could be prised from the chalk for their axes, knives, blades and leaflike arrowheads. The whole family were engaged in harvesting, flailing, winnowing, parching, grinding the wheat and barley into sustaining flour, the men bringing the herds down from the hillsides in Autumn, culling the older, weaker beasts and, as the year darkened to its chilling end, felling trees to expose further land for cultivation, stripping the elms of their bark and leaves for winter fodder, a cycle of laborious husbandry. This round of physical effort was repeated year after long year and its disfiguring strains are apparent in the skeletons of these first farmers.

These were young people, many of them suffering from the hardships of their manner of living. Osteoarthritis was a major affliction, a degenerative condition that affected the cartilage and adjoining bones of the hips, the knees, finger-ends and the lower spine, almost unknown in former times but becoming prevalent in the Neolithic Age with the muscular stress of dragging away tree-trunks, ploughing without traction animals, the carrying of cumbersome loads. It was 'the scourge of the community' from the evidence of bones in the chambered tombs of West Kennet and Lanhill twenty miles north of Stonehenge and it was widespread in the many skeletons under the earthen long barrow of Fussell's Lodge, a burial mound built around 4000 BC, a thousand years before the beginning of Stonehenge, and only seven miles from where the circle would stand.

Bad years for crops led to other illnesses. Malnutrition, spina bifida, loss of teeth, rheumatism also affected these settlers. Poliomyelitis was noted at Cissbury where a man's left arm was 'much shorter and lighter' than his right. Injuries and fractures were commonplace. An old man at West Kennet had a broken arm. At Knook, twelve miles from the site of Stonehenge, when those eminent early 19th century antiquarians, Sir Richard Colt Hoare and William Cunnington, excavated a long barrow with their labourers in 1801, they came upon the skeleton of an elderly man with a thick skull from which all the teeth were missing. His fractured arm had been set 'in a manner as would not convey to us, in modern times, any favourable opinion of the ancient Britons' skill in surgery'.[5]

There were other hazards. At first men were content to make their tools from raw flints, lying on the ground, that could be collected locally and then chipped into shape at home. But over the centuries some communities began mining for the better seams far below the surface, sinking shafts and tunnelling out a web of subterranean galleries along which the miners crawled with crude chalk oil-lamps, levering out glass-sharp lumps of black flint from the treacherously soft walls with antler picks. It was dangerous but it was rewarding. The roughed-out axes of these mine-workers were bartered or exchanged or presented all over southern Britain.

Some early mines were the work of people near Stonehenge. Hardly a mile from the future ring some shallow, opencast pits were dug but the flint was poor and the site was abandoned. Five miles to the SSW at Woodford six similar, open mines were found, also the work of Neolithic groups who eventually allowed them to silt up. Years later a mortuary house was built there which, in turn, was covered by a long barrow.

Much deeper mines are known in East Anglia and in Sussex where some at Church Hill were dug as early as 4200 BC. At Cissbury, in use around 3500 BC, there had been accidents in the pits, some of which were up to 40 feet (12 m) deep. In one, cleared out in AD 1875, there was the skeleton of a young woman who had either fallen in head first or whose corpse had been callously dumped into a disused shaft. In the dark tunnel of a nearby mine the remains of another young woman were found. She had been killed by the fall of three blocks of chalk that had crushed her skull, embedded her hand in her chest and broken her back. In an earlier injury her arm had been broken.

It might be thought that such diseases and dangers are overstated, selected for effect, but the statistics deny this. Most of these people, working under duress, lived brief lives. At the burial centre of Hambledon Hill in Dorset 60 per cent of the skeletons were of children and infants. At Fussell's Lodge the majority of men were dead by 36, women by 31, and only a minority of children survived beyond the age of seven. These were not special cases. The age of death was just as grim at the tomb of Ascott-under-Wychwood in the Cotswolds:

The World's a bubble, and the life of Man
Less than a span.
In his conception wretched, from the womb
So to the tomb.
                     Francis Bacon

Excavations at two passage-graves in the Orkneys revealed a yet more macabre pattern. At Quanterness and at Isbister, both of them used centuries before Stonehenge, the mortality rate amongst infants and children was dreadful. Almost half the Isbister children died before they were one year old, a fifth of them before three months, and most human beings were dead before they reached twenty. Those under that age outnumbered the older people by three to one and hardly one person in a hundred survived the fortieth year. By the time they were fifteen most women were bearing children and, on average, gave birth three times before dying within the next nine years.[6] The Elizabethan essayist Bacon observed poignantly 'that old men go to death, and death comes to young men', a statement the more shocking when applied to Neolithic societies, where 'old' referred to someone barely twenty years of age. Death was no gentle stranger to these people. It was a house-guest.

Appalling though this may seem today, there is no reason to think that these first farmers considered themselves unfortunate. What seems to us a grossly premature age of dying was to them normal. They had laughter, care, compassion and joy. Yet, in their ever-changing society, precariously balanced on the edge of survival, where one outbreak of illness or the spread of disease amongst their cattle or a year of famine could lead to the extermination of a community, it is no surprise that their ritual objects were charms and amulets of fertility.

Modelled from chalk, easily broken or worn away through handling, it is remarkable that any of these talismen have been preserved, crude female figurines, male phalli, a tiny ashwood carving of a being with breasts and erect penis from the Somerset Fens, plaques with undecipherable grooves scratched on their smoothed surfaces. These were some of the tokens through which the people hoped to safeguard their lives.

Little balls of chalk or stone were probably equally explicit sexual symbols, made by people well acquainted with the potency of the bull and its pendulous testicles. To primitive cattle-herders the bull has often been the epitome of reproductive power. In Roman times the blood and testicles of bulls were used in religious ceremonies. Small balls of chalk, usually shaped and often in pairs, have been discovered in Neolithic sites: with a chalk phallus at the Grimes Graves flint-mines; at Windmill Hill causewayed enclosure twenty miles north of Stonehenge; and most commonly, and most significantly, with the dead in megalithic tombs, sometimes joined in lovely double-sphered pendants like those from the passage-graves in the Boyne Valley of Ireland. If such objects were supposed to preserve or perpetuate life, then they provide one of the clues to the purpose of Stonehenge. Several balls of chalk lay in the ditch there.

There is also evidence of an early Neolithic axe-cult, but the symbolism is different from the sexual objects. The phalli and the balls were complete in themselves. Because they were recognisable imitations of human organs they probably acted as articles of sympathetic or homoeopathic magic intended, by their likeness to their bodily counterparts, to bring fertility to the society that manipulated them. This was not true of the axe.

Just as a Christian cross is, this weapon seems to have been a form of shorthand, personifying a powerful but unportrayed spirit or deity. It was closely associated with death, leading some scholars to speak of a Mother Goddess, a fearsome supernatural being who watched over the ghosts of the dead. Except in rare and controversial cases, there are few recognisable images of this being in Britain. In the chambered tombs of Brittany 'she' was sometimes represented by a roughly shouldered stone standing at the entrance to the burial chamber or by the carving on the slabs of the tomb of a sub-rectangular figure with tiny circles for breasts. Sometimes an axe was carved by her, the expression of her guardianship. Often an axe by itself was sufficient. In Britain the axe may have been regarded as the embodiment of such a protectress of the dead. Both 'she' and the axe would appear at Stonehenge.

Actual and perfect axes have been recovered from the foot of standing stones in Brittany, and over a hundred axes of beautiful jadeite, fibrolite and diorite were left in the huge Carnac Mound of Mané-er-Hroek. In Britain a comparably lovely pale-green axe of jadeite was deposited in the

Somerset Fens alongside an insecure stretch of trackway laid down around 4000 BC. The workmanship of this delicate implement was so fine that it may have taken some craftsman over a hundred painstaking hours to finish. At Crudwell in north Wiltshire three 'extremely fine, long, wedge-shaped polished flint Celts' were dug up in 1862. Two of these curiously patterned axes went to Devizes Museum, but the third was sent to Lady Cooper who 'gave it to a collector' and it is now lost.[7]

Axes like these, superbly made, over 9 inches (23 cm) long, frail and slender, are most unlikely ever to have been working tools. One from Lincolnshire had been carefully ground down so that a fossil belenite, perhaps a magical symbol in itself, could be seen on both its faces. Another graceful axe, close-grained and prettily-speckled, was unearthed from a turfpit near Pendle in Lancashire. These were ritual things, a belief strengthened by the fact that several in Brittany were perforated so that they might be hung around the neck like a Christian crucifix.

Some of these objects have been recovered from the burial-places of early Neolithic families. On Salisbury Plain there were earthen mounds known as long barrows, great rectangular piles of earth and chalk under whose eastern end the dead were placed, often in a timber-built chamber. One of the earliest yet known of them was Fussell's Lodge, 7½ miles south-east of the site of Stonehenge and first noticed from the air in 1924 as a ploughed-down spread of chalk. It was excavated in 1957.

In Wiltshire, as in many counties, a detailed gazetteer has been compiled of the ancient monuments.[8] Within each parish the barrows, both long and round, have been given individual numbers such as Amesbury 14 to distinguish them from the others. Sometimes a site already had a local name like the round 'King Barrow', whose parish listing is Amesbury 23, or the rich Bush Barrow (Wilsford South 5). The long barrow, Clarendon Park 4a, is better known as Fussell's Lodge from the name of the farm on whose land it once stood.

Six thousand years ago the forest was dense here, oaks and hazels and hawthorns crowding the sides of the dry valley. In a clearing people constructed a big, oblong shelter 65 feet long, 24 wide and 8 feet high (20 × 7.3 × 2.4 m). Its roof, perhaps ridged, was supported by three massive oak uprights, the ridgepoles across them each weighing well over a ton. With walls of horizontal planking covered with flints and turves, this substantial building could have survived for a century or more. It faced ENE. Outside the entrance four posts may have been the supports for a high, open-air platform.[9]

Even a young oak, perhaps 30 feet high and 3 feet thick (9 × 1 m), would weigh two tons or more even when stripped of its branches. Men would soon have become experienced in the shifting and raising of such awkward loads, learning how deep the postholes had to be, how best to manoeuvre the post into position, how its base had to be packed firmly around with chalk blocks. Shaping the timber with their flint adzes, they must quickly have developed skills in carpentry, the art of chipping out mortise and tenon joints to hold the joists and purlins in place, socketing the planking with pegs and dowels, chamfering the edges neatly together.

A structure like Fussell's Lodge could have been put up by a dozen able-bodied people, perhaps no more than a single family, and in it, over the years, the bones of the dead were laid. When it was excavated the remains of more than fifty bodies were found, men, women and children, the young outnumbering the adults by two to one, many of them with evidence of hardship, some with fractures, many with arthritis, and four in five of the children showing signs of malnutrition.

These were not the simple burials they appeared. Most of the bones were unburnt, but there were a few that were scorched as though attempts at cremation had been made. By one of the bulky posts skulls and longbones had been stacked, a pile of bones had been heaped tidily by another and the bones of two individuals had been assembled into a single skeleton near the entrance. There were some ribs and small bones missing from most of the remains and mixed amongst the bones was soil from an unknown locality. The position of an ox-skull at the eastern end of the vault and bovine footbones outside its walls suggested that an ox-hide, complete with hooves and skull, had been draped over the charnel-house with the horned head jutting above the entrance.

Fussell's Lodge seems to have been a family mortuary house used by a group of a dozen or more people and their descendants for a century or more, men and women who brought the dry bones of their dead there from some distant burial-place. This would explain the missing small-bones, the 'foreign' soil, the weathered condition of some of the skulls.

It is arguable that bones were carried there only when the flesh had rotted, leaving a disconnected collection of bones to be parcelled together. Some bodies may have been exposed on a platform outside the entrance, safe from predatory beasts but not from scavenging birds. Others may have been buried and disinterred when the bones were fleshless. The belief that the spirit or ghost will not leave a corpse until all moisture has gone is a common one among primitive societies who take great care to protect themselves against visitations from the un-dead. Scorching would have hastened this process of desiccation. It is conceivable that even in the early Neolithic period 'burial' did not consist of an immediate interment but, instead, was a protracted ritual extending over months before the bones were taken to the mortuary house. What rites accompanied this final act can be little more than a guess, although the frequent presence of ox-bones from the meaty parts of the animal are indications of funerary feasts.

Excarnation, the digging up of bones from a temporary grave for reburial, has long been suspected in prehistoric Britain. In the middle of the 19th century Dr John Thurnam, of the County Asylum in Devizes, became interested in the shapes of skulls in the earthen long barrows and he dug into many of the mounds. Although his technique of excavation was poor, sinking ugly and often undescribed trenches not only into 22 long barrows but into 61 round ones between 1853 and 1867, he did leave a lot of information about the crania and bones he had discovered.

In 1863 he explored a long barrow on East Down, six miles NNW of Stonehenge. This huge tumulus, unapproachable today in the Military Danger Zone, covered eight skeletons. They were not reverently laid out. Instead, wrote Thurnam, the bones were so 'mingled and so closely packed that it was scarcely possible to regard this as the original place of burial; and it is almost certain they had experienced a prior interment, and had been removed to the spot where they were found after the decay of the soft parts and the separation of the bones'.[10]

It was only after five or more generations that the burials at Fussell's Lodge were sealed off from the world of the living. Around the shelter a trapezoidal stockade of posts was put up, 135 feet (41 m) long, 40 feet (12 m) wide at the eastern end but narrowing to 20 feet (6 m) at the west, a 2½ ton oak log standing massively at each corner. Chalk rubble from two deep ditches along its sides was dumped into this enclosure, filling it and covering the mortuary house which later collapsed, fracturing many of the bones and skulls. The final post-walled barrow looked like a grossly exaggerated Neolithic house, an imposing and conspicuous home for the dead.

For a dozen people it was the work of weeks, possibly months, digging out the chalk, cutting down and dragging the trees, trimming them, erecting the shaped posts in their bedding-trenches. It was a designed project. The northern side of the stockade was straighter than the south, implying that the latter had been laid out by offsets from the former, and the excavator noted that the back end was just half the width of the front 'while the length was roughly three-and-a-half the breadth . . . it seems hard to avoid the conclusion that some reasoned system of proportion lies behind the whole concept'. He added that almost certainly a plumb-line had been used to ensure that the great timbers were exactly vertical. Even as early as 4000 BC engineering practices were being employed on Salisbury Plain.

There are over sixty of these earthen long barrows on the plain (Fig. 3), sixteen within three miles of where Stonehenge would stand (Table 2). Except for the immediate south-east where the River Avon curls and turns through the Amesbury valley, the site of the future circle is surrounded by these old burial-places. Some like Shalbourne 5a, 15½ miles north-east of Stonehenge, are ploughed almost flat and can hardly be made out while others, like its neighbour Shalbourne 5, hidden in the trees of a dense coppice whose overgrown, rusting barbed-wire makes a visit perilous, are still excellently preserved under stands of beeches.

There are monsters, open to the sky, heavy on their hillsides like slumberous whales, but twice the size, basking in a sea of grass: Milton Lilbourne 7, known as the Giant's Grave, the Cold Kitchen barrow (Brixton Deverill 2) with nettles and rush grass and cornflowers and poppies growing

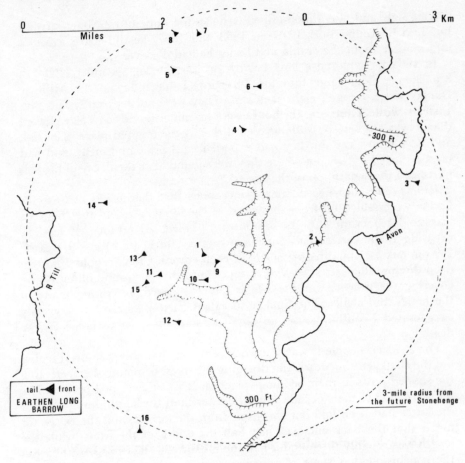

Fig. 3. The Stonehenge Region c. 3700 BC. The numbers refer to the long barrows listed in Table 2.

on it, and not two miles to its east, the beautiful elegance of the low and long barrow on Pertwood Down (Brixton Deverill 7), grazed by foxy-faced sheep, its eastern end pocked and hollowed like a shrivelled apple by some forgotten excavation. Anyone going to see this pair of fine barrows should not be deterred by the sign on the farm-gate at the bottom of Cold Kitchen hill, 'Private Land. Hang-gliding on this site by Flying Druids ONLY'.

There were five major groups of long barrows in Wessex, which includes the counties of Wiltshire, Hampshire, Dorset and Sussex: one on the south coast near Dorchester, another on Cranborne Chase, two on Salisbury Plain, one east, the other west, and a northern group on the Marlborough Downs.[11] These concentrations may have corresponded to five separate regions, each with increasingly distinctive customs.

## TABLE 2. Earthen Long Barrows within three miles of Stonehenge

| | Site | Grid Reference | Distance from Stonehenge | Direction Facing | Length Ft. | M. |
|---|---|---|---|---|---|---|
| 1 | Amesbury 14 | SU 115417 | ½ mile SW | SSE | 100 | 31 |
| 2 | Amesbury 104 | SU 141419 | 1 mile ESE | SSE? | 65? | 20? |
| 3 | Bulford 1 | SU 163431 | 2¾ miles ENE | ESE | 133 | 41 |
| 4 | Durrington 24 | SU 124444 | 1½ miles N | SE | 142 | 43 |
| 5 | Figheldean 21 | SU 108458 | 2½ miles NNW | SE | 148 | 45 |
| 6 | Figheldean 27 | SU 127453 | 2 miles NNE | E | 182 | 56 |
| 7 | Netheravon 6 | SU 114466 | 3 miles NNW | SSE | 111 | 34 |
| 8 | Netheravon 9 | SU 108466 | 3 miles NW | SE | 115 | 35 |
| 9 | Wilsford South 13 | SU 118413 | ¾ mile SSW | NNE | 65 | 20 |
| 10 | Wilsford South 30 | SU 114410 | 1 mile SSW | E | 126 | 38 |
| 11 | Wilsford South 34 | SU 104411 | 1¼ miles SW | ENE | 117 | 36 |
| 12 | Wilsford South 41 | SU 108401 | 1½ miles SSW | ESE | 140 | 43 |
| 13 | Winterbourne Stoke 1 | SU 100415 | 1¼ miles WSW | NE | 240 | 73 |
| 14 | Winterbourne Stoke 53 | SU 091428 | 2 miles WNW | E | 104 | 32 |
| 15 | Winterbourne Stoke 71 | SU 101409 | 1½ miles SW | NE | 170 | 52 |
| 16 | Woodford 2 | SU 100377 | 3 miles SSW | S | 67 | 20 |
| | | | Average Length of Barrows | | 127 | 39 |

Dates, including the earliest yet known for the barrows in Wessex, show that the long barrow tradition endured for over a thousand years (Table 3).

## TABLE 3. Some radiocarbon dates for long barrows in Wessex

| Site | C–14 'Date' | Corrected Date BC |
|---|---|---|
| Lambourn, Berks | 3415 ± 180 bc | 4260 BC |
| Fussell's Lodge, Wilts | 3230 ± 150 bc | 4020 BC |
| Nutbane, Hants | 2730 ± 150 bc | 3510 BC |
| Normanton Down, Wilts | 2560 ± 103 bc | 3320 BC (Mortuary house) |
| Beckhampton, Wilts | {2517 ± 90 bc<br>{2307 ± 90 bc | {3265 BC<br>{2980 BC |
| Alfriston, Sussex | 2360 ± 110 bc | 3050 BC |

To this geographical division can be added a separation in time. Although long barrows began as sepulchres for communal family burials, slowly, almost imperceptibly over the centuries, the tradition was subtly modified until the latest barrows became prestigious monuments for the burial of a single, adult male. From this one might infer an increasingly hierarchical society very different from the egalitarianism of early Neolithic families. It was, however, a social disruption that was concealed by the unchanging outward appearance of the long barrows.[12] Ritual also changed and it is the pattern and the trend of these changes that are the background to the construction of the first Stonehenge.

The siting of a long barrow was chosen for the mound to be conspicuous. Bulford 2, under its old, tall beeches and water-tank, was piled up at the very edge of a steep drop to the north-east. Tilshead 4, the White Barrow, rises at the head of a slope to the north. Bratton, with a chalky snake of footpath along its length and incorporated in an Iron Age hillfort, has a magnificent view over the Vale of Pewsey. Two miles NNE of Stonehenge is Knighton Barrow (Figheldean 27), which the 18th century antiquarian, William Stukeley, called the 'north long barrow'. In 1914 Maud Cunnington, the Wiltshire archaeologist, observed, 'although not of great length this is a very fine barrow, and the most conspicuously situated of any in the county, being a landmark for many miles across the Plain in every direction'.[13] The military put water-tanks on it.

In the absence of any known association of Neolithic houses with these barrows, an explanation for their siting must be cautious. Possibly each of the sixteen near Stonehenge had its own 'territory', a rectangular strip of about 1½ square miles with the barrow on the high ground of the plain and the occupation area lower down on the slopes of the Avon or the little River Till to the west. Allowing 2½ acres per person with as much lying fallow and with some land uncleared, these territories could have supported a family, especially if the inland areas of the plain were regarded as common land for grazing the summer herds. Some form of land organisation must have existed. Although it is unprovable, and probably wrong, the suggested scheme would have been socially acceptable for families inhabiting the same region, would have provided land, water and timber, access to the interior of the plain, and would explain the conspicuous position of many of the barrows, placed where they and their dead overlooked the homes and cultivated plots of the living.

The barrows vary greatly in bulk. A small one like Wilsford South 13, lurking in the Normanton round barrow cemetery near Stonehenge, is estimated to contain no more than 6000 cubic feet (170 cm) of chalk, a midget when contrasted with the enormous, overgrown and rather battered Tilshead 2, 390 feet long, 100 feet wide and still 11 feet high (119 × 31 × 3.4 m), over seventy times the volume of the other. The majority of barrows, however, might be compared with Fussell's Lodge and there are good reasons for believing that the bigger ones were built quite late, when there was a growing emphasis on architectural grandeur. It was only when the tradition was waning that much smaller, rather oval barrows such as Sherrington 1 were put up, in appearance like an egg cut in half and constructed of gravel from the adjacent River Wylye. When William Cunnington explored it in 1804 he failed to find a Neolithic burial, but under a layer of ash there was a neatly cut round pit containing an antler and the skull of an ox.[14]

In a book about Stonehenge what is most noteworthy about the construction of these barrows is the virtual absence of large stones. There is no good building stone on Salisbury Plain except at Chilmark, a full 11 miles south-west of Stonehenge. Roman coins have been found in the quarries whose easily-cut freestone was used for the cool austerity of Salisbury Cathedral and the soft, golden walls of Wilton House. It is known as the architect's stone, for it is without grain and is simple to cut into blocks, but it was not extracted by Neolithic people who, if they wanted stone, took what there was to hand, glacial erratics or outcrops, neither of which was plentiful on the plain.

The local materials were flint, timber, reeds, clay and chalk, and all these can be seen in the older houses of villages such as Stratford-sub-Castle near Old Sarum to the north of Salisbury. Here there are half-timbered houses, flint-walled houses, thatched roofs and walls of mud and clay with thatched tops against the weather. Only the churches and manor houses are of expensive, imported stone.

It was chalk and earth and wood that Neolithic communities used for the majority of the great barrow mounds, although Knook 2 was composed of a cairn of flints and big marl stones lying, as Cunnington discovered in 1802, on 'a regular paved floor of flints'. Heytesbury 1, the famous Bowl's or Boles Barrow, the name deriving from the Saxon *Bodelus Beorh* or 'Boda's Barrow', also had a cairn of stones that was covered with a thick capping of white marl as if in imitation of the chalk barrows to the east.[15] The stones here, which included a Welsh bluestone of the kind later to be set up in concentric circles at Stonehenge, were so loosely stacked that they collapsed during Cunnington's excavation of July, 1801, when 'the large stones came rolling down so fast upon us that we were obliged to desist from exploring it further'.

Boles Barrow is 3 miles north of Heytesbury, where Cunnington lived and where he is buried behind the church. Boyton 1, a conspicuous and substantial barrow, is 2 miles to the south-east. Here, in 1804, on top of a heap of flints Cunnington came upon a stone that 'took the strength of three men to lift out'. At Arn Hill (Warminster 1), another fine barrow at the western edge of the plain, he found a 5 foot (1.5 m) high sarsen standing in the mound near three skeletons. Standing stones such as this, associated with burials, are known in Brittany and have been recorded in Britain at the Tinglestone long barrow in Gloucestershire, and at Lyneham chambered tomb, Oxfordshire, and farther north there were two standing stones in the forecourt of the Bridestones near Congleton.

That only three barrows, all on the far margin of Salisbury Plain, are known to have held stones reaffirms the fact that stone was not readily available to the builders of long barrows, something which makes the presence of Stonehenge all the more remarkable. There is a vague report that a 'cist', possibly a chamber of big stones like the four at Luckington in Wiltshire miles away to the north-west, once existed at Amesbury 104 near Stonehenge, but this barrow has long since been destroyed and nothing positive is known about it.[16] Of the sixty-nine long barrow sites on Salisbury Plain, 16 within 3 miles of Stonehenge, 15 between 3 and 8 miles away, and 38 more than 8 miles distant, only one definitely had a stonebuilt chamber. This is the oddly-named Tidcombe & Fosbury 1, 14 miles away at the remote north-east corner of the plain, a barrow 185 feet (56 m) long, which from its south-eastern end looks like a set of gigantic vertebrae because of the uneven dumps of soil along its spine. It has a strange history.

'The peasants, being persuaded that great riches were hid in this barrow about the year 1750, bestowed almost a summer's labour to dig into it; when at last they found three prodigious big stones. . . . These stood up perpendicular, having two others of like sort laid on the tops of them, and thereby making a sepulchre, for under them was deposited one human skeleton. When I visited it, one of the men presented me with a fragment of the lower jawbone with two or three of the teeth.'[17] The ragged, V-shaped ditch, 8 feet wide and 5 feet deep (2.4 × 1.5 m), hollowed out by those disappointed treasure-seekers, still disfigures this barrow where four largish stones lie half-buried in a cavity at the south-east end. Further excavations by the Rev. W.C. Lukis in 1845 recovered only a big horn-core of an ox.

In construction this stone-chambered tomb belongs with other megalithic barrows like Adam's Grave (Alton 1) on the Marlborough Downs a few miles to its north-west. It was quite different from the earthen long barrows to its south with their mounds of chalk and flint and their timber mortuary houses.

Occasionally on Salisbury Plain there may have been a rare Neolithic round barrow like the one at Black Heath (Mere 13d) in which a cremation was found in an upturned pot, the surface of which 'is shining as if saturated with grease and smoke',[18] but such circular mounds were exceptional. It was the long barrow that prevailed and in some of them, despite the decay of the timbers, the remains of wooden structures have been detected.

It is clear that even within a region as compact as Salisbury Plain, not 30 miles wide from Warminster to Ludgershall and barely 15 long from Salisbury northwards to Upavon and the marshy wetland of the Vale of Pewsey, some 350 square miles of deceptive landscape in which the bleak chalk expanses half hide the sheltered wooded denes of the villages, even in this small area burial habits differed. There were many ways of treating the dead. At Fussell's Lodge some corpses may have been exposed on a scaffold and others temporarily buried. On Normanton Down they were left in an unroofed stockade.[19]

Inside a rectangular ditched and banked enclosure a palisade of oak posts with an entrance at the ESE surrounded a spacious open area. From the excavations of 1959 some ox and sheep bones and eleven antlers were recovered, one of which gave a 'date' of about 3320 BC (2560 ± 103 bc). Standing only a hundred yards away from a long barrow and in plan very like other known mortuary enclosures it is tempting to think of the bones of the dead being gathered up there and carried to the Wilsford South 30 barrow in which Cunnington found 'four other skeletons strangely huddled together', one apparently with no forehead,[20] and perhaps to Wilsford South 13 half a mile north-east. Two other barrows were within 2 miles, Wilsford South 34 to the west and the huge Lake mound, Wilsford South 41, to the SSW. It is feasible that mortuary stockades such as Normanton Down were intended to be used by several families.

Elsewhere ridge-roofed shelters were built. At Nutbane in Hampshire, only 13 miles from Stonehenge, a rather frail and cramped hut was replaced by a larger structure in which the bones of two young men were laid on a bedding of brushwood. Two posts stood by them. Later this building was dismantled and a more massive version, roofed and with entrances at east and west, was put up. The remains of a full-grown man were found in it. Around 3500 BC (2730 ± 150 bc), when the mound of a long barrow was to be heaped over the site, this mortuary house was deliberately set on fire, 'causing the posts to smoulder down to their sockets'.[21]

A similar vault was identified at Woodford 2 with 'a few weathered bones', and others have been suspected from the many sadly-imperfect excavations of the past. At Tilshead 2 the shelter seems to have collapsed. At Tilshead 7 Thurnam came upon 'eight skeletons singularly cemented together, within a space of less than four feet in diameter and about a foot and half in depth'.[22] Evidence of burning, reddened soil, scorched bones, at Winterbourne Stoke 53 on whose floor there 'had been an intense fire', burned skeletons at Tilshead 2 and Bratton 1, charred wood at Knook 2, Fittleton 2 and Sherrington 1, and what seem to have been postholes to support the uprights of a roof, or a tumbled mass of flints when the structure crashed down under the weight of the barrow, signs like these at Boyton 1 and Heytesbury 4 all testify to the rites that ensured that the spirits of the dead had quitted their bones and were powerless to menace the living.

Some skeletons had undergone excarnation having been buried and then dug up. At the Oxendean barrow, Warminster 6, Cunnington and Hoare found the bones of a man in a long, deep grave. He must have been defleshed before burial, because 'his skull lay chiefly upon the breast, beaten into pieces before burial, the limbs otherwise being in regular order'.[23] At Norton Bavant 13 a jumbled mass of at least eighteen skeletons with many missing long-bones suggested the idea of a previous interment to Thurnam. In 1864 he re-excavated Boles Barrow. Examining the skulls in it, he concluded that many of them had been intentionally hacked and broken after death. In a further excavation in 1886, the two brothers William and Henry Cunnington, grandsons of the first William, rediscovered the skulls and remarked, 'it is curious to note that, with one exception, the blows were inflicted on the *left* side of the cranium', indicating that the person or persons responsible had been right-handed. They added, 'in one instance at least, it appears that the victim had been beheaded, as a neck vertebra, found amongst the loose bones, had evidently been cut in two by some sharp instrument'.[24] That the skeletons had previously been exposed was apparent, as 'many of the bones, especially the long bones, had been gnawed by rodents'.

In barrow after barrow excavators have commented on the disarticulated bones, the weathered state of many of them, the absence of arm-and leg-bones, even skulls. At Amesbury 14, only half a mile from Stonehenge, Thurnam found a skull in 1866 that was without cheek-bones or teeth. At the Robin Hood barrow, Figheldean 31, which he dug into in 1864, the bones of a single individual lay in a little pile and it 'appeared to have been disarticulated by the decay of the ligaments before the final interment', and at Tilshead 5, now in the Military Danger Zone, 'there were two skeletons lying not more than a foot apart. The space occupied by each was so very small, that either very unusual means had been resorted to for doubling up the body, or the flesh had been suffered to decay before burial'. The ligaments, however, had not rotted, for the bones were still '*in situ*, joint to joint'.[25]

It seems that a newly-dead corpse was regarded as retaining some life and it was only when all flesh and moisture had gone that the bones were deemed free of any lingering spirit. Perhaps nothing more clearly demonstrates this belief that death had many stages than the almost complete absence in the long barrows of objects for the dead to take with them into another existence. If the ghost or soul had departed, it had no use for material things. It was only while corruption of the body was taking place, while the corpse was exposed or buried in a temporary grave, that it had any need of possessions.

At Normanton Down antlers had been left with the dead inside the mortuary enclosure. Elsewhere, in primary graves whose whereabouts were probably marked by posts, corpses were given pots or other articles, a chalk plaque with a young child at Whitehawk, antlers, deer ribs and a broken vessel with an old woman at Pangbourne, a bowl with another body at Handley Hill in Dorset. Months after the burial, when only the skeleton remained, the dead were disinterred, the bones carried to the mortuary house and the unwanted trinkets and implements discarded.

In contrast to this lack of funerary offerings, animal bones have been found in the barrows, particularly those of oxen, castrated bulls or bullocks whose flesh provided a succulent meal for the mourners as they celebrated the safe deposition of the sterile dead. At Tilshead Lodge two skulls of oxen lay close to the human bones, one with part of the spine still attached where it had been cut 'as if by great violence, probably in the slaughter of the animal'.

Two quite separate aspects of Neolithic ritual are apparent here. The survival of ox bones 'from the fleshy parts' of the beasts seems good evidence of feasting during the funerary rites, an activity little different from modern-day wakes. Also recorded by early investigators, however, were single skulls of oxen set down near the disarticulated bones of the dead. Remembering the presence of clay or stone balls, thought to be representations of testicles, in some tombs, it is plausible to suppose that these isolated skulls were considered to contribute strength or potency or protection to the burial place. They may have been totems. In view of later discoveries at Stonehenge itself, the association of such skulls with the dead is significant, for it is from such seemingly trivial facets of Neolithic burial and belief that clues about the purpose of Stonehenge can be detected.

At Knook 2 an ox-skull from the barrow was pronounced by a butcher 'to have been larger than ever he saw of that species of animal'. A similar skull had been placed in front of the Fussell's Lodge mortuary house. An immense number of bones lay under the great mound of Warminster 14, mostly of pigs. Elsewhere, ribs of deer and boars' tusks littered the debris of the dead, giving the impression of baked meats and thanksgiving as the last acts were performed in the long-drawn-out funerary rites.

These had included the digging of pits near the jumbled bones. Some holes may have been for posts to support the mortuary structure. Others, such as a big cavity at Boles Barrow, 6 feet long, 3 wide and 2 deep (1.8 × 0.9 × 0.6 m), may have been graves in which the corpses were first left to decay. The majority, however, were far too small for this, symmetrically round basins not more than 3 feet across and less than 2 feet deep (1 × 0.6 m), containing only loose grey or black earth. Hoare commented that it was quite usual to come upon them near the heaps of bones, 'one or more circular cists cut into the native chalk, and generally covered with a pile of stones or flints'.[26]

At Winterbourne Stoke 53 two deep pits were filled with 'an immense quantity of wood ashes and large pieces of charred wood', possibly the burnt timbers of a mortuary house, but at Tilshead 2 there was an oval pit as neatly cut 'as if it had been done by a chissel'. From what is known of early Neolithic tools, the hole had probably been hacked and prised out with a pick made from a red deer antler, the crumbling bits of chalk scooped up with the shoulder-blade of an ox, and the sides finally smoothed with a long, sharp flint blade.

Under Heytesbury 4 there was an equally well-fashioned hole filled with black earth, stones and marl with skeletons lying by it. Other finely-made cavities were noted at Knook 2 and Knook 5 where 'just west of the skeletons there was a 3 foot deep pit with neither bones nor ash in it'. At Sherrington 1 an ox skull and a deer antler had been carefully set down in a similar bowl-like hollow. Stockton 1, a well-preserved barrow on a gentle SSW slope, covered the remains of three adults and a child alongside an oblong pit, 4 feet (1.2 m) deep, filled with flints and marl. A fifth human skull had been put down on its far side.

Pits like these have also been recognised under the much later round barrows, at Whitesheet Hill, at Kilmington, at Blackheath, even at the Winterbourne Stoke cemetery, hardly a mile from the circle at Stonehenge, where a skeleton on the old land surface had been laid alongside 'a small oblong cist, without any deposit in it'. Hoare conjectured that these mysterious holes denoted 'some particular ceremony that was practised in these tumuli', and Thurnam added that they may have corresponded to 'the cavities . . . which were excavated in the earth, and in which libations and the blood of victims were offered to the infernal deities by the ancient Greeks'.[27] The proximity of the long barrow pits to the dead and their comparative smallness suggests that this is a feasible explanation for them. They have a remarkable likeness to the controversial Aubrey Holes at Stonehenge.

Filling the pits may have been the last action before the piling up of the huge barrow to cover the bones. The people, probably both men and women, dug out two parallel trenches, 50 or more feet (15 m) apart, each ditch composed of short sections like grotesque bath-tubs quarried out by work-gangs, the segments eventually linked together as their ends were broken down. The excavated material was used to build the barrow between the ditches, its body an inverted image of the trenches. The stripped-off turf was laid out in a thick rectangle to form the base of the mound. When this turf and the topsoil that was spread over it was compressed by the weight of the overlying chalk, it formed a black layer that has consistently been noticed by the excavators of these long mounds. Onto it soft, weathered chalk from the top levels of the ditches was heaped and then harder, deeper chalk was dumped in uneven piles, giving the barrow an undulating profile like the humps of a serpent's back. When the hollows were filled in with chalk the barrow must have stretched bleakly white against the plain like an enormous blanched house as pallid as the bones it covered.

The barrows still loom from the landscape, impressive in their bulk and heaviness, huge mounds clamped at the very edges of steep slopes, grassy and covered in wild flowers and nettles, as ponderous today as they were five or more thousand years ago. Some, like Chapperton Down (Tilshead 10), have been unfortunate, mutilated by military manoeuvres,[28] but damaged or not, almost without exception they have a feature in common. They face eastwards.

'We find', wrote Sir Richard Colt Hoare, 'more generally one end of these barrows broader than the other, and that broad end pointing towards the east'.[29] It is at the eastern end that the majority of skeletons and bones were placed, a situation obviously preferred by Neolithic people. Recent fieldwork by the author and others has shown how emphatic this choice was. Of the 65 barrows still in good enough condition for their orientation to be determined there is only one, at the far west of the Plain, that does not face between NNE and south. Arn Hill (Warminster 1), a fine barrow darkened by beeches and weeds, faces SSW. It lies at the edge of a sharp western slope whose ridge made it impossible for its builders to conform to a more traditional axis. All the other barrows have their wider, higher end between NNE and south, most of them, 90 per cent, between 36° (NE) and 166° (SSE).

**TABLE 4. The orientation of long barrows on Salisbury Plain**

| Direction Faced | No. of Barrows |
|-----------------|----------------|
| NNE | 4 |
| NE | 8 |
| ENE | 8 |
| E | 17 |
| ESE | 5 |
| SE | 12 |
| SSE | 7 |
| S | 3 |

A word of caution is necessary. The weathered, sometimes ploughed-down state of many barrows prevents an exact bearing being obtained from them. After making plane-table surveys of 35 barrows it became quite clear to the writer that the original axis could never be precisely recovered and that it was not possible to attain an accuracy better than ± 2° so that an 'alignment' of 91° at Bratton 1 means that the mound was probably oriented by its builders somewhere between 89° and 93°. It would be misleading to claim anything more definite.

The direction was decided before the mound was built. At Fussell's Lodge the excavator recorded that 'the mortuary house post-sockets lay exactly on the axis of the enclosure and in line with the [entrance] causeway', showing that when the people heaped up the final stockaded barrow they respected the orientation of the earlier mortuary house.[30]

There is a simple explanation for this easterly preference. It was not the direction of the prevailing wind nor was it primarily caused by the lie of the land. Most probably the barrows were planned to face the rising of a celestial object such as the sun or the moon. It is much more difficult to explain why people should want this, although the concept of the sun as a giver of light and warmth is a common one, just as the moon has often been linked with darkness, cold and death:

> God, what a dancing spectre is the moon.
>
> George Meredith, *Modern Love*

The problems of archaeo-astronomy, the study of astronomical practices in the ancient world, are many and often impossible to solve. For the long barrows of Salisbury Plain, however, matters are not intractable. At a latitude just north of 51° N. sunrise in 4000 BC would have occurred around 50° (NE) at midsummer, and over the following six months would have moved steadily southwards, appearing at the east in September, and at the south-east, around 130°, by midwinter.

Its precise azimuth or compass-bearing would be affected by the height of the horizon. At the Stonehenge latitude of 51° 11' the midsummer sun would come up at 49° 35' if the skyline were level with the place where the observer was standing. If, instead, a nearby hill were 3° higher than that place the rising sun would have been concealed for over 4°, climbing above the horizon only at about 54° 16′. As most long barrows on the Plain occupy quite high positions themselves, it is rare for them to be so overshadowed. The sun's range, therefore, can be said to be between about 50° at midsummer and 130° at midwinter. As no fewer than 13 of the 65 barrows face either to the north or south of this narrow arc, it is unlikely that their builders had aligned them on the sun.

The range of the rising moon is wider. Lunar movements are more complex than those of the sun and when calculating the moon's positions it is necessary to take into account the effect of atmospheric distortion. Allowing for such complications, the moon would have risen at its most northerly near to 41° and at its most southerly near 143°. Although this arc covers little more than half of the eastern skyline, over 90 per cent of the barrows are oriented within it. Only the overgrown Weather Hill (Fittleton 5) faces 17° (NNE) to the north of it. Five others were aligned to the south of 143° and these introduce a comment about the nature of long barrows and the changing beliefs of the people who raised them.

From the varying number of bodies in them and from the wide range of radiocarbon dates for the barrows it has been suggested that the first mounds were modest in size, no more than about 150 feet (46 m) long and never more than 80 feet (24 m) in width. Over half of them are to be seen within three miles (5 km) of Stonehenge and all but one, Fittleton 5, were oriented within the lunar arc. It seems probable that they were intentionally aligned on the rising moon. Recalling the quite strong evidence for a female deity or protectress of the dead and the persistent association of the moon with women, it is conceivable that to Neolithic people the moon was in some way connected with death.

This would not account for those barrows facing southwards towards places on the skyline where the moon could never have risen or set. Such mounds are huge: Brixton Deverill 2, 230 feet (70 m) long, facing 149°; Grans Barrow in Hampshire, 200 feet (61 m), 175°; Shalborne 5, 170 feet (52 m), 172°; Tidcombe & Fosbury 1, 185 feet (56 m), 166°; and Warminster 14, a colossus, 266 feet (63 m) long, 56 feet (17 m) wide and still 15 feet (4.6 m) high. It is aligned to the SSE, 166°. All these gigantic barrows and many other outsize mounds such as Boyton 1 and the looming Milton Lilbourne 7,315 feet (96 m) in length, are located in marginal positions on the Plain, often in areas of poorer land; they are considered to be later than their shorter counterparts and put up at a time in the Neolithic when the population was growing. These vast piles of earth and chalk might well have been symbols of power and land-ownership in an age when a cult of ancestors was replacing the old tradition of communal burial. Some of them contain only a single, articulated skeleton, usually male.

Few of the orientations in these great barrows are to the north of east. Instead, there was an increasing tendency to concentrate towards the south, as though to align the barrow not on a lunar rising but towards that part of the horizon between the moon's extreme rising and setting, an area of the sky in which the southern moon would always appear. It was an interest in the south that would become dominant in the later years of the Neolithic.

Ritual was gradually changing. So coarse is our chronology because of the paucity of radiocarbon dates that it is impossible to construct a firm framework for these changes, but it is likely that in the centuries after Fussell's Lodge was closed there developed two major variations in burial customs. Fewer and fewer people were buried in the long barrows and the role of men acquired greater status.

Statistics reveal how communal burial diminished. The average number of bodies in a long barrow is only six. In a tomb built for a family of a dozen men, women and children such a group could expect that number of deaths within fifteen to twenty years, but it is reasonable to suppose that most barrows were in active use for at least a century. By that time nearly fifty deaths would have occurred. The disparity between the bodies actually found and the number to be expected suggests that from being family vaults the later barrows were clan structures in which the chosen members of only one of five or six families were given privileged burial. The gaining of land or herds or even some form of psychological power may have led to these social changes.

It is arguable that aging and friable bones were systematically cleared out of the mortuary houses to make room for others, a practice suspected in megalithic tombs elsewhere in Britain. Yet, as Fussell's Lodge demonstrated, the wooden chamber of a barrow could comfortably accommodate the remains of fifty or more people. Unless the Salisbury Plain barrows had each been open for three hundred years or longer, filled with dozens of disjointed skeletons, there would have been no need for such clearance. Given the decaying strength of the timbers, it is most unlikely that any chamber could have been used for as long as three centuries. An alternative explanation has to be found for an average of only six individuals in the barrows and a form of selective burial seems probable.

Evidence for the growing importance of men comes from the bones themselves. The number of complete skeletons, articulated and presumably carried fully fleshed into the tomb, is small, little more than twenty. This is in strong contrast to the two hundred or more disarticulated remains of which a quarter are of children, a quarter of women and just over half of men. Of the complete skeletons, only one child and one woman are to be set against the score of men.

These male burials are quite commonly found as the only burial and this piece of demographic detective work has revealed a subtlety concerning children. In those barrows where a child was buried alongside an adult it was with a man five times but with a woman only once. 'The burial of children with adult males perhaps suggests that adult males had appropriated to themselves the rôle of ensuring the social reproduction of the group.'[31] Where the ages of the men could be determined they were between 25 and 50 years old, which 'in Neolithic terms could be described as middle-aged'. That age and sex distinctions did exist in the Neolithic is shown at Fussell's Lodge, where of the heaps of bones two were entirely of grown males and a third consisted solely of infants. A fourth collection of bones near the entrance, artificially arranged to resemble a single complete skeleton, turned out to be the re-assembled bones of two women, one of them elderly and arthritic. In front of them was an ox-skull.

The culmination of so many changes led to more casual burials for the majority, sometimes in open-air earthworks known as causewayed enclosures, and to ever more prestigious interments in barrows for special people. Outwardly little had altered. The newer long barrows had the same appearance as the old, but now they were for individual men and with the burials there were personal possessions, often objects that reflected the man's distinction. The moon, the pits, ox-skulls, axes, all these were retained as part of the funerary rites as tradition required, but now they were for one person rather than the group.

Just over a mile (1½ km) WSW of the site of Stonehenge, at the junction of the Winterbourne crossroads, there is a fine long barrow, its ditches still apparent and only its north-west side scarred where labourers dug out chalk in the 19th century. It is an almost perfect mound, 240 feet long and over 10 feet high (73 × 3 m), facing north-east towards a long, low skyline and the most northerly rising of the moon.

Thurnam excavated here in 1863. At the barrow's eastern end he came upon the skeleton of a man lying on its right side, head to the south-west, knees drawn up as though the corpse had been tied. Near the back of the skull was a pit 18 inches (46 cm) across and as deep, 'scooped out of the chalk rock'.[32] Close to the man's right arm was a 'bludgeon-shaped flint about 8 inches long, and well adapted for being grasped in the hand. From one end numerous flakes had been knocked off, and it had evidently constituted an object of considerable importance to its owner'.[33]

Similar but even more impressive articles became commonplace in the centuries to follow.

# 2

# Homes for the living and the dead
## 3500 – 3200 BC

*Twas in that deluge of Historie, the memorie of the British Monuments*
*utterly perished: the Discovery wherof I doe here endeavour (for want*
*of written Record) to work-out.*

John Aubrey, *Monumenta Britannica I*, 20

A thousand years after the first farmers on Salisbury Plain a crisis had developed. The population was growing and by 3500 BC, in the middle of the Neolithic period, anxieties over land and food led to cults of protective ancestors and to new ways of expressing power. Some communities died out but others flourished, perhaps marrying the girls out to nearby groups, clans mingling with kinsfolk, each family only one of a hundred or more little knots in the network of relationships on the Plain. Over the centuries intricate blood ties were established.

Only by widespread marriage could society survive but, given the spread of farming, an increase in population was inevitable. It has been calculated that the descendants of a family of ten people, five men, four women and a child, could have suffered 1735 deaths in three hundred years and still have expanded to a community of 559 people.[1]

We have no reliable means of knowing the number of families on the Plain. What can be suggested, on the basis of what we know about the rate of infant and child mortality and the average age of death among adults, is the ratio by which a society might have increased between 4500 and 3500 BC. An assumption of about eighty families on Salisbury Plain at the beginning of the Neolithic is neither outrageously high nor low, a scattered population of 960 people in the assumed proportions of 300 men, 280 women and 380 children including 56 infants.

Each woman, on average between 15 and 35 years of age, may have had four children, resulting in a population birthrate of 56 infants annually: $(280 \times 4) \div 20$. At the end of the first year, therefore, the number of people would have become 960 + 56, a total of 1016 from which the number of deaths must be deducted.

Men, living about thirty years between the ages of 15 and 45, may have had ten deaths (300 ÷ 30) yearly. Women, with an adult lifespan of twenty years, would have suffered fourteen deaths (280 ÷ 20). Of the 56 children only 26, less than half, would survive to reach 15 years and maturity, the others dying in infancy or early childhood. For an early society this is neither distortion nor demographic pessimism. Rural Brazil in AD 1960 had a population in which fewer than half the people were over twenty years of age and less than 19 per cent were more than forty years old.

The Salisbury Plain statistics, although entirely hypothetical, show a feasible annual increase in population of only two human beings, 960 people plus 56 births less the deaths of 10 men, 14 women and 30 children (1016 − 54 = 962). But this almost imperceptible yearly improvement of a mere 1.002 per cent would in ten years have caused the population to grow to 979, 1.02 per cent more than the original 960. In fifty years there would have been 1060 people, in a century, 1170, in five hundred years, 2584, and by 3500 BC, no fewer than 6962 men, women and children, over seven times the number of the first settlers.

It is not the precise figures but the rate of increase, even with so few children reaching maturity, that demonstrates the problems that confronted any society occupying so small an area as Salisbury Plain. With more people to feed, more crops and more cattle were needed, areas of good soil were over-exploited, poorer regions were brought under cultivation, more forest was cut back and competition for land increased. In such a period of tension there came the emergence of territories, leaders and conflict. It was a crisis that was intensified by a deterioration in the climate with higher rainfall and cooler, darker seasons.

Sometimes known as the Meldon Bridge phase after a heavily-defended settlement in northern Britain,[2] it was a time when monumental building became commonplace perhaps because people believed that the erection of gigantic barrows would proclaim that the territory was well-manned and was guarded by the spirits of the dead. An ancestor cult became widespread. The customs of previous generations were continued but in exaggerated forms. In contrast to the modest volume of an early long barrow like the 28,000 cubic feet (792 m³) of Fussell's Lodge, there now appeared gross monsters such as the Old Ditch barrow (Tilshead 2), 390 feet (119 m) long, swelling out of the eastern slopes of Breach Hill. Its 430,000 cubic feet (12,169 m³) of chalk and earth was fifteen times the size of the other but, significantly, despite its bulk it covered only a single burial. In 1802 Cunnington failed to locate it, but sixty-three years later Thurnam found a small, crouched skeleton, head to the north, under a pile of burnt flints.[3] Near it was an incomplete cremation, deposited there while the bones were still hot.

Other types of monument also were magnified. Mortuary enclosures like

Normanton Down were reproduced, but to a vast scale, no longer compact rectangles but expanded a hundredfold with banks 400 feet (122 m) apart and 1¾ miles (2.8 km) long. As will be seen, the interpretation of these cursuses is relevant to the purpose of Stonehenge.

Ditched and stockaded occupation sites were constructed for safety. Trade extended away from the local flint mines to centres miles away from Salisbury Plain where there was good, tough stone for axes because, all through this period of disturbance and change, men had continued to open up the land. This merging of clearing with clearing, some of them up to 30 square miles (78 km²) in extent, as the forests were cut back over the hundreds of years before 3500 BC, has been compared to a mosaic or the cells of a honeycomb, but this is too geometrical and organised a simile. There was no socially agreed plan to it and its effects were disastrous. It was like flakes of snow settling slowly together, a sheet of blotting-paper on to which there gradually fell more and more spots of green ink until the whole sheet became an expanse of green, a countryside of grassland near the rivers and on the slopes of the Plain. Only sparse stands of oaks, abruptly erect on pockets of clay-with-flints in the bland landscape, remained as relics of where the forests had been.

There were limits to the expansion, for the chalk was surrounded every-where by tracts of heathland and clays and greensands inimical to Neolithic husbandry. On the Plain itself overgrazing and overcultivation had destroyed much of the shrub and tree cover and by 3500 BC huge areas of land were exhausted. No one generation could have realised how much degeneration was occurring, but year by year the land became less capable of supporting the large population. For protection from less fortunate communities those groups that were powerful enough built large defensive earthworks at the edge of their territories.

There were occasional settlements without defences. Not two miles north-east of Stonehenge, on a south-facing slope now overlooked by the ugly Stonehenge Inn, evidence of woodland clearance was discovered at Durrington Walls, whose occupants had planted crops and kept sheep or goats on the freshly-opened ground. When they quitted the site they left behind the rubbish of broken round-based pots, a smoothly-polished flint axe and tiny, leaf-shaped flint arrowheads. Several radiocarbon dates from a midden's charcoal showed the place had been inhabited around 3230 BC.[4] There was a similar undefended settlement at Marden, nine miles NNW amongst the marshes of the Vale of Pewsey.

It is the protected sites, however, that have been more frequently iden-tified. Known as causewayed enclosures, they were laid out on low hills, their large sub-circular interiors encircled by one or more rings of inter-rupted ditches like unstrung beads. The chalk from these ditches was heaped up to make a high inner bank enclosing a space as small as three or four acres (1.6 ha) or as big as 21 acres (8.5 ha) at Windmill Hill in north Wiltshire. One bank or two, one within the other, was normal but

Windmill Hill had three and Whitehawk Hill in Sussex had four, the inner two being fairly neat ellipses. From the distribution of adjacent long barrows these enclosures seem to have been put up at the outer edge of their group's territory.

Like those of the long barrows, the enclosure ditches were dug in sections, and although the inner bank, except for an entrance, was probably continuous, quite wide gaps were left between the quarry ditches rather like pathways and it is these spaces that have given the causewayed enclosures their name.

Where there was more than one ditch it was usually the innermost that was more symmetrical, possibly because it was the first to be planned. A study of their shapes suggests that the rings were laid out as circles or ovals by communities using a unit of measurement. This varied from site to site and there was 'no common unit or, at best, [only] roughly defined common units within limited geographical areas'.[5] This would not be surprising if such units were based on human body-lengths such as the *span* of outstretched fingers (9 inches or 23 cm); the *foot* (12 inches, 30.5 cm); the *cubit* or length of the forearm (18–22 inches, 46–56 cm); or the *fathom* of arms fully extended (6 feet, 1.8 m). These personal lengths would have differed from place to place. It is also possible that whereas the cubit was preferred in one district, it was the fathom that was chosen somewhere else, creating individual systems quite unrecoverable today.

Just as the earthen long barrows were distributed in five main clusters in Wessex, so the great enclosures followed the same pattern, but with only one in each region: Maiden Castle in south Dorset; Hambledon Hill on Cranborne Chase; Windmill Hill on the Marlborough Downs, and, on Salisbury Plain, Whitesheet Hill in the west and Robin Hood's Ball in the east less than three miles from the future site of Stonehenge. All five seem to have been important centres. They lie in areas of better land than the unenclosed occupation sites, often near a source of flint, and in them there are more good stone axes than elsewhere, more decorated pottery, and evidence of feasting as though these were prestigious places inhabited by men and women of high rank in society.

There has been much argument about the function of these enclosures which have been variously thought to be corrals for an annual round-up and culling of cattle, and places of seasonal gatherings and trade. It is just as likely that they were also settlements and retreats, inhabited almost constantly by some people and used as a refuge by others in times of danger. Postholes associated with the ditches and banks at Whitehawk, at Hembury in Devon, at Windmill Hill and other camps hint at the former existence of substantial stockades and gateways. Walls, massively built, at Crickley Hill in Gloucestershire and at Carn Brea in Cornwall and a timber rampart at Hambledon Hill are further indications of the defensive nature of these enclosures.

It has been argued that these were not fortified settlements because the ditches were not deep enough nor the banks high enough to provide a proper defence, but this takes no account of the vanished palisades. It is also a modern interpretation which may have been incomprehensible to the prehistoric mind. The excavator of the Offham Hill enclosure in Sussex commented that 'in many preliterate societies warfare has a strong ritual function. . . . A strong physical barrier need not necessarily be equated with an effectively strong barrier. One has to think only of the invisible but immensely powerful barriers around cult houses in Melanesia',[6] adding that the shallow ditches at Offham may have been accepted as a spiritual wall between the tabu area within and the profane world outside. Centuries later the ditch at Stonehenge may have been regarded in this way, not unsurmountable physically but, to the people of its time, psychologically impassable.

The recutting and cleaning out of their ditches, the refurbishing of their banks, the discovery of human bones and the presence of domestic litter inside the enclosures point to prolonged occupation inside camps big enough to contain humans and their livestock. Not all the material found in them is exotic. Scores of flint scrapers have been unearthed, everyday tools for the cleaning of hides and as ordinary as plastic wrappings in a modern dustbin.

The ditches have revealed another of the purposes of some enclosures. Less privileged folk may have been buried there, especially the young whose inability to walk or talk meant they were not complete members of society. At Offham Hill it was thought that corpses had been exposed inside the earthwork, some of their bones slipping into the ditch as the flesh decayed. Even more telling evidence came from Hambledon Hill,[7] one of the most spectacular sites in Dorset because of the great ramparts of the Iron Age hillfort that were raised there three thousand years after the Neolithic occupation. Captured by the Roman general Vespasian in AD 44, the hillfort later saw fifty of Cromwell's soldiers defeat two thousand peasants in AD 1645. In the following century Wolfe trained his troops on the steep slopes of the hill before they scaled the Heights of Abraham at Quebec in 1749. Neolithic people had lived here, five thousand years earlier, at the western edge of Salisbury Plain.

There were three adjacent enclosures, all of them inside an enormous though incomplete bank surrounding some 60 acres (24 ha). One of them on Stepleton Spur may have been for domestic occupation. Another, to its north, was different. Inside it were pits with splendid ritual objects, finely-made imported pottery, a jadeite axe, other axes of Cornish greenstone, antlers of red deer, and deposits very reminiscent of offerings to the dead. In the ditches there were human bones, 60 per cent of them of young children, even more than the dramatic 40 per cent in other enclosures. That these were the remains of corpses formerly exposed in the open air was confirmed by the disturbed skeleton of a young man whose hips and leg-bones had been gnawed by dogs or wolves before his interment.

Many human skulls were excavated from the ditches, set meticulously upright but often without jaw-bones. 'This main enclosure may have been the site of a gigantic necropolis constructed for the exposure of the cadaveric remains of a huge population . . . a vast reeking open cemetery, its silence broken only by the din of crows and ravens.'[8] One can imagine the inhabitants of the settlement half a mile to the south-east carrying the dead up the hillside to this graveyard, leaving offerings in pits, having their funerary feasts alongside the corpses, the bodies of infants, children and adults left here to rot. Months later the dry bones were buried, the skulls placed along the ditch bottom.

As many as 350 people may have lain here and the communal burial-ground for them was quite different from the long barrow for someone more distinguished on the south side of the enclosure. Aligned north-south, it had been a comparatively small mound, not more than 84 feet (25.6 m) long. A bigger barrow, 225 feet long 48 wide and 8 feet high (68.6 × 14.6 × 2.4 m), also aligned north-south, can be seen between the northern banks of the later hillfort. This barrow, Child Okeford 1, has been dug into, but nothing is known of its contents. Bulldozing of the smaller barrow, Child Okeford 2, badly damaged it, but much human bone was recovered from the wreckage and '*could* have come from one individual'.[8]

This mixture of occupation, defence, ritual and burial may have been repeated in the two enclosures on Salisbury Plain, one at the far west, the other at the east. A small excavation at Whitesheet Hill, NNW of Shaftesbury, produced sherds of a local round-bottomed bowl, flint flakes, a scraper and an almost intact skull of a small, long-horned ox. The egg-shaped enclosure had a long SW-NE axis, an alignment repeated in several later ritual sites on Salisbury Plain, including Stonehenge.

The Whitesheet Hill site was quite small, just over 5 acres (2 ha), and its eastern counterpart, Robin Hood's Ball, was little bigger, the outermost of its two banks enclosing an area of almost 8 acres (3 ha) (Fig. 4). The name of the site actually belongs to the nearby wood and may refer to the round barrow there, 'ball' being Old Norse for a circular mound. 'Robin Hood' may have nothing to do with the medieval outlaw. As late as 1773 the place was known as Robin Wood Ball and there is still a Wood's Butt close to it.

The causewayed enclosure, in a commanding position, lies at the north-east corner of the cluster of long barrows near the River Avon, possibly because strangers, whether traders or neighbours, were reluctant to penetrate far into another's territory. The inner ring is an almost perfect ellipse with a long SW-NE axis[9] and if its orientation of about 38° was intended it may have been deliberately aligned on the northernmost rising of the moon.

Ploughing near the enclosure disturbed two quite distinct areas by its ditches, one with a clutter of flint scrapers, the other with lots of burnt flints and sarsen querns and grain-rubbers for grinding corn, proof of

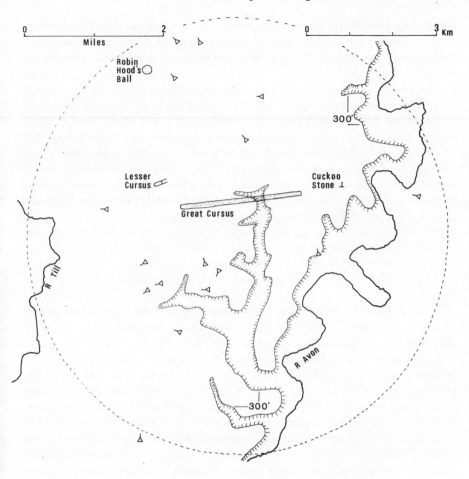

Fig. 4. The Stonehenge Region c. 3500 BC.

domestic activity.[10] Much broken pottery and occupation rubbish was discovered. Postholes in the outer ditch, some of them burnt, hinted at a stockade, and some articulated legbones may have fallen from mortuary scaffolds standing alongside the perimeter of the earthwork. As at Hambledon Hill, there are traces of a second enclosure here, perhaps used for the exposure of corpses. Yet, once again emphasising the contrast between the disposal of the unimportant dead and those of higher status, there is a nearby long barrow on Alton Down (Figheldean 31). When Thurnam dug into it in 1864 he discovered the doubled-up skeleton of a man who, from the eroded state of the skull, had been exposed for a while before burial. Close to this single skeleton was an oblong pit, far too small for a grave and too shallow for a post. It held nothing but brown earth.[11]

Analysis of the soil under the bank at Robin Hood's Ball pointed to a climate in prehistoric times very similar to the oceanic, cool and moist conditions of today. This gradual deterioration of the weather probably accelerated the struggle for any land that had not been badly affected by the heavier rainfall.

There were violent deaths during these unsettled years. A man's skeleton in the Cotswold tomb of Ascott-under-Wychwood had a flint arrowhead in its backbone and a second lay by his chest. An old man in the West Kennet barrow near Avebury had an arrowhead by his throat. A young man buried in a mortuary enclosure at Fengate had a similar missile embedded in his ribcage. 'At his feet were the tiny bones of an infant and beyond the infant were the partially disarticulated remains of a [young] woman and a child about ten.'[12] All the bones, except the infant's which were too frail, are now on display in Peterborough Museum.

As well as such individual killings, there is evidence of attacks on defended causewayed enclosures. At Crickley Hill a rectangular cabin had been set on fire and over two hundred arrowheads lay in its ruins.[13] Other arrowheads have been found at Windmill Hill even though its people did little hunting.

Some prehistoric bows have been preserved in peat-bogs, single pieces of yew 5 to 6 feet (1.5–1.9 m) long, murderous longbows accurate up to 60 yards (55 m) and with a range well in excess of that (Table 5).

Such big bows were surprisingly like the famous English warbows of the Middle Ages, also made from a single piece of yew and with a deadly pulling-power of 100 lbs (45 kg). The medieval arrows were about a yard (1 m) long, not very different from the occasional prehistoric arrow-shafts that have been recovered whose lengths varied from 34 to 40 inches (86–102 cm). Their hitting power may be compared with a modern, light hunting arrow: 'Such an arrow is quite capable of cutting its way right through a deer and will easily penetrate a thousand sheets of paper as used in telephone directories'.[14]

**TABLE 5. Details of prehistoric longbows found in Great Britain**[15]

| Site | Length | | Wood | Date | |
|------|--------|------|------|------|------|
| | Inches | Cm | | bc | BC |
| Meare Heath, Somerset | 75 | 190.5 | Yew | 2690 ± 120 | 3470 |
| Ashcott Heath, Somerset | 63 | 159 | Yew | 2665 ± 120 | 3450 |
| Cambridge Fens | 60 | 153 | Yew | 1730 ± 110 | 2130 |
| Edington Burtle, Somerset | 61 | 155 | Yew | 1320 ± 110 | 1620 |
| Denny, Stirling | 68 | 172 | Oak | 1300 ± 85 | 1595 |

American Indians of the 19th century are known to have put arrows completely through a full-grown buffalo. In 1884 a USA cavalry officer compared their bows favourably with the most powerful Colt revolver, adding that he 'had seen a bow throw an arrow five hundred yards and have myself often discharged one entirely through a board one inch thick'.[16] These bows, with strings of animal tendon, were similar to those of Neolithic Britain. The fragment of a yew longbow, found in AD 1890 in Drumwhinny Bog, Co. Fermanagh, still had a knotted piece of animal gut hanging from a hole at its nock-end.

Like the Indians, people in Britain had both hunting arrows and others, with heavier flint blades, for war. These finely-chipped flint arrowheads, viciously sharp, were probably attached to ash shafts that had been polished between two grooved sandstone rubbers which, when clasped together with the shaft between them, formed a neat cylindrical hole in which the wood could be pulled up and down until it was glassily smooth.

Weaponry like this was probably responsible for the death of a well-built man, aged about 19, whose skeleton lay among the ashes and charcoal of the burnt-down palisade at Hambledon Hill. He appeared to have been carrying a child, maybe trying to save it from the fire, when he was killed by an arrow that hit him in the chest.[17] Signs of another attack were noticed at the hilltop village of Carn Brea with its rampart of colossal stones, some weighing over two tons. More than seven hundred arrowheads lay about the enclosure, many of them around the gateway.[18]

It was not only human dangers that threatened these early people. Theirs was an existence in which the ghosts of ancestors dwelt in an Other-World of spirits who could protect the living. Life was everywhere. It was in the animals, in the rock that gave stone, in the stream with its sustaining water, in the windblown tree, in the storm, in the sun and in the silent moon where the dead might linger. It was a world of humdrum planting and herding, of making pots, of cooking lukewarm gruels with stone pot-boilers hot from the fire, of cutting skins for clothing, a tedious, tiring world. But it was also a life of myths in which tales were recited of the marvel of the beginning when man was born, stories told, things remembered and mingled with magic so that old men became heroes and dead men became almost gods. It was a world of living spirits that slid in and out of existence with the warmth and the snow, with daylight and darkness so that man was never free of them. It was necessary to perform rites, make offerings. There were rituals in the sacred places and there were charms to be carried or worn, the chalk plaque, the coloured pebble, the stone axe.

Such awareness of natural forces and the threat of attack by man probably compelled society to become more organised, with leaders whose prestige was manifested not only through individual burial but through ostentatious possessions such as fine axes. Forest clearance had already increased the demand for axes and it is in this middle Neolithic period that the first really deep pits for flint were dug in southern England. From an early one on Easton Down eight miles ESE of Stonehenge some miners' antler picks had been dated to about 3280 BC (2530 ± 150 bc).

It was the axe of stone, however, that was coveted. Sources of good stone had been known since Mesolithic times, but it was Neolithic people who exploited the so-called 'axe-factories' where loose scree on mountainsides or outcrops of hard but workable stone were used for the manufacture of tools as sharp but less brittle than flint. The club-shaped axes, which could also be adzes or plough-shares, were not perforated for a shaft but were attached to a wooden handle by thonging. Highly polished, daintily symmetrical and with keen cutting-edges, these were objects to be prized not only as implements but sometimes as articles of rare richness.

It has been possible to locate the sites of several factories and they have been catalogued into over twenty groups, Group I at Land's End, Group VI in the Lake District, and Group VII in north Wales being three of the most important.[19] As might be expected, the Group VII factory at Graig Lwyd on a headland overlooking Conway Bay found a demand for its tools all over Wales. Conversely, the Group VI factories on the slithering, perilous Langdale slopes in Cumbria had a wider market. Many of their products of fine-grained tuff were taken across the Pennines to the area near Bridlington in Yorkshire. From there they were redistributed to the Peak District and the Midlands, scattered over a vast rectangle bordered on the west from Liverpool down to Bristol and, in the south, from the Severn across to Sussex.

Few of these axes reached Salisbury Plain. There the supply came from Cornwall, whose Group I source near Mount's Bay provided elegant axes of greenstone, shaped into long triangular forms by pecking and polishing. They were exported, probably by sea, as far away as Wessex and East Anglia. Strangely, not many have been recovered from Cornwall itself, maybe because other local factories offered too much competition but more probably because 'merchants' in southern England had established trading links with the miners of Land's End, taking virtually all their products. On Salisbury Plain over 84 per cent of the axes are Cornish and many of them are objects of beauty.

From their worn-down edges and scratched sides there is no doubt that most of them were used as working tools and were either broken, thrown away or lost. Yet it is equally apparent that others had a symbolic value and were deliberately buried in the earth or dropped in rivers and streams in areas which were considered spiritually potent. In Britain there are concentrations near causewayed enclosures, cursuses and standing stones like that at Rudston near Bridlington, a towering pillar of millstone grit, over 25 feet (7.8 m) high, the tallest stone in the British Isles. It stands at the edge of a terrace on which four cursuses converge. 'Statistical analysis has shown that the monolith occupies the central point in the distribution of polished flint knives, stone maceheads and two forms of stone adze.'[20] In Wessex the majority of stone axes have been found within a few miles of the causewayed enclosures of Windmill Hill, Maiden Castle and Robin Hood's Ball.

Some of them were offerings. Many undamaged axes of flint or stone and of high finish have been dredged from the Thames, and native pottery, known as Peterborough ware, lavishly decorated with birdbone or twisted-cord impressions, have been recovered intact from rivers or in pits alongside them. Underneath a plank of the Sweet trackway in Somerset, laid across a stretch of boggy ground, there was a flawless, slender axe of pale-green jadeite, 8 inches long, 2½ wide but only ¾ inches thick (20 × 6 × 2 cm). It was so perfectly shaped that its craftsman must have spent days on its grinding and polishing and yet it had been deposited in the water under the crossplanks of the track. Another delightful jadeite axe, its end broken, came from Breamore in Hampshire and others are known in Wessex.

It is believed that these beautiful ornaments had a distant origin in Switzerland or the Italian Alps. They are far too thin and fragile ever to have been labouring tools and must have been cult objects. Some from Brittany are up to 18 inches (47 cm) long but barely an inch (25 mm) thick. Others, smaller than this, about 8 inches (20 cm) in length, have a perforation at their tapering end for suspension around the neck. That the axe symbolised a female guardian of the dead has already been mentioned, but it may also have had a developing significance as a giver of life and strength for the living, for the dead and for the forces of nature themselves. This would explain the discovery of so many axes in pits near ritual centres and in water believed to be inhabited by spirits. 'The discovery of several jadeite axes in or near streams or rivers, or in other fluviatile deposits, and the one certainly found in a boat, suggests that they were either lost during transport or deliberately consigned to water.'[21]

With trade and exchange, distant contacts were established, tenuous at first but later becoming strong, vital to our understanding of Stonehenge. Foreign axes, not only of jadeite but of dolerite, a basalt-like stone, black, grey, green, sometimes speckled, and taking a sharp finish, have been found near Southampton and Bournemouth, at Bredon Hill near the River Severn and at Priddy in Somerset. They came from Sélédin in central Brittany, an axe-factory which at its height may have been producing as many as five thousand axes annually. Its first tools were used only in southern Brittany but later, by 3500 BC, the axes were reaching the whole of western France. Their discovery at the mouths of great rivers in southern Britain shows the beginnings of Anglo-Breton links that would eventually develop into close ties between the regions.

Such long-distance transportation involved not only a sea-crossing, even from the Channel Isles, of some 80 miles (128 km), but also some knowledge of the coastline and British centres of population. Organised expeditions are more likely than chance explorations of a little-known land. More locally, the methods by which Cornish axes reached Wessex is debatable but it is permissible to think of parties of young men, in soft skin clothing and carrying longbows and leather quivers, journeying by canoe along the rivers, shouldering the boats across high land to the next waterway, the group taking with it grain or flints or hides to be exchanged as gifts when they arrived at Land's End.

The means by which 'foreign' articles are acquired by recent primitive societies suggests that when the travellers arrived at the settlement of the axe-makers there were meetings and feasts for several days before the Wessex men could leave, taking with them the axes and tools they had been given. Or it may have been the reverse, with expeditions from the axe-factories making the sea voyage to Salisbury Plain, turning up the quiet, wooded waters of the River Avon. Whatever the direction, whatever the method, it can be assumed that such 'trading' involved ceremonies approved by long usage. It can also be assumed that anything novel seen by the visitors would be minutely described when the party returned home, the countryside, the dangers encountered, farming practices, burial customs.

Externally, the tombs of Wessex and Cornwall were very different and the fact that many around Land's End were circular would have been commented on by people from Salisbury Plain. Within a few miles of the principal factory at Mount's Bay and at others near modern St Ives and Marazion, there were many low, round cairns known as entrance-graves with stone-built passages and chambers, the mound edged with granite kerbstones.[22] Such unusual structures would intrigue foreigners, although it is unlikely that any stranger would have been allowed inside these sacred places and he would remain ignorant of their contents.

It was the circularity and the smallness of the entrance-graves, most being no more than 20 to 39 feet (6–12 m) in diameter, that made such a contrast with the gigantic rectangular barrows of Wessex. Elsewhere in the British Isles at this time the circle became increasingly popular. Round houses replaced the traditional four-sided home. Circular chambered tombs, or passage-graves, were erected in Ireland and Scotland. Round barrows, without entrances or burial-chambers, were known in Yorkshire. And by 3500 BC some of the first stone circles and circular earthen henges had been built, open-air enclosures that eventually supplanted the long barrows and megalithic tombs as ritual centres.

It was a time of upheaval, with old customs being abandoned and new ways introduced, links with far-off areas growing, leaders controlling the affairs of their communities and engaging in ever-more grandiloquent projects to proclaim the permanence of their society in an unstable world. Ancestor-cults developed side by side with the glorification of the living.

Because of the need for more food, any outstanding success in its production seemed proof of the intervention of those ancient ancestors whose work it had been to clear the land and grow the first crops. 'Agricultural surplus is regarded as the will of the gods and is attributed directly to the influence of the ancestors in the spirit world.'[23] Those of the living who had the best harvests were believed to be descended from the most powerful ancestors and they were able to demonstrate their fortune and strength by the giving of feasts and presents. This established their superiority in ways both obvious and acceptable to their relatives and neighbours.

In status halfway between men and gods, such people demanded wealth in life, grandeur in death. A laboriously-dug and monumental cursus provided the means for both.

The purpose of these linear earthworks has exercised archaeologists ever since William Stukeley, that fine fieldworker, detected the faint outlines of one just north of Stonehenge: 'Aug. 6, 1723. I discovered the noble Ippodrom ["hippodrome", a course for chariot-and horse-racing] of Stoneheng' for nothing els can I suppose it. tis formd of two parallel lines 10000 feet 700 cubits in length and 350 asunder going in a strait line from east to west, 200 north of Stoneheng. the vallum is inward of both.' Years later Stukeley noted that 'This is the finest piece of ground that can be imagin'd for the purpose of a horse-race',[24] and for 'hippodrome' he substituted the shorter Latin *cursus* from which is derived the English 'course'.

He was mistaken. With its square corners the Stonehenge cursus, like its counterparts, was unsuitable for racing. Nor are any wheeled vehicles known from this period in the British Isles, and despite the presence of horsebones in some southern tombs such as West Kennet and Winterbourne Stoke 1[25] it is unlikely that horses were yet used for riding or traction. People walked. Life was slow and four miles was a long hour across the countryside, something which makes the 3½ mile (5.6 km) perimeter of the Stonehenge Great Cursus all the more astonishing.

Extending WNW-ESE, this long enclosure with its parallel banks was like a monstrous pathway nearly two miles (3 km) long from end to end and over 110 yards (100 m) wide, dipping near its centre into the dry valley of Stonehenge Bottom and then rising eastwards towards the landmark of Beacon Hill two miles away. It was built at the heart of a region. Robin Hood's Ball was two miles to the NNW and near the cursus itself were long barrows, two to the north, one to the south-west and no fewer than eight to its south.

On the same bearing and two-thirds of a mile (900 m) to the ENE a crude block of sarsen, the Cuckoo Stone, lies in a field behind a little wood. Today it is a stumpy 6 feet (2 m) long, rough and thick, but it may once have stood as an outlying marker of the cursus just as many Neolithic tombs in Britain and Brittany had a free-standing stone outside them. Over a thousand years later the timber rings of Woodhenge were set up a quarter of a mile beyond the stone on the identical line as though perpetuating a hallowed alignment. If so, it is strange that the bearing, 263° – 83°, is not astronomically important.

Sir Norman Lockyer, Director of the Solar Physics Laboratory, suggested that the cursus had been oriented so that dawn-worshippers of the May sun would have been warned of its imminent appearance by the rising of the Pleiades around 1950 BC.[26] The sightline is quite good but the date is 1500 years too late. In 3500 BC Alcyone ($\varepsilon$ Tauri), the brightest of this lovely cluster of stars, was rising a long way away from the direction of the Stonehenge cursus.

Instead, the row may have been rather casually laid out to mark the equinoctial sunrises of March and September midway between the midsummer and midwinter solstices. There is a legend about the Cuckoo Stone which says that the bird perches on it on Midsummer Day, but the sarsen was known as the Cuckold Stone in 1790[27] and this suggests that it was human frailty on warm summer nights rather than avian astronomy on cool summer dawns that gave the stone its name.

The elongated interior of the cursus covered 70 acres (28 ha), big enough to accommodate three dozen football pitches laid end to end. Although it was hypothetically possible for a few fanatical families to have dug out the quarter of a million cubic feet of chalk (7100 m³), it would have taken them years. 40,000 man-hours or more were spent on the construction of this incredible structure. Its completion demonstrates the cohesion of a society prepared to undertake such a project.

In plan Stonehenge and the cursus form a gigantic, upside-down triangle, the tip balanced on Stonehenge with the long base of the cursus half a mile to the north, its ends north-west and north-east of where the stone circle would stand. Stonehenge is almost but not quite due south of the earthwork's centre. Stukeley thought that it was: 'The meridian line of Stonehenge passes precisely thro' the middle of the *Cursus* . . . [whose ends] are each exactly 60 degrees from the meridian line. . . . By which we see, the Druids well understood the geometry of a circle, and its measure of 360 parts.'[28]

Like many hopeful researchers after him, Stukeley was distorting facts to suit his belief that the druids were scientists and mathematicians capable of landscape engineering. Stonehenge and the cursus did not form an isosceles triangle. From Stonehenge it is less than a mile to the west end of the cursus but it is more than a mile to the eastern terminal because the WSW-ENE axis of the earthwork is slightly tilted from a true west-east line.

The cursus must have been spectacular. In the beginning the chalk-white lines of its banks stood starkly against the greenness of the plain, sweeping across the landscape like the ski-tracks of a giant. Today they are almost imperceptible. From Stonehenge their outline is hardly visible, the banks eroded, the ditches choked but marked by two hedgerows leading from the trees of the western Fargo Plantation, sliding downhill and then rising gradually to the thin north-south coppice where an imitation long barrow is buried under a farm track.

Cemeteries of later round barrows nestle around the cursus, testifying to its association with death. The Old and New King Barrows are at its east. Mounds, now ploughed-down, lay along its northern edge. Others can be seen to the north on Durrington Down. The conspicuous Cursus group, dug into by Stukeley and Lord Pembroke, hump near its western terminal. Two round barrows were built inside the cursus itself, one of them covering the skeleton of a man, head to the north, the 'curious pebble' commented on by Hoare lying by his side.[29]

The Stonehenge Great Cursus ranks amongst the largest of some fifty cursuses in Britain, most of them in the south and east where the soil is most easily dug. Many have one end near a river as though water were important in their rites.

Some, like that at Stonehenge and the even longer Dorset Cursus, are intimately linked with long barrows, six in Dorset, no fewer than eleven in the vicinity of Stonehenge. Not only do two long barrows abut both the west and east ends of the 6-mile (9.6 km) long Dorset Cursus but two others can be found inside it. Gussage St Michael III lies at right-angles to the banks, its long mound almost blocking the space between them. Pentridge IV was incorporated into the western bank, proving the barrow's greater antiquity. This association with long mounds, as well as the nearness of Bronze Age round barrows and the similarity of cursuses, although hugely bigger, to the rectangular mortuary enclosures, makes it likely that these linear earthworks were centres of funerary ritual with corpses or collections of bones paraded along their length prior to interment or cremation.

With this in mind it is noteworthy that years after its construction Neolithic people deliberately altered both ends of the Stonehenge cursus to make them look like long barrows. The terminal ditches were abruptly deepened, the banks raised, and any stranger would have thought that the cursus had been laid out between two distant long mounds. Such prehistoric 'follies' show how determined people were to establish bonds between the cursus, their ancestors and the spirit-world.

At the east end this architectural illusion was so successful that despite the unusual north-south axis of the 'barrow' it deceived Stukeley, Colt Hoare,[30] Thurnam and modern archaeologists. For years it was known as Amesbury 42 until excavation in 1983 revealed the truth. Thurnam dug into it in 1868,[31] finding only the later interment of a woman and child near the surface and another infant slightly lower down. Significantly, there was no burial of human bones at the bottom, just the leg-bones, pelvis and skulls of oxen put there when the terminal was transformed into the resemblance of an earthen long barrow.

Apart from these indications that cursuses were places in which funerary rites were performed, their other functions remain enigmatic. Access to their interiors was provided by gaps at sites such as the Springfield Cursus in Essex,[32] at the Dorset Cursus', and at Stonehenge where Stukeley was the first to notice 'two entrances (as it were:) gaps being left in the two little ditches',[33] but it is impossible to say what features lie undetected inside the enclosures. Finds of pottery in the ditches suggest a date quite early in the Neolithic and this is partly confirmed by the fact that Late Neolithic henges such as Thornborough in Yorkshire were built on top of their banks. Otherwise, little has been discovered to explain their purpose.

Fortunately, glimmers of light moderate this darkness. A circular ditch at one end of the Dorchester cursus in Oxfordshire with another near the centre,[34] and the truncated bottoms of post holes at the north-east end of the Springfield cursus,[35] show that circular, perhaps roofed structures stood inside some of the earthworks. Excavation in 1947 in the western part of the Stonehenge cursus came upon a dense concentration of dolerite fragments like the stone used for the bluestone circles to be raised inside Stonehenge. The excavator speculated that a ring of standing stones had once existed inside the cursus: 'It will follow that a cursus . . . represents some sort of processional way containing a stone or timber circle with a long barrow or other Late Neolithic ossuary . . . the material embodiment of an attempted connecting link between the living and the dead.'[36]

Signs of burning in many of the cursuses, none of which has been fully explored, and the discovery of human and animal bones are indications that skeletal remains may have been consumed on pyres after exposure within the enclosures. Yet so exceptionally long are some cursuses that it is unlikely that they were limited to any one function as processional avenue, charnel-house or crematorium. It is feasible that they were put up to demarcate a sacred area of land dedicated to the gods, a *temenos* or holy precinct.[37] Separated from the profane world, such a hallowed piece of earth would be a fitting place for the dead to lie before their burial.

Some of the longer cursuses consist of two separate lengths that joined together where their ends lay on lower ground, the junctures indicated by a kink in the line, something very obvious in the Dorset Cursus.[38] Similar combinations exist in stone rows like the famous Ménec lines near Carnac in Brittany and Stall Moor on Dartmoor. The Ménec multiple rows, over half a mile (800 m) from end to end, extend WSW and ENE from the bottom of a gentle fall where the stones are smallest. There is a noticeable bend in the rows at this point. The eastern rows lead up a soft gradient to a partly-ruined egg-shaped cromlech or stone circle. The western lines were connected to a similar but almost destroyed cromlech which, like its partner, seems to have been aligned on the solstitial sun. A plausible interpretation of these settings is that they were for processions and ceremonies at midsummer, and midwinter to commemorate the important divisions of the year.[39]

Stall Moor in Devon is the longest stone row in the British Isles. It is a line over two miles (3 km) in length, composed of two meandering stretches that join together at the watery banks of the River Erme. The northern section ends at a small burial cairn on Green Hill. In the southern sector the stones rise in height to the tallest pillar, which stands against an impressive stone circle whose interior is devoid of any sign of a burial mound. Like the Kennet Avenue linking the Sanctuary stone circle to the great circle-henge of Avebury, Stall Moor appears to consist of a circular enclosure joined to a far-off burial place by a line of stones. It is possible that a cursus had a similar role, with a site for funerary rituals inside a long and impressive promenade along which the mourners could proceed to a barrow or flat grave. Three mortuary structures were found close to the Dorchester cursus, suggesting that cursuses were 'associated with some ritual in connection with the dead and may in fact delimit ceremonial ways along which the dead were carried to their place of final interment'.[40]

Half a mile north-west of the Stonehenge Great Cursus is the lobster-shaped, ploughed-out site of the Lesser Cursus, a quarter of a mile (400 m) long and with two banks like claws reaching out from its ENE end. In plan like an enormous coffin, the main enclosure has a continuous bank inside its ditch, but the eastern extension is open, suggesting that the work was abandoned, something not unusual in prehistoric times. Excavation at the west of the cursus recovered several antlers, regularly spaced apart and deliberately buried when the ditch was backfilled. Similar deposits of antlers have been found with Neolithic burials, at the Tilshead Lodge (Tilshead 5) long barrow not 6 miles (9.6 km) west of the Lesser Cursus, where several fine antlers lay above an ox-skull, and at Norton Bavant 13, 11 miles (18 km) to the west, in which a magnificent antler rested amongst a confused mass of skeletons. Nearly all the skulls were broken. Thurnam wondered if an adjacent battered lump of flint weighing 3¾ lbs (1.7 kg) had been used to smash them.[41]

Antlers, shed by stags yearly and replaced by even larger new growth, may have been regarded by Neolithic people as magical, objects of powerful regeneration and therefore beneficial to the dead. At Winterbourne St Martin 5b in Dorset a skeleton lying on its back had a pot by its left arm and an antler by its right. At Chaldon Herring two corpses had antlers carefully balanced on both of their shoulders.

Native traditions were slowly changing. Cremation, long practised in the eastern parts of Britain, was taken up by some groups on Salisbury Plain. Increasingly, there was a difference in the burial rites accorded to various members of society. Round barrows slowly replaced the long. Flat graves were dug, sometimes in cemeteries like the one at Durrington. 'Besides the barrows there were in 1864 in an arable field approaching our Winter-bourne boundary remains of about thirty graves of common people; but only two of them even then nearly perfect. These were where the body had been laid north to south, looking northwards, upon the chalk rock which there was about a foot below the surface. Flints had been set like a low wall around the body and apparently above it. The teeth of one skeleton were in full number but the cusps had worn off and every tooth was level. In the skull was a triangular flint, but if it belonged to a weapon and had caused death it was one of the rudest ever fashioned.'[42]

Communal burials were also placed under round barrows. In the Soldier's Grave, a large mound only a few yards from the impressive Nympsfield megalithic long barrow in Gloucestershire, a rock-cut pit like a boat contained the bones of between 28 and 44 individuals. At Westbury 7 near Bratton at the north-west corner of Salisbury Plain Colt Hoare noted the similarity between this round barrow and its long predecessors: 'On opening it we found its interior corresponding in great measure with the long barrows, and differing from any of the [Bronze Age] circular *tumuli* hitherto discussed; for amongst several large sarsen stones and flints, we discovered seven or eight skeletons lying in every direction; the thighbones of one by the head of another, a skull on the breast of a second, &cet, &cet, but no trinkets or warlike or domestic instruments.'[43] The skeletons there, probably interred as fleshed corpses, were different from the contents of the Mere 13d round barrow 11 miles (18 km) to the SSW. Also excavated by Cunnington and Hoare, this held only a single person who had been cremated and whose ashes had been gathered into a small pot.

Other individuals, perhaps of high status like those in the biggest long barrows, have been found even closer to Stonehenge. Just north of the circle, at Larkhill, the skeleton of a young man whose corpse seems to have been tightly bound was unearthed from a north-south grave. The nearby construction of a military railway in 1918 uncovered the bones of a middle-aged man apparently buried in a sitting position. Another, near Woodhenge, lay in a shallow, circular pit. The decayed remains, crouched and with the head to the south, were surrounded by Neolithic sherds. The body had been exposed elsewhere, for there was no lower jaw and 'only a few pieces of skull'.[44]

People such as these may have been of sufficient rank to be given elaborate and protracted funerary rites, their corpses carried from the cursus to a circular mortuary house of heavy timbers that stood on the site of Stonehenge.

# 3

# The first Stonehenge
## Stonehenge Ia: 3200 – 2700 BC

*It is thus not only possible, but even probable, that there existed in
the centre of the site, some timber building.*

Richard Atkinson, *Stonehenge*, 170

Long before the circle of sarsens that most people think of as Stonehenge, long before the two rings of bluestones that preceded that circle, around 3300 BC at the very beginning of the monument's history a substantial wooden building stood on the eastern slopes of Salisbury Plain overlooking the cursus. A century or more later a spacious open-air enclosure, ditched and banked, was laid out around it (Fig. 5).

Three things relate these structures to the beliefs and burial practices of earlier people in the region: the animal bones, especially skulls, found in them; their alignment to the south; and their association with the moon. These features were intimately connected with a great charnel-house of timber inside the earthwork, a place intended as a lodge in which corpses would remain until they were reduced to skeletons. Only then would the bones be removed for final interment in one of the cemeteries around Stonehenge.

The earthwork or 'henge' was thrown up by natives, the descendants of the adaptable and inventive families of earlier generations, the short-lived members of an increasingly hierarchical society, people living in an age when the axe and the skulls of oxen were cult objects and when the mundane drudgery of farming was enriched and sustained by elaborate rites of death involving the moon.

From miles around, straggling in from their lonely farmsteads in the sheltered dells, carrying their tools of wood and antler and flint, these were the people who dug out the beginnings of the world's most famous prehis-

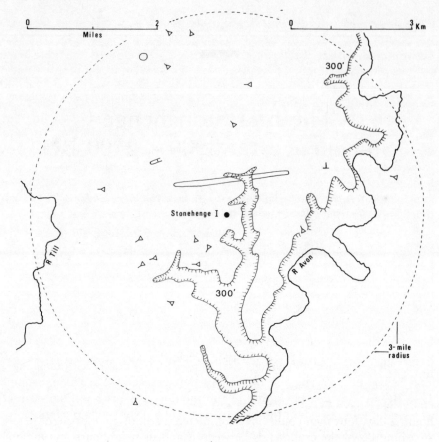

Fig. 5. The Stonehenge Region c. 3200 BC. Stonehenge Ia.

toric monument. It was a time in the later Neolithic when the construction of circular assembly-places was widespread. There were henges such as Arminghall in Norfolk and Maumbury Rings in Dorset on the easy soils of the lowlands. There were circles of standing stones like Castlerigg in Cumbria and Stenness in Orkney on the granite and sandstone uplands of north-western Britain. There were also rings of upright posts, perhaps carved and painted like totem-poles, but these have long since vanished. Today it is usually only from the air, as at Woodhenge, that the lusher vegetation growing on the filled-in postholes of these structures can be detected.

Amongst these early rings the henge from which Stonehenge gets its name was not outstanding either in size or design. From the meticulous survey of 1877 by Flinders Petrie, later to become a great Egyptologist, its dimensions are exactly known.[1] A circle 360 feet (110 m) across was scribed out, probably by means of leather thonging or a fibre rope with a sharpened stake at its end to furrow out the inner edge of a ditch. Eighteen feet (5.5 m) outside this a second furrow defined the ditch's outer side. The turf between these rings was spaded off and the sods stacked up tidily with baskets of topsoil dumped over them to make a low outer bank never more than 8 feet (2.4 m) wide or 2 feet 6 inches (76 cm) high. Traces of this minor earthwork can still be seen today.

With the exposure of the chalk below the grass, the task of digging out the great ditch began. Working outwards from its inward rim, pairs of diggers with antler picks hacked out pits deep enough to stand in and then levered away the jagged lumps of chalk to make elongated hollows like foxholes, steep-sided and flat-bottomed. Pit after pit was quarried by the gangs and from the air the site looked like a child's model railway to which more and more trucks were added, an ever-growing chaplet of holes.

A couple of men, well used to digging on their cultivated holdings, could have shifted half a ton of rubble in an hour. This was shouldered in woven panniers and leather sacks by other labourers up to the bank they were building along the inner edge of the ditch. When finished it was 20 feet (6 m) wide and 6 feet (2 m) high, broken only by two causewayed entrances, one, 35 feet (10.7 m) wide, at the north-east, the other, one-third the width, at the south. Such a bank was a considerable barrier. On it, moreover, from the discovery of postholes in the short sections that have been excavated, there may have been a stockade preventing any outsider from seeing into the enclosure.

Up to twenty-five ditch segments, from each of which came 50 tons of chalk, may have been dug at the same time. Digging and carrying eight hours a day, four men could have completed a section in a fortnight before smashing down the crude ends between it and its neighbours and moving on to the next part to be opened. Hawley, who excavated many of these trenches, likened the result to an irregular polygon composed of nearly a hundred hollows that merged together to form an almost continuous ditch, 4½ to 7 feet (1.4–2.1 m) deep, from which had been taken about 6000 tons of turf, soil and chalk. Even allowing for bad weather and weariness, a workforce of two hundred could have finished in two months, perhaps after the harvest. The remains of flying ants, insects that flourish only in the autumn, have been recovered from another Late Neolithic project, Silbury Hill, and Stonehenge may similarly have been begun around September.

Silbury Hill was erected around 2750 BC. The ditch and bank at Stonehenge were constructed some centuries earlier. Organic analysis of antlers at the very bottom of the ditch has yielded radiocarbon assays of 2180 ± 105 bc, 2440 ± 60 bc, and 2460 ± 60 bc, suggesting that the henge was built around 3200 BC. The erection of the enormous timber building at its centre may have taken place several decades before then.

Hints of it were found during Hawley's excavations in the 1920s, but earlier digging had destroyed many of the clues that would have proved its existence. From what has been recovered the building was apparently just under 100 feet (31 m) across, thatched, with an entrance at the north-east and a second, narrower opening at the south where it was approached at an angle by a long, roofed passageway.

It might seem impossible that anything could be preserved of posts that rotted or were dismantled over five thousand years ago. The wood has gone, the pits that supported them have been filled by man or weather. Rain and wind have worn away a knees-depth of soil from the tops of the holes, leaving only their tapering bases, and even these have been ravaged. In the 17th and 18th centuries antiquarians shovelled out gaping craters at the heart of Stonehenge where the building had stood. Rabbits, intro-duced in the late 17th century, burrowed through the soft soil where the posts had been. Later still, millions of visitors trampled over the area. Yet some postholes survived and excavators came upon the dark rings where soil and decaying vegetation had sifted into the pits. Lt-Col. Hawley discovered scores of them.

In 1915 Sir Edward Antrobus, the owner of Stonehenge, died and the monument was put up for auction. Mr Chubb, who almost casually bought it for his wife, later generously gave it to the nation and the Office of Works decided that several of the dangerously leaning stones should be straightened and gave the Society of Antiquaries permission to undertake research excavations during the work. These began in 1919 under the direction of William Hawley, the experienced Wiltshire archaeologist whose excavation at Bulford has been mentioned. Funds were so limited that he often had to work alone, living on site in a wooden hut that, ironically, was far less spacious and well-built than the building he was to discover. Short, moustached, military and meticulous, he worked with method but little imagination and when asked by Admiral Boyle Somerville, a keen archaeoastronomer, about possible sightlines at Stonehenge, Hawley replied 'that his object has been to report all that he came across during the excavations, and to collect facts without indulging in any theory about them'.[2]

In 1922 he uncovered the holes of 46 posts arranged in six parallel lines across Stonehenge's north-east entrance[3] and in 1923, just south of the sarsen circle, he noticed more holes, 'identical in method of making and in appearance' to those of the previous year.[4] The absence in them of bits of bluestone and sarsen from the stone circles suggested that they were the handiwork of people earlier than the builders of the famous rings. Some of the holes, despite erosion, were up to 2 feet (61 cm) across and 2½ feet (76 cm) deep, big enough to have held tall, thick posts of oak supporting a low, pitched roof of thatch or reeds.[5]

There seemed to be no pattern to them, but in 1924 Hawley came upon two parallel trenches inside the henge starting between Aubrey Hole 20 and the southernmost Station Stone 92 and leading south-north towards the sarsen circle (Fig. 6). In the trenches there were regularly-spaced postholes which he thought were the remains of a stockaded, probably roofed passage about 12 feet (3.7 m) wide. It ended some 45 feet (13.7 m) short of the ditch, but the ground between was 'very flinty and hard from traffic over it'[6] as though the area had been subjected to constant trampling.

Five posts had stood diagonally across the passage-entrance which itself was at an angle to the central building, making it impossible for anyone outside to peer down the gloomy corridor into the interior. At its far end the passage was crossed by a 30 feet (9 m) long arc of nine posts, three to its west, three in it like gateposts, and three to the east. The holes of two more beyond them had been joined together to make a pit in which a grown man had been buried. 'The neck and shoulders were forced into the grave, pressing the ribs together, and causing a very broken condition. The skull was broken owing to its being slightly above the side of the grave.'[7]

As Hawley's excavation neared the sarsen circle, more postholes were found, and as some of them had been cut into by the Y and Z Holes of the Middle Bronze Age they were obviously older than those pits. Inside the circle itself the ground was a honeycomb of postholes, some dug into by later stoneholes, others riddled by rabbits. Yet, as Hawley recorded, the 'whole of this disturbed area coincided exactly with the direction taken by the postholes on the outside of the circle'.[8] Despite his stated aversion to guesswork, he speculated that 'a wooden passage-grave' had stood there before the erection of the stones.[9] Fear of undermining the great sarsens prevented him from investigating further, but his plans and detailed descriptions of the postholes support his interpretation of a large, circular structure that had been carefully dismantled. One hole, 4 feet (1.2 m) deep and 2 feet 8 inches (81 cm) wide, had been packed hard with chalk as though neatly backfilled when its post was withdrawn. At the bottom was 'a little dark brown substance which might have been decayed wood'.[10]

The size of the building can be conjectured even though it may have had several phases, none of them dateable on present evidence. An inspection of Hawley's plans suggests that his south-north passage led to a perimeter fence or palisade about 138 feet (42 m) in diameter, remnants of which were found in an interrupted curve of smallish holes running from Z Hole 7 to Z Hole 11, with the passage terminating on that line near Z Holes 9 and 10. A similar avenue or passage existed at the henge on Saggart Hill 11 miles (18 km) south-west of Dublin.[11] Like that at Stonehenge, it was aligned north-south, 30 feet long and 6 feet 3 inches wide (9×1.9 m) and it led towards a rectangular hearth in which the soil has been burned a deep red 'by the kindling of many fires over a long period'. From the lack of domestic rubbish the hearth seemed to have had a ritual function. It lay near the centre of an apparent round timber building whose walls were supported by two rings of posts, the outer being about 72 feet (22 m) in diameter. Several burials were found in it.

Intriguingly, the excavator of this little-known site, with its many similarities to the early Stonehenge, believed that the Lugg Townland henge had

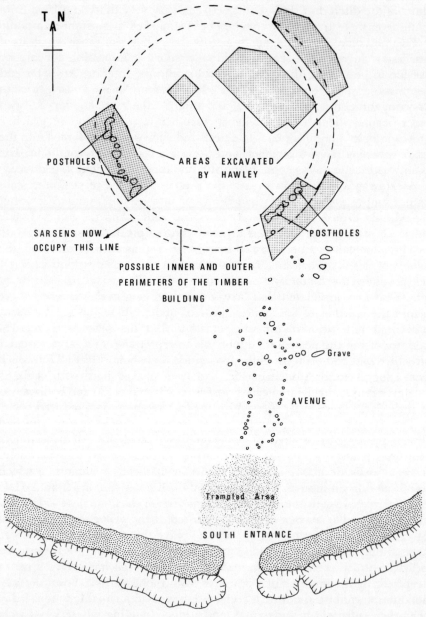

Fig. 6. Surviving Evidence for the Central Hut.

contained at least three 'trilithons', like the five archways in the sarsen phase of Stonehenge III, at Lugg of stout oak posts, each pair having a lintel across its top.

At Stonehenge, inside the palisade there appears to have been a round building of almost the same diameter, 97 feet (29.6 m), as the great stone circle of many centuries later. Excavation in the stonehole of the massive fallen sarsen 12 located a large posthole that had been cut into when the stone was erected. Two other deep postholes were found just to its west, one dug into by Z Hole 13, one to its north, the biggest that Hawley recorded.

These holes may have been part of the building's outer wall. From the fragmentary evidence of other holes in the damaged interior of Stonehenge there had probably been an inner ring, concentric with the first and like that at Lugg, of taller timbers, supporting the roof, on the circumference of a circle some 80 feet (24.4 m) across. Like those of the outer wall they would have been held firmly in place by horizontal ring-beams along their tops. There may also have been a great central post.

The physical proof of such a structure is necessarily incomplete, but some confirmation of its existence comes from two timber buildings, nearly contemporary with it and less than two miles away inside the Durrington Walls earthwork.[12] Here also were circular houses of concentric rings, and a 'passage' with an arc across it. Both were composed of heavy oak posts. The southern setting was a huge one, 125 feet (38 m) across, of six concentric rings of postholes that are presumed to have borne the weight of a sloping roof. The northern ring was smaller but remarkably like the charnel-house suggested for Stonehenge.

Starting as quite a large building, 98 feet 5 inches (30 m) in diameter, it was rebuilt more modestly as a hut 47 feet 3 inches (14.4 m) across with a central setting of four big posts twice as thick as those in its outer wall. To the south of the entrance there was an arc or façade of closely-set posts, nearly 80 feet (24 m) across with a 10 foot (3 m) gap at its middle. Here a hinged gate may have given access to the building. Beyond the arc was an avenue or passage 80 feet 8 inches (24.6 m) long. Like the Stonehenge passage, it also followed a north-south line. The existence of such a structure gives credence to the suggestion that something comparable once stood at Stonehenge.

Assuming that the dimensions proposed for the Stonehenge building are near the truth, then its height can tentatively be reconstructed. Sixty or seventy 2 foot (60 cm) thick but untreated oak posts would have been adequate to hold a roof pitched at a low angle of 25°.[13] Thirty of them in the outer wall need have been no more than 8 feet (2.4 m) tall, the other thirty in an inner ring being taller, perhaps 12 feet (3.7 m) high, with four more at the corners of a central four-sided setting rising to a maximum height of 25 feet (7.6 m). With the spaces between the outer posts being no more than 10 feet (3 m) wide, it would have been easy to peg horizontal planking across them to make a solid wall, weatherproofed with sheets of birchbark, and with gaps left in it for the two entrances and to let in light.

Construction of such a lofty and spacious building would have given little difficulty to the Late Neolithic inhabitants of Salisbury Plain. With more than a thousand years of accumulated experience in woodworking, the techniques of estimating stresses, of jointing beams together and making them stable would have been well understood. Only 40 miles to the west in the Somerset fens other people were selecting particular types of wood for specific tasks, easily-split oak for planks, hazel for lightweight posts, hazel or alder for the pegs and dowels, chipping out mortise-and-tenon joints with flint chisels. One of their mallets, made of yew, a tough and heavy wood, was found preserved in the peat there.[14]

Indications of an improvement in the standard of living comes indirectly from the native pottery. Hand-built as before and still incapable of tolerating the naked flames of a cooking fire, these were nevertheless fine vessels, abundantly decorated with bird-bone impressions or fingernail impressions. Used for the storage of grain and as containers for liquids, the increasing number of flat-bottomed pots suggests that homes now had shelving, dressers and tables. Stone versions of such wooden furniture have been preserved in the Neolithic village of Skara Brae in the Orkneys.

Wooden objects, five thousand years old but surviving in waterlogged conditions, tell the same story of more comfort and technical expertise. A broken bowl came from Ehenside Tarn in the Lake District. Thirty miles (48 km) to the south, at Storrs Moss, several remarkable bits of wood were recovered, including an oak plank and a grooved and tenoned post that had 'been intended for an upright in a timber building, slotted into a floor board', the groove having been designed to 'receive the ends of horizontal rods forming a wall-screen'.[15]

Shabby and weatherworn as they are today, such fragments of antiquity show that people had the skill and the workforce to erect the Stonehenge mortuary house. The mutilated plan of the postholes points to its former existence. Hawley's limited excavations inevitably missed some. Of those he found, some may have been for scaffolding when the stone circles were put up, others for the market-stalls and fun-fairs of more modern times, but these would not have been so big nor so tidily refilled as many of Hawley's were. There is, as Atkinson observed, no reason to doubt the likelihood of a timber building, the surviving postholes offering positive evidence in its favour. 'It is reasonable to suppose that so large a sanctuary would have had something at its focal point, a *"sanctum sanctorum"* in which resided the numinous principle of the place.'[16] That it was a place for the dead depends on different evidence.

Although it was impossible to date it, a burial was unearthed by Hawley in 1926 close to the centre of Stonehenge.[17] The grave had been disturbed in Georgian times, but it could be seen that the corpse had been placed in a shallow, 8 feet (2.4 m) long pit lying exactly across the major NE-SW axis of Stonehenge. A post had stood just outside the grave, suggesting that the burial belonged to a period after the decay of the hut when the henge's interior was open to the sky. Its presence shows that the association of the monument with death and funerary rites continued over the following centuries.

Whether there had been other human remains in this central area will never now be known because a frenzy of unmethodical diggings has ruined the middle of Stonehenge. Many of these plunderings, undertaken surreptitiously, left only rough hollows and pits with no word of what had been found. Others are well-known and reveal just how limited any presentday researcher is when trying to reconstruct this early phase.

The Elizabethan historian William Camden mentioned in his *Britannia* 'that men's bones are frequently here dug up' by the treasure-hunters in the vicinity, adding 'ashes and pieces of burnt bone here frequently found',[18] and Hawley discovered that Tudor fortune-seekers had dug across the north-east entrance wrecking two postholes and leaving broken pots and bottles behind them.[19]

In 1620 there is a record of an 'excavation' inside the stone circle itself. In that year James I visited the Earl of Pembroke's great house at Wilton, seven miles south of the circle. Some of the royal party rode out to the ring and, not content with looking, dug into various parts, finding skulls of bulls, oxen 'or other beasts'. Prominent amongst these primitive archaeologists were Dr William Harvey, discoverer of the circulation of the blood; Inigo Jones, the royal architect; and George Villiers, Duke of Buckingham and favourite of the king.

Years later, Britain's first great field-archaeologist, John Aubrey, wrote that Buckingham 'did cause the middle of Stonehenge to be digged; and there remains a kind of pitt or cavity still; it is about the bigness of two sawe-pitts . . .',[20] a saw-pit being wide and deep enough to accommodate a standing man holding one end of a two-handed saw, his partner on a platform above him as they cut through a log. On a sketchplan of 1666 Aubrey marked the hole at almost the exact centre of the circle where it would effectively have removed any sign of a post. It was a disaster to be repeated by later diggers. Buckingham actually wanted to buy Stonehenge and would have given 'Mr Newdick (then owner of this place) any rate for it, but he would not accept it', wrote Aubrey.

The 18th century antiquarian, William Stukeley, believed that by his time at least one of the sarsens had fallen because of 'digging near it' and lamented the harm done by plunderers who had delved into the north-east side of the ring. This outrage did not prevent Stukeley himself, on 5 July 1723, from burrowing alongside the Altar Stone, '4 foot along the edge of the stone, 6 foot forward towards the middle of the adytum [the innermost part of a temple]. At a foot deep we came to the solid chalk, mix'd with flints which have never been stir'd', [21] an observation which shows that he had extended the destruction of an area already spoiled by Buckingham.

And it was in Stukeley's time that Thomas Hayward, the owner, encouraged rabbits to inhabit the ring so that he could hunt them for his larder. Stukeley was distressed to see how quickly they bred, with warrens appearing at the Winterbourne Stoke barrow cemetery over a mile away: 'They are the nearest barrows planted with rabbits, which do much damage too at Stonehenge, and threaten no less than the ruin of the whole.'[22]

The circle was attracting ever more visitors and by 1740 an elderly but enterprising carpenter from Amesbury, Gaffer Hunt, had set up a hut by the tumbled trilithon 59–60, keeping a 'cellar' of wines and ales under a leaning stone causing even more disturbance.[23] In 1925 Hawley came upon his traces, broken crockery, glass and clay pipes and, worst of all, holes that had been dug for the posts of Hunt's stall.[24]

At the beginning of the 19th century those indefatigable diggers, Sir Richard Colt Hoare and William Cunnington, excavated under the Slaughter Stone at the north-east entrance 'so completely as to be able to examine the underneath side of the stone'.[25] They also explored two of the Four Stations, 92 and 94, interfering with one of the Aubrey Holes with 'its single interment of burnt bones'. In November, 1802, Cunnington sank a pit close to Stukeley's central hole 'to the depth of nearly six feet',[26] finding charred wood, animal bones and 'three fragments of coarse, half-baked pottery'.

The chances of any recognisable order of postholes surviving these onslaughts by men and rabbits were slight and further diminished when, in 1839, a Captain Beamish, to satisfy the curiosity of a Swedish Society, quarried out an area reputed to have been about 8 feet square and 6 deep (2.4 × 1.8 m) in front of the Altar Stone.[27] If true, this would have been the equivalent of removing a 20-ton lorryload of solid chalk.

The obvious result of these devastations was the irreparable ruin of the most sensitive part of Stonehenge. Yet there was some compensation. The objects found and discarded in these sorties reveal how closely the rituals inside Stonehenge had corresponded to the funerary activities of earlier Neolithic people at their long barrows. Time after time, quite casually because of the triviality of the things, the diggers remarked on the finds they had made. Inigo Jones, 'who digged throughout all the Foundations',[28] recalled that he had discovered 'Bulls and Oxen, and several sorts of Beasts, as appears by the Heads of divers kinds of them, not many Years since, there digged up'.[29]

Such skulls, unaccompanied by other ox-bones, are comparable with the finds in the earthen barrows of former centuries. There, like the ox-hide complete with skull draped over the mortuary house at Fussell's Lodge, skulls had been placed with the Neolithic dead. Two complete ox-skulls were found at Tilshead Lodge barrow, a huge skull was discovered by Cunnington at Knook 2, and another together with an antler was found in a neat pit under the barrow of Sherrington 1. The discovery of ox-skulls at Stonehenge makes it likely that rituals of death were performed there also.

The skulls also give support to what archaeologists have suspected for a long time, that it was only certain members of society who were privileged to be buried in the later long barrows or to be laid in the Stonehenge charnel-house. In the causewayed enclosures and in settlements, places used by all ranks of the community, bones of cattle are plentiful, but mixed with them are the bones of pig and sheep or goat. But alongside the dead under the mounds and at the centre of Stonehenge it is the ox-skull that is dominant, perhaps as a totem, perhaps as the epitome of strength, perhaps even as the emblem of a richer, more powerful member of the group, the badge of an emergent aristocracy in what had previously been an egalitarian society.

Inigo Jones believed the skulls to be the remains of sacrifices: 'Now that there hath oftentimes been digged out of the Ground at Stone-Heng the heads of such Beasts, in all probability in that Place sacrificed, I need not again remember, it being so well known.'[30] His nephew, John Webb, using Jones' posthumous notes, revealed that the skulls had lain in pits. Many had been dug up by Harvey and Buckingham, both of whom noticed the 'great Quantities of burnt Coals or Charcoals digged up likewise; here lying promiscuously together with the Heads, there, in Pits by themselves apart, here more, there less', both inside the circle and outside it in the henge, 'in several Parts of the Court surrounding Stonehenge it self'.[31]

A hundred years after Buckingham, more skulls were unearthed. 'Mr Hayward, late owner of *Stonehenge*, dug about it. . . . He found heads of oxen and other beasts' bones, and nothing else.'[32] and William Cunnington in the next century dug up 'parts of the head and horns of deer' similar to the antlers left in some long barrows and carefully set along the ditch bottom at the Lesser Cursus.

These early investigators almost compulsively confined their explorations to the middle of Stonehenge inside the ring of stones and it can be assumed that it was here that the ox-skulls had been buried inside the timber charnel-house. In this their distribution was different from that of other ox-bones from the edible parts of the animal. Hawley recovered many carcase-bones from the bottom of the encircling ditch where they had been placed after the meat on them had been eaten by mourners. An identical dichotomy between the situation of skulls and cut meat-bones had existed in the long barrows, the former alongside the dead, the latter in the ditch as leftovers from the funerary feasts.

Also in the Stonehenge ditch were the bones of pig and deer and these tell something about the environment on Salisbury Plain. Hawley noted the abundance of red deer bones and the contrasting scarcity of those from roe deer.[33] This creature, dainty and small, likes to browse in open woodland, whereas the bigger red deer prefers the margins of dense, deciduous forests. It seems likely that even late in the Neolithic period there were still some thick spreads of trees in the neighbourhood of Stonehenge on land unfarmed, holy and for the dead.

Other things in the ditch also were significant. In 1920 the horn-core of an ox was found lying near a round piece of chalk 'showing signs of cutting', and in 1922 Hawley dug out the 'small horn core of a young bison and two roughly round objects of cut chalk, perhaps intended for balls'.[34] He also came across broken human skulls, one near the west terminal of the north-east causeway, a second near the south entrance in a bowl-shaped cavity which held 'many pieces of a very large ox-skull'.[35] Like the human skulls along the ditch at Hambledon Hill, they may have been set near the entrances to Stonehenge to provide spiritual power to a physical barrier. Of the chalk balls lying near the bones in the ditch the interpretation of such globules as representations of testicles has already been made. With the ox-skulls symbolising strength and potency it was a conjunction entirely fitting in a monument dedicated to death and rebirth.

If this were the purpose of the building, to act as a focus for ceremonies of death, it would answer the second of the twelve questions about Stonehenge, the problem of its latitude.

There has much argument about the choice of site for the circle and whether it was specifically selected for astronomical reasons. The controversy is complicated because it has two aspects, one macrocosmic concerning the significance of certain latitudes in the British Isles, the other the local question of why the builders chose such an awkward location which sloped down both from south to north and from west to east when there was level, seemingly more suitable land immediately to the south and west.

It was Charrière in 1961 who first pointed out that Stonehenge stood on a unique astronomical latitude, 51° 11′ N. (51°. 18), at which the midsummer sun rose at the north-east of the horizon almost exactly at right-angles to where the extreme northern moon set at the north-west.[36] His observations were refined by Newham in 1963 and, quite independently, by Hawkins in the same year.[37] In his interesting book, *Stonehenge Decoded*, (1965), Hawkins wrote, 'It seems unlikely that the choice of 51°. 17 as a location for Stonehenge was made by chance'.[38]

That the situation was intentionally chosen to incorporate this solar-lunar right-angle is apparently corroborated by the four stones that once stood at the corners of a megalithic rectangle surrounding Stonehenge, the Four Stations. The short sides of this oblong are in line with sunrise at midsummer and the long sides are quite well-aligned on the northerly setting of the midwinter moon. The Station Stones, however, almost certainly belong to a secondary phase of Stonehenge and cannot be used to prove that astronomical considerations determined the site of the henge. It is feasible that the 90° phenomenon was recognised only centuries after the earthwork was built. Nor is the latitude exactly right. Some miles to the south would have been better, as Atkinson's calculations have demonstrated.[39]

There is nothing surprising about celestial events occurring at right-angles to each other. Because of the involved relationships between the sun's and moon's movements, particularly the moon which swings through an 18.6 year cycle between its major and minor extremes, there are several latitudes in the British Isles at which two skyline settings or risings happen at 90° to each other. Just north of latitude 54°, near the lovely stone circle of Swinside in the Lake District, an observer might see the minor northern moon rising at the ENE 90° away from the major southern moonrise at the SSE. On the Mull of Kintyre, around the latitude of 56° where the astronomically-publicised stone row of Ballochroy stands, the midwinter and midsummer sunsets take place at right-angles to each other. In the extreme north of Britain, level with the Iron Age broch of Mousa in the Shetlands, the sunrise at midsummer would appear on the horizon some 90° from where the minor moon would come up.

Stonehenge stands where it does quite simply because people were living nearby. The timber building was erected in an occupied region, set at the heart of a cluster of long barrows, and it was centrally placed for the inhabitants of the eastern part of Salisbury Plain. Within three miles there were no fewer than sixteen barrows: Bulford I and Amesbury 104 to the east; Winterbourne Stoke 1, 53 and 71 to the west; Durrington 24, Figheldean 27 and 31, Netheravon 6 and 9 to the north; and, to the south, the concentration of Amesbury 14, Wilsford South 13, 30, 34 and 41, and Woodford 2. Within the same radius, bounded on the east by the River Avon and less than an hour's walk in any direction, there was the causewayed enclosure of Robin Hood's Ball and the Greater and Lesser Cursuses. It was these places and the needs of their users that decided where Stonehenge was to be. To believe in an astronomical explanation is to believe that Neolithic natives had known about the solar and lunar right-angle centuries earlier when they opted to build their long barrows on that latitude, or, even less probably, that astronomically-minded incomers had purposefully searched out the right latitude and raised a sun-and-moon monument in the middle of an inhabited territory. It is noticeable that in other occupied regions of southern Britain on the same latitude, in Kent, Somerset and Exmoor, not one henge or stone circle was constructed to incorporate this dramatic right-angle event. Most probably, it had never been recognised.

The problem can be resolved by considering the local question of why the Stonehenge builders accepted a site that was so uneven. A visitor approaching the circle from east or west may be puzzled to notice that the ring stands not on the highest ground but somewhat down a slope that falls steadily to the north. On the site itself one can also see that the stones were put up on land declining north-eastwards towards the dry valley of Stonehenge Bottom a quarter of a mile away where the main roads now converge. Whoever agreed on the place deliberately rejected the flatter ground nearby despite the difficulties entailed in constructing a roofed building on a distorted part of the Plain. The cause appears to have been the Great Cursus half a mile to the north.

It will never be possible to enter the minds and understand the motives of a society that existed five thousand years ago and whose only surviving message exists in a half-destroyed pattern of holes on a hillside, but two simple hypotheses about the location of Stonehenge can be tested. The people who dug out the postholes, cut down the trees and erected the shaped timbers may have wanted their building to be conspicuous from all directions and also to overlook the cursus. If those conditions were to be fulfilled, together with a third to be considered shortly, then there was only one place for the structure.

Although the posts vanished long ago, the sarsens of Stonehenge remain to show where the wooden building stood. The stones can be seen from quite long distances from the east, west and north, but it is from the south that their position is critical. Were the ring to stand much farther down its north-facing slope it would have been concealed from the Lake barrow cemetery 1½ miles (2.4 km) to the south. Conversely, were it to be higher up the slope much of the cursus would have been obscured. The entire line of the cursus can be seen from the centre of Stonehenge, but if an observer moves back a mere 60 yards (55 m) to the southern causeway across the henge-ditch a great proportion of the cursus's western sector is hidden by the curve of the hillside. It is likely, therefore, that the building was situated as high on the slope as possible in order to be observable from all the surrounding countryside without losing the prospect of the cursus to its north.

It might be asked why it was not constructed a few hundred yards to the west where the ground was more level, where the cursus was still in full view and where the site was still visible from all around. The answer may rest with the third of the builders' requirements.

The Stonehenge cursus is almost 1¾ miles (2.8 km) in length, so long that from Stonehenge one had to turn one's head to look from one end to the other. Yet Stonehenge lies almost exactly south of its centre, the south being a direction already noticed as being important in the later long barrows. The error is no more than 246 feet (75 m) out of 3033 yards (2774 m) but would have been much greater had Stonehenge been put up on the level ground to the west.

It would have been exceptionally difficult to calculate the midpoint of the cursus from anywhere to its north or south because the lines of its banks ran WSW-ENE and not at right-angles to an observer. It is likely that it was from the estimated centre of the cursus itself that a sightline was projected due south with a surveyor giving directions to people on the far side, waving them to left or right until the correct position was established. By whatever means they did it, their near-success demonstrates the intimate relationship, physical and spiritual, between the timber building and the older cursus.

If funerary rites had taken place in the latter it is probable that related ceremonies were intended to be held on the site of Stonehenge. It is permissible to imagine processions inside the sacred confines of the cursus, a corpse being borne along its length from west to east and then carried southwards towards the great mortuary house on the hillside, the mourners trailing up the slope, taking the body into the building where it would lie during the protracted days, weeks or months, skulls of oxen set down near it and its companions until, finally, the life-drained bones could be lifted and taken along the dark, southern passageway for burial somewhere in the vast necropolis that surrounded Stonehenge.

The rising of the midwinter moon was essential to these rites of death.

# 4

# Moonlight on Stonehenge
# Stonehenge Ia continued

*There can be no doubt that Stonehenge was an observatory; the impartial mathematics of probability and the celestial sphere are on my side.*

Gerald Hawkins, *Stonehenge Decoded*, vii

There are subtleties to the first Stonehenge unsuspected by the casual visitor who sees only the stupendous sarsens resting on the cushion of the Plain like a tremendous and petrified crown. These spectacular stones divert attention from the unobstrusive width of the entrance through the bank and ditch, its orientation, the reason for the fossilised bulk of the Heel Stone that rises outside the entrance like a grotesque, hooded figure, scabrous and rough, the oldest surviving stone of the monument.

Today, from the bottom of the dry valley that divides Stonehenge from the cursus, the earthwork is invisible, hidden by the slopes of the hillside. Even when the bank was new and higher it would still have been concealed from mourners making their way towards the henge and the mortuary house, but they would have been guided by the stone's silhouette standing white against the skyline. Moving up the slope the procession would have passed this outlier before coming to the entrance, precisely laid out towards the rising moon and flanked by the domineering portals of four more sarsen uprights. Behind them the people would see the long lines of the cursus, its eastern end interrupted by gaps through which they had taken the corpse on its bier. On 6 August 1723, when he was the first person to recognise them, William Stukeley, wrote, 'the eastern end of this Cursus . . . appears very plainly at Stonehenge and there are two entrances still visible thereabouts across each ditch almost answering the direct part of the avenue'.[1]

These gaps, opposite each other but obliterated today, were about 600 yards (550 m) from the end. An early 19th century plan by Philip Crocker shows them very clearly with the avenue of Stonehenge's second phase leading towards the southernmost. 'You will', noted Sir Richard Colt Hoare, Crocker's employer, 'perceive its [Stonehenge's] connexion, by means of the AVENUE, with the cursus',[2] the northern gap being level with a now-destroyed round barrow, Durrington 62a, at grid point SU 131432.

The avenue, laid out around 2200 BC, led towards the north-east entrance of the henge. In turn, the henge, which had been constructed a full thousand years earlier, had that entrance in line with the timber building's main doorway. This faced towards the major rising of the full midwinter moon. Proof that this lunar alignment was intentional comes both from the causeway across the ditch and from the interpretation of the postholes Hawley discovered on the causeway itself. To understand this it is necessary to explain the movements of the sun and moon.

Unlike the sun, the moon has a complicated cycle which varies from year to year. It is doubtful whether prehistoric communities had any comprehension of the celestial mechanics that caused these lunar eccentricities. At a time when all people were country-dwellers, their life-rhythms those of the slowly-changing seasons, they would have noticed that the sun never rose farther up the horizon than the north-east, near 50° from True North on Salisbury Plain, and at that time the daylight lasted longer, the weather was warmer and the crops were nearing full growth.[3] For three or four days sunrise occurred at the same place on the skyline, its 'standstill' or solstice, and then day after day it rose ever more to the south, reaching due east, 90°, three months later, and six darkening months after the summer solstice it attained its most southerly rising, 130°, at the south-east. This was its midwinter standstill near the end of modern December. People soon became aware of the difference between the midsummer solstice's warmth and growth, and the darkness, cold and sterility that came with the days of midwinter. At the latitude of Stonehenge, almost 51° 11′ N, daylight at midsummer lasted about sixteen and a half hours, but at midwinter there were fewer than seven hours before the blackness of night returned.

Year after year the sun was predictable, always rising at the north-east and setting at the north-west in summer, always rising and setting at the south-east and south-west in the bleakness of winter. The moon was more capricious.

Whereas the sun took a year to complete its cycle from midsummer back to midsummer, the moon took only a month, the time in which it circled the earth. Its risings and settings moved rapidly from one extreme to the other in about fourteen days, dwindling from a full moon into a right-facing crescent and then completely disappearing, only to reappear a few nights later with the thin horns of its crescent now pointing towards the left. Such transformations may have seemed magical to the Neolithic mind.

It has been claimed that these lunar variations were recorded in semi-abstract carvings in Irish chambered tombs such as Knowth and Newgrange.[4] Crescents chipped and pecked into the stones of the passages are supposed to portray the moon in its phases with wavy lines like snakes representing its oscillations over and under the regular path of the sun. No such megalithic art is available for scholars studying the Neolithic period in southern Britain. The debatable Irish evidence serves only to show that in the British Isles other people, centuries before Stonehenge, apparently considered the moon so deeply associated with death that they carved its movements on the walls of their tombs.

There are difficulties about observing the extremes of moonrise. Sometimes this happens in daylight and is almost undetectable by the human eye. Its seasons, moreover, are literally opposite those of the sun. There can only be a full moon in the northern half of the sky when the sun is at the south in midwinter, for it is the reflected light of the sun that illuminates the moon. There is a third problem.

Whereas the sun has a constant annual swing from north-east to south-east back to the north-east for its risings and a similar western cycle for its settings, the moon does not. Instead of one extreme rising at the north and one at the south the moon has two, its major and minor positions. These positions at both north and south widen and contract like heavenly concertinas over a period of 18.61 years in arcs which at the latitude of Stonehenge are about 20° wide. The moon's most northerly or major rising occurs near 41° (NNE). On each of the following years it rises a degree or so farther south until 9.3 years later it attains its minor northern rising around 61° (ENE) before starting on its steady swing back to the NNE. The same is true for its southerly risings and for both its northern and southern westerly settings.

Depending on the height of the skyline, which in the saucerlike landscape of Stonehenge is a fairly even 0.5°, the rising and setting positions of the sun and moon on Salisbury Plain can be summarised (Table 6).[5]

### TABLE 6. Azimuths of solar and lunar extremes on Salisbury Plain

|  | SUN | | MOON | | | |
|  | Rise | Set | Rise | | Set | |
|  |  |  | Major | Minor | Major | Minor |
|---|---|---|---|---|---|---|
| Midsummer | 50° | 310° | 143° | 123° | 217° | 237° |
| Midwinter | 130° | 230° | 41° | 61° | 319° | 299° |

Early Neolithic people who wished to set out alignments on the midsummer or midwinter positions of the sun at Stonehenge would have found this a relatively uncomplicated procedure because after two or three years they would have realised that the midsummer sun never rose farther north than the landmark of Sidbury Hill 8 miles away nor the midwinter sun farther south than the 7-mile distant Battery Hill. It would have been easy to set up a stone or post in line with these natural features.

The wisdom gained over a thousand years by their forefathers as they oriented their long barrows on the moon warned later observers that to find the place where the most northerly moon rose in relation to Stonehenge would be a lengthier undertaking. Fortunately, they did not have to concern themselves with the minor lunar rising, an event so intermingled with other risings of the moon as to be virtually undetectable and probably unrecognised by Neolithic people.

From generations of watching the vagaries of the full moon they knew that at its most northerly the moon rose well to the north-east or left-hand side of where the sun came up at midsummer and this could be used as a starting point for observations of the moon. There were to be unsuspected complications, described later, but men probably thought they could erect a marker, perhaps the Heel Stone, in line with the summer solstice and then, year after year, set up a post showing where the northern moon had risen. Each post would be a little farther north. Eventually the moon would begin its southerly return towards the Heel Stone and beyond. All the posts but the northernmost could be removed and their pits backfilled. Nine years later the rising moon reappeared to the left of the solar marker and a new line of sighting-posts could be started. After six full lunar cycles a single row of posts, one from each line, stood pointing to the NNE and the proven direction of the major northern moonrise.

That this was their procedure has been revealed by Hawley's excavations and by Newham's intuition. It is corroborated by all the features known to have existed around Stonehenge's north-eastern entrance: the width of the causeway; the postholes there; the two stones on the axis of the henge; and the four great posts beyond them.

In 1922, stripping off the turf across the causeway, Hawley noticed a series of dark rings that proved to be the tops of 46 filled-in postholes. They contained nothing but dirty chalk. The following year he found eight more 'making the total number 53',[6] a remark which speaks badly either of his memory or of his arithmetic. Spreading across the entrance, the holes had been arranged in six irregular lines, and being anything from 1 to 2 feet (30 – 60 cm) in diameter they could have held quite substantial posts. Apart from suggesting that they might have formed a palisade, Hawley made no further comment about the mysterious cluster and for several decades the holes remained enigmatic and unconsidered.

It was Newham,[7] believing that Stonehenge in its earliest phase 'was essentially a site for the investigation of lunar phenomena', who put forward the best explanation for them, that they had been for posts aligned on the moon (Fig. 7): 'Their arrangements are similar to what could be expected if the "Stonehenge Astronomers" planted poles on successive midwinter full moon risings when observed from the enclosure centre. The number of such moon risings appearing in a cycle of 18.61 years . . . would usually be

nine. Apparently, some are missing, probably on occasions when the rising
moon could not be seen because of cloud or mist.'

He added that from the number of rows it was likely that observations
had taken place over six full lunar cycles, or more than a century
($6 \times 18.6 = 111.6$ years), and he buttressed his argument by comparing
Hawley's plan of the prehistoric holes with a reconstruction of 'known
moon risings over the past hundred years. . . . There is a resemblance
between the patterns as a whole.'

If Newham was correct then the people who made these sightings must
have realised that what they had started would never be finished in their
lifetimes. Even a man old beyond normal expectancy would have been
unable to make more than about thirty years of observations and it would
have been unusual for him to have seen more than one of the extreme
risings he was searching for. Indeed, uncertainty was inherent in the process
from its beginnings, relying for its accuracy on the decaying poles and a
knowledge passed by word of mouth from one generation to the next,
always susceptible to human error. But perhaps exceptional accuracy was
not an important consideration.

Reactions to this lunar interpretation have varied. Heggie thought
'Newham's explanation a poor one', Atkinson believed it 'possible, but
clearly the observations thus marked were not made systematically with
respect to time', while Wood concluded that 'the evidence on balance
supports the view that Stonehenge was a lunar observatory from its earliest
times'.[8] Such differing responses from scholars add point to Hinks' acerbic
assessment, many years ago, about Lockyer's and Penrose's hope to date
Stonehenge by astronomical methods: 'One may well doubt whether
anything is gained by these attempts to help out the deficiencies of archaeology with the aid of astronomy.'[9]

Extreme caution is demanded when analysing such imperfect and
ambiguous evidence as a straggling set of postholes, but several additional
factors support Newham's theory. Not only do the holes on the left-hand
edge of the group line up with the major northern moonrise, but those on
the right are neatly directed towards midsummer sunrise, as could be
expected if that was where the observers began their sightings. There are
no postholes to their right, showing that there had been no attempt to
follow the moon along to its minor rising.

The ends of the ditch run up to but do not encroach upon the postholes,
implying that the group had been respected both by the causeway and by
the gap through the bank behind it. Here two stones had stood, side by
side, 8 feet (2.5 m) apart, like a gunsight straddling the axis of the henge
which exactly bisected the rows of holes.

Well outside the henge's entrance and 83 feet (25 m) beyond the pair of
stones there was further indication that Newham was right. Here, in 1924,
Hawley discovered a line of four great postholes parallel to the group in
the causeway. They were twice as wide as those and so deep that 'the first

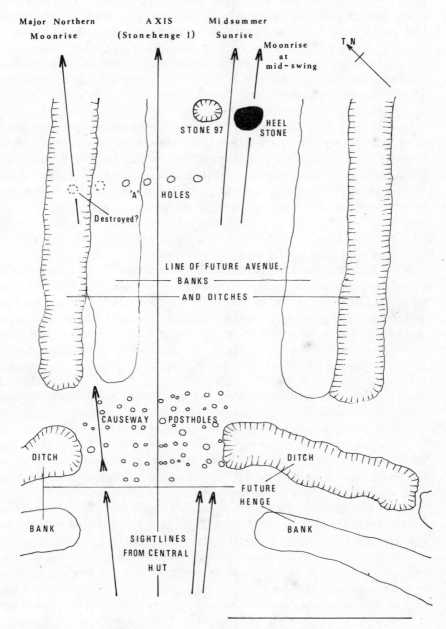

Fig. 7. The Lunar Postholes of Stonehenge Ia. Only 52 of the causeway postholes can be identified from Hawley's notes.

hole, owing to its depth, had given the person who made it some difficulty in removing the soil, and to facilitate this an indentation at the side had to be made, thoroughly spoiling the shape of a hole symmetrically round like the òthers'.[10] These large holes certainly belonged to the first Stonehenge. The avenue bank of the second phase had been heaped over one of them and, moreover, 'a line drawn from the centre of the earthwork through the centre of its entrance appears to bisect this line of postholes at right-angles',[11] something which would have been impossible with the changed axis of later periods.

Spaced tidily 6 feet (1.8 m) apart, the four holes presumably supported thick, heavy posts as much as 10 feet (3 m) high. After the more ephemeral causeway posts had been withdrawn and their pits backfilled, these tall poles may have served as lunar sighting-devices, acting as guides to the moon's progress along the horizon. When the moon came up in the gap between the first or right-hand post and its partner, it was a quarter of the way between the midpoint of its cycle and its northern extreme. When it rose between the second and third posts it was one-third of the distance, each post indicating a stage in its movements.[12]

Such signalling markers enabled watchers to estimate how long it would be before the full moon reached its major northern position. Yet there is a paradox. Observers in the charnel-house obviously needed a post in line with the extreme rising and it can be calculated that had two more equally-spaced uprights been added to the left of the four, the sixth would have indicated the major moonrise. There is no such marker, but inspection of Hawley's plan shows why. Not appreciating its significance, he stopped excavating just where the fifth posthole would have been uncovered. And even if he had located that one, he would not have found the sixth and most tell-tale hole of all, because when the ditch of the later avenue was trenched out the posthole would have been dug away with it.

These markers were never very accurate. Spaces about 1° wide between the four (or six) posts permitted no more than an approximation of where the moon was on its journey. To Neolithic people that may have been all they required, but to the archaeoastronomer it is a trap. If he claims to have detected sightlines accurate to only ±1° he is likely to be accused of uncritical enthusiasm and slipshod research. If, in defence, he excludes all but the most exact of alignments, he may well be rejecting a mass of others laid out, rather casually, by prehistoric people with no concept of 20th century precision. An escape from this predicament is to study large groups of similar monuments sharing a common orientation. When this is done, as with the numerous recumbent stone circles of north-eastern Scotland, it is clear that although their builders aligned them on the major southern moon, variations of several degrees were quite acceptable.[13]

Three hundred years ago William Stukeley understood this. Writing about the design of the gigantic rings at Avebury he commented: 'This is done with a sufficient, tho' not a mathematical exactness, where preciseness would have no effect'.[14] The same seems to be true of Stonehenge. There are alignments, but they are not honed to the stiletto sharpness of a laser beam. They are as diffused as bars of sunlight through stained glass.

It was only when the alignment had been determined that the ditch and bank of the henge could be constructed. The position and breadth of the north-east causeway were decided by the space taken up by the arc of lunar postholes and until the sightings were concluded it was not known how wide the entrance of the henge was to be. The charnel-house, however, with its southern passageway probably had existed for a long time before this. Scores of years observing the midwinter moon in the icing exposure of Salisbury Plain demanded some form of shelter and the obvious solution was a hut through whose apertures the moon could be watched.

Stonehenge was never used for scientific observations. It was never inhabited by astronomer-priests searching for explanations of eclipses or detecting tiny lunar oscillations. As long as the moon was caught rising above the great posts this may have been enough. In its pallor, bleakly white on the frosty grass, people may have perceived the image of death itself, a place to which the dead would go, or from which Death came, protectress of the dead and slayer of the living, to be venerated, feared and appeased.

It is well-attested by classical authors such as Pliny that in the Iron Age, two thousand years later, druids in Britain held their major ceremonies by moonlight. Mistletoe, their sacred plant, with its white, moonlike berries was thought to have curative properties and it is significant that the recently-discovered body of Lindow Man, garrotted and stabbed and thrown into a bog, had pollen grains of mistletoe in its stomach. It has been suggested that he had been given a potion containing the juices of mistletoe in order to give his sacrifice more meaning and so safeguard his community.[15] In Neolithic times also, when many 'Iron Age' festivals began, the moon may have been looked on as the giver and taker of life and the goddess of healing. In medieval times the stones of Stonehenge were reputed to possess medicinal powers, a garbled memory of the moon whose temple this had been.

'How wonderful is Death,
Death and his brother Sleep!
One pale as yonder wan and horned moon. . .
Percy Bysshe Shelley. *The Daemon of the Wild*

That Stonehenge was a place of death is shown not only in the pits and posts and ox-skulls but in the entrances. The encircling bank was no more than a barrier to exclude the world and to confine the spirits of the dead, but the ditch with over a hundred antlers discovered in its excavated sections, perhaps as symbols of life and growth, was different, and where the ditch was broken by its two causeways extra care was taken to ensure its potency.

Portal stones gave it dignity. Inigo Jones, presuming Stonehenge to be a temple of Roman design, thought there had been three entrances placed geometrically at the north-east, north-west and south at the corners of an equilateral triangle: 'At each of which was raised, on the Outside of the Trench aforesaid, two huge Stones gatewise, parallel where unto on the Inside two others of less Proportion'.[16] Forty years later John Aubrey called this 'absolutely false'[17] and on the plan he made for Charles II drew in only the north-east entrance with two stones inside the bank and another outside the ditch.

Three of the stones have gone, removed by 1719 when Stukeley first came to Stonehenge, but Hawley believed he had found two of their holes. With known standing stones at the entrances of other henges such as Mayburgh and King Arthur's Round Table in the Lake District, Avebury, and Maumbury Rings in Dorset, it is likely that at Stonehenge the space between the ditch terminals was enhanced by rough sarsen pillars taken from the Plain and erected to form an impressive portal to the enclosure.

This was a matter of architecture. It is the concentration of objects at the ditch-ends, deliberately placed by the entrances, that the nature of Stonehenge is revealed, in the carved balls of chalk, the horn cores, traces of fire, animal bones, antlers and parts of a large ox-skull. There were, even more significantly, human bones. Low down in the ditch, when its sides were only just beginning to weather, the skeletal remains of a man had been buried. There were fragments of his skull, parts of his jaw with two teeth still in it, arm-bones, fingers, all mixed with antlers and the bones of a young ox, including a large piece of skull and a horn core. It was by no means a reverent interment and may have been a sacrifice, but it reaffirms the association of death with Stonehenge. Nor was it the only human burial to be found.

Already, farther along the ditch to the east, Hawley had dug up some bones. They lay in a shallow grave close to the iron lever of a padlock and it was guessed that they were 'those of a [modern] criminal hung in chains, and what was left of him had been hastily buried'.[18] Other human remains were different. Where a portal-stone had stood at the inner end of the ditch its hole 'was filled with white chalky rubble in which . . . were bones of a young person about the age of eight or nine', and on the other side of the causeway there were the cremated ashes of an adult and a child about five years old 'placed there without ceremony . . . perhaps contained in a bag of fabric or skin'.[19]

Human bones have been recovered from the ditch-ends of other henges and earthwork enclosures in southern Britain, at Gorsey Bigbury in Somerset, at Marden, Durrington Walls and Avebury. Although those at Stonehenge possibly belonged to a period when the ditch was beginning to silt up, their presence there, so close to the entrance, suggests that they had been assigned to safeguard the sacred enclosure, maybe sacrificed for that purpose.

Recalling the hints in early Neolithic times of a female deity or spirit connected with death, it is significant that it was almost invariably women's bones that were deposited at the entrances or in special parts of a ritual circle, a young girl's corpse placed at the bottom of a stonehole at the east of the Sanctuary stone circle, or the body of a dwarfed female at Avebury nearby, ceremoniously set down in the ditch at the very edge of the southern entrance. The Neolithic mind may have conceived such female burials as personifications of the 'goddess' herself, acting as surrogates for an Other-World presence. At Gorsey Bigbury, a henge with a single entrance some two days' walk west from Stonehenge, the bodies of a man, woman and child were buried in the ditch, but when the flesh had decayed it was the woman's skull that was disinterred, detached from her skeleton and reburied right against the entrance.[20] It is unlikely that the position was accidental any more than the cremations at the north-east entrance to Stonehenge were there by coincidence.

This entrance is obvious to all visitors because of the Heel Stone outside it. What is less well-known is the smaller entrance at the exact south of the earthwork, although it is still clearly visible as an unbroken causeway across the ditch. Hawley excavated there in 1924, finding antlers, signs of burning and scatters of flint but no human bones or postholes. He thought, however, that the causeway had been paved with flint. The entrance was in line with the passageway of the central hut and it was the area by it that Hawley considered had been trampled down: 'The ground was very hard near the outside and also on the inside, from the causeway to where a line of postholes ended'.[21]

It might be asked why there should be two entrances to the henge, not opposite to each other, and of different dimensions, but in this Stonehenge was no different from some other contemporary enclosures. The early stone circles of Cumbria also possessed two alignments, one to a cardinal point of north, south, east or west, apparently used in the laying-out of the ring, the second alignment defining a calendrical event such as midsummer sunrise or an important feast day. The quaintly-named Long Meg & Her Daughters near Penrith has its two bulkiest stones set almost due east-west of each other, but the entrance was erected at the south-west with a thin outlying pillar beyond it in line with the midwinter sunset. Similarly, Swinside, arguably the most perfect of all the evocative circles in the Lake District, had its highest stone at the north and its entrance of double portal-stones at the south-east in line with the midwinter sunrise. At Castlerigg near Keswick, in the numinous setting of a mountainous landscape, the high stones of the entrance stand at the north, but the tallest stone is at the south-east, angled radially to the circumference to point towards sunrise in early November.[22]

This was not a random arrangement corresponding simply to the time of year when the ring was erected. Early November was the occasion of the festival of Samain, when the ghosts of the dead rose from their graves, our Hallowe'en, when the sun rose far down the horizon at the ESE. The celebration of the November sunrise, therefore, may have an ancestry extending back to Neolithic times, commemorated in the alignments of some of Britain's first stone circles and revealing something of forgotten prehistoric customs. The beginning of May, when the sun rose at the ENE, was another Iron Age festival, Beltane, just as Lughnasa, or Harvest Day, was observed in early August. Early February saw the festival of Imbolc, or Oimelg, the time when ewes came into milk.

Alignments to these events are to be found in early stone circles intermingling with the two other great divisions of the year, the midsummer and midwinter solstices, all of them important times for farming communities: February for ewes, May for driving the cattle on to the Spring grass, August for the harvest and November for the culling of the herds and the return of the strongest to their stalls. This dimly-remembered heathen calendar of pastoralists has been christianised, Imbolc into Candlemass, Beltane into Whitsuntide, Lughnasa into Lammas and Samain into All Saints' Day.

In Cumbria prehistoric people used the sun for their calendar, but on Salisbury Plain it was the moon that was observed. It is no surprise at Stonehenge to find the major alignment towards the moon's most northerly rising, and with the interest already shown by the builders of earthen long barrows in the cardinal points of east and south one could also expect a second alignment to one of those positions. Hardly a mile from Stonehenge the long barrows of Wilsford South 30, Winterbourne Stoke 53 and Tilshead 4 all looked to the east, while Shalbourne 5, Warminster 1 and Grans Barrow had their higher ends at the south. There was a remarkable absence of orientations to north or west, as though these were directions to be avoided.

East and south are both of lunar importance. East is the place on the skyline midway between the moon's most northerly and southerly risings. South was where the moon reached its highest point in the sky between its rising and setting and where, possibly, it was thought to be at its most vital. How, in pre-compass days, when there was no Pole Star to guide them, people were able to determine where True North and South were at Stonehenge has been shown by Alexander Thom.[23]

From a survey of the horizon Thom deduced that from the henge the midsummer moon at its most southerly rose near Figsbury Ring, an Iron Age hillfort 3½ miles (5.6 km) north-east of Salisbury. It would set behind Chain Hill at the south-west.

## TABLE 7. Major southern lunar alignments from Stonehenge

|  | Distance in miles from Stonehenge | Height above Stonehenge | | Azimuth | Declination |
|---|---|---|---|---|---|
|  |  | Feet | Metres |  |  |
| Figsbury Ring | 6.6 | 148 | 45 | 141° 54' | −29° 0' |
| Chain Hill | 3.7 | 114 | 35 | 216° 16' | −29° 24' |

Thom suggested that at these places foresights had been constructed so that people might record and analyse the moon's movements from Stonehenge, but in this he was probably mistaken. What matters is that if Stonehenge observers had aligned posts on those positions and then marked the point midway between them they would have produced a line less than 1° from True South, a line, moreover, looking towards Rox Hill, once Rocks Hill, 2¼ miles (3.6 km) away and a convenient landmark for 'catching' the moon on its path across the night sky.

This must have been the first sightline established at Stonehenge, for without it there would have been no possibility of laying out the timber passageway that led to the hut. One or two postholes discovered by Hawley near the later sarsen stones 8 and 9 may be the relics of sighting-posts towards the southern moonrise, but the ground has been so disturbed that nothing definite can be claimed.

From its beginnings Stonehenge was a place of death. Stonehenge was the mortuary chapel of a great necropolis, claimed Ramsay in 1894, and almost a hundred years before him Hutchinson, discussing the purpose of stone circles, wrote, 'we presume that Stonehenge is a sepulchral monument, the Mausoleum of kings, and as in those days great veneration was paid to the memory of the dead . . . we doubt not that at Stonehenge, sacrifices had been made to the MANES [the souls of departed ancestors] of those who there lay entombed'.[24]

In fact, very few were buried there. The building had been raised as the first resting-place of the dead, set up at the heart of an extensive burial-area that may have been used by as many as two or three thousand people. Everything there touched death, the barrows, the cursus, the balls of chalk, the antlers, the meat-bones in the ditch, the skulls of oxen and the pits in which they lay with marks of fire around them. One entrance looked towards the cold winter moon, the other faced southwards towards the moon when it was highest in the sky.

Even before the henge was constructed the best-known feature of Stonehenge, the Heel Stone, Stone 96, had probably been set up as an astronomical marker. A sherd of Windmill Hill ware, a native style of early Neolithic pottery, was found near the bottom of its stonehole, showing that it belonged to the first phase of Stonehenge. Standing about 80 feet (24 m) beyond the north-east entrance this raddled block of sarsen slumps towards the earthwork, its unshaped top 16 feet (4.9 m) above ground with a further 4 feet (1.2 m) hidden in its stonehole. Weighing some 35 tons it could have been dragged by oxen from ground nearby where other largish stones have been recorded, but it took a communal effort by human beings to erect it. Once it was almost upright it had a dead weight of seven tons or more. Even with each labourer exerting a pull of 100 lbs (45 kg), at least 150 people would have been needed to haul it into the vertical, their ropes of leather or plaited fibre straining dangerously taut while other men jammed timber props against its underside to prevent it toppling backwards.

At one time this outlier was misnamed the Hele Stone in the belief that it was associated with Helios, the Greek sun-god, but this was romanticism. The name is derived from 'the friar's heel' and, ironically, is given to the wrong stone. The Devil is reputed to have thrown it at a holy father, striking him on the back of the foot, leaving a heel-shaped indentation on the slab, a mark which does not exist on today's Heel Stone. Instead, with the eye of faith, one can make out the depression on the fallen stone 14 at the south-west of the sarsen circle. John Aubrey knew this: 'One of the great stones that lies down, on the west side, hath a cavity something resembling the print of a man's foot',[25] and, showing how unreliable folk stories can be, added that it was Merlin, not a friar, at whom Satan had hurled it, furious that the magician had transported the pillar from Ireland 'by Art Magick'. Of Merlin more later.

It has long been accepted, rather uncritically, that Neolithic people aligned the Heel Stone on sunrise at midsummer. Even in recent times locals claimed that 'immediately before sunrise on the longest day a bird perches on the gnomon stone, and flies away as soon it has seen the sun rise, and that throughout the rest of the year no bird ever alights on that stone',[26] not surprising with the roar and racket of the main road so near.

The discovery of this solar alignment is usually attributed to Dr John Smith, who reported it in his *Choir Gaur* of 1771. Smith, an inoculator against smallpox, began an astronomical survey of Stonehenge in 1770 as an escape from hostile neighbours. The practice of smallpox inoculation, injecting the cowpox virus directly into the vein, had been known in England since the 1720s, but it was never very successful or popular, being as likely to kill as cure. This probably explains the apprehensive antagonism of Smith's villagers, 'malevolent villains, NOYSEY WRETCHES!',[27] who were preventing him from making a living.

Thwarted by their abuse, Smith started on the first systematic analysis of sightlines at Stonehenge, an activity which has since grown almost into an industry. There were obvious problems. The circle was already ruinous with stones fallen or leaning like bluestone 48, 'incumbered with Dung' and 'much injured by ignorant people', making the proof of any alignment very difficult. Nor did Smith have any surveying equipment or assistant. Nevertheless, working alone, he decided that the Heel Stone was the key that 'would disclose the uses of this Structure' because it marked the place at midsummer where the sun would rise at its solstice for 'three days together'. He went on to make other observations about the Four Stations and the trilithons of the sarsen ring and these will be considered in later chapters.

It was William Stukeley, however, who anticipated Smith by twenty years. 'The Entrance of Stoneh. is 4° from the true N.E. point, they set it to the N.E. loc[ation] that is the suns utmost elongation in Somer Solstice when they held a grand festival', adding in the book he wrote later that the entrance faced the skyline 'where the sun rises, or nearly, at the summer solstice'.[28] With his 'nearly' Stukeley was more scholarly than some of his astronomical successors and this leads to the third and fourth questions about Stonehenge, why the Heel Stone does not stand exactly in line with midsummer sunrise and what its purpose was.

At the end of June modern observers at the centre of Stonehenge, given clear weather, will see the sun appear on the horizon to the left of the Heel Stone. Five thousand years ago the discrepancy was greater. Nor does the stone stand on the first axis of Stonehenge, 46° 33′, but well to its right. Either its erectors had been very clumsy or they had reasons for this apparent displacement.

In 3200 BC the midsummer sun would have risen almost exactly 50° from True North, but the Heel Stone has an azimuth of 51°.3,[29] over a degree from its position if it were a solar marker. Differing explanations have been given for this.

In 1979 an unexpected stonehole was discovered near the Heel Stone.[30] It was 10 feet (3 m) north-west of the outlier and as the hole, now known as Stone 97, had been cut into when a prehistoric ditch had been dug around the Heel Stone, it was almost certainly a contemporary of that pillar. Stone 97, however, had been removed in antiquity and its hole neatly backfilled.

Two possibilities of almost equal weight can be applied to this discovery. Either the stones had stood side by side as a pair, aligned upon the sun, or the missing stone is not missing but is the present Heel Stone that had been shifted several times before Neolithic observers were satisfied with its present position.

If there had been a second stone then, with an estimated azimuth of 48° 21′, it would have stood just to the left of the solstitial sunrise. Together with the Heel Stone it would have formed a setting like a gunsight through which the midsummer sunrise would have been quite well seen. From this two things follow. It would explain why the Heel Stone is not in line with the sunrise, something that has puzzled astronomers since Stukeley's 'nearly'. It also implies that the Heel Stone was erected only very late in the first phase of Stonehenge when the prehistoric community was quite intentionally re-aligning the axis of the henge by over 4° in order to create a solar orientation. As the sun has always been connected with masculinity and dominance such an adaptation might reflect the social changes that occurred during the Late Neolithic period and which will be described in the next chapter.

It is also possible that this change was accompanied by the construction of an avenue of standing stones leading up to Stonehenge and enhancing what had previously been a plain hillside. Inigo Jones claimed to have seen four stones like portals at the north-east entrance and although forty years later one of them had gone, John Aubrey drew the remaining three on his plan of 1666. Referring to these and the outlying Heel Stone he wondered if they might be 'the remains of the avenue, or Entrance to this Temple;

which will appeare very probable, by comparing it with the Temples of Aubrey, Kynet [the Sanctuary], and ye Wedding at Stanton Drew . . .'.[31] In the 1720s Stukeley also believed in such an avenue but had either rejected or forgotten it when, years later, he wrote his book about Stonehenge. His friend, Roger Gale, reproved him for the omission, 'which is that the avenue up to the chief entrance was formerly planted with great stones, opposite to each other, upon the side banks of it, for I very well remember we observed the holes where they had been fixed'.[32]

Only excavation could prove the existence of such stoneholes. Magnetometer and resistivity surveys in 1981 did detect anomalies in the underlying ground but they were inconclusive.[33] Moreover, if Gale were right about depressions in the banks of the earthen avenue of Stonehenge's second phase these would have been about 55 feet (17 m) apart, much wider than the 10 feet (3 m) gap between Stone 97 and the Heel Stone. The evidence for a former stone-lined avenue, therefore, is unsatisfactory, especially as there is a more plausible explanation for 'Stone 97'.

It is feasible that it was no more than a stonehole in which the Heel Stone itself had once stood. The pit was improbably large for a single stone, 5¾ feet wide, 3 feet deep and no less than 16½ feet long (1.8 × 1 × 5 m). The excavator observed 'that the possibility exists that it consists of intersecting pits, each of which, at different times, contained a stone'.[34]

Well before the discovery of this hole J. E. Wood suggested that the Heel Stone had never been a solar pillar but had been used to mark the midpoint of the northern moon between its major and minor extremes.[35] Knowing that it took nine years from the time it appeared to the left of the midsummer sunrise for the moon to reach its most northerly rising, Neolithic people needed only to begin their sightings when the moon rose to the left of the summer solstice. This position could be marked by a standing stone.

The moon, however, was not so easily trapped. The observers would have been disconcerted to find that a pillar just to the left or even directly aligned on the midsummer sun obscured one or more of the very moonrises they wished to record. Fine adjustments were needed. Even moving the stone less than 5 feet (1.5 m) altered the angle from the centre of Stonehenge by a full degree and it may have been only after several replacements more and more to the right that the people could be sure that the lunar stone would fulfil its function.

The Heel Stone did indicate the midsummer sunrise but only because that direction could be used for observations on the moon. If this had not been the case then the axis of the henge would surely have pointed to the outlier rather than be over 4° to its north-east. As will be seen later, when a solar cult developed at Stonehenge its adherents actually changed the axis and widened the 35 foot (10.7 m) wide entrance to 60 feet (18 m) to bring it more into line with the Heel Stone.

Predictably, the first causeway with its central axis of 46° 33′ had its two edges in line with the northern moonrise and the Heel Stone respectively. When it was widened by 25 feet (7.6 m) and the axis changed to 49° 54' ± 3' the Heel Stone became its major feature, framed midway between its sides, emphasising how the people's interest had shifted to the sun. It is likely, therefore, that Stukeley's 'nearly' was more percipient than even he realised. The Heel Stone was not originally a sighting-mechanism for observing the midsummer sunrise but a counting-device for people wishing to know how far up the horizon the northern moon rose.

If the Heel Stone had been intended as a sun-stone its ideal position would have been just to the east of midsummer sunrise, 20 feet (6 m) from where it may first have stood.[36] This is so gross a mistake that a lunar explanation is more probable, with the stone moved once or twice but never more than a few feet. A similar relocation was noticed at the Stripple Stones circle-henge on Bodmin Moor, seemingly in an endeavour to align upon the equinoctial sunset.[37] It is possible that extensive excavations in the interiors of other henges and stone circles would reveal comparable re-alignments.

Even so, to think of the Heel Stone only as a sighting instrument is to oversimplify the Neolithic conception of the world in which poetry and science were never separate but were a unity in which every object was a duality of self and spirit. The stone marked the sun and the moon, it proclaimed that the land around it was inhabited and possessed, it stood sharply on the skyline as a signpost to the henge, and it embodied the ancestral ghosts.

Speaking of the Heel Stone Hoare commented that 'its original purport is totally unknown, though conjecture has not been idle in ascribing various uses to it',[38] but the erection of a stone or post outside a burial-place was common practice in Neolithic times. Hoare wrote that at the long barrow of Warminster 1 'at the south end was a sarsen stone 5 feet high, terminating almost in a point, and placed in an upright position. Near it lay the bones of three skeletons.'[39] It has been thought that such stones were representations of the female guardian of the dead, sometimes in southern France realistically carved, but more often, in Brittany, crudely shaped or even simply a coarse slab standing in the burial chamber or just outside the tomb.[40]

Such protective pillars have been found in Breton megalithic chambers such as Ty-ar-Boudiquet and Crech-Quillé, and outside others such as Les Pierres-Plates, sometimes, as at Manio, with stone axes deposited at their bases. In Britain there are too many sites where burials and standing stones are associated for more than a few to be mentioned, the Tinglestone barrow in Gloucestershire, the Long Stone at Gatcombe in the same county, or posts set up at the ends of long barrows like Thickthorn Down and Badshot Lea.

At Wor Barrow in Dorset a heavy sarsen stood immediately inside the entrance close to a clutter of human bones, just as some roughly-shouldered blocks in Brittany looked down the tomb's dark interior where the skeletons lay, watching over the dead. At Lyneham in Oxfordshire, close to the Rollright Stones circle, a pillar once 10½ feet (3.2 m) high stood at the entrance to a chambered tomb in which skulls and human bones were unearthed. Only 13 miles (21 km) south-west of Stonehenge a little henge at Tisbury surrounded a tall standing stone. Buried at its foot was a skeleton. In the chamber of Bryn Celli Ddu passage-grave on Anglesey there is a smoothed, elegant pillar over 8 feet (2.4 m) high. Near it were skeletons. Other bones, cremated, had been scattered around the chamber intermingled with human teeth and other unburnt human bones.

Stones outside henges and stone circles may also have been the embodiment of this protective spirit. A slab once stood in a ring of cremations beyond the entrance to a henge at Llandegai by the Menai Straits. In the same way as the Heel stone, other outliers may have combined an astronomical function with that of a guardian pillar. Long Meg in Cumbria, at the south-west of an enormous stone circle, not only marked the midwinter sunset but has also been likened in shape to a female deity. It is an interpretation that has its critics. 'The vulgar notion that the largest of these stones has breasts, and resembles the remainder of a female statue, is caused by the whimsical irregularity of the figure, in which a fervid imagination may discover a resemblance of almost anything.'[41]

The Neolithic world was not our world in a simpler form. To us it is a complex and elusive world, not because we cannot understand the farming methods or the carpentry techniques but because we cannot comprehend how the people themselves regarded those activities, what rituals were performed to make the wheat grow, what magical acts were needed before a house could be built. It was a half-world of natural forces and phantoms of which man had only imperfect ripples of perception like images glimpsed in running water. There was an awareness of an Other-World in which the dead lingered and where the spirits dwelt, more powerful than man, sometimes wilfully destructive, but to be reached and coerced through the intercession of the dead.

The Heel Stone remains as a symbol of the Neolithic mind, the only survivor of the charnel-house and the bones it safeguarded. The building has gone, but sufficient is left for it to be reconstructed in the mind, the sturdy worked uprights of its walls, the heavy thatched roof surmounted by a 'lantern' like a roofed crow's nest for the admission of light and for ventilation, something essential in the reeking decomposition that pervaded it. Inside, possibly on elevated platforms, were the corpses, their decay hastened by fires glowing below them, ox-skulls by their sides during the drawn-out months before the desiccated bones could be removed for burial.

It was the first Stonehenge and it was to change.

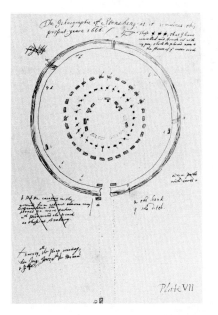

1. John Aubrey's 1666 plan of Stonehenge showing three stones at the north-east entrance

2. Inigo Jones' 1620 plan of Stonehenge, drawn by John Webb, showing four stones at the north-east entrance

3. Aerial view of Stonehenge from the north-east (copyright English Heritage)

4. Aerial view of Stonehenge from the east (copyright English Heritage)

5. Warminster 14 earthen long barrow from the south (Aubrey Burl)

6. Neolithic digging tools: antler pick, ox shoulder-blade; wickerwork basket (Aubrey Burl)

7. Bluestones 49 ('male') and 31 ('female')
at the entrance to Stonehenge (Aubrey Burl)

8. Stonehenge: the causeway of the south entrance is in the foreground;
beyond it, the short sarsen Stone 11 stands in front of Trilithon 53–54
(Aubrey Burl)

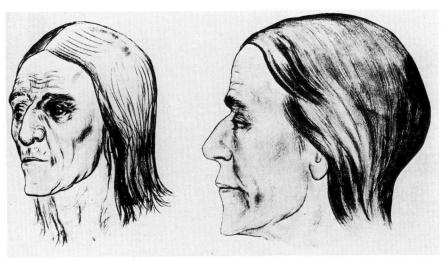

9. Reconstruction of neolithic faces from the skulls
in the Lanhill chambered tomb, Wiltshire

*Prospect from the west end of the Cursus of Stonehenge.*

A. the eastern meta. B. the eastern wing of the avenue. C. Stonehenge.

10. Stukeley's drawing of the Stonehenge Cursus from the north-west: the
curved end is imaginary; A and B are the Old King and New King barrows;
C is Stonehenge

11. Spiral-decorated antler macehead of the grooved ware cult;
from Garboldisham, Suffolk (Bury St Edmunds Museum)

12. The macehead found
with a cremation at the
east of Stonehenge
(Aubrey Burl)

13. Casts of French female statue-menhirs: left, St Sernin, Aveyron, Guyenne,
southern France; right, Mas Capelier, Aveyron (Aubrey Burl)

14. Collingbourne Kingston earthen long barrow, Wiltshire (Aubrey Burl)

15. The Heel Stone from the south; the Cursus round barrows are in the background (Aubrey Burl)

# 5

## Prestige, pottery and pitfalls
## Stonehenge Ib: 2700 – 2200 BC

*If the Aubrey Holes were really intended for eclipse prediction, it shows a degree of sophistication for the Late Neolithic Period that is not paralleled at other sites.*

J. E. Wood, *Sun, Moon and Standing Stones*, 163

*And the woman said to Saul, 'I saw gods ascending out of the earth'.*

1 Samuel, 28:13

Near Tilshead, a few miles north-west of Stonehenge, the rivulet of a tiny winterbourne, a stream that flows only after a wet autumn, twists delicately across Orcheston Down. Here it is swollen by other rills and brooks and becomes the River Till, which in turn swirls into the River Wylye, trebling its size. Some miles to the south this joins the River Nadder in a writhing tangle of channels, only shortly to be overwhelmed by the even heavier River Avon. By then the primal trickles of the Tilshead winter streamlet are no more than flecks of spray in the flood of water that pours down towards the south coast. The story of Stonehenge from its inconspicuous beginnings has a similar pattern.

> Time, like an ever-rolling stream,
> Bears all its sons away;
> They fly forgotten, as a dream
> Dies at the opening day.

Isaac Watts, *Hymns and Spiritual Songs*

Comparable surges affected Stonehenge. The beliefs that created it were enriched but warped by a changing society and by ideas from outside the region. The roots of its birth were never killed but they became entwined in a myriad of strands of time and strange customs so that what we see today is the result of minglings and conflicts that encompassed two thousand years of change.

There was the fading climate and there was the exhaustion of agricultural land. There was the tension between those who were gaining wealth and those who had nothing. The power of ancestors seemed to have failed and their cult gave way to the worship of gods. Gods demanded priests and opulent presents and it was the powerful men of society who could provide both. Alliances were agreed between leaders in distant parts, exchanging rich gifts which they took with them to the grave, breaking with tradition while persuading their followers that everything was as it had always been, a deception more easily practised in a non-literate society whose myths and legends could be modified and manipulated as the teller desired. Like some musical heirloom on which any tune could be played, Stonehenge was used to show that nothing had changed, the instrument was still the same. But the melodies were different.

The later Neolithic was a time of unrest. There had been widespread disturbance that ultimately was followed by many readjustments of the old ways of life. Whether such upheaval was caused by over-exploitation of farming land, or famine, or plague, or struggle over territories is not clear. One might speak not of medieval but of deserted prehistoric villages and of people struggling to return to a settled existence. In Wessex several vague territories became more sharply defined, first with causewayed enclosures as their foci, later with small henges: Maumbury Rings in south Dorset, Knowlton Centre on Cranborne Chase, Stonehenge on Salisbury Plain, and perhaps the stone circles at Avebury on the Marlborough Downs. Objects from far away are found with local products close to these new gathering places.

Influential regions emerged elsewhere in the British Isles. The Boyne Valley of eastern Ireland with its great passage-graves and formalised art may have been the spiritual birthplace of the grooved ware cult that was briefly to dominate at Stonehenge. The Yorkshire Wolds, whose inhabitants largely controlled the distribution of stone axes from the Lake District, was another of these 'core' regions. Salisbury Plain, producing nothing exotic, but having prairies of rich soils, deep sources of good flint, and sprawling at the middle of a network of navigable rivers and accessible hill-ridges and trackways, was a third.

There, superficially, the native way of life continued unchanged. Pottery, almost indestructible and a helpful indicator of period and patterns of existence, slowly developed from the simple, round-based Windmill Hill ware into heavier, decorated bowls ornamented with impressions all over their bodies. This Peterborough ware had three overlapping phases known as Ebbsfleet, Mortlake and Fengate. It is the second of these that is commonplace during the Late Neolithic on Salisbury Plain.[1] It was widely spread from the south coast right up to Cumbria and Yorkshire and its popularity may have been accelerated by the movement of the potters themselves, women who were married out or exchanged as gifts to consolidate the bonds being made between different parts of England.

Little is known about this 'dark age'. The damaged foundations of three claustrophobic round huts were found at Winterbourne Dauntsey south-east of Stonehenge and the Mortlake pottery in them showed that they belonged to this period. Their filth discouraged any idea of a prehistoric golden age. Although they were situated on a low hill, the ground appeared to have been continually sodden, bare of anything but patches of grass and scatters of decaying food thrown out from the cramped, squalid shacks. Each of them had a sunken floor littered with bones of pig and sheep, ashes, pot-boilers for heating water. Cores of flint and flakes struck from them indicated where someone had squatted, making tools. Outside there were rubbish-pits containing the shells of carnivorous snails that had fed on the mouldering refuse, 'and the picture of unsanitary conditions deduced from the remains of masses of slugs was no savoury one'.[2]

It is salutary to realise that being only six miles from Stonehenge the occupants of these dirty hovels almost certainly went to and used the ceremonial enclosure. It is likely that some other people lived better, but even the best of them would be well acquainted with insects, cattle-droppings, dust, hard floors and the bitter chilling air of a winter morning when rising from the comfort of a hide-covered sleeping-place.

Burials are rarely identified in the vagueness of this time, although those that are known emphasise the increasing tendency towards adult males being given precedence. When General Pitt-Rivers excavated the Wor long barrow in Dorset, a mound which may have been used for executions in Roman times from the presence of decapitated bodies high in the ditches, he found six Neolithic skeletons under the barrow, all of them male. Like many other Neolithic people they were dolichocephalic with long narrow heads, and were slight and short, their average height being only 5 feet 2 inches (1.6 m). Two other skeletons lay deep down in the ditch, one with a lozenge-shaped flint arrowhead below his ribs, providing yet another probable instance of violent death.

When Pitt-Rivers later investigated two round barrows near the tumulus he found that they were Neolithic also. One covered a man's skeleton with a Mortlake bowl beside it. The other had two more males, one with a finely-finished jet 'slider' like a narrow black buckle for fastening a belt around the waist.[3] An origin in Yorkshire is not unlikely and it could have been an exotic and prestigious object exchanged between men of high rank. The fashions of a single or a very restricted number of burials in a grave, of priority for men, and of luxurious grave-goods were to become prevalent over the following centuries.

The land was failing and the old beliefs in kinship and the protective powers of ancestors weakened. Confronted with this dilemma, communities could choose: they could reaffirm their faith in their ancestors, building more elaborate tombs, stressing their loyalty to tradition; or their leaders, as on Salisbury Plain, could imperceptibly take control of ritual, invoking gods and powers of nature, turning away from an ancestor-cult which linked them too closely with their followers; or, as in Yorkshire, the leaders could blatantly annexe wealth for themselves, taking it into death with them in defiance of all that had gone before.

On Salisbury Plain small henges, almost like the assembly-places of fiefdoms, were built, enclosures that demanded large workforces. Their presence hints at a reshaping of society, with local 'chieftains' controlling districts and accumulating riches. 'It is through these regional monuments that the leaders justified their power. Local problems could be controlled by re-writing the history of the ancestors but real power now required the control of a larger area and the ancestors were too localised. Claims had now, therefore, to be made to the "gods", the "natural" powers of the world, who were ranked above human and ancestral claims.'[4]

Unlike the ancestors, the gods demanded offerings and, because of this, in the phase known as Stonehenge Ib, changes were made. Just within the henge's bank a ring of pits was dug. Then, almost immediately, the empty holes were backfilled. Nothing of any kind, post or stone or article, was left in them. Such apparent irrationality has led to all sorts of interpretation from the astronomical to the asinine but, in fact, there was nothing illogical about it.

In 1666, while making a survey of Stonehenge for Charles II, John Aubrey noticed five faint depressions irregularly spaced around the inner edge of the bank and on his plan he marked 'b b b &c little cavities in the ground, from whence one may well conjecture the stones c c were taken'.[5] They are known as the Aubrey Holes after him.

Some people have doubted that he could detect the tops of such ancient, grass-covered pits, but their scepticism betrays the result of inattention during history lessons. 1666 was the year of the Fire of London, which followed the Great Plague of 1665, both of them years of exceptionally hot summers when, as Leasor wrote in *The Plague and the Fire* (1962, 94), 'the sun shone with Italian fierceness, roads crumbled into dust . . . dunghills steamed' and prayers were uttered daily for rain. The dry earth and parched grass would have made the richer, greener turf growing over the pits stand out, although only to the eye of an observant fieldworker such as Aubrey.

By 1720, in different weather conditions, the depressions were no longer visible but this did not prevent Stukeley from some sanguinary thoughts: 'The cavitys in the plain of Stonehenge were to make their fires in and hang the kettles for boyling the flesh of their sacrifices in their anniversary feasts in memory of the dead'.[6] Some of the pits would prove to be too small and shallow for Neolithic barbecues, but it was not until they were excavated that their nature could be appreciated.

In 1920, after inspecting Aubrey's plan in the Bodleian Library, Oxford, Hawley and his colleagues searched with a steel bar for the 'cavities'. After locating one, 'and subsequently more, all apparently at regular intervals round the earthwork',[7] he began to empty them. Altogether fifty-six were detected, roughly 16 feet (5 m) apart, all round the circle. Hawley started at no. 1 by the north-east causeway, excavating twenty-three in the first year. He dug thirty-two in all, nos 1–30 clockwise and nos 55 and 56 at the far side of the main entrance. In 1950 Atkinson, Piggott and Stone excavated two more, nos 31 and 32, from the latter of which charcoal supplied a radiocarbon date of 1848±275 bc.[8] Because this was one of the very first C–14 assays its chronological range was very wide and offered a broad span for the sample between 2123 and 1573 bc (2700 – 1950 BC). There are reasons for believing that it is the earliest date, 2700 BC, that is to be preferred, a time before any stone circle was put up inside Stonehenge. Bluestone fragments, sarsen and other material from later phases lay only in the very tops of the holes. Newall, moreover, pointed out that it was possible to draw an exact circle through the holes from the middle of the ring, something which would have been impossible in later centuries when the stone circles had centres several feet away from that of the henge.[9]

Despite this symmetry there was little geometrical about the pits. Lying on the circumference of a ring with an average radius of 142 feet (43.3 m), they were anything from 30 to 70 inches (0.8 – 1.8 m) wide, sub-circular or misshapen, and from 24 to 45 inches (0.6 – 1.1 m) deep. Nor were they evenly spaced, but varied by as much as a foot between their centres. Whatever the reason why they had been dug, it had obviously not been obligatory to make them identical in size, shape or position.

These hollows have been claimed as the stoneholes of an unknown circle, as the postholes of a timber ring, as places where fires burned so that the blinding sun could safely be observed through the smoke, as ritual pits and as markers for the prediction of eclipses.[10]

Some of these ideas were hardly less fantastic than astrology and ley-lines and have been condemned. 'The astronomer, in his quest for alignments, might convert barrows into observation mounds without reference to their uses and contents, and without allowing for the ignorance of the period, while the anthropologist allows his imagination to carry him beyond the limits of actual fact.'[11] Frank Stevens, former Curator of Salisbury Museum, concluded that 'the true solution will be for the field archaeologist, rather than the weaver of theories and the student in his library'.

Although unfair to most astronomers and anthropologists, Stevens had some excuse for his outburst. Too often, precise alignments have been 'discovered', accurate to 1', dated within a century, the fore- and backsights neatly indicated, when, in reality, the foresight is only one of several skyline notches and the backsight is an overgrown barrow, lopsided and spread-out from antiquarian explorations. Such over-zealous 'astronomy' seems as hit and miss as the notorious gunfight in the OK Corral when 34 revolver shots and several buckshot blasts achieved only three accurate hits, four fair ones and missed four of the nine large targets altogether even though fired at pointblank range.[12]

Similar objections can be made to some of the slipshod theories about the Aubrey Holes. Their ragged spacing and the latitude allowed in their width and depth warns us that their diggers may not have been concerned with geometrical precision. One question, however, that has arisen and which is not susceptible to accusations of ramshackle thinking is whether the actual number of Aubrey Holes mattered. This raises the fifth of the questions about Stonehenge.

It has been suggested that Neolithic people, well aware of the moon's movements and realising that 56 was a significant lunar number, purposely laid out that number of pits to use them as markers for eclipse-prediction. It was an idea put forward by Hawkins in 1964 and later elaborated by Hoyle.[13] Asking why the people had not simply bisected quadrants of the henge, Hawkins hypothesised that the Aubrey Holes had 'provided a system for counting the years, one hole for each year, to aid in predicting the movement of the Moon', over its 18.61 year cycle.[14] Although close to 18.61, the multiples of numbers such as 19 (19 × 3 = 57) or 18 (18 × 3 = 54) would soon have resulted in errors. 'The smallest time unit that would have remained accurate for many years would have been the triple-interval measure, 19 + 19 + 18, or a total of 56 years.'[15]

If three black and three white stones had been placed on holes spaced 9, 9, 10, 9, 9, 10 apart and moved sideways one hole each year, they could have foretold lunar eclipses. 'This simple operation will predict accurately every important lunar event for hundreds of years', claimed Hawkins. Three holes were critical: nos 51, 56 and 5. Whenever a stone arrived at Hole 56 on the major axis of the henge, that would be the year when a solar or lunar eclipse would occur within fifteen days of midwinter. It was also the year of an eclipse of the summer moon. Equinoctial eclipses would happen whenever a white stone reached Holes 5 or 51.

The astronomer Fred Hoyle devised a more intricate scheme after calculating that the first method would permit the prediction of eclipses only a short two or three months before their occurrence. Other critics argued that 47 would have been a better number than 56. Nevertheless, the theory has been discussed here because, unlike some ill-considered notions, it is mathematically and astronomically tenable. Recognising Neolithic man's interest in the moon, it is possible to argue that he worked out a system for anticipating a phenomenon as dramatic as an eclipse. Archaeologically, however, the hypothesis is less convincing.

It depends on the choice of 56, and what has been generally overlooked in the debate is that there are other henges with 'Aubrey Holes' but never with 56 of them. 56 is fundamental to the eclipse argument. 'There has never been put forward a satisfactory account to explain the presence of these holes – except as receptacles for human cremation, but why then the number 56?'[16] The implication is that 56 was the number uniquely wanted, but 56 is a number peculiar to Stonehenge. In similar British henges of the same period with similar pits containing similar material, all of which was probably inserted later, there is nothing to confirm that their makers had anything but an animistic interest in the sun or moon. Despite the reluctance to accept that, later on, the Aubrey Holes were 'receptacles', yet in every comparable site from Cairnpapple in Scotland down to Maumbury Rings in Dorset broken objects and bone were buried in the pits (Table 8). There is no justification in singling out Stonehenge from the group. All the sites are henges, with banks and ditches, with entrances, all are Late Neolithic and all have central spaces where people assembled for their rituals. The pits were just one part of those rites.

The Aubrey Holes were not components of a prehistoric computer. Instead, they were related to the pits under early Neolithic long barrows, bowl-shaped hollows having only loose earth in them. Against these basins were the bones of the dead – at Tilshead 2, at Heytesbury 4, at Knook 5 whose pit 'had neither bones nor ash in it', and the nearby Knook 2 'of semi-circular form, neatly cut in the solid chalk' and with nothing more than 'vegetable mould, charred wood and two bits of bone in its filling'.[18]

This long-established custom of making pits near the dead provided a persuasive method for effecting the transformation of Stonehenge from an ancestral mortuary house into a temple of the gods. Pits, dug out all around the timber building, and almost identical to those of the long barrows, would be acceptable in this sacred place. By now the building was surely in a ruinous state, needing repair or, more practically, removal. The presence of pits would allow this alteration, for they would create an alternative barrier around the precinct, a ring open to the sky but composed of hollows like those of the ancestors, bowl-shaped, empty of everything but their own chalk and earth but so disposed that they honoured the old alignments of the henge.

A charnel-house was no longer needed. From the evidence of complete skeletons in the latest long barrows, corpses in the Late Neolithic were being buried shortly after death, still fleshed and after a fairly brief period of mourning. The building's rotting timbers could be dismantled. It is possible, but unprovable without excavation, that in their place the people set up free-standing concentric rings of posts, perhaps carved or coloured, an outer circle as wide as the former mortuary house, with a ring of even taller posts inside it. Such wooden rings, years later supplanted by stone circles, have been discovered not only on Machrie Moor and at Moncrieffe, Croft Moraig and Balfarg in Scotland but much closer to Stonehenge at the Sanctuary near Avebury. Here just such a posthole setting was uncovered by Maud Cunnington, a ring of hefty uprights replacing an earlier mortuary house[19] and itself succeeded by a stone circle. It is a sequence that may have been duplicated at Stonehenge, the new tall posts standing like the framework of a new house, of the same size as their forerunner, lintelled but without walls, roofless, open to daylight, admitting the sky. To the symbolism of the Neolithic mind this could have been the mortuary house rebuilt, a ring of pillars within a ring of pillars and it would have given more credence to the illusion that nothing had changed, especially if those open rings of posts became the focus of the new burial rites. In those short-lived generations there would soon have been very few

**TABLE 8. Henges in Great Britain with 'Aubrey Holes'**[17]

| No. | Site | No. of Pits | Diameter | | Spacing | | Miles from Stonehenge | Contents of the Pits |
|-----|------|-------------|----------|--------|---------|-----|------------------------|----------------------|
| | | | Feet | Metres | Ft | M | | |
| 1 | CAIRNPAPPLE, West Lothian | 7 | 56 | 17.1 | 25 | 7.6 | 330 | Bone pins, cremations |
| 2 | LLANDEGAI, Gwynedd | 5 | 25 | 7.6 | 16 | 4.9 | 170 | Cremations |
| 3 | MAXEY A, Northamptonshire | 10 | 44 | 13.4 | 14 | 4.3 | 125 | Cremations |
| 4 | MAXEY B | 10 | 31 | 9.5 | 10 | 3.1 | 125 | Cremations |
| 5 | DORCHESTER I, Oxfordshire | 13 | 21 | 6.4 | 5 | 1.5 | 45 | Bone pins, flints, antlers |
| 6 | DORCHESTER IV | 8 | 20 | 6.1 | 8 | 2.4 | 45 | Cremations |
| 7 | DORCHESTER V | 13 | 34 | 10.4 | 8 | 2.4 | 45 | Cremations, Peterborough ware, antler picks |
| 8 | DORCHESTER VI | 12 | 39 | 11.9 | 10 | 3.1 | 45 | Cremations, flints, Late Neolithic sherds |
| 9 | DORCHESTER XI | 14 | 40 × 36 | 12.2 × 11.0 | 9 | 2.7 | 45 | Animal bones, antler picks, cremations |
| 10 | MAUMBURY RINGS, Dorset | 44 or 45 | 169 | 51.5 | 12 | 3.7 | 45 | Antlers, carved bone, animal bones |
| 11 | STONEHENGE, Wiltshire | 56 | 284 | 86.6 | 16 | 4.9 | — | Bone pins, flints, cremations |

who could remember what had stood there before the spacious wooden circles.

Bearing in mind that ultimately two concentric rings of Welsh bluestones would be set up at Stonehenge, it is significant that exactly the same pattern occurred at the Sanctuary only 16 miles to the north in a steady transition from mortuary house to timber rings to stone circles, each stage being an imitative mutation of its predecessor. In such a manner every change became no more than a reaffirmation of the past.

Whatever changed at Stonehenge, its traditions were preserved. Even though the mortuary house had gone, the NE-SW axis survived. The burial mentioned in the last chapter was discovered exactly placed across it. In 1926, his final year at Stonehenge, Hawley noticed that to the north of the circle's centre the ground had been disturbed. As he removed the loose soil, 'a quantity of human bone was come upon in a disordered mass', grotesquely jumbled with prehistoric sherds, a Roman coin, the nail of a horseshoe, broken glass and a clay pipe, a turmoil produced by 18th century treasure-seekers who had accidentally shovelled into a grave. Hawley's workers cleared out a hollow 8 feet (2.4 m) in length, in which a single human arm-bone remained. The pit lay NW-SE at right-angles to the axis of the old earthwork. In it a corpse had been placed, head to the north-west and with a post at its feet, a post that from the centre of Stonehenge would have stood in line with the Heel Stone. There was nothing to date this interment but, as Atkinson observed, 'there is no reason to suppose that it is not prehistoric',[20] nor is there any reason why it should not belong to this early open-air phase. Placed where it was just inside the new ring of posts and on the original axis, one that would be altered by later generations, this was not a pious burial but a votive offering that acted like a threshold to the interior of the timber circles.

Outside these rings the people reduced the height of the henge's bank by spading and scraping much of the grass, earth and chalk back into the ditch. Hawley recognised the 'fallen white chalk over the ditch floor' and 'an earthy chalk rubble layer' above the silt that had accumulated on the ditch bottom as the sides had been worn away by rain and ice.

Rendering the bank less of a barricade gave more prominence to the Aubrey Holes. In 1973 Alexander Thom undertook a survey of them and demonstrated how their diggers had respected the cardinal positions of their forebears: 'Since the position of the first Aubrey Hole is 3° 7' from geographical north and the mean spacing is 6°.429 the north point is very nearly midway between two holes, and since there are 8 × 7 holes then all the cardinal points and the four intermediate points (NE, SE etc) lie midway between holes.'[21]

This might explain how the holes were set out. Pairs of holes were first dug astride the north, south, east and west cardinal points. Then each of the intervening arcs was filled with twelve more holes along the perimeter of the planned circle. If this is what happened, then the number 56 was entirely fortuitous, being no more than the unconsidered total of (4×2) + (4×12), a chance combination arrived at by semi-numerate people with no thought of eclipse prediction.

Nor is there evidence of the use of a precise measuring-stick. Thom, who believed that prehistoric people in Britain and Brittany employed a yard-stick of 2.72 feet or 0.83 m in length, his 'Megalithic Yard' or MY, some-times multiplied by 2½ to make a staff of 6.8 feet or 2.07 m, his 'Megalithic Rod' or MR, pointed out that the circumference of the Aubrey Hole circle was exactly 131 MR. The radius, however, of which he had said 'the holes were placed more accurately' than they were along the circumference,[22] was an unconvincing 20.8 MR and the holes were some 2.4 MR apart, an error of over 8 inches (20 cm) or nearly 10 per cent if the intended spacing had been 2½ MR. It is possible, instead, that a local measure of about 4 feet (1.2 m) was used but not, as Stukeley said, with 'a mathematical exactness'.

Once the holes were dug, offerings could be poured into them, sanctifying the pits, dedicating the temple to the gods, 'the opening of a symbolic door down to the nether world'. As Richard Atkinson goes on to remark, at the hengiform site of Dorchester XI 'more than one of the pits showed signs of having been filled with a pool of liquid', though perhaps only prosaic rainwater.[23]

Two thousand years later, on his long and troubled voyage, Odysseus described how he had consulted with the spirits:

' . . . with my sword
I dug out a pit a cubit round and deep,
and poured three libations to the countless ghosts,
first honey mixed with milk, then wine, and water,
throwing down barley on these gifts
before calling to the spirits of the spectral dead.'
Homer. *The Odyssey*, Book XI

At Stonehenge chalk was rammed back into the pits, sealing the evan-escent offerings. For decades the tops of these entries to the Other-World must have been kept clean of grass, always white, always maintaining the power of the magical ring inside the spoiled bank. Bodies were still brought there, but now for only a short while and probably only those of the leaders. Then, abruptly, once more things changed. Stonehenge was abandoned.

As long ago as 1921 Hawley suspected that something unusual had happened: 'At some time in the history of Stonehenge, and perhaps for a long period, there must have been a considerable amount of vegetation covering the site. I conclude this from the great amount of small snail-shells occurring throughout the excavations.'[24] These were not the large garden variety but much tinier species, just as restricted in their mobility and very sensitive to their habitat. The presence of the carnivorous snail, *Cecilioides acicula*, in some long barrows shows that it was a corpse rather than a skeleton that had been buried there. The little *Oxychilus cellarius* snail was found amongst the human bones in the Wayland's Smithy barrow, 'where it was attracted by the rotting flesh of bodies'.[25] Other snail-types provide information about their prehistoric environment, some liking daylight, others dark, some warmth, some cold, others damp or dry conditions, so that their shells are like a barometer of the local landscape at the time they died.

At Stonehenge a cutting through the bank and ditch in 1978 recovered hundreds of shells and amplified Hawley's remarks. Dug just west of the north-east causeway it exposed ten distinct layers from the modern turf down to the bedrock of the ditch. Just above it was the evidence of the later, partial backfilling. There were few snail-shells at the bottom of this thrown-back chalk, suggesting that for a time the loose rubble had remained dry and grassless before, gradually, some weeds and vegetation had grown, inhabited sporadically by a snail, *Vallonia costata*, with a preference for open-air conditions. This period was presumably contemporary with the digging of the Aubrey Holes. But it was followed by a quite different sequence in which light-loving varieties of snail diminished and shells of *Zontidiae* became abundant, thin-shelled and fragile, a type common in ungrazed grassland and in the shady litter of woodland leaves. Around Stonehenge there were still some clearings and open spaces but 'nevertheless, on a local scale, it seems clear that this episode reflects human abandonment of the site'.[26]

During those years, around 2600 BC, trees and scrubby undergrowth spread across the Plain and where there had been tracts of agricultural land now there was a wilderness. At Stonehenge the enclosure was deserted to the wind and the rain, and the posts of the circles sagged in slow decay, untidy as a huddle of javelins in the earth.

Within the shabby outline of the bank a few trees and bushes rooted and flourished. Hawley had come across the misformed cavities left when they died, quite different in shape from well-cut man-made postholes. He named them Holes F, G and H, dismissing them as natural hollows, and later attempts to use them as astronomical markers have not been convincing. Other thickets overshadowed the grasses of the ditch. Except for a few natives piously visiting it, Stonehenge lay neglected.

Salisbury Plain was apparently no longer settled by a unified population, confidently existing in a net of blood-ties and kinship bonds. Now there were separate zones as though there were one for the commoners, another for the socially élite. Not two miles to the north-east of where Stonehenge mouldered, the vast and irregular earthwork of Durrington Walls was heaped up alongside a bend of the River Avon. A mile and a half (2.4 km) to its south a small, single-entranced henge was constructed in a clearing on the low summit of Coneybury Hill. This henge seems to have become the accepted ritual centre of the region. Four miles away, separated from it and Durrington Walls by the brambles and bushes bristling along

Stonehenge Bottom, people using native pottery were living in an almost industrial area of flint-working. Other men and women were occupying commodious timber buildings in Durrington Walls. Here the pottery vessels were not local but of the style known unromantically as grooved ware.

It was an uneasy time everywhere, a time of innovation and of struggle, with defended sites replacing the old open settlements. Great field-systems were developing. In Ireland the first metalwork in the British Isles was being manufactured, cast perhaps by immigrant smiths from the continental mainland with their distinctive beaker drinking-pots. The earliest metal tools were flat, broad-butted axes of copper named after a hoard of Castletown Roche in Co. Cork, a region rich in copper deposits. Aging axe-factories in Cornwall and Wales and Cumbria continued to produce stone axes and fresh sites were exploited as people prospected for further sources of hard, workable stone. Almost everywhere the entrances of earthen long barrows and megalithic tombs were being blocked and few new long mounds were built. In what was known as the Mount Pleasant phase after the stockaded enclosure in Dorset other gigantic earthworks were erected in Wessex at this time, at Knowlton, at Marden, Avebury and Durrington Walls, the last three having almost identical 'territories' of about 14 miles (22 km) across, some 150 square miles (390 km²) with the earthwork enclosure at its centre.

Excavation and geophysical surveys have revealed the former existence of many timber structures inside Durrington Walls, put up on land occupied eight centuries earlier by people with no fear of attack. The Late Neolithic was more threatening. Around 2600 BC a deep ditch and a mile-long outer bank was constructed with a wide entrance left at the north-west and another at the south-east facing downhill towards the river. Inside the enclosure, to which the term 'henge' is often misapplied, there were circular buildings of stout oak, one, at least 125 feet (38 m) across, of concentric rings of postholes. It may have been the equivalent of the timber rings conjectured to have stood inside Stonehenge. Also inside Durrington Walls, nearly a quarter of a mile across, there were perhaps twenty other round wooden huts and buildings varying in size and as randomly arranged as an African kraal.

On the supposition that the earthwork was an embanked village and assuming the high number of ten occupants to each dwelling, some two hundred people may have lived there. Allowing for the elderly, the very young and the crippled, one might guess at an active work-force of seventy able-bodied men and women. So small a group is unlikely to have built the earthwork and put up the structures by itself and this provides yet another hint that these people were a privileged minority.

It has been estimated that the ditch and bank alone took 500,000 hours of labour to make. For seventy people toiling eight hours daily every day of the year, the work would have gone on for two and a half years. They would then have had to fell the oaks, transport them to the site and put up the buildings, some of which contained tree-trunks weighing nearly four tons. Rather than seventy it is arguable that up to fifteen times that number was involved, a thousand or more workers digging and carrying the chalk in gangs like a scurry of ants, unregimented in the scuffle of constant, dust-murkened movement as basketload after basketload of rubble was dumped on the hump-banked ridge of the bank.

Others searched miles away for tall trees in the alluvial valleys by the river where the best oaks grew, hacking them down with heavy axes of stone from Cornwall, hauling the logs to the Avon, floating them downstream like prehistoric lumberjacks, a thousand tree-trunks from clearings which, if patchworked together, would have formed a quarter of a mile square of denuded forest.

One wonders what power it was that granted people the ability to organise so many others supposedly not by compulsion but by persuasion. One also wonders why it was that those leaders, who were of native stock and not invaders of whom there is no sign, had turned away from Stonehenge. The simplest, most cogent answer is the appeal of a novel cult. It was a cult connected with grooved ware.

Where it originated in the British Isles is not certain, although the Boyne Valley of Ireland is a strong candidate from the similarity of the symbols carved on the walls of its passage-graves to motifs channelled on the sides of many grooved ware pots. Wherever the style began, its vessels, decorated with panels and bands of incised lines in geometrically stiff patterns or occasional swirling spirals, have been found as far north as the Orkneys, in mainland Scotland, in Yorkshire and in much of lowland Britain.

Unlike the finely-made beakers that appeared in Britain not long after-wards, grooved ware was a phenomenon with very few individual associations. Usually the flower-pot shaped vessels have been found with articles of local origin. They do not lie in a particular type of barrow or settlement, they were not placed with a unique form of burial, no special assemblage of tools or weapons or ornaments has been discovered with them. No physically distinctive human beings used them. For these reasons it is more likely that the pots were part of an attractive cult rather than the property of an intrusive people. In this they were different from beakers.

The fact that grooved ware has been recovered from some early stone circles and henges supports the idea that the vessels were elements of a new ritual that was rapidly adopted. The one strong association with the pottery, maceheads of antler or stone, confirms this. These implements, made of material chosen for its attractive appearance and sometimes decorated with coiled spirals, seem more like the equipment of ceremonial rather than temporal authority, the symbols of a cult that has left almost nothing behind it.

The pots in themselves were not impressive. Their flat-bottomed, poorly-fired bucket shapes were far inferior to the native Mortlake bowls. It was the ritualistic associations of grooved ware, the beautiful objects that could be worn or paraded ostentatiously, the arcane symbols and the votive rituals that enthralled the highborn males who were admitted to the mystery.

We shall never know the ethos of this cult. Hints come from the way in which its devotees ceremoniously deposited disparate things together. What was once considered rubbish has been reconsidered as the deliberate juxta-position of distinctive articles in the belief that such arrangements, acts of sympathetic magic like sticking pins into wax effigies, would guarantee the well-being of the community, creating order in times of disorder such as the Late Neolithic was.

Of the three aspects of this cult, the objects, the symbols and the rites, it is the objects that are most easily understood today. These were pres-tigious items: maceheads of antler or exquisite stone, often chosen for its bands and swirls of colour and then polished and perforated to receive the wooden shaft on which it could be displayed; finely-chipped flint arrow-heads shaped like the blade of a guillotine for slicing through the hide of hunted game; flint knives; flat plaques of chalk the size of a postcard and incised with grooves and lines whose meaning eludes the modern mind; these were some of the things to which people of status had access. Made by skilled craftsmen, they may have been carried scores of miles to a distant kinsman or ally and presented to him as a gift and token of continuing friendship.

They were evidence of rank and they were for more than everyday use. Tabus attached to them. No pot was placed with a burial. Nor was any axe or carved stone ball. Maceheads, to the contrary, have been found on settlements and in graves as articles permissible to take into death, perhaps to ensure that the role of its possessor would not be diminished in the Other-World. Some have been discovered as offerings, buried or thrown into rivers, enhancing the prestige of its owner who had given it to the gods.

This may have been the case with the macehead of lustrous red antler that was dredged from the River Little Ouse at Garboldisham in 1964. It had lain deep in the sludge amongst animal bones and was incised with what may have been the most potent of all grooved ware symbols, the spiral. This motif is carved on stones at the entrances and in the interiors of Irish chambered tombs, on pottery and, now and then, on maceheads, including a superbly fashioned one of multi-coloured flint from the Boyne passage-grave of Knowth.[27]

There has been speculation that the spiral represented two aspects of the sun, arranged clockwise in narrow coils to show how the sun's shadow would be cast day after day as it moved from midsummer to midwinter, whereas it would make wider anti-clockwise rings from midwinter back to midsummer.[28] It is the faintest of suggestions that by this time the sun itself was venerated. Other symbols, the meander, lozenge, small dots and lines, although common to the passage-graves and the grooved ware pots, have no recognisable resemblance to anything, although to their society they must all have a ritual significance.

Of grooved ware rites our knowledge is meagre. The burial of objects, including sherds, in postholes and pits was widespread. So was the custom of demarcating zones in which only selected things could be deposited. At Durrington Walls several of these zones have been detected.[29] There were concentrations of decorated sherds, flint tools, scores of antler picks and the meat-bones of pigs, the relics of feasting on this succulent animal. The ox was still a beast of importance to the economy for traction, for its hide, for everyday work, but it was pork, not beef, that was preferred by the élite, as the proportion of animal remains inside the earthwork shows (Table 9).

### TABLE 9. Numbers of individual animals found in Durrington Walls

| Domestic | | | Wild | | |
|---|---|---|---|---|---|
| | No. | | No. | | No. |
| pig | 228 | aurochs | 3 | red deer | 14 |
| cattle | 97 | roe deer | 2 | badger | 1 |
| goat | 1 | horse | 3 | fox | 2 |
| sheep | 7 | beaver | 1 | pinemarten | 1 |

The manifestly selected contents of ritual pits suggest that this was not rubbish but material deliberately gathered together in magical combinations that would generate power and protection. There is an opaque vision of a secret society, its leaders flaunting their superiority, living in some luxury, engaging in ceremonies that have left few traces behind them. In every region, the Orkneys, Yorkshire, Wessex, the cult merged with native customs in different ways so that it is no more than a blurred picture that we have of it. In the vicinity of Stonehenge offerings were buried in grooved ware pits in a profligacy quite different from the austere emptiness of the Aubrey Holes and the hollows by the long barrow skeletons.

A quarter of a mile south of Durrington Walls in the gardens of houses facing the road to Amesbury four pits were found, all carefully dug and then promptly filled with upturned basketloads of flint tools in almost perfect condition. With them was a Welsh stone axe, another of flint, sharp-edged arrowheads, bones of ox, pig, roe deer and fox, nutshells and, astonishingly, marine food brought by people from the coast over 30 miles away, the jaws of chub and the shells of scallops, mussels and oysters, signs of good living four and a half thousand years ago. Amongst these enticing gifts to the gods were three large flint balls with 'little or no signs of use'.[30]

At Ratfyn, a mile from Durrington Walls, where snail-shells intimated a damp climate, two pits contained some exceptionally large cattle bones, bones of a brown bear, and some delicately-chipped arrowheads intermingled with hundreds of flint flakes and some fire-crackled pot-boilers. Such an esoteric mélange is unlikely to have been refuse. The brown bear, an immensely strong creature of the forest, and the very heavy cattle may have symbolised strength just as oxen had done in the early Neolithic centuries before. Another pit on the King Barrow ridge just east of Stonehenge held a collection of the footbones of young pigs, a selection unlikely to be the leftovers of feasts – unless, of trotters!

A further pit in Stonehenge Bottom where the busy roads converge in sight of the stone circle was one of the most informative.[31] It was a small and shallow basin which had several clearcut layers in it. A broken antler and a sheep's shoulderblade lay side by side near the top. Below them was a medley of grooved ware sherds and animal bones but, at the very bottom, there were two thin plaques of chalk, each about 2½ inches (64 mm) square, with designs of lozenges, chevrons and triangles carved on them. Lumps of chalk lay nearby. The designs on the tablets had been executed with care and, resting where they did, it seems clear that they had a powerful meaning. Their motifs were those of the Boyne Valley. They were also very like some carved stones in the Neolithic village of Skara Brae, of the same period but over 500 miles (800 km) to the north. Such far-off links display the ubiquity and strength of the grooved ware cult.

In his stimulating book, *Science and Society in Prehistoric Britain* (1977, 168), Euan MacKie wrote, 'Durrington Walls . . . had a permanent population of non-farming specialists who lived off a surplus of food provided by the surrounding peasant population', and although he perhaps overstressed the part played by astronomer-priests his list of 'classes of skilled specialists – wise men, magicians, astronomers, priests, poets, jurists and engineers with their families' might well approximate to reality if each of these categories had 'prehistoric' and 'non-literate' placed in front of it to remind us that technology, scientific investigation and religion would have had quite different connotations then from what they mean to us today.

While the élite dwelt in the comfort of Durrington Walls the rest of the population seems to have inhabited areas peripheral to that, on the downs at Wilsford, Normanton, Knighton, Alton, Lake, or on the other side of the Avon on Earl's Farm Down and Figheldean, grazing their herds, growing wheat, flint-working, existing at a time when life was returning to the normality of previous centuries. Of their homes almost nothing is known. Structures within an obvious earthwork such as Durrington Walls are relatively easy to locate, whereas the vestiges of a single, wooden-walled farmstead somewhere on Salisbury Plain are discovered only by chance. Finds of pottery prove this. Only a third of the native Peterborough ware has been found on domestic sites. Two-thirds of the fragments have been stray finds from ploughed fields, rabbit burrows and the banks of streams.[32]

That there were social differences is apparent in the equipment of these followers. Not for them the maceheads, the long bone pins, Cumbrian axes and belt-sliders of black jet. From their areas of flint-knapping on Wilsford

Down and elsewhere have come flint axes, stone axes from Cornwall, chisel-ended flint arrowheads and knives, tools and weapons, but little of anything exotic. Yet amongst them some people must have prospered, their crops better, their herds larger, and by hard work and good luck they may have acquired the status of 'Big Men', providing gifts and feasts for the less fortunate, respected, emulating the élite but never permitted to join them, living in a social limbo, envious and resentful. In turn, the élite, ever more aware of tension, may have decided to emphasise that everything was as it had always been by returning to Stonehenge in 'an attempt', Bradley suggested, 'to re-establish the unity of society through an explicit link with the traditions of the past'. The same writer added that 'the continued use of [this monument], even after a period of desertion, may involve a reference to the past as a source of legitimate authority'.[33] Grooved ware sherds, grooved ware objects and human cremations were ritually interred at Stonehenge.

When Hawley was excavating in the ditch alongside the south causeway he unearthed half a dozen sherds from a little pit dug 10 inches (25 cm) into the silt that had accumulated there. Four were badly eroded but two could be joined together and on them was a typical grooved ware motif, a rough chevron pattern very like those from the Ratfyn pit.[34] That they lay so close to the causeway indicates the special attention prehistoric people gave to the entrances and alignments of their ceremonial monuments. It is significant that a fragment of a tiny grooved ware pot had been put into Aubrey Hole 29 close to the south-west end of the henge's axis.

The importance of the entrances was also stressed by other deposits, but not by the use of pottery. Apart from the single Windmill Hill sherd near the Heel Stone, these were the only bits of pottery to come from this early phase of Stonehenge. They demonstrated the re-use of the enclosure during the shadowy Late Neolithic period, a time when the site retained its old associations with the dead but in a changed way, by receiving cremations.

Cremating the dead, a custom long practised in the east of Britain, was gradually adopted in the south, and during the early 3rd millennium BC it was accepted in the Thames Valley. There, at Dorchester-on-Thames, less than 50 miles from Stonehenge, several earthen rings like miniature henges surrounded scatters of pits. In these and in the encircling ditches were scores of cremations.[35] The earlier Neolithic pottery, Abingdon ware, with them showed that the earliest of these burials were made some time before the Aubrey Holes were dug at Stonehenge, but the later presence of Mortlake and grooved ware sherds proved that the Dorchester cemeteries and the henge on Salisbury Plain were eventually in use at the same time.

Cremation was a more certain method of drying dead bones and driving out any lurking malicious spirit than the protracted technique of allowing the flesh to decay naturally. It is not surprising, therefore, to discover that it became popular in Wessex. For celebrants of the grooved ware cult who may have revered the sun and whose rituals were embedded in the belief of associations between different symbols, the link between fire and the sun may have been so strong that cremation, with its heaped fires and flames, rapidly replaced the burial of entire bodies or skeletons. It was the burnt bones of the dead that were put into the Aubrey Holes whose tops must have been still visible, perhaps kept clean by natives.

The first cremations were messy, with large splinters of charred bone and lumps of wood-ash bundled together and packed into hollows dug down to the bottom of the Aubrey Holes. Hardly anything was found with these first interments, but many of the holes were disturbed yet again to receive not a crude mass of dirty bone and charcoal but a neater, more ritualised offering of tiny bone fragments from which the ash had been washed. With some of these later cremations there were characteristic grooved ware objects.

The cleansing of burnt bones was noticed at Dorchester-on-Thames. From the manner in which even the hard enamel had flaked off teeth it was clear that the pyres had generated intense heat, reducing the long bones and skulls to minute scraps. When the ashes were cooling, personal articles were thrown onto them, which explains the contrast between the comminuted bones and the slightly scorched condition of such combustible things as bone pins. Finally, the cold ashes were raked and the mourners picked out bits of bone, washing and crushing them even smaller before wrapping them with the pins inside leather bags.[36] At Stonehenge Hawley often remarked on the compacted state of the secondary cremations, speculating that they had been buried in a container of skin or fabric.

Such meticulous preparation of the bones was in contrast to the first grubby deposits and it was a difference reflected also in the grave-goods (Fig. 8). Only in one pit was anything discovered with a primary cremation.[37] Here, in Aubrey Hole 55, two antlers rested under a thick layer of ash and bone and, significantly, these exceptional offerings were in the pit alongside the north-east axis of the earthwork, perhaps deliberately put there to add vitality to the entrance. Elsewhere, it was with the secondary cremations that objects were found, long bone pins in Aubrey Holes 12, 13, 24, with two in no. 5; flints in 13, 16, 19 and 29; a chalk ball in no. 21; antlers in 5 and 21; animal bones in 5, 13, 21, 32. It is obvious, once again, that people had paired items in ceremonies of fetishism, believing that together the objects would combine to animate the magical powers of the Other-World. It was the evocation of supernatural spirits by association and exclusion. A chalk ball could be placed with antler and animal bone; flint flakes could not be grouped with anything else; bone pins could lie with antler, with animal bone and with finely-made flint fabricators.

In the context of a cult in which combination and situation were so vital it is interesting to find that Aubrey Holes 5 and 21; at the east and south of the henge respectively, each had a rich assortment of articles, both containing antler, animal bones and long bone pins as though to enhance

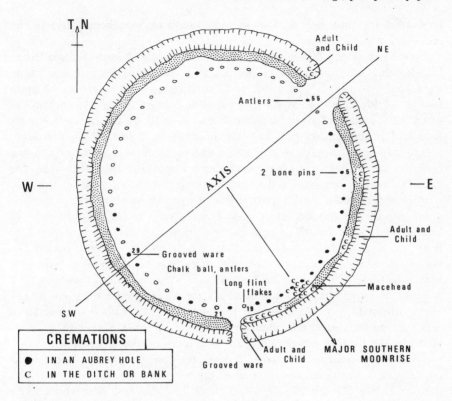

Fig. 8. Cremations and Deposits in Stonehenge Ib.

two of the cardinal points that had been so fundamental to the beliefs of the people who had built the henge nearly nine hundred years before.

There is uncertainty about what the bone pins were. As with so many things in prehistory, their function is disputable. From regions as far apart as the Orkneys, eastern Ireland, Yorkshire and Wessex, manufactured out of whalebone, antler or walrus tusk and anything from 4 inches (10 cm) to 10 inches (24 cm) long, they are usually found with burials.[38] There have been suggestions that they were skewers for securing the tops of leather bags in which the cremations were parcelled, but as the pins themselves were charred from the pyre this is questionable. Others, with carved heads, were so unevenly balanced that they are unlikely to have been nose decorations. Although it is possible that they were for tying back the hair, some at Garton Slack in Yorkshire, over 5 inches (14 cm) long, were found with infants, making this interpretation debatable also. Many of the pins are plain but some have a perforated end for a thong and others have poppy-or mushroom-shaped heads, apparently to prevent them slipping through an eyelet. It is feasible that in the days before weaving they were fasteners for leather cloaks or tunics, symbols of distinction worn by the grooved ware élite. Seven of them were found at Stonehenge, five in the Aubrey Holes.

Thirty-five of the fifty-six holes have been explored, one of them twice. Hawley dug out thirty-two (1–30, 55, 56); Atkinson, Piggott and Stone excavated two (31, 32) in 1950; and Cunnington and Hoare came upon two by accident, no. 46 when digging near Station Stone 94, and no. 56 when burrowing under the Slaughter Stone in 1810. Of the thirty-five holes nine had no cremation but, not unexpectedly in a cult which placed so much emphasis on association and position, there was a pattern to the contents of the pits. The east was more important than the west, the cardinal points were treated specially, and the holes nearest the two entrances received deposits quite different from those elsewhere.

So regular is the occurrence of cremations on the eastern side of Stonehenge from the north-east entrance down to the south, every hole from no. 2 to 18 containing one, that it is likely that people buried the bones systematically in a clockwise direction, placing a deposit in hole after hole in a regular and organised procedure. Whether these activities took place at one great rededication or as a series of isolated events over many years cannot be proved, although the interrupted burials on the western side suggest the latter, a sequence of sporadic interments year by year, or death by death, in a ritual that gradually declined and petered out.

There is a noticeable difference between the continuous arc of cremations on the east and the broken-up stutter on the west. Of the excavated pits there only nos 20, 23, 24, 28, 29, 31 and 32 contained burnt bone. The intervening holes were never disturbed. Except for nos 46, 55 and 56 the remaining Aubrey Holes have not been investigated.

When digging at the north-west Cunnington happened upon no. 46. 'Much to our surprise', wrote Hoare, 'we found within it a simple interment of burned bones'.[39] Hawley discovered ash and calcined bone in no. 55, the hole with the two antlers, but when no. 56 was emptied by Cunnington in 1810 he made no mention of any finds. From this it may be assumed that the rather haphazard run of cremations on the western side is an indication of a practice that was slowly dying out.

Position was important. The NE–SW axis was stressed by the antlers in no. 55 at the north-east and by the unusual presence of pottery in Aubrey Hole 29 at the south-west. Here there was the base of a small grooved ware vessel like a Breton vase-support, resembling an enlarged napkin ring, which Hawley thought might have been a 'lamp, as the surface of the upper part is blackened as if greasy matter had been burned upon it'.[40] Originally this small pot had four protruding lugs, each pierced for suspension from a house-beam where it may have given dim light.

The entrances also were emphasised. The only other grooved ware sherds were discovered in the ditch by the south entrance, and the complete absence of cremations in the Aubrey Holes immediately to the east of both entrances suggests a refusal to have human bones situated there. Hole 1 on the eastern side of the north-east causeway had only chalk in it. Hole 19 by the south causeway held 'a mass of white flint flakes . . . discarded by an implement-maker' who had squatted there skilfully striking 'thin and delicate implements' from a block of flints whose core and waste flakes were buried under the chalk rubble that filled the hole. Some pieces fitted together. It may have been this craftsman's industry that created the 'elegant long flint blades', found by Hawley, 'so clean and sharp that they could be used to cut the bread at picnic lunches'.[41] Sadly, they are now lost.

Everything had purpose. Every offering, every action was conditioned by the demands of the cult, everything was ordered by association and exclusion.

All things counter, original, spare, strange,
Whatever is fickle, freckled (who knows how?),
With swift, slow; sweet, sour; adazzle, dim. . . .
      Gerard Manley Hopkins. *Pied Beauty*

Even the burials were kept apart. The Aubrey Holes and their contents have frequently been described as a cemetery but to deem them no more than that is to misunderstand the reasons for their deposition. These were ritual offerings. What is less well-known is that there were other cremations at Stonehenge, in the ditch and along the inner edge of the bank, cremations different from those in the Aubrey Holes but just as punctiliously positioned.

Whether in the grass-covered ditch or just under the turf of the henge itself, the majority of these pockets of bone were so small that Hawley believed them to be the remains of children. Hardly any ash or, indeed, anything else lay with them, just one or two bone pins and some blackened antlers. They seemed so insignificant that they have generally been disregarded. Yet in some respects they are more informative than the famous cremations in the Aubrey Holes. It is possible that it was the bones of men that were buried in the holes. Women and children might have merited less prestigious parts of the enclosure. Even so, inside the henge the situation of their interments was no less carefully planned, not for the benefit of the dead but to the advantage of the living.

At the exact east two cremations lay side by side in the ditch. Also in the ditch, alongside both entrances, there were arrangements of an adult, a child and animal bones, one group just west of the north-east causeway, another by the south entrance where two adult cremations were accompanied by the smaller limbs and teeth of a child lying by a long bone pin. Nearby was a minute collection of burnt bone, no more than 5 ounces (142 gm), mixed with animal bones. Hawley remarked that 'this is the third instance of human and animal bones occurring together'.[42] Another adult, probably a woman, and a child were buried in the ditch at the south-east close to where Station Stone 91 would stand.

Hawley also noticed that, unlike the Aubrey Hole burials, there was not a single example, either in the ditch or by the bank, of a cremation to the west of a line drawn north-south through the middle of the henge even though he had cleared out 150 feet (46 m) of the ditch west of the south entrance. 'Perhaps they may some day be met with beyond that spot, but probably not far beyond it, as the people they belonged to seem to have had a superstitious reason for selecting the eastern area.'[43] For a man who, professedly, would not speculate this was imaginative and it was right. It was the rising not the setting of the moon and sun that dominated people's vision of the world. The west, as the orientations of the long barrows showed, was a direction to be avoided.

If the cremations in the ditch were small, those along the inner edge of the bank were slighter, mere handfuls of bone set in hollows often no deeper than a saucer. Yet with the people's obsession with arrangement it is noteworthy that they concentrated no fewer than nine of these cremations, cramped together, at the ESE between, and just outside, Aubrey Holes 13 and 14. The position must have been important. It is an idea underlined by the fact that it was here that Hawley came upon the loveliest object ever to be found at Stonehenge.

It was a beautifully polished macehead of hornblendic gneiss, shaped like a doll's cushion and little bigger, with a shafthole drilled through it. 'The trueness of the boring is quite wonderful when it is remembered that there was only sand and a revolving cutter of wood or bone held in a bow-drill for making it'.[44] It is now displayed in Salisbury Museum.

Maceheads were vital to the grooved ware cult. They were often made of attractive stone or gleaming antler, and there is even one of red pottery from Longtown in Cumbria. The excellent quality of many of them has suggested that they were 'the products of a specialised craftsman or a small number of skilled workers'.[45] One of Cornish greenstone tumbled from the earth of a round barrow that Cunnington and Hoare were digging at Winterbourne Stoke barely a mile from Stonehenge. 'We found a perforated pebble-stone, about 2 inches long, and very neatly polished; it has one corner broken off, and some cracks as if it had been burned . . . the Britons seem to have attached particular qualities to certain stones; and this, probably, may have been suspended as an amulet from the neck.'[46]

The Stonehenge specimen, although smaller than average, was no less delightful, striped in thin wandering ribbons of beige and brown, as smoothly hard as planed teak. Hoare was probably correct that such charming articles were not for mundane use but were fetishes or talismen.

One might wonder why such a precious and potent object was left at the south-eastern circumference of the ring, lying amongst a group of children's cremations in scoops not 'deep enough in the more solid ground to cover all the bones'.[47] The cult is the connection. From what we know about the fixation of its adherents on position and pattern, only an important location could have justified such a luxurious offering being left there. It has never been commented on, maybe because Hawley's report is vague about it, but it is unlikely to be coincidence that the macehead and the cremations marked a critical lunar event.

They were on the line between the centre of Stonehenge and the point on the horizon, 12′ above Stonehenge, where the midsummer moon rose at its most southerly near 142° from True North. This was a crucial orientation. It continued and elaborated a lunar tradition established centuries before with the midwinter postholes of the north-east causeway. The children, like the girl at Woodhenge, may have been sacrificed to sanctify the ground, perhaps placed there by native people reasserting their right to the hallowed enclosure.

The alignment possibly was marked by a heavy post. In 1924 Hawley recorded 'the largest posthole yet found',[48] some 100 feet (30 m) south-east of the centre of the henge and a little to the right of the major southern moonrise. Two smaller postholes were found near it.

It was the old creed in a new form. The charnel-house had gone but there were still human bones. The sun might be honoured but the lines to the moon were made stronger. Precious objects were buried in secret rites understood by only a few, but more traditional things continued to be brought to the earthwork. Rough stone balls were buried in the ditch, even in the Aubrey Holes, spheres that resembled others in chambered tombs and in the passage-graves of the Boyne Valley. There they were often found in pairs. In the East Anglian flint-mine of Grimes Graves comparable objects were associated with a phallus carved out of chalk. At Skara Brae they were fashioned from stone and had delicate spirals incised on their polished surfaces. At Tara in Ireland thirty such balls had been left in a tomb by whose mound a phallic granite pillar stood. Balls like these, so often found with the dead and with male organs alongside them, can plausibly be interpreted as symbols of rebirth, of an awakening from the dead. Their presence at Stonehenge reveals something of the monument's purpose.

So too does the chalk disc lying in the ditch near the entrance. It was a 'flat piece of chalk rather round, with a hole through it, which might have been a spinning whorl, but more likely to have been a child's toy as there was a roughly cut chalk ball, more oval than round, not far from it. Both objects showed signs of cutting but the ball is much rubbed down. It may be remembered that a very perfect chalk ball was found in Aubrey Hole no. 9.'[49]

It was not a toy, even for a remarkable child. Similar discs have been recovered near the corpses in megalithic tombs.[50] One of stone, at Brackley on the Kintyre peninsula, lay by the stains of long-vanished bodies on the sandy floor of the burial chamber. The position of the flat disc at Stonehenge, so close to a chalk ball, is yet another reminder of the henge's death links.

So also were the antlers and the object discovered by Hawley in the loose earth around the tallest stone of the sarsen circle, lost there when the stonehole was dug. It had been cut into the shape of a stone axe, but it was made of chalk, useless materially but powerful as the representation of an axe cult whose origins reached far back into the Neolithic. Near it was an even cruder axe of rhyolite and some pieces of antler. Chalk axes like Hawley's came from two postholes at the neighbouring Woodhenge, both of them in astronomical locations. Here it is only necessary to reiterate the funerary associations that some axes had in the Neolithic period, their outlines carved on the kerbstones that surrounded Newgrange passage-grave in Ireland. In Brittany, tiny axes of prettily-coloured stone were perforated for hanging around the neck like a crucifix. They were amulets, miniatures of the axe known to be carried by the female guardian, the protectress of the dead. Real axes were often buried with the dead. And, like the 'figurines' of the 'goddess' carved at the entrances and in the passages of Breton megalithic tombs, they could be put down in front of other burial places, personifying the spirit of the watchful deity.

At Perth Chwarau in Clywd, a cave used as a prehistoric graveyard had an axe buried at its mouth. At Gop not far away an unused stone axe was set upright in a pit outside the entrance to a cavern containing fourteen burials. The chalk axe at Stonehenge presumably belonged to the same system of beliefs, repeating that throughout its many changes the theme of death, burial and rebirth survived on Salisbury Plain.

To us, looking back over more than four thousand years, the grooved ware cult seems almost an interlude, perhaps no more than four centuries, sixteen generations in which it flourished, reacted to tension and collapsed. It disappeared. Then, in place of its incised and patterned pots, there were beakers. Groups of Beaker people from the continent, using finely-burnished drinking vessels, infiltrated the exchange networks.

# 6

# Beakers, burials and bluestones
## 2500 – 2200 BC

*The Beaker invasion ranks as one of the most important of all movements from the continent into Britain.*

E. F. Lincoln, *Britain's Unwritten History*, 67

*. . . the Beaker Folk have no substance as a special population group.*

R. Harrison, *The Beaker Folk*, 166

*This is not the occasion to embark on another dissection of the Beaker Folk, even though they are so prominent in death.*

R. Bradley, *The Social Foundations of Prehistoric Britain*, 65

It has been supposed that it was Beaker men, prospecting for copper, who were responsible for constructing the two bluestone circles at Stonehenge, ferrying heavy stones nearly two hundred miles from the Preseli mountains of south-west Wales and erecting them in concentric rings where the ancient mortuary house had stood.

Until recently there was no argument about the users of Beaker pottery. The makers of these well-fired, finely-shaped vessels were invaders from the continent, stocky, round-headed archers, skilled in metal-working, who built the first stone circles and who gave their dead individual burial with valuable grave-goods under the novelty of a round barrow. Gordon Childe entitled their coming 'the invasion by Round-Heads' and suggested that the pots of these bowmen had held beer, 'a source of spirituous authority by which their users maintained their dominion'.[1]

It was believed that the Beaker folk were of Nordic stock, speaking a form of Indo-European language from which our own is descended, 'energetic conquerors' who 'soon occupied the greater part of Britain, ruthlessly dispossessing the Neolithic communities of their best pastures, and also, no doubt, of their herds and sometimes of their women'.[2] These alien plunderers were physically different from the small, dark 'Celtic' natives, as the evidence of their skeletons proved, demonstrating that there had been an invasion of foreigners. 'There is no intention to question', wrote Grahame Clark, 'that the appearance of Beaker pottery in this country, along with cultural innovations on a broad front, indicates some intrusion of actual people.'[3]

That amiable eccentric and former Cambridge archaeologist, Tom Lethbridge, airily speculated that these newcomers were spacemen from Mars 34 million miles away, but this was a far-fetched notion.[4] More mundanely, David Clarke concluded that there had been two primary waves of immigrants around 2500 BC followed by several later bands filtering into these islands over several centuries. It was one of these, the Wessex/Middle Rhine warriors, with some of the most beautifully burnished and elegantly decorated beakers, who 'may have had 'the Prescelly stones brought along the copper/gold route to Wiltshire and Stonehenge'.[5]

Except for the Martians, all these explanations were plausible, based on data from pottery, radiocarbon assays, gold and copper objects, flint arrowheads, human bones, round barrows and finds from stone circles such as Stonehenge and Avebury. A Beaker invasion of the British Isles seemed to be one of the rare, established truths of our prehistory.

Nevertheless, every item of such 'evidence' for foreign intruders has been questioned by researchers who reinterpreted this disruptive episode in the late Neolithic as the result not of warlike incomers but of yet another cult like that of the grooved ware zealots or the 19th century Peyote Cult in North America. According to this re-thinking there were no Beaker people, only beaker pots, there was no invasion, only the gradual percolation of an idea, and the round or brachycephalic skulls were no more foreign than the long or dolichocephalic skulls that had been so consistently found in the long barrows of the early Neolithic. The round barrows were also indigenous. Even the Welsh bluestones, part of the folklore of Stonehenge, might have reached Salisbury Plain by glaciation rather than by an epic Beaker undertaking. Everything associated with beakers could be explained as the adoption of a new system of beliefs which brought with it new paraphernalia, just as the Peyote Cult had its own ritual objects of rattles and fans and carved staffs, a drum and a crescentic altar.[6]

The lure of the Peyote Cult for the defeated and oppressed American Indians on their reservations lay in the eating of the hallucinatory cactus that induced visions and euphoria. In Britain a substitute for the cactus could have existed in some toadstools, especially the commonplace but poisonous Fly Agaric (*Amanita muscaria*) with its enticing bright-red, white-spotted cap. This tempting fungus, often portrayed in fairy stories as a seat for grey-bearded dwarves, can be found all over these islands. Although highly dangerous it could, if eaten sparingly, be infused in the juices of the stomach and then urinated into a beaker. 'The drug could be offered in solution from persons who had previously ingested it. It is well documented that rites involving *A. muscaria* have included the drinking of urine from intoxicated priests. . . . Thus, with no irreverence we might well examine the possibility, if the beaker is held to be central to the rites, of the beaker as a urinal.'[7] A similar *soma* or alcoholic infusion was important in the Vedic rituals of prehistoric India, and in the British Isles it could have produced prolonged periods of transcendental ecstacy and illusions of the spirit-world for its followers.

Alternative explanations, however, are not invariably more persuasive than a long-established one. When sediment from beakers has been analysed it has proved to be the remains of a beer rather than a fungal concoction. Despite the many objections, none of them trivial, the old idea of an actual infiltration of Beaker people in the mid-3rd millennium BC still seems likely. Beakers are widespread over Europe and it must have been people who brought them across the North Sea into these islands, people whose way of life was somewhat different from that of the natives and who, at first, may have kept themselves apart. Apparently, though, they quite rapidly assumed a dominant role in regions as far apart as eastern Scotland, Yorkshire and Wessex.

There is nothing to show that they were any healthier or longer-lived than the people of earlier centuries. On Overton Down near Avebury the bones of four adults and seven young children contained signs of hardship and disease, several of the men and women having arthritis, and three children had suffered from malnutrition. An even more extreme example of physical distress was encountered in November, 1915, when a flat grave was accidentally bulldozed away at the Upavon Flying School eight miles north of Stonehenge. From it bits of a well-fired, cord-decorated W/MR beaker were recovered together with the bones of a heavy-jowled old man. There were abscesses in many of his teeth and his back was deformed, 'for he had suffered from severe rheumatoid disease of the spine'.

A study of short-cist Beaker burials in Scotland, most of them brachy-cephalic, showed that although just over half the men lived beyond 36 years of age, no fewer than 85 per cent of the women died before 25, probably through inferior diet and childbirth. Many children must have grown up motherless in a male-dominated society. Fractures, osteo-arthritis and spondololysis were detected, but the plague of those Beaker communi-ties may have been toothache and septicaemia. Consistent calculus around the teeth indicated a lack of dental hygiene and 'acute infection remains the most likely cause of death at all ages'.[8]

The man in the central grave at Overton Down had apparently been a leather-worker, judged by the tools near his beaker, and such an occupation shows that whether his ancestors had come to Britain as aggressors or peaceful immigrants they were not all aristocratic warriors. It is better to think of an influx of several small farming groups around 2500 BC, penetrating the country down the great rivers of the east coast, the Humber into Yorkshire, the Thames into the heart of Wessex. The earliest of these incursions may have come from the Low Countries, bringing with them their squat, flared-mouth beakers known as All-Over-Corded (AOC) vessels from the impressions of cord or animal gut that had been twisted round and round the wet clay before being burned away during the firing.

Such families may warily have settled on Salisbury Plain in an uneasy co-existence with the natives not unlike the mixing of Britons, Boers and Bantus on the South African veldt. There were probably not enough newcomers to offer a threat, but presumably they were well enough armed to defend themselves even against greater numbers much as 140 British soldiers had done at Rourke's Drift in 1879 against several thousand Zulus or as 28 American hunters had fought at the Adobe Walls settlement in Texas five years earlier, fighting off several hundred Comanches from dawn to early evening, killing scores of Indians by use of their powerful buffalo rifles.[9]

A vital part of a Beaker man's equipment was the bow. He may also have had a horse, but any picture of braves riding tall in the saddle would be mistaken. Although horse-bones have been found on Beaker sites across Europe and although it is possible to explain 'the wide and rapid spread of beakers as being linked to the spread of domesticated horses',[10] not one piece of riding tackle has been discovered anywhere. Nor were Beaker horses thundering stallions. They were the size of Exmoor ponies and even if they had been ridden, to the consternation of strangers as Cortes' Spaniards had terrified the Aztecs, in Beaker times it would have been less overbearingly so, with the rider's legs dangling to the ground.

Yet the absence of riding equipment may mean no more than that it was made of organic material and has perished. The Comanches, some of the finest horsemen ever to have lived, had bridles of horsehair, a saddle of hide, and reins and stirrups of leather. Once discarded such things would not have lasted long in the moist conditions of the British Isles. Interestingly, the Comanche mustang was hardly bigger than an Exmoor pony, not exceeding 13 or 14 hands (4 feet 8 inches or 1.4 m) yet this shaggy, ugly, tough little mount could outrun the bigger European military horse over short distances.[11] From this it does not follow that Beaker people did ride horses, only that absence of evidence of horse-gear is not evidence that it never existed.

Interestingly, amongst the Scottish short-cist burials 'the only female in which a healed fracture was noted had broken her clavicle or collarbone some considerable time before her death. This type of injury commonly occurs when the weight of the body is taken on the outstretched hand and often happens when a rider is thrown from a horse.'

Even so, rather than the horse it was probably the bow that safeguarded Beaker communities. Unfortunately, unlike the Neolithic longbow, none of these weapons has been recovered. There do, however, appear to be tiny continental replicas in the form of pendants, and proof that there must have been bows comes from the numerous flint arrowheads with Beaker burials. If the pendants do represent bows, then these may have originated in countries where yew was absent and longbows could not be made.

Beaker bows seem to have been a short, composite variety, about three feet (1 m) long, thick and crescent-shaped, of wood stiffened with antler or bone and backed with sinew. With a finger-hole at their centre and notched at both ends for the bowstring, they could be fired rapidly just as the Scythians, using the same kind of bow, were reputed to be able to fire five arrows before the first hit the ground. Such bows could conveniently be carried slung across the chest.

That it was this kind of bow that Beaker archers used is likely because some of their grave-pits containing arrowheads were too short to accept a longbow unless it was broken. On the continent, moreover, wristguards akin to those of Beaker bowmen are known to have been part of the equipment of shortbow warriors. They have never been discovered with a longbow.

In Britain, at Thwing near Bridlington, a Beaker barrow contained an adult skeleton, very probably male as it lay with its head to the east, a custom for men in Yorkshire. In the curled fingers of the man's left hand there was 'a small article, so much decayed that nothing could be made out regarding it beyond the fact that wood had entered into its composition', maybe a rare fragment of a Beaker bow like the traces of sinew, wood and leather discovered with a Beaker burial at Borrowston in Aberdeenshire.

By coincidence, hardly 20 miles east of Thwing, at Callis Wold in 1864, John Mortimer, the Yorkshire archaeologist, came upon another possible bow. In a round barrow lacking any burial there were five flint arrowheads and a dark, curved streak in the ground which, as it was 'little more than three feet in length, and was close to the arrowheads, it was thought it might mark the remains of the' longbow'.[12]

What seem to be the relics of quiverfuls of arrows have often been found, in Germany, in groups of 5, 10 and 15, indicating some elementary numeracy. At Thwing in Yorkshire three fine, flint arrowheads lay under the skeleton, their bases neatly chipped to leave a central tang for the arrowshaft and a sharp barb on either side of it to prevent a hunted animal – or human – from shaking the missile loose. Such barbed-and-tanged arrowheads are a hallmark of Beaker weaponry.

As with the grooved ware cult, something of a fetish was applied to the deposition of these weapons. An archer's equipment consisted of the bow, a quiverful of arrows and a 'bracer' of stone, clay or bone, perforated at its ends for thonging and to be worn as a wristguard for protection against the lash of the bowstring. These bracers, rectangular, waisted, even elliptical, have also been interpreted as bracelets, but a function as a wristguard is equally plausible.

It was rare for all these items to be left with a burial in Britain. Of forty Beaker graves with archers' gear, sixteen contained only a single arrowhead, no more than a token that the dead man had been a bowman. Of the fourteen graves with bracers, only five had arrowheads. The symbol was the essence, whether of a single article representing the group or of specially made objects that would have been unusable in life.

Thirteen flint arrowheads were found in a barrow at Breach Farm in Glamorgan. Seven were a translucent grey-black, five were a pellucid pale yellow and one was opaquely golden. All of them had delicately serrated edges and were so uniformly thin and fragile that they could never have been projectiles. They had been made for the Other-World. Like the single arrowheads and the weaponless bracers, they were symbols, ghosts of reality that the dead would recognise.

### TABLE 10. Beaker graves in Britain with arrowheads and/or bracers

| Beaker Type | No. of Arrowheads in the Grave | | | | | | | No. of Graves with | | | No. of Bracers |
| | 1 | 2 | 3 | 4 | 5 | 6 | 7 | Arrowheads only | Arrowheads and Bracers | Bracers only | |
| --- | --- | --- | --- | --- | --- | --- | --- | --- | --- | --- | --- |
| AOC | 3 | – | – | – | – | – | – | 3 | – | – | – |
| E | – | – | 2 | – | – | – | – | 2 | – | – | – |
| W/MR | 2 | 1 | – | – | – | – | – | 1 | 2 | 3 | 5 |
| N/MR | 2 | – | – | 1 | – | – | 2 | 5 | – | – | – |
| E. Ang | – | – | – | – | – | – | – | – | – | 1 | 1 |
| BW | 1 | – | – | – | – | – | – | 1 | – | – | – |
| N2 | 1 | – | 1 | 1 | – | – | 1 | 3 | 1 | 2 | 3 |
| N3 | – | 1 | – | 1 | – | – | – | 2 | – | 1 | 1 |
| N4 | 1* | – | – | – | – | – | – | – | 1* | 1 | 3 |
| S1 | 1 | – | 1 | – | – | – | – | 2 | – | – | – |
| S2 | 3 | – | – | 1 | – | 1 | – | 5 | – | – | – |
| S3 | 2 | – | – | – | – | – | – | 2 | – | – | – |
| Others | – | – | 1* | – | – | – | – | – | 1* | 1 | 3 |
| TOTALS | 16 | 2 | 5 | 4 | – | 1 | 3 | 26 | 5 | 9 | 16 |

\* = grave with two bracers

It is obvious that very few burials were accompanied by a quiverful of arrows or a bracer and it was even rarer for arrows and bracers to be buried together. The complete absence of any collection of five arrows is also a surprise, for five could have been expected to be a popular number in those days of simple counting systems.[13]

It is this sudden accumulation of distinctive traits that makes it difficult to believe that the Beaker 'package' was no more than the chance convergence of native traditions. Some articles of the assemblage might have developed in such a way, but it seems improbable that so many should have merged together fortuitously. To the beaker itself, a form of pottery and decoration unknown previously in the British Isles, and fired by an unprecedentedly skilful technique, has to be added the novel barbed-and-tanged arrowheads, the bracers, copper knives and small articles of gold, the emergence of round-headed people, a preference for single burial in flat graves or under very low round barrows, the deposition of grave-goods, the brewing of beer, a knowledge of metalworking, the domestication of the horse and the herding of a smaller breed of cattle, *Bos longifrons*, unlike the bigger indigenous *Bos frontosus* of the British Neolithic. It is unlikely that all this, like Topsy, just 'grow'd' rather than being introduced into Britain as the customs and possessions of a continental society. Communities of people rather than cults of pots seem more probable.

During this later part of the Mount Pleasant phase the climate was improving, with drier summers, perhaps 2° to 3° Centigrade warmer than today, and with winters rather less cold. Great areas of Salisbury Plain were under cultivation, with field-systems in which wheat and other crops were grown. Industry was expanding. Flat axes of copper, broad-butted and heavy, were being fashioned in simple moulds in Ireland, where a hoard was discovered at Knocknague in Co. Galway, perhaps left there by Beaker smiths. Stone axes were still being produced, but demand was increasing for shafthole implements like the Stonehenge macehead, and such holes could be drilled only through certain rocks for which the once-popular tuffs and greenstones of the Lake District and Cornwall were not suitable. Slowly the ancient axe-factories were losing their markets and in their place new sources flourished, one of them in the Preseli mountains of south-west Wales.

Quite possibly, in the beginning around 2500 BC, there were only a few Beaker settlers in the vicinity of Stonehenge, keeping well way from the hamlets in the hollows of the Plain and from the lonelier farmsteads on the higher slopes, foreigners who looked curiously at the tall posts of the Stonehenge circles and the chalk-capped pits that surrounded them, wondering but not encroaching on a forbidden place.

Although the flat or low-mounded Beaker graves are inconspicuous and their settlements are elusive, it does seem noteworthy that only seven AOC pots have been found on Salisbury Plain. Even adding the nine 'European' (E) beakers of roughly the same period and making the assumption that twice as many lie undetected, and further assuming that each vessel represents a single burial from a community of twenty people, this still amounts to fewer than a thousand men and women for the 250 years, or eight generations, that such beakers remained in vogue. An average of six beaker burials each generation suggests only six of their groups on Salisbury Plain at any one time, a hundred or so people who would cause little anxiety amongst the natives, especially if the strangers brought with them the peace-inducing art of brewing.

Such figures contrast tellingly with the 28 Wessex/Middle Rhine and Northern/Middle Rhine beakers of the years from 2400 BC onwards. These were pots, moreover, that accompanied burials with warrior equipment and with some of the richest grave-goods known from the Beaker period. By their time the growing Beaker occupation might have been recognised as a threat and this could explain the body that was dumped in the ditch by the main entrance to Stonehenge.

In 1978 while recutting a trench 30 feet (9.1 m) west of the causeway to obtain environmental material, archaeologists uncovered the skeleton of a young man. His 'grave' was a crudely dug pit and in it his skeleton lay on its back with its right arm across the chest. The bones were those of a healthy male, about 25 to 30 years of age, whose slight deformation of the spine would have given him a rather twisted posture but not one which would have limited his movements. He had been somewhat bow-legged, and the wearing-down of some of his ankle-bones showed that, like many of his contemporaries, he had been accustomed to squatting rather than sitting when eating or talking with friends.[14] Tissue from his left femur was dated to 1765 ± 70 bc, around 2180 BC for the time of his death, the years when the bluestone circles were being erected at Stonehenge and when resentment between native and Beaker groups may have been strong. Fragments of bluestone were actually found in his grave, some of the debris scattered about the site when the stones were being shaped.

A dark slate wristguard rested halfway up the man's arm and three broken arrowheads lay by the skeleton. When the bones were cleaned the tips of the arrows were seen embedded in the man's ribs. They had been fired at short range, one from the right into the chest, another into the side and a third from behind to the left, penetrating the heart and killing the man instantly.

Bracers such as his are otherwise known only from Scotland and northern Ireland, suggesting that he may have been a stranger who had offended by breaking some tabu. Equally, antagonism between newcomers and natives may have been the cause of his death, local people angry at the desecration of their sanctuary by the building of unwanted stone circles there. Two of the killing arrows were not of Beaker type but of the native Conygar style and it is possible to imagine an unexpected encounter, a panicking flight with at least three enemies in pursuit, and the casual burial, the body dumped almost contemptuously in the ditch of the despoiled earthwork.

Violence was never unknown in prehistory. Under a cairn near the stone circle of Glenquickan in south-west Scotland there was a stone cist of slabs arranged like a coffin. It held 'the skeleton of man of uncommon size. One of the arms had been almost separated from the shoulder by the stroke of a stone axe, and . . . a fragment of the axe still remained in the bone.'[15] Any belief in a golden age in ancient times must be tempered by such examples.

Conflict may also have arisen over disputes about land and territories. By 2400 BC this could have been the case on Salisbury Plain, where users of W/MR beakers may have been coming to power through straightforward physical coercion. Little is known about the origins of these people and some have claimed that theirs was a ceramic style that had developed from the earlier 'European' beakers. Clarke, however, believed that their pots were part of the possessions of people who had arrived in Britain from the area of the middle Rhine, a great majority of them, 80 per cent, settling amongst their kindred within sixty miles of Stonehenge. Hence the name. So similar is the decoration on these unique pots to others around Koblenz and Mainz that it gives some credence to Clarke's view.[16]

These were tall, slim pots, large enough to hold a quart and with a lip thin enough to be used for drinking. Many of them had a bright 'sealing-wax' finish attained by the careful choice of clay and by wet-burnishing the coil-built body before firing. They must, in Clarke's words, 'have glowed like burnished copper in the firelight'. Neat, horizontal bands of triangles impressed with a sharp-toothed comb, 1–2 inches (26 – 48 mm) long lattice patterns and ladder motifs surrounded the body, and often a ring of triangles like flames ornamented the base.

So fine are these lovely pots, far better than anything else in Britain, that their potters must have devised a purpose-built clamp, or rudimentary kiln, with a controlled fire to allow just so much air to reach the vessel and oxydise its surface into a red as perfect as the famous Samian ware of Roman times. Some beakers, like that from Upavon, were fired upside down on their rims, excluding oxygen from the inside which turned jet black in startling contrast to the vivid exterior. These were fine wares. Whereas a local Mortlake vessel might have walls half an inch (12 mm) thick, the sides of the superb beaker from Berwick St James, 15 miles from Stonehenge, were less than half that. This was because of another Beaker innovation. The fabric of these pots was composed of selected clay mixed with a grog of well-ground sand or other material, the first example in this country of using a pre-firing tempering agent to allow a thinner wall and to lessen the time needed for firing.[17]

Most of these beakers have been recovered from graves and there are considerable social differences between what seem to be burials of artisans with flint axes, antler picks and fire-making or leather-working equipment and the few rich interments, almost always of men, lying with their heads to the north, in a flat grave probably once marked with a post. With them there is sometimes a copper dagger or a barbed-and-tanged arrowhead, a wristguard with two or four holes for the leather lacing, and, very rarely, a tiny disc of gold, the first precious metal to be exploited in the British Isles.

Little is known about the homes of these people, whether peasants, craftsmen or warriors. No house remains were found in a Beaker 'settlement' at Downton on a gravel terrace near Salisbury. Its medley of post-holes was more suggestive of a spatter of tents seasonally erected there year after year. At a flint-mining site, worked by beaker users, at Easton Down a few miles east of Stonehenge, there appeared to be the remains of a huddle of frail, hurdlework huts where a more substantial timber house had stood. Of sturdy dwellings nothing is known on Salisbury Plain. Other even more lightweight shelters were detected as scattered stakeholes under some round barrows at Snail Down just to the north of Stonehenge. 'They can only be interpreted as the remains of a flimsy tent, or tents, abandoned before the barrows were built.'[18] Beaker sherds and the flake of a battle-axe of stone from near Nuneaton were discovered near them. One can hardly consider such structures as normal homes unless Beaker people led semi-nomadic lives, wandering with their herds and flocks, restlessly moving across the open downs, avoiding the tilled lands and ripening crops of the natives.

This absence of occupation evidence is so little different from that for native settlements that it is very likely that subsequent erosion of the chalk has worn too much away of the postholes for anything to be detected or else it is not on the upland slopes that we should look but where today's villages sprawl, by the wooded streams and in sheltered valleys a long way from the round barrows on the hillsides overlooking these elusive hamlets.

The 'settlement' at Easton Down was at the heart of a mining area that had been worked for centuries if the radiocarbon date of 2530 ± 150 bc, around 3300 BC, from an antler is reliable. Some 250 filled-in pits covered nearly forty acres. They had been dug into the chalk to reach the deep, unweathered layers of flint. Two miles away, at Martin's Clump, there was another group of pits showing how necessary flint was in the everyday life of Neolithic people. Unlike the 30 foot (10 m) shafts with radiating tunnels at their bottoms at Grimes' Graves in Norfolk, the Easton Down miners had found it more economical to dig no deeper than 16 feet (5 m), after which it was easier to sink a fresh shaft, tipping its rubble into its disused neighbour. In 1929 archaeologists found 45 grey, red and yellow pebbles on the floor of one, 'possibly collected by miners' children for a primitive game of marbles'.[19]

The presence of many beaker sherds showed that flint extraction continued here as late as 2000 BC and from this long activity come other glimpses of domestic life such as the skeleton of a dog like a fox terrier. It had been so glutted on animal bones that its droppings were rich in calcium salts and had hardened so much that they were preserved in the chalk where the dog lay. Similar dogs are known elsewhere in the British Isles and so is a form of labrador.

Other animals at Easton Down included the bones of the straight-horned *Bos longifrons* cattle, the first to be recognised of this breed and unlike the forward-thrusting, twisted-horned *Bos frontosus* of Neolithic farmers. Some sheep also are known. Such animals were scarce at Durrington Walls, but at Mount Pleasant in Dorset, where beaker sherds lay in the ditches, they were ten times as plentiful. The grazing of sheep would have kept grassland free from reverting to a wilderness, but the paucity of weaving articles in Late Neolithic Britain suggests that flocks were kept more for their meat than their wool, although patterns on some beakers are virtually identical to what might be expected on textiles and weaving was known on the continent.

As well as the animal bones at Easton Down there were other hints of a home industry. Near the temporary shanties there were three perplexing drumlike pits, no more than 2 feet six inches (76 cm) across or deep, symmetrically cut, flat-bottomed and half-filled with a mixture of finely-pulverised ash and wood that 'could be cut like butter'. This may have been the sediment of highly alkaline lye, produced by steeping the ash in water and useful in leather-working. The hairs and epidermis of any hide soaked in the pits would soon have been loosened sufficiently to be combed away before the pelt could be tanned to make a pale and supple skin to be cut and sewn for clothing.[20]

From such scraps of information it is a temptation to visualise this humdrum life of farming, mining, making clothes and pots as the work of people with beliefs like ours, but this is to force them into an unnatural mould. These were the years when the Aubrey Holes at Stonehenge were still being visited, redug and used by grooved ware adherents, when strange deposits were being laid down at Durrington Walls, when the waking day was from dawn to dusk, when the moon divided the year, when the seasons regulated life and when most people's world was no more than two or three hours' walk in any direction. There were the open, airy spaces of fields and pastures but there were dark places, forests where few explored, there were springs and streams inhabited by powerful spirits, and there was the world of the dead. To understand the changes that were to be imposed upon Stonehenge the burial customs of Beaker societies must be known.

Just a few yards north of the flint-miners' hovels on Easton Down there was a round barrow so small and low that it was not noticed until 1929. Unobtrusive mounds such as this over a grave, or no mound at all, are typical of early Beaker burials and are quite unlike the impressive tumuli of the succeeding Early Bronze Age. The barrow, Winterslow 20, now on a bare upland but put up by some woods, covered a large, shallow pit. It was big enough to accommodate a complete body but inside it there was only 'an almost complete skull', brachycephalic, from which two vertebrae fell when it was moved. Propped against it was a bar of flint, 'never a tool but purposely chipped' in the shape of a phallus,[21] another example of a belief that models of male sexual organs had regenerative powers.

Such cephalotaphy or skull-burial was probably a fertility offering to ensure that the mines nearby would provide plentiful flint. In the same manner, a pit at Grimes' Graves contained a group of antlers, chalk balls and a female figurine against a pile of flints, because the shaft in which these offerings were made had not exposed the expected rich seam of flint. Gifts to the Other-World safeguarded the miners against future misfortune. It was through the medium of imitative magic that Neolithic people manipulated their world, in their farming, in their mining and in their treatment of the dead.

Such beliefs could be world-wide. In Assam, where there are many megalithic tombs, it was the custom periodically to remove the blocking stone so that another corpse could be taken inside the chamber. While the vault was open, no work of any kind was allowed in the village 'lest the paddy should rot as the corpses in the grave had rotted. This is interesting as yet another example of the close connection between death and fertility in primitive communities.'[22]

The skull-burial at Winterslow was paralleled by another discovered in 1849 at Winterbourne Monkton 9 near Avebury. Here a child's skull had been added to a round barrow, supposedly placed inside a beaker with a small sarsen ball, another symbol of fertility. Sexual objects, antlers, heads of bulls, all were believed to give protection and strength. The first burial in the barrow was of a man with a beaker behind his head, an arrowhead by his feet and with two ox-skulls over his body.

Neither of these early Beaker barrows was anywhere near a Neolithic long mound, the Winterslow tumulus being two miles SSW of the nearest at Martin's Farm in Hampshire. This is true of all known early Beaker burials on Salisbury Plain. There was a deliberate avoidance of native cemeteries, a further reason for thinking that there were actual Beaker people who, at first, existed apart from the indigenous population. One of the very first, a burial at Amesbury 89 with a 'European' beaker in it, is isolated from any long mound, and of the fourteen burials with W/MR beakers the nearest to a long barrow is Wilsford South 2b, which is a full three hundred yards from Wilsford South 30, a distance involving almost five minutes' walking across the downland.

Like a small family graveyard to which burials were added over several generations a site was chosen, almost timidly, for four of these early barrows, Wilsford South 51–54, nearly half a mile from the monstrous Lake long barrow (Wilsford South 41). Although this vast Neolithic mound is now nettle-covered in an untidy beech wood it remains a massive and impressive pile even though it is broken-backed where someone has sunk a shaft. Yet from its battered ridge Stonehenge can be seen a mile and a half to the north and so strong were the native traditions attached to this ancient place that no fewer than nineteen round barrows were put up around it in the Early Bronze Age.

Sir Richard Colt Hoare did not touch the long barrow but he did ask William Cunnington to dig into the four 'small barrows, scarcely elevated above the soil' that Beaker people had raised well away to the north-east. All were early with pieces of an AOC pot, a 'European', one N/MR, two W/MR and a handled beaker like a little pottery tankard. On a slight south-facing slope from which the outline of the Stonehenge earthwork could just be made out the barrows lay at the corners of an irregular rectangle no more than 100 yards (90 m) apart. They were midgets compared with the later Lake cemetery round barrows which, on average, were forty times bigger. One of the Beaker group had no covering mound and the biggest was hardly a foot (30 cm) high, perhaps a reflection of the small numbers of people available to construct these modest burial places. Four or five workers could have dug out a grave-pit and heaped up the overlying

## TABLE 11. Distances of W/MR and N/MR Beaker barrows from Neolithic long barrows on Salisbury Plain

| Round barrow | Size Feet Diam Ht | Metres Diam Ht | Beaker type | Clarke Corpus No. | Nearest long barrow | Distance away |
|---|---|---|---|---|---|---|
| Amesbury 51 | 60 × 4 | 18 × 1 | W/MR (2) | 1035F; 1036 | Amesbury 14 | ½ mile |
| Berwick St John 12 | 17 × 1 | 5 × 0.3 | W/MR | 1075 | Tarrant Hinton 1 | 3 miles |
| Boyton 4 | 50 × 1 | 15 × 0.3 | W/MR (2) | 1081; 1082 | Boyton 1 | 1½ miles |
| Bulford 71a | ? | ? | W/MR | 1084 | Bulford 1 | 500 yards |
| Heytesbury 4e | Destroyed | | W/MR | 1115 | Imber 4a | 1¼ miles |
| Longbridge Deverill 3b | Destroyed | | W/MR | 1143 | Warminster 14 | 1½ miles |
| Mere 6a | 33 × ½ | 10 × 0.2 | W/MR | 1125 | Brixton Deverill | 1 mile |
| Monkton Farleigh 2 | 74 × 4 | 23 × 1 | N/MR;W/MR? | 1111; 1112F | Giants Grave | 3 miles |
| Upton Lovell 2c | 30 × 2 | 9 × 0.6 | W/MR | 1151 | Knook 2 | 1 mile |
| Wilsford South 1 | 39 × 1½ | 12 × 0.5 | W/MR (6) | 1156F; 1157; 1158F; 1159; 1160; 1161 | Amesbury 14 | 500 yards |
| Wilsford South 2b | Destroyed | | W/MR | 1162 | Wilsford South 30 | 300 yards |
| Wilsford South 51 | 44 × 1 | 13 × 0.3 | N/MR | 1169F | Wilsford 41 | ½ mile |
| Wilsford South 52 | 25 × 0 | 8 × 0 | W/MR | 1171 | Wilsford South 41 | ½ mile |
| Wilsford 'Lake' 21 | Destroyed | | W/MR | 1175F | ?Wilsford South 41 | ? |
| Winterslow 3 | 132 × 4 | 40 × 1 | W/MR | 1204 | Idmiston 26 | 1½ miles |
| AVERAGES | 50 × 2 | 15 × 0.6 | | | | 1 mile |

mound in less than a week, scraping up the turf and chalk from the shallow, circular ditch that demarcated the funerary area, using antler picks and ox shoulderblades, moving from segment to segment just as Neolithic people had dug out the ditch at Stonehenge eight hundred years earlier.

Such unspectacular barrows, however, are deceptive about the obsessive determination of their builders to keep the dead away from the living. At Bulford 71a, four miles from Lake, a crouched skeleton with a W/MR beaker lay under 'an immense sarsen' weighing several tons that needed a score of men to drag it over the grave-pit. In another Beaker barrow the grave had been quarried deep down into the solid chalk, emptied of over 100 cubic feet (3 cm) or five tons of rubble. Other barrows, seemingly trivial piles of chalk, concealed wooden structure erected skilfully and purposefully like prisons to contain the dead. The mound of Amesbury 51, half a mile north-west of Stonehenge and close to the Cursus, covered an enormous pit in which there was a mortuary house of jointed timbers that were preserved only as impressions of planks and posts in the tumbled chalk that had hardened around them. 'Mortuary houses . . . were a far more regular feature of beaker, and beaker successor graves, than has hitherto been supposed.'[23]

Mortuary houses have been suspected at Sutton Veny 4a and at Mere 6a, a lonely little barrow where pieces of wood were found near the skeleton of a robust man with a young person at his side, their skulls almost touching. From this diminutive barrow came some of the richest of W/MR grave-goods, a tanged copper dagger, a bone spatula, a convex slate wrist-guard and two thumbnail-sized discs of sheet gold, their cruciform patterns hinting at a cult of the sun for which there is evidence in Beaker societies. The mound of Mere 6a was so low that after its excavation around 1800 no one could find it until that doyen of barrow-seekers, Leslie Grinsell, rediscovered it in 1950 from 'the exuberant growth of buttercups' on its top.

In September, 1804, Cunnington dug into Amesbury 51 and uncovered three skeletons lying north-south, one above the other, the lowest, in the mortuary house, being big-boned and with perfect white teeth. 'But the most remarkable circumstance', wrote Colt Hoare, 'was, finding a piece of the skull, about five inches broad, that had apparently been sawn off, for I do not think that any knife could have cut it off in the manner in which this was done.'[24] When the barrow was re-examined in 1960 the roundel was recovered near two pieces of the skull from which it had been detached.

Such surgery, or trephination, was not uncommon in Beaker times, over seventy cases being known from France and Britain, horrifying though it is to imagine the fear and pain that accompanied the operation. The technique consisted of scraping out a deep groove round and round part of the skull, using a sharp flint knife, until the incision was deep enough for a hole to be made through the bone and the roundel prised and snapped off. 'The Stone Age inhabitants of France almost certainly culled plants from the juice of which they squeezed their drowsy anodynes',[25] a practice which, if true, must have been one of the earliest uses of anaesthetics.

In the Snail Down barrow cemetery near Stonehenge an adult cremation had a cranial disc alongside it suggesting that a trepanning operation had failed. The lack of healing on the Amesbury 51 skull tells the same story. At Amesbury 71, a barrow well to the east of Stonehenge on Earl's Farm Down, a well-built man seems to have survived his trephination for some time, but at Crichel Down in Dorset another male, thick-skulled like the man under the Amesbury 51 barrow, did not recover and may have died from infection.

Why anyone should submit to such treatment is unknown, but the many instances of success show that the 'surgeons' with their flint knives must have been quite proficient except when becoming over-ambitious about the amount of skull to be removed. Headaches, epileptic fits, insanity, cataracts, all may have been thought the work of evil spirits that could be expelled only through a cavity in the head of the afflicted person. Then, like the frightful rituals of witch-doctors performed on superstitious tribesmen, their operations accompanied by the rattling of bones and amulets and by the incantation of spells, the dreadful process of trephination would begin.

Surprises of a different nature came from the Amesbury 71 barrow with its trepanned skull. No fewer than four separate phases of activity had taken place there, ranging from the primary burial inside a cramped enclosure down to a final cremation a thousand years later. The bones of the first body had been respectfully rearranged alongside a big grave pit that was aligned north-south. Powdered wood and stakeholes in the cavity showed that some form of mortuary house had stood inside it, the skeleton of a man who had suffered from osteoarthritis as well as undergoing trepanning being laid there under a lightweight wooden canopy. Centuries later when the barrow was overgrown and when the grassland had been windswept into patches of bare chalk, a pyre was lit, a memorial post was set up and the barrow was transformed into a family necropolis. Bodies, including that of a woman some of whose hair was preserved, were added before the mound was enlarged, and even after this cremations and inhumations were put into its ditch at a time when the great sarsen circles of Stonehenge were already weathered and old.

Such continuity in a burial site was not unique. In the Lake cemetery the Wilsford South 52 barrow had a central pit deep enough to contain four burials superimposed one above the other like the shelved corpses in the catacombs of Rome. This resulted from the early Beaker dead being given individual burial only for other bodies to be inserted into the barrow later, the custom of corpse inhumation gradually giving way to cremation. 'The number of "certain" human cremations with British beakers is very small indeed',[26] and these few were probably put into an old barrow when Beaker pottery styles had been accepted and imitated by native people many generations after the first Beaker settlers on Salisbury Plain.

Just south of the Wilsford barrow was an even less obvious one, not six inches (15 cm) high. Dug into by Cunnington, who found only a few bits of scorched bone in a cone-shaped pit, it also was re-excavated in 1958 and a token left by Cunnington discovered. Up to 1804 his habit had been to put a newly-minted coin into a grave as dating evidence of his work, but in that year he had small, square lead tablets made inscribed 'Opened 1804 W.C.'. For 1805 he selected brass discs with 'Opened by Wm. Cunnington 1805'. For later years different tokens were manufactured, but unfortunately, if there were any left over, Cunnington used them in ensuing years contributing confusion rather than clarity to his successors.

Finds from these unpretentious barrows were varied and interesting because of their associations. From barrow 54 came six barbed-and-tanged arrowheads. In the same grave was a heavy shafthole battle-axe from the Preseli mountains of south-west Wales, the presumed source of the famous bluestones and another reminder of the links between early beakers and the first stone circles on Salisbury Plain, although those links were not straightforward as it was once believed.

Bodies were not casually laid in their graves. Strict laws, conditioned by a solar cult, determined the disposition of a corpse. Under barrow 51 the long grave-pit was aligned north-south, a custom that became prevalent with the development of W/MR beakers. At Heytesbury 4e a skeleton was found five feet (1.5 m) down, lying on its face 'with the head to the north'. An interest in the cardinal points has already been noticed in the orientations of the final long barrows, in the southern entrance to Stonehenge and in the layout of the Aubrey Holes there. By early Beaker times it became almost a rule to dispose a corpse with its head towards the north. It was not, however, a trait adopted by Beaker communities from native traditions in Britain.

On the European mainland in the Saale Basin of Germany there were preferred orientations, sexually distinguished, for Beaker graves, all bodies arranged north-south, but men on their right sides with heads to the south, women on their left sides with heads to the north, both groups facing east towards the rising sun.[27] Elsewhere on the continent there were similar alignments. It is arguable that such orientations were the result of a developing cult of the sun among societies in which the fires of metalworking smiths, the rippling gold of molten copper and the eye-blinding brilliance of the sun may have mingled in a rich, entrancing solar cosmology quite unlike the cold, lunar mysticism of Neolithic people. Such opposing creeds could also explain why the axis of Stonehenge was to be changed.

On Salisbury Plain the practice for W/MR burials was for the body to be laid in a crouched position, as though asleep, with head to the north and the beaker set down in front of the body, usually near the feet. As early as 1803 Cunnington was writing that 'the head to the north is the most ancient position', and in 1804, 'in primary interments at a great depth the head generally lies to the north, or nearly so'. It was a custom that

Stukeley had recognised almost a hundred years before. Such orientations were not precise nor could they be expected to be. In times when there was no Pole Star, nor a compass, an alignment to north or south could be attained only be bisecting the distance between two related celestial events. On Salisbury Plain the midwinter sun rose at the south-east around 130° and set some eight hours later near 230° at the south-west. If the skyline were level, south would be midway between these points and by setting up posts at these extremes, stretching a rope from one to the other and then folding it in half, people would have been able to establish the midpoint even though the hills and dips of the horizon distorted this 'centre' by a few degrees.

This might not have mattered. It was the halfway point between the actual sunrise and sunset that was wanted rather than astronomical south. The same would be true between the midsummer and midwinter sunrises with east at their centre, or between sunsets with west between them. Near Stonehenge, as an example, the midsummer sun would have risen near 50° but if, at the south-east where the sun rose at midwinter, there was a hill 3° higher than the place where the observer stood, he would have seen the sun rise there not at 130° but at 136°. Halfway between that place and the midsummer sunrise would not have been at the east, 90° but a little to the ESE at 93°. This, however, was the direction wished for by prehistoric mourners. If it was necessary for the dead person to face the sun this was presumably because the sun was considered to be the giver of life or the world to which the dead returned. To have a corpse looking eastwards between the midsummer and midwinter sunrises would be to 'tie' it into this solar wandering, its eyes seeing not geographical east but that spot on the skyline exactly between the summer and winter risings of the sun.

In Yorkshire, Beaker graves were oriented east-west, men with their heads to the east, women to the west. This difference may have been related to their roles. Tribesmen in Nigeria placed 'the male on his right looking to the East and the rising sun so that he will know when to get up for the morning's hunt or the day's work on the farm, and the female on her left looking to the West so that she will see the sun set and know it is time to prepare the evening meal'.[28] Other societies believed that the sun had power over the dead. In Assam anyone dying an unnatural death was buried west of the village so that the setting sun, as it sank below the hills, would carry the evil spirits away with it.

To understand the nuances of any prehistoric religion is almost impossible, but for Beaker people it is not only the alignment of their burials that suggests the sun was important to them. There is also the material and decoration of some of their personal ornaments, little discs of gold, possibly from the Wicklow mountains of Ireland. The colour itself was reminiscent of the sun and the discs were embossed with circular patterns around a central cross like solar rays. One from Farleigh Wick in Wiltshire, only 1¼ inches (30 mm) across, was made of two pieces of gold foil beaten together. It was very like the pair found by Cunnington in the Mere 6a barrow. 'These discs are believed to be connected with Sun-worship – a cross within a cross being a well-known solar symbol.'[29]

About a score of these delightful objects are known in the British Isles and others of mother-of-pearl or bronze have been discovered on the European mainland where there are also bronze racquet-headed pins with the same motif of a cross. In Britain Beaker people had no need of pins. They preferred buttons as clothes-fasteners. But they kept the circular shape with its sun's rays like a religious emblem, transforming the pin into a decorative disc that could be stitched onto the tunic of its wealthy owner.[30]

Gold and copper were the first metals to be worked in these islands, the ores almost certainly being Irish and possibly brought into Wessex by Beaker prospectors. A gold disc from Kilmuckridge on the coast of south-east Ireland where voyagers may have crossed from Wales to Wexford harbour is similar to the one from Farleigh Wick, 'providing an interesting link between northwest Wessex, only 18 miles from the Bristol Channel, and the extreme south-eastern corner of Ireland, only 170 miles away along Welsh coastal waters'.[31]

Gold discs, copper knives and tubular bronze beads have been found with W/MR and N/MR burials. Proving the Irish connection, similar beakers have been discovered in the Irish counties of Limerick, Meath and Londonderry. The route taken from Wessex by their owners is revealed by the beakers in barrows along the south Welsh coast up to the Preseli mountains overlooking St David's Head. From there to cross the Irish Sea to Wexford was only 50 miles and this probably was the way chosen by men searching for the precious gold and copper.

The gold may have been panned from rivers in the Wicklows. 'The prehistoric metallurgist may soon have discovered that it was simpler to collect small particles at a constant rate in a hardened hide or in a wooden pan, than it was to walk miles and wade fathoms, searching for elusive pebbles.'[32] So little gold is known from this period that only small amounts would have to be located.

Copper was easier to trace. Rich deposits existed in south-western Ireland and experienced miners would recognise likely sources from the plants that flourished in copper-rich soils, the pinks, mints, mosses, the stands of birches and oaks with dead lower leaves and purple stems, and trees and bushes with stunted roots.[33] Such signs made it easier to locate the copper oxides whose brilliant blues, greens and reds would have been obvious once the prospectors had been guided to them, and the men would smash lumps from the outcrops with massive axe-hammers, some of which still lie in the debris of early copper-mines. Oxide ores were quick to smelt, heated by charcoal and then either moulded or hammered into the uncomplicated shapes of the first metal implements.

Returning homewards the expedition would steer their wooden-framed, leather-lined boats towards the silhouette of the Preselis. These mountains were the source of the Group XIII and XXIII axe-factories, most of whose products of perforated maceheads, battle-axes and axe-hammers were used locally, but there are a few specimens on Salisbury Plain, perhaps taken there by a group on their way home from Ireland.

If Beaker communities with their fine pots had not already awed the Big Men or chieftains of native groups in Wessex, then surely the appearance of copper daggers and glittering discs of gold persuaded some that these were powerful leaders and worth following. Grooved ware domination, exclusive and resented, was already waning. Beaker influence would hasten its end. Copies of Beaker pots would be produced by native people. Even the solar cult was taken up, although never to the complete eclipse of traditional faiths. Nowhere, at first, were these changed more obvious than at Woodhenge.

The rings of postholes inside this worn-down earthwork just south of Durrington Walls were noticed from the air by Squadron-Leader Insall in 1925, and in 1926 and 1927 Maud Cunnington and her husband Benjamin, great-grandson of Hoare's colleague, excavated the site.[34] In the first year when dark, earth-filled postholes were appearing below the stripped turf, the place was called 'Wood-henge' in a jocular comparison to 'Stone-henge' two miles to the south-west. The 'joke' evoked no more smiles than the old village nickname for Woodhenge, the 'Dough Cover' from the earthwork's former domed appearance. It is now flat – like the joke. Today, Woodhenge is quiet and unexpressive, fenced, mown, with ankle-high concrete pillars of varying widths to show where posts once stood. Yet, dull though it appears, it contains a paradox and a tragedy.

The henge and the rings of posts inside it lie uneasily together. The NNE causeway across the ditch and the NE axis of the rings do not coincide but are a full 40 feet (12 m) apart. The shapes, moreover, are different. In plan the bank and ditch, like a square with rounded corners, resemble a squat brandy bottle with the entrance at the neck. The rings are almost perfect ellipses, very slightly narrowing into egg-shapes at their north-eastern ends.[35] Radiocarbon assays of 1867 ± 74 bc and 1805 ± 54 bc from antler and bone at the ditch bottom suggest that the henge was built around 2280 BC when the grooved ware occupation of Durrington Walls was still strong. This is confirmed by the discovery of grooved ware deep in the ditch and under the bank, and by the contents of two pits outside the entrance filled, characteristically, with animal bones, burnt flints, charcoal and potsherds.

The date of the timber rings is not known. The posts could have been erected at a later time by a different people who slighted the bank, shovelling some of the earth and chalk back into the ditch. This had been a wide, deep trench and there had been a rapid silting from its rims followed by a more gradual weathering 'finally so slow that a thick band of turf clothed the surface'[36] nearly 3 feet (1 m) above the base of the ditch. Just under this turfline there were sherds of an AOC beaker. Elsewhere there were fragments of W/MR and 'European' pots, dropped there years after the henge was built. There are reasons for thinking that the place had been taken over and converted to beliefs entirely alien to those of its first users.

Six concentric rings of posts were raised, the outermost, 146 feet 8 inches × 131 feet 10 inches (44.7 × 40.2 m), being composed of light poles set only 2 feet (60 cm) into the ground, perhaps an outer stockade with a gap at the NNE opposite the causeway. Inside it there was a roofed structure or, more probably, five free-standing rings open to the sky like the framework of a large, unfinished house.

The first to be put up was the fourth from the centre, Cunnington's Ring C, with long and short diameters of 96 and 83 feet (29 × 25 m), constructed of thick oak trunks weighing five tons or more. The ramps down which these cumbersome posts were manoeuvred showed that they had been hauled upright from the outside, twenty or thirty men straining at the ropes until the timbers were vertical, their tops some 24 feet (7 m) above the ground. Blocks of chalk were jammed into the holes around their bases. Then the two inner rings, F and E, of more slender posts, were set up, followed by D whose postholes were measured off from E. Rings A and B were similarly laid off outside C.

The respective long diameters of the four innermost rings were 38 feet 5 inches, 57 feet 7 inches, 76 feet 10 inches and 96 feet (11.7, 17.6, 23.4 and 29.3 m). Cunnington suggested that a unit of measurement, a 'Short Foot' of 11½ inches (29.2 cm), had been used, transforming the Imperial lengths into multiples of 10, 40, 60, 80 and 100 Short Feet. This is an appealing idea, implying as it does semi-numeracy and mathematical planning on the part of the designers, but it conflicts with the numbers of posts in the rings, only one of which, Ring A, is a multiple of 10. Ring F had 12 posts, E had 18, D – 18, C – 16, B – 32 and F – 60. Nor are the multiples exact (Table 12). Instead of a counting base of 10, one of 4 would fit better and if instead of 11½ inches the unit of measurement had been a 'Beaker Yard' of 2 feet 4¾ inches (73 cm) then both the units used in the diameters and the numbers of posts would be whole or half-multiples of 4.

### TABLE 12. Woodhenge: units of measurement and counting-systems

|  | The Six Rings of Posts | | | | | |
|---|---|---|---|---|---|---|
|  | F | E | D | C | B | A |
| Long Diameters in: |  |  |  |  |  |  |
| (a) Imperial Feet | 38.4 | 57.6 | 76.8 | 96.0 | 125.0 | 144.0 |
| (b) Metres | 11.7 | 17.6 | 23.4 | 29.3 | 38.1 | 43.9 |
| (c) 'Short Feet' of 11½ inches | 40.1 | 60.1 | 80.2 | 100.2 | 130.5 | 150.3 |
| (d) 'Beaker Yards', 2′ 4¾″ | 16.0 | 24.0 | 32.0 | 40.0 | 52.1 | 60.0 |
| Number of posts | 12 | 18 | 18 | 16 | 32 | 60 |
| Number of posts ÷ 4 | 3 | 4½ | 4½ | 4 | 8 | 15 |

Some confirmation that this is correct comes from the spacing between the rings, on average 9 feet 7¼ inches (2.93 m) or 4 'Beaker Yards'. A counting-system based on 4 would have been easy to use for small sums, 5 being reckoned as 4 + 1 and 11 as 4 + 4 + 1 + 1 + 1, but it would have been clumsy for any figure larger than 20 and there is evidence that errors did occur when prehistoric people attempted anything more ambitious than that. Counting-bases of 4, 5 and 6 have been deduced for Neolithic and Bronze Age societies in the British Isles but, rather unexpectedly, there is no suggestion of a radix or counting-base of 3.[37]

Nor is there any support for the use of Alexander Thom's Megalithic Yard of 2.72 feet at Woodhenge, where the four diameters would have been 14.1, 21.2, 28.2 and 35.3 M.Y, although, showing how numbers can be played with, if a unit of 2 feet 9 inches (0.88 m) had been employed the diameters would have been multiples of 7, namely, 14, 21, 28 and 35. The spacing of the rings, however, would have been an unconvincing 3.33 units and this hypothetical length can be rejected.

Cunnington believed that the groundplans for the rings had been scribed out as circles and then changed into ovals by bringing in the sides, a process inevitably creating inaccuracies. She did not ask why such ellipses were required. Thom thought that the rings were intended to have perimeters which were multiples of 20 of his Megalithic Yard.[38] His dimensions, however, were based on a survey of the modern markers and differ from Cunnington's published lengths, his diameter of Ring C being almost 2 feet (60 cm) shorter. As Maud Cunnington made a point of commending her nephew, Lt-Col. R.H. Cunnington of the Royal Engineers who 'surveyed and made all the measurements', it is wiser to accept her figures.

The probable reason for the non-circular shapes was the wish to lay out a long axis that would act as an astronomical sightline. This was a method often used by builders of stone 'circles' at sites such as Cultoon on Islay, the Twelve Apostles near Dumfries and the Druids' Circle in North Wales.[39] At Woodhenge it altered the monument completely. Sighting-posts were set towards the midsummer sunrise and the long diameters of the rings were aligned on it. Cardinal points also were marked. Posts were erected at the south and the west where the equinoctial sun would have set behind the Cuckoo Stone a quarter of a mile away. Woodhenge, however, was not an observatory.

Close to the centre of the rings a small grave was found 'lying on the line of midsummer sunrise and at right-angles to it'.[40] In it was the skeleton of a 3½ year old child, probably a girl, lying on her right side facing the sunrise. Her skull lay in two halves, 'cleft before burial', one of the clearest examples of sacrifice in prehistoric Britain, and one which suggests that she may have been killed in a ceremony of rededication when the henge was transformed into a place of the sun. In 1934 the skull was sent for further examination to the Royal College of Surgeons in London and it was destroyed by fire in the Second World War.

The people who used Woodhenge left traces behind and when the posts eventually rotted, objects fell into the cavities, scraps of animal bones, flints, some worked, some burnt, and an analysis of the rubbish produced some interesting patterns. Scores of ox and pig teeth were recovered, most of them in the holes of the two outer rings, A and B, those of the ox mainly in the NE and SW quadrants whereas the majority of pigs' teeth were in the NW and SE. Jaws of these animals were closer to the centre. Flint flakes, scrapers and burnt flints were concentrated around the outer rings, mostly to the south of the grave and, with the flints, scraps of animal bone occurred in posthole after posthole. Heavier meat-bones, including part of a pig's skull, lay closer to the middle. It is unlikely that Woodhenge, with its solar alignment, was an abattoir for the inhabitants of Durrington Walls. More probably it was a place where the dead rested in a symbolic mortuary house, open to the sky and the sun, rituals performed around them, funeral feasts held by their mourners, their possessions lying by their sides during the days or weeks before their final interment.

That Woodhenge was a special place is proved by the chalk objects buried there. Unlike the flints, these could not have survived long if exposed in the open and they must have been intentionally deposited in selected postholes before the posts were erected. In Ring C a chalk 'cup' was found in Hole 9 precisely east of the centre. Such objects, known from other Neolithic ritual sites, are too small to have been cups or lamps for oil. Often in them there is a tiny artificial depression, no deeper than a thumb-mark, and this may be the clue. Frequently found with chalk phalli, these 'cups' may have been the female counterpart of the male organ, talismen of fertility, life-giving and appropriate for a house of the dead. In Ring C a second chalk 'cup' was found in Hole 7 in line with the southernmost moonrise. It is demanding too much of coincidence to question the astronomical interests of the Woodhenge people when every one of the carved chalk objects discovered there was in a hole related to a solar or lunar event.

Chalk 'cups' such as these have been found in Neolithic causewayed enclosures and flint-mines as well as in ritual centres like Stonehenge, Woodhenge and Maumbury Rings henge in Dorset. 'We prefer to consider them not primarily as lamps but as belonging to the same class of votive or ritualistic objects as the phallic carvings ... and other unexplained things with which Neolithic tribesmen attempted to make their corn grow, their cattle multiply, and their trade thrive.'[41] Symbols became the reality of life and through them the world could be manipulated.

With the second 'cup' at Woodhenge there was a palm-sized rectangle of chalk with a hole bored through it. These perforated plaques and discs, like the phalli and the 'cups', are also associated with the Neolithic dead. It will be recalled that a similar disc was found with a chalk ball in the ditch at Stonehenge. A further link with that circle was provided by a second disc at Woodhenge, its perforation only half-finished. With it in

Hole 16 of Ring A was a chalk axe like the one found by Hawley near the tallest sarsen pillar in Stonehenge. A second 'axe' lay at the bottom of Hole 21 of Ring B. Recollecting the obsession with calendrical and cardinal points both at Stonehenge and in many stone circles, particularly those in Cumbria, it is significant that the post of Hole A16 had stood due south of the centre of Woodhenge and the post of B21, with a chalk axe in its hole, was in line with the midsummer sunrise.

The association of the axe with the sun and with death is widespread in primitive societies and the chalk axes at Woodhenge are reminders of an axe-cult in prehistoric Britain. A fragment of a chalk axe was discovered in a barrow at Westbury in Wiltshire and 'does not make sense unless votive' and 'the small size and soft material [limestone] of the little axe from Hengistbury Head likewise suggest a votive purpose'.[42] Other 'axes', specially made as ritual objects, have been found with burials. An axe, believed to be of pottery, came from the chambered tomb of Tara in Ireland, and at Brownstone Farm near Kingswear in Devon a miniature axe of jadeite had been left in a cist with two cremations. The chalk axes at Woodhenge and Stonehenge are indications that those places were powerful centres of ritual and death.

Nothing was still. Sherds of late beakers at Durrington Walls have been 'interpreted as evidence for the eclipse of the ritual authority structure, and the annexation of the monument by peripheral groups of [native] and Beaker users',[43] ending the grooved ware cult.

Around 2200 BC the erection of stone circles began at Stonehenge and the axis there was turned away from the moon and towards the sun.

# 7

## Not far from Naas
## Stonehenge II: 2200 – 2000 BC

*If there was any central timber construction in period I, it was probably
destroyed and replaced by the double circle. . . . The new builders of
period II had a religious and cultural tradition very different from
that of their predecessors and cremation-burial played no part in it.*

R. J. C. Atkinson, *Stonehenge*, 67

Everything changed and yet nothing was changed. The timber rings that
had replaced the mortuary house were themselves replaced in this phase
II of Stonehenge, the posts taken down and substituted by stones. Yet the
rings were the same, a circle within a circle, the skeleton of a house whose
walls and roof had been dismantled centuries before (Fig. 9).

Now there were to be two rings of bluestones from Wales, upright pillars
on whose tops lintel-stones would rest like the ring-beams of a roofed
building. There would be a passage-like entrance at the NE; opposite it,
at the other side of the circles, a tall stone would stand, towering over the
others. Outside the rings and against the bank of the earthwork four more
stones, not bluestones but local sarsens, would be placed at the corners of
a rectangle whose long sides pointed towards the midwinter moonset. The
entrance of the henge was to be widened by filling in part of the ditch and
changing the axis of the monument from NNE to NE. Outside the henge
an avenue lined with chalk banks would run NE downhill for over a quarter
of a mile, as straight as a falling stone in the direction from which the
stones had been dragged from the river. The changes were incisive but did
not destroy. It was metamorphosis rather than demolition.

A series of C–14 determinations, including that from the murdered man
in the ditch, make this the most closely dated of all the phases at
Stonehenge. The combination of 1770 ± 70 bc (c. 2190 BC) and 1728 ± 68
bc (c. 2130 BC) from antlers in the avenue's ditch; 1765 ± 70 bc (c. 2180
BC) from the skeleton; and 1720 ± 150 bc (c. 2120 BC) from an antler
near the Great Trilithon of sarsens when the bluestone rings were being

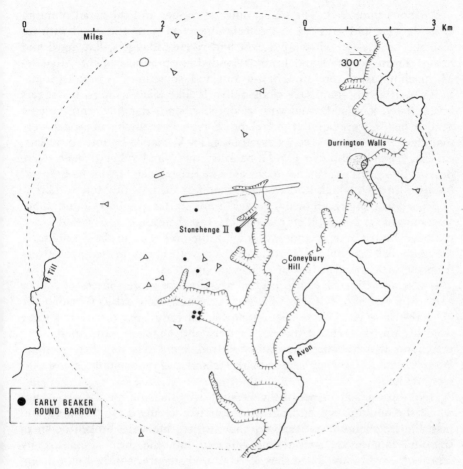

Fig. 9. The Stonehenge Region c. 2200 BC. Stonehenge II and early Beaker barrows.

taken down, offer good evidence that the circles and their associated features were undergoing construction in the years between 2200 and 2100 BC.

It was a time of tension. Burials with even richer grave-goods hint at a strengthening of grades and ranks in society. Craftsmen, producing lovelier, more intricate articles of adornment, could have flourished only under patronage and protection. Rivalry between cults was matched by rivalry between neighbouring groups, each greedily asserting its growing power, and the heaping up of massive banks around previously undefended settlements is an indication of how disturbed the times were. Forty miles south-west of Stonehenge, at Mount Pleasant near modern Dorchester, an enormous ditched earthwork was piled up to safeguard its inhabitants,[1] and dates of 1784 ± 41 bc and 1778 ± 59 bc, around 2200 BC, show that the fortification was a contemporary of the first stone circles on Salisbury Plain.

Weapons improved. The malleability of copper and the rapid blunting of its daggers and axes led to the technique of alloying the metal with tin to make bronze for thin-butted axes and rivetted daggers, flat, hard and heavy. From Scotland and from Ireland these products of the Migdale-Marnoch industry were brought into England, sometimes by traders, sometimes by itinerant smiths. Vicious halberds, like pikes with great daggers jutting from long staffs and with coloured ribands dangling and dancing at their heads, were popular in Ireland. Personal ornaments of bronze were manufactured – armlets, cones as cappings for V-shaped buttons, bracelets, ear-rings like diminutive garden-baskets; these and other trinkets were devised by smiths in response to the ever-increasing demand for flamboyant luxuries through which leaders could manifest their wealth and authority.

Bronze-working could be dangerous. Some smiths gradually found themselves unable to control their movements, lost their appetites, wasted away, poisoned by the arsenic and antimony in the ores that, in their ignorance, they handled casually, wiping the toxins into their mouths with the sweat from the fires and crucibles of their working-areas.

It was an active time. Prospectors searched for more sources of copper and tin, for outcrops of stone for the maceheads and battle-axes that the chieftains coveted. Where such stone had already been discovered there were organised forces of miners, carriers and knappers, and there were merchants who travelled the trackways and rivers to barter their goods in Wessex from as far away as Scotland, Ireland and the mountains of south-west Wales.

Here, on the soft breast of the Preselis, was the summit of Carn Meini where the outcrops spiked from the crests like fossilised pin-cushions, and here the fragments of attractively spotted preselite were broken down to size and laboriously pecked and dimpled into the form of an axe by repeated, hard blows. Then they were ground smooth, polished to a sheen, and finally, slowly, carefully, bored with a bow-drill and sand, first from the top, then from the underside, to make an hourglass-shaped perforation into which the shaft could be fixed. So tedious and protracted was this process that it was probably undertaken as a cottage industry on the plain that surrounded Carn Meini.

Preselite was a bluish stone, sometimes speckled white or pink, and it was ideal for ostentatious regalia. One magnificent axe-hammer, found at Fifield Bavant 12 miles SSW of Stonehenge, weighed over 5 lbs. Like other preselite objects, it is likely to have reached Wessex by transportation along the Welsh coast and then along the rivers of the Bristol Avon and Wylye.

Not every piece of preselite, or bluestone, arrived there as a finished article. A big block nearly collapsed on William Cunnington when his workers were digging out the eastern end of the Boles long barrow (Heytesbury I) in 1801. He had already uncovered fourteen human skulls, 'one of which appeared to have been cut in two by a sword', and the horned skulls of at least seven oxen, but because large stones were continually tumbling down he had to stop the work. Recognising that one boulder was of the same material as the smaller pillars at Stonehenge, he took it for his garden in Heytesbury. It is now in Salisbury Museum.

Its presence in a long barrow has provoked much argument because it must have reached Salisbury Plain many years earlier than the bluestone circles. The custom of long barrow building was dying out by 3000 BC and this suggests that preselite may have been present in Wessex centuries before the end of the Neolithic period. There is another mystery. Near the Preselis there are several stone circles, Meini-gwyr and Gors Fawr among them, and their stones are not of preselite, which could have been obtained quite easily, but of ordinary, unremarkable igneous rock from the vicinity. This suggests that the Welsh workers on Carn Meini regarded the stone much as modern miners regard coal and oil, useful as providers of income for food and shelter, sometimes dangerous to extract but certainly not magical. This is quite different from modern interpretations of the Preselis as magic mountains that exercised a magnetic attraction to the wayfarers and sea-goers who used this landmark as a guide. 'I believe, therefore, that the awe-inspiring character of Prescelly Mountain is alone sufficient to account for the special significance of the rocks which crop out along its crest.'[2]

One asks what justification there is for believing that groups of Beaker adventurers dragged and rafted scores of bluestones along two hundred miles of seas, rivers and countryside of southern Britain. There are two questions about the problem, where the bluestones came from, and how they reached Stonehenge. For hundreds of years it has been realised that their source was different from that of the sarsens of which, as early as 1655, Inigo Jones remarked, 'the same kind of Stone whereof this *Antiquity* consists, may be found, especially about *Aibury* in North *Wiltshire*'.[3] This was not true of the bluestones and in 1721 William Stukeley contrasted the appearance of the sarsens with the Altar Stone which was composed of 'a kind of blue coarse marble'.[4] This did not explain their origin and since his time Devon, Cornwall, Wales and as far away as Normandy have been suggested. It was not until 1923 that, following an analysis of the variety of bluestones at Stonehenge – spotted dolerite (preselite), rhyolite, volcanic ash and others – Thomas noted that just such a mixture was to be found near the crest of Carn Meini.[5] The fact that the Altar Stone, a block of micaceous sandstone, had also come from south-west Wales, from the Cosheston Beds near Milford Haven and only twenty miles south of the Preselis, apparently confirmed this as the likely source.

It also provided some substance for an otherwise fantastic account by Geoffrey of Monmouth of how the stones had been brought to Stonehenge, not from Wales but from Ireland. Over eight hundred years ago this medieval 'historian' explained why the circle had been built.[6] In his *History of the Kings of Britain* (AD 1138) he reported the advice given by the magician Merlin. Three hundred British nobles had been massacred by

Saxon treachery. 'If', said Merlin to his king, 'you want to grace the burial-place of these men with some lasting monument, send for the Giants' Ring which is on Mount Killaurus in Ireland.' Accepting that the stones would form a dignified cenotaph, the king had them transported to Salisbury Plain where Merlin erected the circle. As the Preselis lay almost exactly halfway between eastern Ireland and Wiltshire and on just the route that prehistoric people might have taken from one to the other, there was the enticing possibility that Geoffrey of Monmouth had chanced on a story of some mighty megalithic feat that survived, distorted and misunderstood, in folk memory. So romantically appealing was the idea of this bold enter-prise and so well did it fit with Thomas's identification of the bluestone source that it soon became part of archaeological thinking. 'The tradition relative to this event was narrated by Geoffrey of Monmouth',[7] and 'In the story of Stonehenge in Geoffrey of Monmouth we may have the only fragment left to us of a native Bronze-Age literature'.[8]

There was nothing inherently implausible about the reconciliation of Geoffrey's story with the Preselis as the bluestone source. The saga of the stones' journey from Wales to Wiltshire was so dramatic that it could well have been recounted from century to century, albeit warped and tinged with interpolations of magic and Merlin. Geoffrey may have seen Stonehenge for himself. Equally, from his undetailed description, he may only have read about it. Eight years before the completion of his own book the *Historia Anglorum* of Henry of Huntingdon had appeared, a work which contained the famous paragraph about Stonehenge as the second wonder of Britain whose stones 'of a wondrous size have been erected after the manner of doorways', the earliest surviving reference to the antiquity.

With great religious houses and cathedrals such as Old Sarum and Winchester near Stonehenge and with clerics travelling between them, it is unlikely that the circle was unknown. But what passers-by remarked on were not the insignificant bluestones, dwarfed by the trilithons and half-hidden inside the ring, but the incredible sarsens that overshadowed them, three times their height, titanic pillars so bulky that it seemed no mortal men could have raised them. Not one bluestone is shown in either of the 14th century sketches of Stonehenge, and that it was indeed the impressive sarsens to which Geoffrey referred is plain from his description of them.

'The stones are enormous and there is no one alive strong enough to move them.' This could not be a description of the bluestones, which on average weighed no more than 4 tons, very different from the 20 to 50 tons of the sarsens. The Britons, said Geoffrey, tried to shift the stones of the Giants' Ring with hawsers, tackles and ropes, the same equipment he had seen used by cathedral masons, 'but none of these things advanced them an inch' and it was left to Merlin to move the stones by magic.

From this it seems that there can be no straightforward connection between Geoffrey's legendary account and the source of the bluestones. Indeed, if the stones' derivation had been Snowdonia rather than the

Preselis[9] then they could have been shifted towards Salisbury Plain by glaciation, as Kellaway had suggested, a geological explanation which would eradicate all reason for believing in a long-lasting recollection of a prodigious effort of transportation. Judd, who doubted whether prehistoric people could have moved heavy weights any great distance, thought the stones had reached Salisbury Plain by glacial drift.[10] This would account for the undressed condition of many of them. Human beings, he argued, being sensible, would have lightened them at their source rather than hauling the jagged, unshaped boulders to Stonehenge where they were 'reduced to something like half their bulk'. It is also true that there is no other stone circle among the more than a thousand that are known in the British Isles to which stones have been dragged from more than five or six miles away.[11]

It can be claimed that Geoffrey, credulous and uncritical, had been misled by stories he had heard. The crucial question is why he said Ireland was the country from which the ring had been taken. The answer may be simple. It begins with the location of Mount Killaurus where the Giants' Ring had stood.

Killala in Co. Mayo and Ushnagh Hill in Co. Westmeath have recently been suggested, but earlier writers thought the site to be in Co. Kildare. It is noteworthy that near the town of Kildare there is the Hill of Allen, famous in Irish legend for its links with the Other-World. Churchmen would have known it. There was a rich monastery at Kildare, founded by St Brigid in the 5th century, and often visited by English and Welsh clerics. There was nothing unusual about this. Anglo-Norman priests had been travelling to Ireland since AD 1074 when Lanfranc, William the Conqueror's Archbishop of Canterbury, asserted the authority of Rome. From the 11th century onwards Irish priests were sent to Canterbury or Winchester to be consecrated as archbishops. The Irish Sea was a busy monastic thoroughfare.

The natural port for travellers from Britain to Kildare was Dublin, 30 miles from the monastery. From there the wayfarer would skirt the Wicklow mountains to the south and pass through Naas ten miles from Kildare. In Geoffrey of Monmouth's time several monasteries existed there.

When he visited Ireland with Prince John in 1185 another churchman, Gerald of Wales, saw many megaliths in the area. 'In Ireland, in ancient times, there was a collection of stones called the Giants' Dance, that demanded admiration . . . and on the plains of Kildare, not far from Naas [giants] set them up as much by skill as by strength. Moreover, stones just like them, and raised in the same way, are to be seen there to the present day.'[12]

Many of these stones are still standing. They are the well-known pillars of Wicklow granite and are amongst the tallest stones in the British Isles, concentrated in quite a small area of the counties of Carlow and Kildare. The highest are close to Naas, Craddockstown West over 14 feet (4.4 m) tall, Longstone Rath, a slender needle, its top more than 23 feet (5.3 m) above the ground, a Beaker cist at its base, and the Punchestown pillar, the second tallest menhir in the British Isles after Rudston in Yorkshire. It stands a soaring 26 feet 5 inches (8 m) in height, and when it fell in 1931 it was found to be 31 feet (9.5 m) long and to weigh over 9 tons. The dimensions of these great stones compare well with the average 17½ feet (5.3 m) height of a Stonehenge sarsen.

These scattered stones around Naas were surely the huge pillars commented on by medieval scholars. It is easy to imagine that Gerald of Wales and others before him visualised in these lofty menhirs, so similar in size and appearance to the sarsens of Stonehenge, the remnants of a vast stone circle, the work of giants, the majority of whose stones had been taken to Salisbury Plain to be erected in another ring of exceptionally big uprights. 'Merlin . . . put the stones up in a circle . . . in exactly the same way as they had been arranged on Mount Killaurus in Ireland, thus proving that his artistry was worth more than any brute strength.'[13] Geoffrey's Stonehenge story is not a relic of folk memory but a 12th century attempt, blemished by geological incompetence, to explain how the ponderous sarsens had been set in place, and the legend is no more than a monkish mixture of Merlin, magic and imagination. It has nothing to do with the bluestones.

The actual place where men found these stones is still debatable, but the nature of the stones themselves offers an explanation. They are not identical. As well as the pillars and stumps still visible at Stonehenge, there are innumerable chippings dropped and scattered when some stones were battered into shape. Most are preselite, spotted or plain, but there are fragments of rhyolite, of volcanic and calcareous ash and there is sandstone. All these may have come from the Preselis, but pieces of welded tuff did not. Nor did they occur naturally in the chalk landscape of Salisbury Plain. The 'Snowdonia area of north Wales, however, is rich in rocks of this type'.[14]

Whether from the Preselis or Snowdonia or elsewhere, how the bluestones reached Salisbury Plain is still unclear. Three possibilities have been put forward. Beaker prospectors, returning from Ireland and looking upon the spectacular Preselis as the home of the gods, undertook the awesome but spiritually rewarding task of taking the holy stones to Wessex. Alternatively, 'the ancient men of Dyfed, realising that the centre of neolithic society had moved from the West to Salisbury Plain, were taking with them the stone of their native land, or perhaps even stone circles that had already existed in fourth millennium Dyfed', having 'a liking for the blue-grey rock which bordered on insanity'.[15]

The third and most likely answer is glaciation. If this were not so and men really did transport the stones hundreds of miles, one wonders why they did not roughly shape them in the Preselis, removing half the weight. They would also have chosen the hardest, most durable of the rocks available rather than such a mixture of stones, some of which would weather and crumble very quickly. Many of the Stonehenge bluestones were 'too soft or fissile to have been of any value as building material. The inference is plain. . . . Glacial action is the only reasonable solution.'[16]

There can be no doubt of the competence of those prospectors and stoneworkers to recognise a stone's quality. Centuries of selecting tuffs and greenstones for their axes gave them experienced eyes. Yet, in 1880, a few inches below the turf at Stonehenge, Henry Cunnington, grandson of William and father-in-law of Maud, found the base of an overgrown and worn-down schist, one of the original bluestones, weathered into a mere stump.[17] Before then Stukeley had grumbled about how bits of bluestones were 'knock'd off by [the] wretched hands'[18] of credulous souvenir-hunters who thought they were acquiring amulets that possessed medicinal virtues. It is unbelievable that any prehistoric group would have chosen stones as soft as this when so much good material was at hand, and the alternative must be that much nearer the chalky, stoneless area of Salisbury Plain men had chanced upon a litter of bluestones and others, some from the Preselis 'but probably fetched proximally from a site, as yet undiscovered, in West Wiltshire',[19] in a clutter of rocks and boulders of which only a limited number were of the ideal shape and texture.

The stones cannot have been far away. Within twenty miles there were alternative supplies: to the north on the Marlborough Downs there were hundreds of sarsens, big and small; and to the west around Bradford-on-Avon there were masses of oolitic limestone on the valley sides of the River Bristol Avon, the same pass through which the bluestones were thought to have been ferried. The Welsh rocks and boulders were much closer than that, perhaps on the slopes above the River Wylye, three miles from Boles Barrow and twelve miles west of Stonehenge in a part of Salisbury Plain well-known to its natives.

From there the stones could have been taken downriver to the junction with the Christchurch Avon. Here the steersmen turned northwards, paddling and poling upstream a twisting ten miles along the quiet, forest-shaded waters to a landing near present-day West Amesbury. This was not a foolhardy undertaking. A raft would have been unwieldy, but experiments in 1954 proved that when an average 4-ton stone was laden onto a form of lightweight trimaran of three canoes lashed together the displacement was no more than 9 inches (26 cm), leaving the craft high enough in the water to navigate the slow snakes of the river.[20] Once on land the stone could be lashed to a hardwood sledge and dragged by thirty or forty men or, more probably, harnessed to a team of oxen, and trudgingly pulled up the mile and a half slope to Stonehenge.

There has been disagreement about the sequence of the various circles, some scholars preferring the idea that the bluestones and the sarsens were erected together in a unified plan that involved stones of different heights and appearance.[21] In the absence of conclusive evidence it is better to accept Atkinson's detailed hypothesis that the bluestone rings were the first to be put up, an argument based not only on logical conclusions from the archaeological evidence but also upon his long, personal experience excavating on the site.

Two rings, of which no sign can be seen today, were planned for the centre of the henge, their stoneholes possibly arranged to correspond with where the timbers of the mortuary house and the posts of the subsequent circles had stood. By creating a replica, the past did not die but was immortalised. Although the stones were smaller than the posts, about 7 × 2 × 1½ feet (2.1 × 0.6 × 0.5 m), their durability made them acceptable substitutes for their wooden predecessors. In other parts of Britain similar transformations were taking place, in Scotland at Croft Moraig and Moncrieffe in Tayside. At Balfarg in Fife, inside a henge, as many as six concentric timber rings, associated with grooved ware, were succeeded by two concentric stone circles with an entrance at the west and with a central pit containing a cremation with a handled beaker like a coffee mug.[22] And only eighteen miles north of Stonehenge and at about the same time, the upright posts of the Sanctuary, once a small thatched hut near Avebury, were pulled down and two rings of sarsens were erected, the body of a young girl with a 'Barbed-Wire' beaker buried under a stone at the exact east.

These were houses of the dead where the dead no longer had to lie for days or weeks or months. The absence of a roof and walls and a doorway mattered no more than the absence of scenery in a classical Greek play. The symbol of the house was more powerful than the uncovered reality of a stone circle.

At Stonehenge the first bluestone rings have gone, taken down even before they were complete, but proof of their resemblance to a roofed building survives and so does evidence of where they had stood. In his final season there, while digging in the central area, Hawley had come upon a long oval hole with another near it, both of which seemed to have held stones. This part of the ring was re-examined by Atkinson, Piggott and Stone between 1954 and 1956 and the significance of the holes was realised.[23] There was a great arc of elongated hollows, each about 10 feet (3 m) long and with a deep cavity at either end as though a great dumbbell had been pressed into the chalk. These 'dumb-bells' were set radially to the circumference of a circle, 86 feet (26.2 m) across, like a spoked wheel from which the large central hub had been removed. The cavities were the inner and outer settings of two rings from which the stones had been withdrawn. That they were earlier than the great sarsen ring was clear from the way that one hole had been cut into by the later pit for stone 3 of the outer sarsen circle.

Not knowing at first how many 'dumb-bells' there had been they were called the Q and R Holes, R being the inner ring, after the 'Quaere' so often appearing in John Aubrey's manuscript when he wanted to 'query' the number of stones or posts or measurements of a monument. 'Quaere Mr W Rogers at Paynswick the dimensions' of Beacon Camp near Gloucester.

From the spacing of the stoneholes it could be calculated that each ring was planned to contain 38 stones with extra ones lining the entrance at the north-east. Here, passing from the earthwork's causeway, a visitor would have walked into the circles along a narrow stone-lined corridor with five stones on either side, the first two belonging to the circles with a further three extending into the open central arena like a passage into a chambered tomb. As though to emphasise this, extra stones were to have been added on either side of this passageway giving a ponderous, dark impression of portal-stones inside a temple and similar to the stones that had lined the entrances of earthworks such as Mayburgh, Balfarg and Maumbury Rings in Dorset. As will be seen, it is plausible that the 'corridor' at Stonehenge was capped with lintel-stones adding to the feeling that one was entering a roofed building.

It has been noticed that this bluestone phase is often attributed to the users of W/MR beakers. Years ago this idea was based on the supposition that it was Beaker folk who built the British stone circles but this is now an outdated view. Otherwise, the evidence is largely negative. No grooved ware material has been discovered with either the Q and R Holes or the avenue, but one W/MR sherd was found in a Q Hole. Another beaker sherd lay there and a later piece of beaker rested high in the silted-up ditch. As many as 135 beaker sherds of various periods were recovered from the excavations at Stonehenge, but none of them was in a position that showed when it had been dropped. The best that can be said is that the C–14 dates are in accordance with W/MR presence in the region, and as Stonehenge had previously been a grooved ware ceremonial site in which beaker sherds suddenly appeared it is plausible that it was Beaker groups in conjunction with native people who took over the henge, building the first stone circles there.

The Q and R rings were not well laid out and their centres were a little different. From the small published plan Ring R was the more symmetrical with an inner diameter of about 72 feet (22 m), interestingly, very close to 30 of the 'Beaker Yards' suspected at Woodhenge. The stoneholes of Q deviated more from the line of a perfect circle and it is arguable that their holes had been offset from R which, being the innermost, was set up first.

The rings were never finished. Two stoneholes at the entrance were left half-dug and when, between 1956 and 1958, the SW quadrant of the circles was investigated 'it was clear that hardly any of the Q and R Holes had been dug', so that when 'Stonehenge II was dismantled at least a quarter of its circumference was incomplete'.[24] On its axis, however, at the south-west opposite the entrance there was a huge pit and it is tempting to believe that it was here that the biggest of the bluestones, the Altar Stone, over twice as long and four times as heavy as the others, had stood, a great pillar dominating the rings. At the very bottom of the disturbed hole, maybe intentionally deposited there, was a worndown stone axe, not from Cumbria like those of the grooved ware cult but of Cornish greenstone, the type used by the natives.

This leads to the sixth question about Stonehenge, the reason for the Altar Stone being so much bigger, so out of proportion with the other bluestones when it could easily have been reduced in size. The answer seems to lie, as usual, with earlier funerary traditions. In some earthen long barrows like Arn Hill (Warminster 1) a single standing stone had been erected against the human bones as though watching over them. In chambered tombs huge stones at the far end of the passage overlooking the chamber where the dead lay are known in Brittany, and even in Britain where a tall monolith stands inside the chamber of Bryn Celli Ddu on Anglesey. Some of them have crudely-hacked shoulders and breasts to emphasise their femininity. In other tombs there are carvings apparently of a 'guardian-goddess' of the dead, sometimes holding an axe or dagger like a jealous protectress of the spirits inside the tomb. Not far from Bryn Celli Ddu the passage-grave of Barclodiad y Gawres, 'the apronful [of stones] of the goddess', has just such a carving, perhaps inspired by Breton prototypes. On the chalklands of Salisbury Plain posts, now rotted and almost undetectable, may also have stood in the mortuary houses, unnoticed by primitive diggers like William Cunnington.

The intimate associations of Stonehenge with the dead suggest that the Altar Stone may have had a similar function, rising opposite the entrance, higher and wider than all the other stones, dominating the ring. This second Stonehenge was an imitation in stone of the first charnel-house. It too was a house of the dead, although now it was open to the sky and now the corpses were brought to it for no more than a few hours or days for a symbolic period of decomposition before burial. The Altar Stone, looming over the new rings, was as much a part of the funerary tradition, changed but never abandoned, as any other aspect of the bluestone circles, and the stone axe found at its base restates its role as the guardian of the dead.

No immense effort had been demanded in this re-construction of the henge. The Altar Stone could easily have been raised by 30 or 40 men, and even allowing for the setting up of the four Station Stones, the filling in of part of the ditch and the digging and piling up of the earth-banked avenue, no more than 350,000 man-hours of labour were required. With a work-force of 200 labourers the entire project could have been finished in eight or nine months. But time was also needed for the everyday tasks of agriculture and herding, for the vagaries of weather, for seasonal gatherings and for the occasions when all work was forbidden. The pace may have been a leisurely one and one which gave opportunity for the shaping of some stones.

This leads to the seventh of the twelve questions about Stonehenge, why it had a circle inside a circle unlike most other rings in the British Isles. It is a question rarely, if ever, asked and yet the answer is critical to an understanding of the monument. There are few concentric stone circles in these islands, perhaps thirty out of the thousand or more megalithic rings that are recorded,[25] and of those the sites in north Britain with their widely-spaced circles are different from those in the south. In Wiltshire, at Winterbourne Bassett, at the North Circle inside Avebury, at the Sanctuary and at Stonehenge the circles are closely set together in a plan similar to those of real houses at Durrington Walls, the outer ring symbolising the wall of a house, the inner representing the posts that supported the roof. Such concentric rings, therefore, are best interpreted as imitations of a wooden building.

That this was so at Stonehenge is indicated by the bluestones there that once were lintels to be placed across the tops of standing stones. Mortise-holes had been ground out on their undersides to receive the tenons, or crude pegs, bashed and shaped out of the solid tops of bluestone pillars. These stones are no longer in their original places. They have all been moved and with the possible exception of the Altar Stone it is impossible to know where they once stood. Stone 150, by current numbering, lying at the north-east partly under another bluestone, has two mortises in it, 41 inches (104 cm) apart but not quite equidistantly positioned from the stone's ends. At the ESE Stone 36 with its sophisticated curvature and smoothing has two oval mortises in it. Other bluestones have the broken, ground-down bases of their tenons still clear to view on their tops, three at the south-west, 67, 69 and 70 being the most obvious examples. Other bluestones have been smashed and carted away and it will never be known whether similar pegs and holes existed on them. In 1740 John Wood, while making the first good survey of Stonehenge, lamented how 'incumbered with Dung and other Rubbish' bluestones 46–8 were and how others were 'wasted by the Weather, as well as barbarous Hands', while Stukeley twenty years before grumbled at the way that people broke pieces off 'with great hammers' to test whether the stones were artificial or natural.[26]

Even earlier, John Aubrey was informed that 'Philip, Earle of Pembroke . . . did say, that an Altar-stone was found in the middle of the Area here: and that it was carried away to St James's (Westminster)'. Thinking that this referred to the Court of St James near London the Wiltshire Archaeological Society wrote to the Clerk of the Works there in 1868 asking the stone's whereabouts. 'No such stone exists there', was the reply.

Aubrey had been misled. Another informant, Mrs Trotman, told him that 'one large stone was taken (caried) away to make a Bridge' by 'the inhabitants about the Amesburies'. It was probably this stone that Pembroke had remembered, taken not to London but to the hamlet of Berwick St James only four miles west of Stonehenge. In 1933 a local man reported that two stones, once lying across a stream, had been set up in the middle of the village.[27] They are still there, in the main street at the corners of a drab lane, both of them with footworn troughs along their faces. If these are the broken bits of Pembroke's stone they survive as a memento to 17th century vandalism.

It will never be possible to reconstruct the first bluestone rings, but the lintels and the tenons suggest that at least some of the stones lay across the tops of others, the work of native wood-workers struggling to shape the almost intractable preselite into duplicates of upright posts and ring-beams socketed together as timbers would have been. This was a technological challenge a determined adaptation by men unaccustomed to working in stone, but the most spectacular change, literally, was at the entrance to the earthwork, set out there a thousand years before.

Here the narrow causeway had been aligned upon the northernmost moon where it rose, full and white at midwinter. The Heel Stone had marked the midpoint of its swing from major to minor rising and observers had counted the years until it reached its furthest position once again. All that was to be altered. Men tipped basketloads of chalk into the ditch to widen the entrance and re-align the axis of Stonehenge. The causeway had been about 35 feet (11 m) wide, flanked by the ends of the ditch but now some 25 feet (7.6 m) of its south-eastern terminal was backfilled with 'clean white chalk which had been brought from elsewhere and cast into the ditch', chalk perhaps dug out of the Q and R Holes and which set so hard that it 'gave the idea of the chalk being wet when cast into the ditch'.[28]

The result was drastic. Whereas the middle of the original causeway had an azimuth or compass-bearing of 46° 33' the new midpoint was almost 4° clockwise from that, aligned about 49° 54' almost in line with the Heel Stone, and very close indeed to coinciding with the rising midsummer sun when half its disc was above the horizon.[29] 'This is one alignment in the structure of Stonehenge which is long enough to be measured with an accuracy sufficient to justify the assumption that it was adopted deliberately.'[30] So far from being a halfway pointer for the moon the Heel Stone was transformed into the stark symbol of the sun. The sun in late June had always risen about midway between the northern moon's major and minor risings but what had been no more than fortuitous was now made into a solar triumph. The orientation was not quite perfect, being only 'where the sun rises, or nearly so, at the summer solstice'.[31] Stukeley was right. The alignment was not exact but it sufficed. It turned Stonehenge into a solar monument in which the former lunar sightlines were almost eliminated. Another would replace them.

A ditch was dug around the Heel Stone, protecting this pillar of the sun from the profane world outside, and from the new entrance to the henge deep ditches were dug to lay out the lines of an avenue that extended, as straight as a ruler, downhill for over a quarter of a mile. Little could show more emphatically the indifference its makers had for the previous lunar alignments. The northern sides of the avenue's inner bank and ditch cut right through where a midwinter moon post may have stood, eradicating the line as though it had never been.

Not unexpectedly, it was Stukeley on his first visit to Stonehenge who first detected the low banks of the avenue: 'Nor is there the least notice taken of the avenue, tho' the two ditches that formed the outside of it are very visible the whole length.'[32] Today they can just be made out, with the eye of faith, by the thistles that grow more thickly upon them. Inside its banks the avenue was about 40 feet (12 m) wide, running up to the widened entrance, suggesting that the two were contemporary. Two sarsens, B and C and now vanished, were set up on a SW-NE axis in the middle of the avenue between the Heel Stone and the causeway, and there may have been two parallel rows of standing stones lining the inner edges of the banks like megalithic railings. Stone avenues such as that already existed at the nearby circles of Stanton Drew in Somerset and Avebury in north Wiltshire. In 1740, just after the publication of Stukeley's book about Stonehenge, his friend, Roger Gale, wrote rebuking him for not mentioning the stones: 'I think you have omitted a remarkable particular, which is that the avenue up to the chief entrance was formerly planted with great stones, opposite to each other upon the side banks of it.' Gale claimed that they had seen the stoneholes. In 1979–80 surveys were made with technical equipment to trace these filled-in holes, but the results were inconclusive.[33] As neither John Aubrey in 1666 nor Inigo Jones in 1620 saw any stones in the avenue, Aubrey referring only to the Heel Stone, the question must be left unresolved.[34]

Various explanations have been offered as reasons why an avenue should have been constructed: that it provided a dignified processional way for mourners and worshippers; that it commemorated the route by which the bluestones had been brought to Stonehenge; and that it signified a symbolic pathway along which the sun entered the sacred rings.

All may be correct. Many other avenues, stone-lined or formed of earthen banks, are known in these islands and some are connected to stone circles.[35] In such cases, one end of the avenue is frequently close to a river, as is true of Stonehenge near the Avon, suggesting that water had a role in the rites within the rings. It is also not uncommon for the higher end of an avenue or of a single or multiple rows of stones to be adjacent to a burial cairn, an indication that human bones were central to the function of the stones, a conjunction of water and funerary activities in keeping with what has already been claimed for the purpose of Stonehenge. This early section of the avenue – for it was to be extended centuries later – was undeviatingly straight, a masterpiece of landscape surveying. From Stonehenge it pointed directly to that part of the Cursus where there was an entrance gap. It 'proceeds in a straight line towards a valley . . . leading in a gentle curve towards the CURSUS'.[36] Even hundreds of years after it was laid out the Cursus was still to be part of the ceremonies inside Stonehenge.

Nothing in the bluestone phase is more enigmatic than the rectangle of of stones, 91–94, known as the Four Stations, inconspicuous, ignored by most visitors and yet vital to an understanding of what Stonehenge was.

The name was given to them by E.P. Stone in 1923[37] but it derived from observations made by the Rev. Edward Duke in the mid-19th century. Although today only two stones remain, four once stood at the corners of an oblong whose longer sides were arranged NW-SE, each stone erected just within the bank of the henge. Even in John Aubrey's time two had gone. He believed the survivors to be the remnants of an outer circle of stones that had stood in his 'cavities', but Hawley's excavations of the Aubrey Holes disproved this. Those holes had never held stones or posts, and this leads to the eighth of the questions about Stonehenge, why people should have so meticulously placed four stones, not bluestone but sarsen, in a rectangle that neatly contained the bluestone circles.

Today Stone 91 at the ESE, 9 feet (3 m) long, is prostrate, Stone 93 at the WNW is a reshaped stump no more than 4 feet (1.2 m) high, and Stones 92 and 94 have disappeared, their positions overlain by low mounds. Hoare and Cunnington dug into these 'barrows', finding a 'simple interment of burnt bones' in 94[38] where they had unknowingly cut into an Aubrey Hole, and recovering nothing from 92 at the SE. When Hawley re-excavated this 'South Barrow' two facts emerged. A large stone had stood there, its base imprinted in the bottom of a pit 4 feet (1.2 m) deep. Around it a ditch similar to that around the Heel Stone had been trenched, interrupting the edge of Aubrey Hole 19, something not anticipated by the prehistoric diggers 'as the trench had to be deepened in consequence'.[39] The area of this encircling ditch ran round Aubrey Holes 17 to 19 and this suggests not only that Stone 92 was later than the Aubrey Holes and therefore later than phase Ib of Stonehenge but also that the Aubrey Holes were by now so overgrown that they had not been noticed. At the other side of the henge the hole for the missing Stone 94 was found in 1978. It was cleared only to its top, but this was sufficient to show that it too may have cut through an Aubrey Hole, no. 46, the one investigated by Cunnington.

In the early 18th century Stone 91 was still upright, leaning slightly, and Stukeley noticed 'two semi-circular hollows' from which Stones 92 and 94 had been withdrawn before Aubrey's time. In 1740 John Wood remarked on the same two holes, 'one with a simple Bank of Earth about it; and the other with a double Bank separated by a Ditch', perhaps the result of rubble being spaded out during the removal of the stones. Thirty years later John Smith confirmed this: 'Directly north and south of the temple, just within the vallum of the ditch, is the appearance of two circular holes encompassed with the earth that was thrown out of them but they are now almost effaced by time.'[40] It seems likely that the mounds at 92 and 94, reported by later writers and still recognisable today, were no more than upcast trampled down by cattle, sheep, horses and the feet of visitors. E. H. Stone thought so. 92's barrow was 'mostly the soil thrown out by Colt Hoare in making his excavation'.

The date of the Four Stations has not been proved, but there are reasons for believing that the stones were later than Stonehenge 1b. At least two Aubrey Holes already existed when Stones 92 and 94 were put up. Furthermore, where the diagonals of the rectangle intersected, they coincided nicely with the centres of Stonehenge II and III but were 3 feet (1 m) north of the centre of the Aubrey Hole circle. They also crossed within a mere fifth of a degree of the new axis.[41]

So well-placed is this centroid that the Four Stations have been interpreted as a template or surveying-frame for establishing the centre from which the circumferences for the two bluestone rings were to be plotted. Of the regularity of the rectangle, laid out by eye with ropes and staffs over 200 feet (60 m) of uneven turf, there is no doubt, just as the directness of the avenue testified to the skill of its designers. Yet if the Four Stations were no more than corner-stones from which the diagonals intersected at the midpoint of the intended rings, then a square would have been as effective and might have been easier to lay out. It has been claimed, therefore, that the stones were sighting-devices from which astronomical observations were made along the rectangle's long and short sides and along its diagonals, not of 45° from the corners like those of a square but of angles subtly calculated to be in line with the sun or the moon.

This would provide justification for the view that the Four Stations belong to the bluestone phase of Stonehenge. They were later than the Aubrey Holes but had to be earlier than the sarsen circle of Stonehenge III because its high, wide stones would have blocked any sighting across the ring. R.S. Newall, who often dug with Hawley, was perhaps the first to realise this. In his little guidebook, *Stonehenge. Wiltshire*, of 1953 he wrote, 'Since [the diagonals] cannot be seen from each other, their careful planning diametrically opposite each other, suggests that they were earlier than the [sarsen] monument'.

Only in phase II could the diagonals have been used as sightlines with an observer looking over the tops of the bluestones which, with the exception of the Altar Stone, seldom stood more than 5 feet (1.5 m) above the ground, with the higher Station Stones rising above them. Indeed, this might explain why sarsens had been chosen for the Stations, simply because they were longer than the available bluestones.

Wondrous things have been deduced for the Four Stations which have been considered marvels of prehistoric engineering, their positions pinpointed by surveyors with a knowledge of Pythagorean triangles and who incorporated no fewer than thirteen celestial alignments into the rectangle. The fantasia began two hundred years ago when John Smith wrote that the mounds of 92 and 94 were due north and south of each other. Their axis, in fact, was closer to NNW-SSE From this unpromising beginning the astronomy and geometry of the Four Stations have been subjected to elaborate analyses, some of which have been more elaborate than analytical.

It was the Rev. Edward Duke, whose father had delved into several round barrows of the Lake cemetery in Colt Hoare's time, who suggested in 1846 that Stones 91 and 93 were 'astronomic gnomons', like the pin of a sun-dial, to which a priest looked from the observing-platform or 'station' of the mounds at 92 and 94. Standing at 92 he would have seen the midsummer sun rise over Stone 91 whose top was level with the horizon. Six months later, standing on 94's station, the astronomer would have observed 'at the winter solstice, the setting sun descend exactly behind' Stone 93.[42]

To the astronomy geometry was added. In 1880 Flinders Petrie, having completed the first accurate survey of Stonehenge, noted that the diagonals of the Four Stations 'cross each other at $45° ± 6'$, or just half a right angle. . . . This also shows that the circle was divided into sixteenths, or $22\frac{1}{2}°$, as each diameter is $^1/_{16}$ from the right angles to the axis, or $^3/_{16}$ from the axis'.[43]

Twenty years after Petrie Sir Norman Lockyer made a special study of Stonehenge in which he attempted to date the monument from astronomical computations. Amongst other considerations he suggested that from the centre of the circle May Day sunset would have been seen over Stone 93 and the early November sunrise over Stone 91, respectively the dates of the Celtic festivals of Beltane and Samain. It was not implausible that alignments on such solemn calendrical events should have been built into a ritual centre like Stonehenge. Lockyer's thesis, based on some misconceptions, was ridiculed by archaeologists. 'To attempt to produce the date from the axis of Stonehenge is to argue in a circle.'[44]

However witty the criticisms, non-archaeologists continued to examine the Stations, seeking explanations for them, sometimes coming to convincing conclusions that were founded on treacherous evidence. In 1966 the car park at Stonehenge was extended and three enormous postholes were discovered. Their tops are now painted white at the lower end of the area. 'Peter' Newham, scholar and retired Gas Board manager, who for years had puzzled over the complexities of Stonehenge, thought they had been distant sighting-posts 'in line with important setting phenomena of sun and moon when observed from the four Stations and Heel Stone positions'. Identifying alignments to the midsummer sunset, the major northern moonset and to the midpoint between the moon's northernmost settings, he added that 'these can be considered as the most positive "astronomical" discovery yet made at Stonehenge'. It was the present writer who had to point out that there were two unpublished radiocarbon dates for the postholes, one of $6140±140$ bc, the other of $7180±180$ bc, long before Stonehenge, in the Middle Stone Age when Salisbury Plain was covered with coniferous forest. Not surprisingly, the wood from the holes was not oak, so widespread in the Neolithic, but pine, the trees that had flourished in the Mesolithic period.[45]

It was in 1966 also that Gerald Hawkins' *Stonehenge Decoded* was published in Britain. Having developed and checked ideas first put forward in 1963, and using not only the Four Stations but the circle-centre and Holes G and H that Hawley had considered pits left by trees or bushes, Hawkins proposed nine individual alignments to solar and lunar risings and settings.[46] Ten years later Dibble observed that the Station rectangle would split into two right-angle triangles which were 'close to 5, 12, 13 Pythagorean right triangles'.[47]

Thirteen alignments, accurate subdivisions of a circle, right-angled triangles, they are all correct and nearly all quite unintended by the people who put up the stones. The entire problem comes from the elementary fact that at the latitude of Stonehenge the midsummer sunrise and the major northerly moonset occur virtually at right-angles to each other. Because of this, when people at Stonehenge included two simple alignments in their new circle they constructed a 'marvel of geometry and astronomy' without being aware of it.

It appears that they wanted one sightline to the most northerly moonset and another to the May Day sunset, the occasion of a vigorous pastoral festival later to be known as Beltane. Although the procedure they adopted will never be certainly known, a reconstruction can be attempted. There were four simple stages (Fig. 10).

(1) They put up a post at what they believed to be the centre of the earthwork. They were in error by about 3 feet (1 m).

(2) From this post they observed the May sun at the WNW and erected a second post, just inside the bank, in line with its setting. This would be the position of Station 93.

(3) Using '93' as a backsight and the centre post as a foresight, they set up a third post on the far side of the henge at the ESE. This would be Station 91.

(4) From there they aligned on the major northern moonset at the NW. The post they raised there would later be replaced by Station 94. No measurements were needed, no protractors were used, just posts, human eyes and the moon and sun.

Little more was required except that, perhaps for the sake of completeness, a fourth post was raised at 92, as far from 91 as 93 was from 94, and as far from 93 as 94 was from 91. Despite over-enthusiastic claims for the geometry of this 'rectangle' it was far from exact. No two sides matched. Clockwise from 91 they measured 112.1 feet, 262.2 ft, 107.3 ft and 263.3 ft (34.2, 79.9, 32.7, 80.3 m). The 'right angles' are almost as bad, being 89° 25′, 89° 33′, 91° 2′ and 90° 1′,[48] considerable deviations from an 'ideal' rectangle of 90° corners and with sides of 263.3 × 109.7 feet (80.3 × 33.4 m).

The lengths of the short sides show that the Four Stations were not intended merely to stand at the ends of diagonals whose intersection fixed the centre of the new bluestone rings. The outermost of those circles was only 86 feet (26.2 m) across, not the 110 feet (33.5 m) width of the Four Stations. The same objection would apply to the 97 feet (29.6 m) diameter

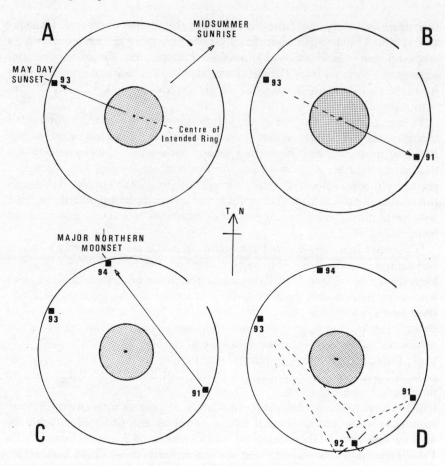

Fig. 10. The possible construction of the Four Stations.

of the sarsen circle of the third phase of Stonehenge. The width of the Four Stations setting had little to do with those diameters. A rectangle 263 feet (80.2 m) long and 86 feet wide would have had a WNW diagonal at an angle of 18° from its long side, or if 97 feet wide, an angle of about 20°. Neither of these was appropriate. By an astronomical chance, and quite unrealised by the men laying out the Four Stations, an alignment to May Day sunset in the latitude of Stonehenge produced an angle of 22½° and for this the short sides of the rectangle had to be about 110 feet long.

Once permanent stones replaced the corner-posts of this uncomplicated near-oblong everything else followed. The two simple sightlines, one to the moon, the other to the May sun, by chance subtended an angle of about 22½° between them, explaining Petrie's contention that the circle had deliberately been divided into 16 equal parts (16 × 22½ = 360°), something never imagined by the builders. Because the major northern moonset, on which the long sides of the rectangle were aligned, happened to occur almost at right-angles to the midsummer sunrise the short sides of the rectangle had to point towards that event and, in reverse, rather imprecisely to the midwinter sunset. Because it was nearly a rectangle it inevitably also formed two Pythagorean triangles even though that Greek mathematician would not be born for another 1600 years.

In the bluestone phase of Stonehenge there were three straighforward, rather casual alignments, one to the midsummer sunrise with the Heel Stone and the axis fairly well in line with it; one to the major northern moonset, again not exactly set out; and a third to the May Day sunset, in error by almost a degree.[49] It was good enough for the people. They were not astronomers searching for a means of predicting eclipses but men and women engaged in rituals of life and death in which the sun and moon were essential.

This was a transitional time. From the Late Neolithic onwards, orientations towards the rising of celestial bodies, so commonplace in the chambered tombs and earthen long barrows of previous centuries, would give way to alignments towards their settings, and ceremonies would be held not in the light of dawn but in the darkening of night, lit by the flames of burning torches.

Other megalithic 'rectangles' are known, in southern Britain and Brittany, and these also may have been orientation-devices to record an astronomical event or a cardinal point. One at Mattocks Down on Exmoor is now almost destroyed but a description in 1630 spoke of two stones 147 feet (44.8 m) apart, and 66 feet (20 m) to the north there were 23 other stones 'in a straight and equal line . . . equally proportioned, but double as long in length than square and more (which, as I am told, is called a Parallelogram)'. The longer sides were reportedly WNW-ESE, but lacking good information we can make no deduction from this.[50] Other possible quadrilaterals on Exmoor are associated with Bronze Age round barrows, 'as at Chapman Barrows, where a stone quadrilateral has a stone in the middle and an outlier'.[51]

In the British Isles such settings seem confined to south-western Britain. On Bodmin Moor there is a well-preserved example at King Arthur's Hall where there is an oblong of closely-set stones which, alternately tall and short, line the inner edges of a rectangular earthwork with a possible entrance in its SW corner and aligned almost exactly N-S. Nothing more is known of this unusual site except that it exists in a region of several stone circles such as the Trippet Stones, Fernacre and Stannon and close to some early prehistoric settlements.[52]

Its surveyor, A.L. Lewis, was reminded of apparently related structures in Brittany, also with gaps at their corners and associated with rites of human cremation. Perhaps the closest comparisons to the Four Stations are to be found there, a thought all the more interesting because of other evidence of Breton influence in the later phases of Stonehenge. A square enclosure once stood at Lanvéoc on the Crozon peninsula, and at Morgat nearby there was a double line of large and small stones reminiscent of those at King Arthur's Hall, paired together around a rectangular core. Another rectangle with a row of menhirs down its centre was known on the Île d'Ouessant, an island almost within sight of Britain. 'From Ushant to Scilly is thirty-five leagues.'

All these sites have been ravaged for their stones and nothing remains of them, but at Crucuno, 3 miles NW of Carnac in the Morbihan, a magnificent rectangle has survived, protected by the gorse and bramble impenetrably bristling in and around it. It was ruinous in the 19th century but was restored in 1883. So well were the long sides arranged E-W that the validity of the reconstruction was questioned, but there are several reasons for believing that Gaillard did not 'improve' the monument. It was elegantly proportioned, its sides of spaced stones measuring 108 feet 7 inches × 81 feet 7 inches (33.2 × 24.9 m) which the Thoms pointed out were the equivalents of 40 × 30 Megalithic Yards of 2.72 feet.

Looking westwards from the eastern corner stones, the long sides would have indicated the equinoctial sunsets in March and September, and the same would have been true, although less neatly, of the sunrises in the opposite direction Charrière calculated, moreover, that the Crucuno diagonals were designed to point to the risings and settings of the sun both at midsummer and midwinter and this was corroborated, with some reservations, by the Thoms' survey.[53] They added that it was also possible 'that the moon in its eight "standstill" positions was indicated', although Crucuno, 'unless it had foresights some distance away, could never have been more than a symbolic observatory'. If the lines, as at the Four Stations, were less for men to look along than for the sun or moon to travel into the rectangle, there would have been no need for longer alignments.

Crucuno, spacious and open to the sky, was erected in an area in which there were several earlier megalithic tombs, all with rectangular burial chambers: in the hamlet of Crucuno itself; at Mané Groh and at Mané Bras.[54] It was a transmutation from cramped, dark burial-place to larger, lighter ceremonial centre, a metamorphosis already suggested for Stonehenge, an association with death and with the sun and moon contained in a structure that continually changed and yet always remained the same. Nothing was separate. Everything was part of the world just as it was with American Indians.

> The whole universe is sacred, man is the whole universe, and the religious ceremony is life itself. Every morning, prayers are offered to the sun, earth, and the powers of the four directions, the water that brings life, and the Creator: this earth teaches us, takes care of us, and nothing is wasted, even the common clay.[55]

The same world-picture may have enriched the minds of the Beaker and native groups who were raising the stones at Stonehenge. The sightlines were laid out, the Four Stations were set in place, maybe only after years of observations to ensure their accuracy, and the bluestone circles were begun, were three-quarters finished, and then the work stopped. Why is not known. There could have been disagreement and conflict between adherents of the lunar and solar cults, never more than uneasily co-operating. Beaker dominance may have become as resented as that of the grooved ware zealots before them. Maybe, after seeing the gigantic sarsens at Avebury, it was decided that the bluestones were too small, no more than midgets in the open spaces of Salisbury Plain. Whatever the cause, Stonehenge was rebuilt. When it was finished many of the sightlines had gone.

# 8

## Early Chieftains in a landscape
## 2000 – 1500 BC

*Round about Stoneheng one may number 43, or 45, Barrowes, some much bigger than others.*

John Aubrey, *Monumenta Britannica, I,* 83

*bush-barrow, a barrow planted by the shepherds. 'Tis south of* Stonehenge, *and commands a pleasant prospect of the temple, the* cursus, *the avenue, and of all the barrows arounds this plain.*

William Stukeley, *Stonehenge,* 46

The age was deceitful. Seen from a distance it was like the sea, calm and enticing but, closer, eddies and waves and tidal-races were visible in society. Nothing was still. People changed. There were conflicts and alliances, inventions and archaisms, sudden movements and years of stagnation. Life, like a creeping vine, retained its roots, but its growing tendrils twisted and turned, spread wide, overshadowed the lower, older leaves.

Around 2000 BC men removed the unfinished rings of bluestones from Stonehenge. Work-gangs supervised the dragging of ponderous sarsens from the Marlborough Downs miles away to the north. Perhaps in cold, dry winters when the ground was hard teams of oxen were led across the plain, hauling stones yard by yard over the slopes, across the frozen, shallow streams, heads down, slowly, dully plodding towards the henge where the pillars would be shaped and raised and where many still stand today in an edifice like a gaunt, wrecked cage of Time.

The change was not the work of Beaker communities. Since the years when the owners of those pots had assumed leadership, their power had diminished, partly through the mixing and intermarrying of their descendants with the people of Salisbury Plain. As the years passed there was a resurgence of local traditions a return to old ideas as the intrusive influences weakened and were modified and absorbed. By 2000 BC all that remained of Beaker glory, like sparklets of flame in a dying fire, was the making of pots, similar to the early vessels but less well-shaped, with taller cylindrical necks, lavishly but clumsily decorated by native women. 'Whereas a circle of thirty-five miles radius, centred on Stonehenge, formerly included thirty-eight Developed Southern beaker sites', of about the time when the building of the bluestone rings was abandoned, 'the same area now includes only six Late Southern beakers . . .'.[1]

What yesterday had been an article of prestige today was old-fashioned, the relic of an outworn cult. Grooved ware had gone, beakers were disappearing. In place of them and their wristguards, little bronze knives and flint arrowheads, now, at the beginning of the Early Bronze Age, chieftains coveted vicious bronze daggers, metal axes, helmets, shields, stone battle-axes, and the luxurious superiority of ornaments of gold and amber, belt-fittings and spiralled pins, ostentatious military equipment and brightly-coloured trinkets that they took with them to the grave. Burials with beakers were outmoded. It was not a drinking-vessel that dead leaders wanted by their side but weapons and finery. During this re-emergence of native customs it was the warrior chieftain who dominated, pompously accoutred in emulation of the 'dagger-princes' in Brittany whose way of life was the envy of leaders in southern Britain.

Burials of the early beaker period had avoided the ancient long barrows as though they were to be feared. Now the new Wessex Chieftains were interred under round barrows that crowded around the old burial-places in cemeteries that expanded over the centuries, reaffirming a return to the land of the forefathers. By a prehistoric irony some late beakers have been found in the long barrows themselves, inserted in the Neolithic mound at Figheldean 31 2½ miles NNW of Stonehenge and at Wilsford South 34 whose barrow, like that at Thickthorn Down in Dorset, 'may have been [deliberately] raised to house the beaker burials set along their axes: they could conveniently be called "over-grave" long barrows'.[2]

Such secondary burials may be indicative of a loss of status, even of the sacrifice of some beaker users. For the emergent native leaders it was a round barrow covering a grave-pit that was demanded, not the low, tiny barrows of previous centuries, but swelling domes of chalk as much as thirty long paces across, the height of two men, sometimes surrounded by an earlier ditch and outer bank. It was as though a sacred circle had been laid out to safeguard the grave and its corpse before the final, imprisoning barrow was piled up.

Nor were the dead the short, gracile men of Neolithic times. More often they were tall, large-boned figures, so much so that medieval treasure-hunters believed the skeletons were those of giants. Colt Hoare often remarked on the size of the human bones Cunnington had disinterred. Stukeley was told that a few miles south of Stonehenge labourers had found 'in a barrow between Woodford and Lake a scull so large that it was kept in Wilford church upon the bier for many years as a sight'.[3] As early as 1538 Sir Thomas Elyot, the Tudor scholar, remembered 'about fifty years since, I myself, being with my father, Sir Richard Elyot, at a monesterie of regular Canons (three or four miles from Stonage) beheld the bones of a dead man, found deep in the ground; which being joyned together, was in length 13 feet and 10 inches; whereof one of the teeth my father had, which was of the quantity of a great wallnut. This I have written because some men will believe nothing, that is out of the compass of their knowledge.'[4]

Such claims, of course, were exaggerated. There were no Goliaths or Fee-Fi-Fo-Fums in the British Bronze Age and physical differences may have developed only slowly over the years between 4000 and 2000 BC. Nevertheless, there is a contrast between the taller, heavier people of the Early Bronze Age and the slighter men and women of the Neolithic. The leaders in Wessex were big men in any meaning of the words. An excavation by Cunnington in 1808 revealed an especially impressive example.

Less than a quarter of a mile west of Stonehenge is an unmetalled track, tolerable for sturdy cars and walkers. To the north, across the A344, it leads to Larkhill Barracks. Southwards, beyond the A303, it continues half a rutted mile to a low ridge on Normanton Down. Further on it becomes a footpath sloping down to the A30 and the anachronistic Druid's Lodge. It is the ridge that matters.

From the A303 the track, grassy and uneven, falls very gently then rises quietly, its sides lined with open barbed-wire fencing in an airy countryside of long broad fields. Halfway up the slope a copse on the right has a handsome round barrow by it, Amesbury 15, 'the most beautifully bell-shaped barrow in the plain of Stonehenge'.[5] Farther on still, at the top of the ridge and to the left, there is another large barrow, Wilsford South 5, wire-fenced, and flat-topped where Cunnington plunged a shaft down into it. It is, perhaps, the most important of all the important round barrows on Salisbury Plain for this may have been the burial-place of a man who ordered and organised the building of the sarsen circles at Stonehenge.

His barrow stands on solemn ground. Today sheep graze on it, safely, peacefully, but this was once the place of a great cemetery whose line of barrows still extends eastwards with the overgrown, inconspicuous long barrow of Wilsford South 13 near its centre. Of the round barrows in this Normanton group there are simple 'bowls' without surrounding ditches, and there are the peculiar 'fancy' barrows of Wessex, 'bells' with encircling ditches and banks, a twin-bell near the middle, a 'saucer' at the far end like an upturned plate, and several 'discs', spacious banked rings with a flat interior at the heart of which is a diminutive mound. Two of these skirt the track by the great round barrow.

Stukeley saw it, 'what I call the bush barrow by the country people the green barrow',[6] where blue-flowered heathers 'exhaled the sweetest smell imaginable much like a honey comb and very strong'. Eighty-five years later, on July 11, 1808, William Cunnington delved into this now-famous Bush Barrow with no success. Two months later he returned, without Sir Richard Colt Hoare who was ill with a migraine, and instructed his labourers to dig down from the top in the usual manner until they neared the level of the natural soil.[7] It was a hit-or-miss method no modern excavator would consider employing, but on this occasion Cunnington achieved a spectacular triumph.[8]

On the old ground surface, lying on its back was the skeleton of 'a stout and tall man lying from south to north: the extreme length of his thigh bone was 20 inches'. To the south of his head were rivets and bits of bronze and wood, most probably the decomposed remains of a wooden-framed helmet. By his right shoulder was a bronze axe that had rested on some woollen textile, perhaps on a fold of the man's cloak or on a blanket underneath the body. Fragments of the axe's wooden handle survived in the chalk.

The axe was not alone. There were other prestigious weapons. By the man's right forearm were two daggers side by side, one of copper that had been in a wooden, leather-lined sheath, another of bronze, heavier and a full foot (33 cm) long with a central midrib to give it added strength. These were killing blades. They were also attractive. Part of one of their wooden pommels was preserved. It was ornamented in a design that 'could not be surpassed (if indeed equalled) by the most able workman of modern times'. On it were zigzag patterns 'formed with a labour and exactness almost unaccountable, by thousands of gold rivets, smaller than the smallest pin'. So fine and hairlike were these slivers of gold that Cunnington almost missed them. John Parker, one of his most experienced diggers, 'with his trowel had scattered them in every direction before I had examined them with a glass'.[9]

It was filigree work of almost incredible precision, the craftsman perhaps using crystal or quartz as a magnifying glass to ensure the accurate positioning of each pin. Near the daggers a gold 'belt-hook' was just as artistically created. With convex sides and concave top and bottom, this gold foil plaque was engraved in a series of curving lines that gracefully followed the contour of the plate, lines that had been incised by a hand that had never wavered during the operation. Although this lovely object had a hook, attached by hammering two pieces of gold together, presumably for a belt or a scabbard, 'the excellent condition of the piece as a whole suggests that [it] was never used'.[10]

Under the fingers of the man's right hand was an article, probably a third dagger, 'so much corroded that it broke to pieces on moving'. On the man's chest and originally attached by thread to his woven tunic was a thin, hand-sized lozenge of gold. Its face had been engraved with the outlines of four more lozenges, one within the other. A similar but much smaller gold-foil lozenge was found by the man's right hand. Near it was all that was left of a sceptre or macehead, the head composed of a rare, flecked limestone from Devon, perforated and polished into a smooth egg-shape. Its shaft had perished, but six short cylinders of bone were recovered, each of them dentated like a wolf's teeth and intended as mountings to be set equidistantly along the handle of the sceptre.

The daggers, the axe, the sceptre, the exquisitely fashioned gold pieces, the woven cloth, the enormity of the barrow itself, they all testify to the high status of the person buried under Bush Barrow. And, despite the 4000 years since the man's death, the results of recent archaeological research have added even more information about him and the changes at Stonehenge.

Amongst the hundreds of round barrows in southern England there are fewer than twenty that can be considered rich in terms of goldwork. The majority of them are on Salisbury Plain and in north Wiltshire in the heartland of Wessex.[11] Seldom occurring together in one cemetery, they are considered dynastic tombs, the burial-places of powerful chieftains or princelings in a heroic age where authority was obtained through warfare and manifested through the display of exotic and unique regalia.

A single golden grave was usually sufficient to establish the prestige of its family. There is only an isolated instance of a cemetery with more than one rich barrow. Close to Bush Barrow in the Normanton Down group were two other burials with gold. There was the bowl barrow of Wilsford South 7 with a gold-wrapped shale bead, shale and amber pendants, pieces of sheet gold and two tubular fossils like minute concertinas and perforated for beading. These may have been the possessions of a woman. So too may the articles in the adjacent bell barrow of Wilsford South 8. Here, with a cremation, was the cornucopia of a gold-bound amber pendant, a gold-covered shale button and bone pendant, six amber pendants, two perforated, circular gold-bound amber discs and a gold-sheathed bronze pendant like a miniature neck-ring. There was also a low pot with open-ribbed sides like a 'present from Stonehenge' bought at the shrine by a gullible pilgrim. 'No barrow that we have yet opened has ever produced such a variety of singular and elegant articles', wrote Colt Hoare.[12] Standing as they do only two hundred yards (180 m) from Bush Barrow, the existence of two other lavishly-provided barrows suggests that the occupants of the Normanton cemetery, their burial-mounds conspicuous on a ridge overlooking Stonehenge and clearly visible from there, may well have been the most privileged of all the families on Salisbury Plain, and one in which women were not excluded from high rank.

The origins of the objects from Bush Barrow are, indirectly, very informative about the sarsen structures at Stonehenge. The decoration on the gold and the combination of gold and amber is native workmanship and can be likened to other objects from Little Cressingham and Bircham in East Anglia. As amber from the Baltic was probably washed onto the east coast of England by the currents of the North Sea, it seems likely that Wessex gold was exchanged for East Anglian amber and that both materials were shaped and decorated locally. Indeed, so similar is the gold-working technique on jewellery found at Upton Lovell and Manton in north Wiltshire, at Bush Barrow and at Clandon near Maiden Castle in Dorset, that all the pieces may have been made by one master craftsman working in Wessex itself. This, however, is not true of the Bush Barrow bone mounts and the gold-pinned pommel. These were derived from influences in Brittany, and part of the design of the new Stonehenge also was inspired by Breton architecture.

Connections between Wessex and Brittany have already been indicated by the similarity between the Station Stones at Stonehenge and the Crucuno rectangle near Carnac. By the Early Bronze Age other likenesses were shared by the two regions: rich 'dagger-graves' and the burial of corpses under huge mounds whose size, perhaps, was inspired by the monstrous Carnac Mounds of earlier times with their opulent offerings. With many graves, also, there was sheet-gold; triangular bronze daggers; the use of gold pins not only for ornamentation but for the practical purpose of holding gold-foil firmly in place on the pitch that coated the dagger's hilt; and dentated mountings to embellish the haft of a mace.

Dagger-graves were not uncommon in western Brittany, lying beneath mountainous cairns anywhere from the Morbihan in the south up to the Côte-du-Nord 160 miles south of Wessex across the Channel. The weapons in them, rivetted bronze daggers, some flat, some with a midrib, and known prosaically as Armorico-British A and B, closely resemble the pair from Bush Barrow. At Lescongar in south-west Brittany chemicals in the soil had so blanched the weapons that at first they were believed to be bone imitations of proper bronze daggers. Such weapons testify to the development of a warrior caste in the centuries around 2000 BC both in Brittany and Wessex.

There is a cluster of Breton dagger-graves in the north around Lannion. There, under a well-preserved tumulus at La Motta two miles west of the city and close to the sea, a strange 'box' of gold-foil was found in 1939, decorated as skilfully as the Wessex plaques.[13] Gold-studded pommels are almost abundant in Brittany, indeed may have been created there around Lannion. They are known from Kergourognon, Mouden-Bras, Tossen-Maharit and other barrows in the north. At Kernonen, 10 miles south of Roscoff on the north coast, a burial-vault held boxes of daggers and superbly chipped flint arrowheads, three of the daggers having hilts geometrically patterned with gold pins so fine that a thousand of them would have weighed less than one-tenth of an ounce (1.7 gr).[14]

From northern Brittany across the Channel to the Needles and the mouth of the Avon was a voyage of two or three days in favourable weather. In their wooden-ribbed boats, lined with skins like the Irish curraghs and with long, lifting bows, capable of carrying a crew of nine or ten, men had safely been crossing the northern seas for centuries. In his *Ora Maritima* the late Roman poet Rufus Festus Avienus specifically mentioned seamen from north-west Brittany and their boats:

Skilled and adroit, perpetually employed
In trafficking on ships not built, but sewn. . . .
Nor yet of firwood do they curve a craft

But wondrous fit together skins and hides
On which to sail across the vasty deep.

In the National Museum of Wales in Cardiff there is actually a little
model of such a boat. Known as the Caergwyle bowl, it is made of oakwood
inlaid with gold foil. It has patterns of round shields hanging from its
gunnels, oars below them, waves etched in zigzags along its keel and pairs
of 'eyes' to guide it to its haven. Carvings of what appear to be similar
vessels can be seen on the sideslabs of some Breton passage-graves. Flexible,
light and easily dragged ashore, craft like this carried not only men, copper
and tin but also ideas and traditions between Brittany and Britain. Trade
in metals and rich articles led to alliances and the exchange of gifts, and
the splendours and rituals of one region were imitated and surpassed in
another as Bronze Age society blossomed into ever greater displays of
wealth and power.

The probability of links between Wessex and Brittany is further enhanced
by the presence in the megalithic tomb of Kerlagat, 3 miles north-east of
Carnac, of four gold plaques, dentated like wolves' teeth, flat when excavated but intended to be rolled around a macehead shaft like the dentated
bone mounts at Bush Barrow. These and the daggers and the gold pins
demonstrate the Breton-Wessex associations during the years when
Stonehenge was undergoing its sarsen transformation.

Because of these connections it was once believed that Wessex had
actually been invaded by aristocratic warriors from Brittany, but this is no
longer accepted. There are too many native and too few Breton objects in
the rich Wessex graves for such an incursion to be credible. There is a
simpler explanation.

The Early Bronze Age was a bustling time when the novelty of metal
caused an outburst of exploration into the far ends and backwaters of the
British Isles. Men prospected for copper and tin and gold, finding the
lodes, smashing the rocks that bore them, transporting the ores to industrial
centres where smiths practised their mysteries. Brittany had tin. Cornwall
had tin and copper. Ireland had copper in the south-west counties of Cork
and Kerry where miners drove galleries into the slopes of cupriferous hills,
and eastern Ireland had gold in the Wicklow Mountains. Boats carried the
ore-rich rocks to other parts of Ireland and Scotland where the metals were
smelted and cast in flat moulds to make the axes and daggers and halberds
that leaders craved. Then the finished weapons were taken along the rivers
and trackways and the sea-crossings to Yorkshire and the Peak District
and Wessex, with movement and contact everywhere, and regions once
scarcely known to each other were suddenly linked by this eruption of
search, travel and trade.

Beautiful crescent-moons of beaten gold known as lunulae were manufactured in Ireland and were almost restricted to that country. Such lovely
objects were never popular amongst beaker communities. Although these

lunulae were decorated with the motifs of later 'Southern' beakers in Wessex, none has been found there. Several, however, are known from northern Brittany. 'This concentration linking Ireland to Brittany illustrates the recurring pattern of contact that continued throughout the Bronze Age.'[15]

In reverse, customs from Brittany touched Ireland as well as Wessex. In the west, in Cork and Kerry and counties to their north, late megalithic tombs were built that were almost identical to others in the north of the Armorican peninsula of which Brittany forms the greater part. Late in the Breton Neolithic *allées-couvertes* were constructed, long, rectangular and roofed galleries of stone slabs rising in height towards the north-west, sometimes with carvings of metal axes and daggers or spears in the burial-chamber. In Ireland such tombs were reproduced in the wedge-graves of the west, lying close to the areas where copper was to be found. 'We have previously stated that the *allées-couvertes* of Brittany provide excellent prototypes for the Irish wedge-tombs. . . . The finds . . . indicate a Late Neolithic-early Bronze Age date for the Breton tombs and support the view that these monuments are ancestral to the Irish series.'[16]

In a different way Wessex also was affected, though only slightly in its monuments, for this was a region already well-populated and with strong traditions of its own. But its native leaders greedily adopted the concepts of princely equipment and elaborate burial ceremonies that were long-established in Brittany. It was imitation, not invasion. But it led to the creation of the 'Wessex Culture' with its military gear and its obsession with burials under massive round barrows, inhumations rather than cremations at first, and with the luxurious grave-goods of daggers and small bronze axes, sheets of gold foil, amber, fine stone battle-axes, necklaces of animal teeth and tusks, and tiny 'grape-cups' with nodules of clay all over the surface.

It was an age of grandiloquence, more monumental than mystic, and, fittingly, it was the time when the towering sarsens of Stonehenge were set up, tall as trees, thicker, capped with lintels that themselves were heavier than the bluestones, a dark circle that was visible for miles in the landscape around it. It was dominant and it was meant to be seen and to impress.

The man under Bush Barrow may have intended this. We shall never know if he was the architect or the impresario who supervised the raising of the stones, but there were unusual aspects to his burial. He lay on his back, his feet stretched out in front of him, and he was not in the customary crouched position of most of his contemporaries, his head to the south rather than the normal north. 'In some tribes, when the head is placed south and the feet north, the deceased is in fact orientated to look north at the land of the dead, for this is the position which he will be facing when he rises up.'[17] In Christian burials the head is to the west so that the dead will sit up and look eastwards at the Day of Judgement, but their priests have their heads to the east so that, when the last trumpet sounds, they will rise and face their flocks. A similar wish may have been the reason for the man in the Normanton cemetery having his head to the south, eternally gazing northwards to his own temple of everlasting stone.

Before his time there may have been a long period of struggle and uncertainty between rival groups, with the construction of the bluestones halted as conflicts spread and hindered further work. During those forgotten years people began, diffidently, to re-use the old burial-grounds, heaping up round barrows near but never very close to the long barrows. From the custom of taking the dead to Stonehenge for a ritual lying-in may have developed the practice of digging out smaller circles of earth and chalk, ditched and banked, in which the dead would remain for the period of mourning before their barrow was piled up over them, its great bowl shape surrounded by the earlier bank and ditch to form a 'fancy' Wessex bell-barrow.

This tentative process of returning to the grave-lands of the forefathers can still be seen less than two miles to the west of Stonehenge. There, the fine lines of round barrows near the Winterbourne Stoke crossroads extend north-eastwards from the primary mound of the long barrow in which Thurnam discovered the rough phallus of flint, like a bludgeon, and the single burial of an old man. A full hundred of more feet (30 m) from it were the earliest round barrows, the simple bowls of Winterbourne Stoke 10 and 13,[18] the first with one skeleton, perhaps buried with a beautiful cushion macehead like the one from Stonehenge, the second with two skeletons, side by side in a large grave, buried with two 'Developed Southern' (S2) beakers whose tall, cylindrical necks showed that they were native wares of around 2100 BC.

This early phase of what is known as the Overton period saw the waning of Beaker influence. Flint arrowheads became rare, wristguards were no longer made, and bronze everywhere took the place of copper. Now Beaker burials were often accompanied by artisan tools of flint, stone, bone and antler, indications that the status of the beaker had declined. In richer graves great battle-axes became common. 'Evidently the manufacture of maceheads, which were perhaps eventually intended to be ornamental rather than functional, was abandoned in favour of the later form of battle-axe. . . .'[19] New axe-factories, Group XII at Cwm Mawr in Shropshire, Group XVIII at the Whin Sill in northern Britain, extracted stone suitable for perforating and shaping into those brutal weapons, picrite in Shropshire, quartz dolerite in Yorkshire, and their products were distributed widely in Britain. Battle-axes from as far away as Cornwall, Wales and Yorkshire reached Wessex, at Bulford, Codford St Peter, Shrewton, Tidworth, Upton Lovell, at Wilsford and near Woodhenge, showing that such fearsome Early Bronze Age war-gear was supplanting the lighter, lovelier maceheads of the late Neolithic. It was an aggressive age and in it things were bigger, more flamboyant, the battle-axes, the daggers, the barrows of the élite.

By the time that Bush Barrow was built at the beginning of the Bronze Age, cemeteries of round barrows were developing around Stonehenge, some near long barrows, others in previously unoccupied locations. Even today, 4000 years later and after generations of weathering and ploughing, the rows and clusters of these mounds still ripple the landscape, sited on ridges and near the heads of slopes in the vast burial-ground that the eastern part of Salisbury Plain was becoming. Over the centuries, however, the barrows have changed. Once chalk-white with sloping sides and flat tops like lampshades, they are now furred with grass and smoothed by rain, wind and snow into green domes, sinking and mellowing into the countryside from which they came.

Most of them are ordinary 'bowls', but there are also Wessex 'fancy' barrows including some bells, each of them high, broad and cut off from the profane world by its encircling ditch and outer bank. These were the burial-places of powerful men. Later, the female counterparts of these barrows were the 'discs', tiny mounds inside a wide ring. There were also low saucer barrows, the tombs of less privileged women, and there were 'ponds' scooped into the ground, late, uncommon and more probably ceremonial than sepulchral (Table 13).

Over the long years of the second millennium some cemeteries grew, others were abandoned. Scattered on the plain between them were solitary barrows, some of them the sad, silent memorials to forgotten chieftains whose successors had died out or had been killed in the cattle-raiding and feuding of the times. Other families flourished and in their cemeteries was every kind of barrow. 'The manner in which disc-barrows occur with round barrows of bell, bowl and other types in most barrow cemeteries in Wessex makes it abundantly clear that all types in each cemetery are, as it were, normally of the same dynasty. . . .'[20]

None of them is near Stonehenge, never closer than a respectful half-mile or more to the circle. To the west are the two Winterbourne Stoke groups. To the north, near the end of the Cursus, is a line of bells and to their west is a muddle of bowls with one huge bell, Amesbury 55, beyond them, perhaps the founding barrow of the group and 'the monarch of the plain, being evidently the largest barrow upon it'.[21] Despite its impressive appearance, Cunnington twice failed to find human remains there.

To the north-east of Stonehenge, on rising ground overlooking the sarsen rings, are the tree-shadowed lines of the Old King and New King barrows, most of them bowls. To the south is the rich Normanton group and beyond it on higher ground is a collection of mounds near the gigantic Lake long barrow. Further away still are the lesser-known cemeteries of Wilsford South and Lake Down, the latter with no fewer than five pond barrows near one small disc.

**TABLE 13. Barrow types in the cemeteries around Stonehenge**

| Group | Bowls | Bells | Discs | Saucers | Ponds | Totals |
|---|---|---|---|---|---|---|
| Cursus | 13 | 7 | 0 | 0 | 0 | 20 |
| Lake | 14 | 4 | 2 | 0 | 0 | 20 |
| Lake Down | 10 | 0 | 1 | 0 | 5 | 16 |
| New King | 5 | 2 | 0 | 0 | 0 | 7 |
| Normanton | 13 | 5 | 7 | 1 | 0 | 26 |
| Old King | 9 | 0 | 0 | 0 | 0 | 9 |
| Snail Down | 18 | 5 | 2 | 1 | 1 | 27 |
| Wilsford South | 10 | 1 | 5 | 1 | 0 | 17 |
| Winterbourne Stoke. Crossroads | 19 | 2 | 2 | 2 | 2 | 27 |
| Winterbourne Stoke. West | 7 | 0 | 3 | 1 | 1 | 12 |
| TOTALS | 118 | 26 | 22 | 6 | 9 | 181 |

Barrows are the main source of information about the beliefs and way of life of prehistoric people in Britain and it is regrettable that so much of their contents has been forgotten or lost through the inadequate reports of early excavations. Ever since medieval times barrows have been plundered for treasure, something which has not stopped in these days of metal-detectors. A sketch of 1575 shows tracks intersecting inside Stonehenge with Elizabethan sightseers pointing at the ruin and two labourers digging into a barrow at the west, a skull by their feet 'wher great bones of men ar fownd'. Lucas de Heere, a Dutchman who copied the drawing a few years later, recorded that 'one finds here-about many small hillocks or monticules, under which sometimes are giants' bones (of which I possess one) from which it can easily be perceived that the giant was as much as twelve feet tall. . . '. As an historical aside, it is just possible that de Heere engraved his name on trilithon 53, 'IOH: LUD: DEFERRE'. It is still visible today.[22]

Digging into barrows continued through the 17th and 18th centuries, usually without record. Stukeley bemoaned the destruction that was taking place, at Avebury for the stones, on Salisbury Plain for the land. 'More southerly all the hill-tops, as far as the eye reaches, are covered with an incredible number of Celtic barrows. . . . So foolishly greedy are the country people of an inch of ground, that they have levelled several barrows lately in the neighbourhood, which cost more than the spot they covered will pay in fifty years.'[23] To his own credit, when he dug into a barrow he not only described what he found but also made one of the first drawn sections showing how the mound was composed of layers of turf, chalk, earth, flints and a chalk core.

Cunnington and Hoare were uninterested in the structure of the mounds. Worse, although Hoare did publish two volumes with woodcuts and descriptions of their investigations, Cunnington's method of sinking a central shaft or driving a trench through a barrow inevitably missed many objects and skeletons at the edges of barrows. Grimes proved this in 1959 when re-excavating some of their barrows in the Lake cemetery, already wantonly looted by the Rev. E. Duke, a contemporary of Hoare's, who left only the vaguest of notes to justify his depredations. It is only in the decades of the present century that excavations have had detailed records made of their progress and even now there are some, undertaken years ago, that have not been published.[24]

Nor, even in a more leisurely age when digging could be financed by private patronage, was every excavation enjoyable. In 1803, when opening a bell barrow, Wimborne St Giles 9 on Oakley Down in Dorset, from which came four flint barbed-and-tanged arrowheads like some superb specimens from Brittany, Hoare remembered, 'During the tremendous storm of thunder and lightning by which my friend and companion Mr Fenton, my surveyor Mr Philip Crocker, etc etc, were surprised, our only place of refuge was the barrow, which had been excavated to a considerable depth; the lightning flashed upon our spades and iron instruments, and the large flints poured down upon us from the summit of the barrow so abundantly and forcibly, that we were obliged to quit our hiding-place, and abide the pelting of the pitiless storm upon the bleak and unsheltered down'.[25]

To archaeologists water is not always undesirable. It can preserve organic material that would otherwise rot and this was proved brilliantly in 1968 by the excavation of a bell barrow, Sutton Veny 4a, 13 miles west of Stonehenge. It was a low-lying and waterlogged site, one of a small cemetery near a long barrow, and its contents revealed how elaborate funerary rituals could be, how superstitious people were, and how violent the Bronze Age was.[26]

To prepare the ground for the burial of a young man around 1500 BC bonfires were lit around the area where his grave would be, burning off the scrub and undergrowth from what was then a dry site. A neatly rectangular pit was dug and two low stacks of turves were put at its ends. Men carried a planked but lidless coffin to this grave, supporting it on a bier of two runners and four cross-timbers of rough branches. In the open coffin, displayed to the view of the mourners, was the partly dismembered skeleton of a young man, 28 to 35 years of age, his skull, jaw-bone and right arm detached from the rest of his bones. The bier, the coffin and the body were lowered into the pit, the coffin resting on the turf stacks.

With the man was a bronze dagger, a miniature pot and an Early Bronze Age food-vessel with twisted-cord decoration around its rim and upper body. This vessel was almost identical to another at Bishops Waltham 45 miles to the south-east, made of the same clay and presumably fashioned by a professional potter. Finally, when the rituals of death had been performed a mound of turves was heaped over the open grave and a wide, deep ditch, circular and about 106 feet (32 m) across, was dug to enclose the low mound and its burial.

Then, perhaps deliberately sacrificed to accompany the dead person, a second young man was buried in a pit at the north-west edge of the barrow. He had suffered an earlier injury to his mouth but this had healed. His death, instead, had been caused by two violent blows to the head with 'a sword-like weapon', the first stroke cutting into his right-temple, the second cleaving the skull and killing him. On his chest, like a magic talisman perforated to be worn as a lucky charm, was a tooth of the large, fierce mako shark that may accidentally have beached itself on the south coast only 30 miles away.

Antlers also were used as amulets. They were placed in barrow after barrow, not the worn-down picks used to dig out ditches but undamaged branches that were symbols of regrowth and rebirth to go with the dead to the Other-World. Some of the antlers in the ditch at Stonehenge were undamaged, Hawley writing of a roebuck antler, 'the first yet discovered', and there were many other antlers of the red deer, including 'a fine stag-horn' near the south entrance. At the round barrow of Amesbury 4, dug into by Stukeley who noticed 'red and blue marble chippings', bits of bluestone from Stonehenge in it, Cunnington found pieces of antler by two skeletons. At the 'most beautiful' barrow of Amesbury 15, antlers lay at the head and foot of a skeleton resting on an elm plank beneath a wigwam-like arrangement of poles. At Fovant 1, a few miles SSW of Stonehenge, antlers were set down by the skull and hips of a young man in an oak coffin. Antlers were recovered from Wilsford South 1. At Winterbourne Stoke 56 a man's body had been arranged N-S 'on his right side, and about a foot or more above the bones, was an enormous stag's horn'. In the Lake cemetery Hoare and Cunnington found nothing 'but the skeleton of a dog and the head of a deer'. One of the strangest results of such an antler-cult was encountered on a hill overlooking Chaldon Herring village in Dorset, where a barrow covered the skeletons of two adults, buried either crouched or sitting up in a deep grave, with antlers resting on their shoulders. An adjoining barrow covered another skeleton, also with antlers on its shoulders. Magic and manipulation of the forces of the Other-World was the essence of spiritual belief in early prehistoric Britain.[27]

Other revelations of faiths alien to modern thinking come from barrows such as Amesbury 22 where two infant skeletons were found, each lying over the skull of a cow like the strength-giving ox-skulls from Neolithic long barrows. At Huish Idmiston 25e, only 6 miles south-east of Stonehenge, one barrow had the bones of a young man with 'magnificent teeth' and another held the remains of a girl, no more then seven years of age, who had died from hydrocephalus, 'water on the brain', fluid causing gradual expansion of the skull, a debilitating disease leading to mental failure and death. A woman with her, probably her mother, had a similar tendency. All the bodies in this small cemetery lay with their heads to the east, which would seem to indicate that they were sun-worshippers'.[28]

Short-lived, prone to accident and illness, these people feared death but feared the dead more. Exaggeratedly deep grave-pits, heavy stones over the bodies, deliberate removal of arms to cripple the ghosts, these were some of the methods they used to avert the return of malevolent spirits. The three men under the bowl barrow of Bulford 27, trussed up and with their forearms missing, and the man at Litton Cheney 3 whose amputated hands had been buried first, were mentioned in the Introduction. A comparable desire to incapacitate the dead and render them harmless to the living may account for the skeleton at Collingbourne Ducis 9 lying inside a wall of flints. He had no right hand or arm. It is ironical, considering the desperate actions of prehistoric people to stop the dead from coming back, that on Boyton Down in the late 18th century four skeletons were discovered by labourers cutting down the trees on a round barrow. They were reverently reburied in Boyton churchyard.[29]

One of the greatest paradoxes in British prehistory is that while we have the graves of these people and the incredible monument they built, the hardest, most ponderous structure of massive stones in the whole of Europe, we know even less about their habitations than those of their predecessors. Durrington Walls had been abandoned and the area would not be reoccupied until Late Bronze and Iron Age times almost a thousand years after the erection of Bush Barrow. It might be supposed that the man buried there had lived in palatial comfort, in some spacious, well-built dwelling of heavy carved timbers, the walls daubed smooth, the roof rising above the roofs of his followers, with the wealth of cattle and sheep and pigs in pens around the village like some Zulu kraal of prehistory.

If so, there is no sign of such a settlement. Its traces may be submerged under towns like Amesbury. Rains lashing across Salisbury Plain may have eroded all evidence of its postholes. Possibly, in the warmer, drier conditions of the Early Bronze Age, the prospering herders and shepherds led semi-nomadic existences, moving from summer to winter pastures, avoiding the sacred land around Stonehenge, eating and sleeping in lightweight structures that were easily dismantled and re-erected, the chieftains leading their retinues of warriors and priests, smiths and craftsmen, men, women and children, moving their herds and flocks across the dust of the Plain, keeping away from the grounds already territorially claimed by others but not averse to rustling and skirmishing when opportunities were favourable, all the groups meeting at agreed times to settle disputes over land, animals and trade.

In this the lifestyle would not have been dissimilar to that of 19th century Zulus in southern Africa. In semi-permanent kraals built on dry, sloping land near water and firewood, a tribe would live in a medley of sturdy huts whose thatched roofs were coated in greasy soot from the central hearth. Round this fire the family slept, wrapped in warm ox-hides, lying on an earthen floor into which beef fat had been rubbed and polished by stones to make a hard surface that shone like black marble. The hut was always dark. Without windows and with only a low door, very like the cramped entrances to the houses at Skara Brae and the Knap of Howar in the Orkneys, through which a person had to crouch, these huts 'had a most dismal and dungeon-like appearance on first entering'. Although the chief's hut was larger 'so that a whole cluster of poles had to be used to support the roof, he still had to scramble in and out on his hands and knees, and the royal eyes watered just as badly from the smoke. He also, undoubtedly, had many more cockroaches.'[30]

There were no sanitary arrangements to these villages. In and around them the cattle wandered, their droppings everywhere, but as they grazed solely on grass, quite unlike the modern chemically-nourished cattle-feeds, their dung was almost pulp, odourless, soon drying and useable for fuel. Human beings simply went to the areas of scrub reserved for the men and the women in zones well below any springs and rivers.

Something akin to this may have been the way of life of many prehistoric people in southern Britain around 2000 BC, people like the ordinary folk of the Middle Ages who lived in malodorous shanty towns but who helped to build the resplendent minsters and cathedrals whose majesty and glory astonish us today. Like the Bronze Age settlements, the unhealthy shacks and hovels of a medieval city have long since disappeared.

The commoners of the Bronze Age, the labourers and masons who heaved the sarsens of Stonehenge upright, had few possessions. Children were sometimes buried with no more than a flint or a single pebble. Women had little more, a clumsy beaker or a bronze leather-working awl as a record of their lives. It is easier to pick out the aristocrats of society, the leaders, the warriors, the artisans and, perhaps, the priests.

Not only the gold and amber and jet distinguish the graves of leaders. At Wilsford, in the green shade of a spinney 1½ miles south of Stonehenge, there is a bell-barrow, Wilsford South 58, overgrown and pocked with rabbit-holes. In June, 1807, Cunnington plunged into 'the monarch of this group', finding the skeleton of a very tall, robust man lying on his right, with his head, unusually, to the south-east. With him was a bronze flanged axe, a massive dolerite battle-axe. an enormous boar's tusk, a grooved whetstone of Forest Marble and a strange bronze object like Neptune's trident with the middle prong absent. The two outer prongs, 5 inches (13 cm) long, had been twisted clockwise by a right-handed craftsman and also were slightly curved into a horseshoe shape. At the base a small projection with three rivet-holes showed where a wooden shaft had been. Three bronze rings or links hung from a perforation near it. 'It is unlike any thing we have ever yet discovered', wrote Hoare. It has been described as a hanging-chain for a cauldron, but these were unknown before the late Bronze Age. A more recent interpretation has seen this unique object as a royal standard with the links designed to hold a pendant blowing in the breeze, an impressive addition to the other articles of Bronze Age regalia.[31]

Woollen cloth is also found in these rich Wessex graves, the first woven material in the British Isles. At a time when skin clothing was still the normal apparel the appearance of cloth is another sign of privilege. Forest clearance had opened the landscape, providing spacious tracts on which sheep could graze, and it is noticeable that whereas on grooved ware sites the pig had been preferred for the feasts and offerings, with the return of native customs cattle once again were favoured, the herds sharing the countryside with growing flocks of sheep.

Spinning and weaving were already known on continental Beaker settlements and may have been introduced into Britain many years before the Bush Barrow burial. The frequent occurrence of cloth in Early Bronze Age barrows, however, suggests that it was not until then that such material was readily available. Hoare found fragments in two barrows on Oakley Down, in Dorset, but only 17 miles SSW of Stonehenge. The first, Wimborne St Giles 17, contained 'several pieces of decayed linen, of a reddish-brown colour, lying like cobwebs' on the bones, and the other had 'a considerable quantity of decayed linen cloth, the filaments of which, at first sight, appeared like hair'. In the western Winterborne Stoke group there was 'a considerable quantity of linen cloth' and in a nearby disc barrow ashes in an urn 'had been wrapped in a linen cloth to protect them'.[32]

The British climate is not conducive to the preservation of such perishable material, but Bronze Age burials in Denmark, surviving in waterlogged tree-trunk coffins, showed that high-ranking women had worn summer outfits of short, woven skirts and bodices with wrap-around belts and a winter costume of ground-length skirts, blouses and cloaks. Men of the same class had calf-length woollen tunics, short cloaks, caps, leather moccasins and thonged sandals. Buttons of jet and pins fastened the belts and the cloaks.[33]

Attention was paid to personal appearance. Hair, particularly among the women, was carefully groomed with horn combs that dangled from the waist, and hair-nets and hats and bonnets protected the coiffures. In Britain the frequent discovery of bone points immediately below the skull of a burial indicates a similar concern for the hair to be done up tidily in a bun. For the wealthy, life must have been almost dandifed.

A social grade below these preening leaders of fashion were the warriors, buried in dagger-graves, lacking the precious gold and amber but having the battle-axes and bronze weapons that set them apart from commoners. At Durrington 7 a male skeleton with a late beaker had a huge battle-axe of Cornish tourmaline granite, its point touching the skull as if the man had been holding its haft in his arms. The elegant bell barrow of Amesbury 15, already mentioned for its antlers, also yielded two daggers, the larger in the decayed remnants of a wooden sheath. On the western shoulder of Coneybury Hill near Stonehenge a monstrous bowl barrow, Amesbury 23, known as the King Barrow, may have held a three-riveted bronze dagger and a foot-long whetstone for sharpening the blade. Of the same mound Stukeley was told by his friend, Lord Pembroke, that in 1722 'in that very old barrow near little Amesbury was found a very large brass weapon of 20 lbs weight like a pole-ax',[34] a description sounding very like a halberd with a great dagger fixed at right-angles to a long shaft, a slicing, chopping weapon that in the Middle Ages was used with murderous effect against mounted, armoured French knights at the Battle of the Spurs in AD 1302.

A reminder that prehistoric warriors were not a full-time militia came from a low barrow at the end of the Normanton cemetery nearly half a mile east of Bush Barrow. Cunnington dug into it in 1808, coming upon a cremation, two fine bronze daggers, a bronze crutch-headed pin or cloak-fastener, a whetstone and a broken but carefully-smoothed swan's leg-bone, no more than 8 inches (20 cm) long, hollowed out and having at least two small perforations like fingerholes for a simple flute. One can imagine this part-time warrior piping to his flock during the lazy hours of a Wessex summer, indolently watching the distant labours of sarsens being dragged and heaved upright at Stonehenge. Other flutes from near Avebury and from eastern Britain, one fashioned out of a crane's tibia and with a blowhole and four fingerholes, reveal that such instruments were part of the musical apparatus of Bronze Age Britain.[35]

One aspect of these warrior-graves, like those of the leaders, emphasises the importance that people placed on the orientation of the body. From Stukeley and Hoare and from modern excavators comes a consistent recognition of cardinal alignments, mainly with the head to the north, but with south, east and west not rejected. It was the inter-cardinal positions that were disliked (Table 14).

**TABLE 14   Orientation of bodies in Wessex round barrows**

|  | N | NE | E | SE | S | SW | W | NW | NNW | TOTAL |
|---|---|---|---|---|---|---|---|---|---|---|
| Beakers. (Early to Middle stages) | 5 | 0 | 2 | 1 | 2 | 0 | 0 | 0 | 0 | 10 |
| Beakers (Late stage) | 5 | 1 | 1 | 1 | 0 | 0 | 0 | 0 | 0 | 8 |
| Wessex I | 2 | 2 | 0 | 1 | 1 | 0 | 0 | 0 | 0 | 6 |
| Wessex II | 3 | 1 | 3 | 1 | 1 | 0 | 2 | 0 | 0 | 11 |
| Uncertain | 19 | 6 | 10 | 0 | 5 | 0 | 5 | 5 | 1 | 51 |
| TOTALS | 34 | 10 | 16 | 4 | 9 | 0 | 7 | 5 | 1 | 86 |

It is possible to make rough chronological divisions for these orientations. Where the period of the barrow is uncertain because of a lack of grave-goods, it is likely that the majority belong to the Early Bronze Age phases of Wessex I/II when most of the round barrows were erected.

From the Table it can be seen that no fewer than 40 per cent of bodies were laid with the heads to the north, and 50 per cent to either north or south. Hoare noted that the perfectly preserved skeleton with its skull to the south at Kilmington in west Wiltshire 'grinn'd horribly a ghastly smile', perhaps in frustration because its prehistoric sextons had erred in the orientation.[36]

If east and west are added to the north and south orientations this would account for over three-quarters of the burials, far too many to be accidental. The majority of the people lay on their left sides, but there was an important distinction between the sexes. Where it has been possible to decide whether a burial was male or female well over half the men had their heads to north or south, but women were laid to north, east, west and north-west in equal numbers and children's bodies were even more randomly positioned. Men, it seems, were still afforded the most care and of the men it was the leaders and the warriors who received the greatest attention.

Burials of artisans and craftsmen, specialists hardly known before this time, can be recognised by the tools in their graves, the flint adzes of carpenters, the bone spatulae of leather-workers, flint strike-a-lights for the group's fire-carriers when the herds and flocks were moved from grazing ground to grazing ground. Moss for tinder and flints for sparking and kindling the flame were found with a burial at Shrewton 5k. A sandstone axe-hammer for metal-working came from Bulford 27, part of the equipment of a smith whose work was probably performed in private just as the iron-working smiths of the Zulus protected the mysteries of their craft.

'It was a trade which, generally speaking, was hereditary because much of their work was shrouded in mystery; there were certain sinister secrets attached to it which were jealously guarded and only handed down to a son who had been trained in this craft. Consequently smiths carried out their work in isolated spots, far from the homes of their tribesmen who were strictly forbidden to approach. . . .'[37] Many of them were feared because of their powers. Some used the blood of sacrificed animals, even of men, in the manufacture of special weapons such as the assegai made for Shaka Zulu the despotic war-chief. Undisclosed rites accompanied the forging of the spears. This was not prosaic metalworking but an art that invoked the spirits of the dead and in this the smiths were akin to the witchdoctors whose role it was to foretell the future, cure ills and ward off the evil forces of the Other-World.

Priests or shamans, as powerful and as dreaded, probably existed at the time that the colossal circles were being erected at Stonehenge. Identification of such physicians, lawgivers, soothsayers and bards is difficult because often a leader and a priest were one and the same person but, very occasionally, hints come from the clothing, the burial in a coffin and the articles of witchcraft and divination found under the barrows.

In the small bowl barrow of Upton Lovell 2a a heavily-built man had been buried in an oval grave, his head to the north, and near him was another slighter skeleton, 'probably a female, and perhaps his wife'. The man had a toolyard of articles with him, flint axes, a grooved whetstone, a bronze awl, a pebble hammerstone, a dolerite battle-axe, a sarsen grindstone and also 'several stones and pebbles of different sorts, not to be found in the neighbourhood',[38] a collection to be considered shortly. Five hollow nodules of iron oxide, so-called 'eagle-stones', which had been broken in two 'so as to form a rude kind of cup' lay near his legs. Here also was a row of 36 bone points, all of them perforated to be attached to the hem of a long, leather tunic. There was a row of boars' tusks, also perforated, near his knees. A comparable assemblage of perforated wolf's teeth, ground flat on both sides for necklets around the wrist or ankle, were recovered from the South Newton 1 barrow. In Derbyshire Thomas Bateman found kindred perforated bones in a barrow near Kelmslow.

Comparisons have been made between these objects and the old-fashioned clothing of shamans or medicine-men of southern Siberia, men skilled in forecasting the future, whose traditional costume of fringed tunics had long gone out of fashion amongst their tribesmen. Stuart Piggott hesitated to take the parallel too far but added, 'what sanctioned the bearing of a Wessex Culture battle-axe or the Bush Barrow mace we shall never know, but we can be sure that the authority it denoted was as much spiritual as temporal, for priests and kings, magicians and princes, were not in the ancient world so sharply separated as they are in our latter-day scientific minds'.[39]

There are other suggestions that some Wessex burials were of men deemed to have powers beyond those of ordinary mortals, beings who may have been the forerunners of the Iron Age druids. Even in the Bronze Age there are hints of a tree-cult not unlike that of the druids. Some men were interred in oak treetrunk coffins, lying there not crouched as though in sleep but extended on their backs like the man under Bush Barrow. The association of the druids with the oak is well-known, particularly with those oaks entwined with the round, pallid and moonlike mistletoe. In his *Natural History* (XVI, 249) Pliny the Elder recorded that 'the Druids . . . hold nothing more sacred than the mistletoe and a tree on which it is growing, providing it is Valonia oak'. Branches of oak and burials were conjoined long before the Iron Age. Kendrick pointed to the Bronze Age 'oak-burial' at Gristhorpe in Yorkshire and to others 'in Brittany where in many of the megalithic tombs the funeral deposits were laid on a bedding of oak leaves'.[40]

On the cliffs at Gristhorpe near Scarborough the corpse of a robust man was buried in an oak coffin together with his bronze dagger, a bone pin for his hair, flints, a small wooden bowl and, on his chest, 'a double rose or riband with two loose ends', maybe a sash or girdle which 'fell into small fragments immediately on removal' in 1834. What seemed to be flowers or reeds had been strewn in the coffin and after the lid had been heaved into position a mass of oak branches was spread over it before the clay and stone layers of the barrow were constructed.

Branches had been laid over a treetrunk coffin found in 1878 in a peat-bog near Oban. At Old Sunderlandwick in Yorkshire three skeletons lay in a coffin over which two lengths of black, decayed oak had been left. In the Winterbourne Stoke cemetery near Stonehenge Cunnington came upon a wooden coffin, lying north-south, made of elm, 'yet we also found some pieces of oak'. Next to this fine bell barrow, no. 4, its companion, Winterbourne Stoke 5, contained an elm coffin overlain by 'a heavy piece of fossil wood . . . resembling a bunch of twigs'.[41] A five-handled, glossy red pot was discovered in this barrow, an unusual vessel in Britain but of a style known in Brittany like the two daggers also in the coffin.

Even more evocative of magic and spells are the otherwise inexplicable objects found in some barrows. Two tree-trunk burials in Denmark produced articles of this nature, a man at Hvidegard having a bag filled with dried roots, a seashell, a flint and, more sinisterly, the tail of a snake and the claw of a falcon. At Maglehøj a bronze box near the body of a woman held two horse's teeth, weasel bones, a claw, perhaps from a lynx, mammal bones, snake's vertebrae, quartz pebbles and a piece of a bird's windpipe.

Nothing as explicit as this has survived in Britain, although a 'witch's brew' was suspected in the chambered tomb of Barclodiad y Gawres on Anglesey, but during his ravages at the Lake cemetery in 1806 the Rev. E. Duke chanced upon 'some very singular and curious relicks . . . [which] are cautiously preserved, at his venerable and picturesque old mansion-house'. Amongst these were four tiny bone tablets very like others from a barrow at Folkton in Yorkshire. One of them was plain but the others were incised with geometrical patterns on both sides. The motifs are too shallow for them to have been stamps or moulds and Hoare speculated that 'the custom of casting lots existed amongst the Britons', and that the tablets, flat on one side, convex on the other, had been used for divination. They are now in the British Museum.[42]

Even closer in kind to the Danish witchcraft bundles are the stones and pebbles known from several Wessex barrows. Near the Stonehenge avenue the bowl, Amesbury 101, had been looted before Hawley and Passmore examined it in the 1920s. Despite the damage, they were able to recover an extraordinary pile of natural flints, 'of all sorts of odd shapes, each chosen for its curious projecting knobs and lugs. It suggested a witch doctor's outfit.' The pebbles, stones and white flints at Upton Lovell 2a, the 'curious pebble' at Amesbury 56, speckled, kidney-shaped, which turned sea-green when dipped in water, and the small red pebble at Collingbourne Kingston 19 are tantalising wraiths of witchcraft practices of an age very different from our own. With the cremation at Collingbourne Kingston were five fine flint arrowheads in a wreath of red deer antlers and the skeleton of a dog. The mound is called the Hunter's Barrow, 'and the bones of the dog deposited in the same grave, and above those of his master, commemorate his faithful attendant in the chase, and perhaps his unfortunate victim in death'.[43]

Leaders, warriors, craftsmen and commoners, priests and shamans, all these lie in the barrows around Stonehenge, their burials and grave-goods acting like an opaque film through which their lives, ceremonies and beliefs can just be made out. Through them Stonehenge itself can be reincarnated. Within a region no more than four miles in any direction from the circle there are ten or more cemeteries and over a hundred isolated mounds scattered like gravel across the slopes and ridges of the countryside. But at the middle of this sprawling burial-ground there is a void. An area a mile wide has scarcely a barrow in it. Instead, Stonehenge rises at its centre, the mortuary-house at the heart of this land of the dead.

Around the barrows were the fields of the crop-growers and between the fields were the droveways along which the herds and flocks passed in the autumn when the grass was lush, a leisurely time after the harvest when barrows could be built. Flying ants were trapped under Silbury Hill in a Late Neolithic August, and acorns and pellets of buzzards fell in the Snail Down cemetery in a similar season, a time for renovation and a time between summer and winter when territories could be expanded or taken over.

To south, west and north the realm of the Wessex chieftains seems to have spread out, taking in the former independencies of Dorchester and Cranborne Chase and the Marlborough Downs where the authority of Avebury had waned. Whether in a loose federation or under tyrannical rule, the region covering Wiltshire, Somerset, Dorset, Hampshire and parts of Gloucestershire and Sussex came together. Perhaps as a deliberate flaunting of this new power sarsens, from the same source as Avebury's astonishing stones, were brought from the Marlborough Downs to Salisbury Plain, replacing the puny Beaker bluestones with gigantic blocks and slabs.

One little round barrow, now destroyed, epitomises this annexation of land. Just west of Marlborough and only four miles east of Avebury the Manton barrow, Preshute 1a, was being ploughed away in 1906 and it was excavated under the direction of Maud Cunnington's husband, Benjamin. It was Mrs Cunnington's first dig. The mound was a low one. Beneath it, lying on the old ground surface under a turf-stack, was the skeleton of an old woman, frail, short and with worn-down teeth. The body had been 'wrapped in some coarsely woven material' that had left clear impressions in the clay. The cloth was of two qualities, one much rougher than the other, and it was this that was most clearly visible under the body, extending beyond the head like a shroud. A piece of wood had lain under the head, perhaps to protect the woman's face from the earth and clay of the barrow.

The funerary articles with the woman were amazing. As well as food-bones there was a bronze dagger and amber pommel with 'vestiges of its wooden handle', a miniature cup studded all over with nodules of clay as though covered with grapes, another small 'incense' cup punctuated with clumsily arranged holes, three bronze awls for leather-working, and by the woman's neck was a small pottery object exactly like a collar-stud for fastening a cloak. Near it was a barrel-shaped bead of shale wound around with gold wire and also near the neck were one hundred and fifty beads of jet, shale, amber and fossil, a tiny imitation of a halberd with a bronze blade, an amber shaft encircled with more gold wire, and finally a disc of red amber, an inch (25 mm) across, set in a gold casing delicately embossed with six concentric rings each marked out with a series of exquisitely neat dots.[44]

The most significant fact about this glorious treasure was that the gold-bound amber disc was almost a reproduction of the pair found by Cunnington in the Wilsford South 8 barrow in the Normanton cemetery 20 miles to the south. That barrow also had a little halberd pendant. With it was another near-duplicate, a cone of gold which Hoare remarked was 'similar to the one discovered in the Golden Barrow at Upton Lovel' (2e) 11 miles west of Normanton and over 20 miles SW of Manton. Hoare added that the amber discs 'bear a very strong resemblance to some articles found by Dr Stukeley in a barrow, north of STONEHENGE'. This was Amesbury 44e, the eastern of a pair of twin-bells in the Cursus group, 'which I open'd', remembered Stukeley, '5 July, 1723', finding a dagger, its pommel, jet and amber beads and the gold-bound disc. 'Female Celtic ornaments', he called them, left with a cremation 'in a little heap, not so much as a hat crown would contain'. They were the ashes 'of a girl of about 14 years old. . . . This person was a heroin [*sic*], for we found the head of her javelin in brass'.[45]

Yet another amber pendant came from the Lake cemetery. Such like-nesses between precious objects found miles apart at Manton, Upton Lovell, at the Cursus and in barrows at Lake imply a freedom of movement between distant parts of Wessex as though the entire region was now under one rule. 'It seems very likely that we are witnessing the work of one master goldsmith'[46] whose products, with the expansion of the Wessex 'empire', could now reach out to west and north Wiltshire.

Wealth and power, prestigious leaders, both male and, in later times, female, followers and petty chieftains owing allegiance to a paramount chief, links with Brittany, priests, the positions of north, south, east and west, a fear of the dead, an axe-cult, guardian spirits of the grave, the sun, moon and funerary rites, all these aspects of Bronze Age society were reflected and incorporated in the architecture of the third Stonehenge.

# 9

## House of the dead
## Stonehenge IIIa: 2000 – 1600 BC

*Can a building be arrogant?. . . . It is the building and, perhaps, the*
*purpose to which the building is put. There is a hint of tyranny,*
*more than a little contempt, and something which could be called*
*brazenness. The building itself tries to crush by its very presence.*
*Standing there – before you even enter it – it seems to try to intimidate*
*you.*

John Wainwright, *Man of Law*, 1980, 51–2

It is a dark place, oppressive as though Death were lurking in its shadows. The sarsens are thick, crowding against each other, forced deep into the ground by the lintels heavily pressing down upon them. It is a jostle of stone, monumental but overbearing, and the gaps between the pillars are no more than slits of light through the dark stonework of the circle. Inside the barrier of the sarsens the trilithons climb tightly together, shadowing the sky, grim, sombre, elegaic as though mourning the twilight of mortality.

Thomas Hardy knew it. In *Tess of the d'Urbervilles* his heroine slept there under a dying moon before the Immortals ended their pitiless sport with her. Blake and Constable and Turner saw the darkness, painting the damp, dreary stones against skies of stormy clouds. A forgotten poet, Thomas Stokes Salmon, sensed its dark presence like the atmosphere of a walled vault,

> Wrapt in the veil of time's unbroken gloom,
> Obscure as death, and silent as the tomb. . . .
> *Stonehenge.* 1823

It is overpowering and monstrous and there is nothing like it. Avebury, bigger and wider, is filled with light, the stones spread apart in the spacious setting of the Marlborough Downs. Stonehenge is dark and narrow, dungeonlike. If ordinary mortuary-houses were for the dead, then this was a gigantic mortuary-house for the mighty dead. To build it was an undertaking that would continue far beyond the lifetimes of any who began it. And before it could begin the bluestones had to be removed.

The Welsh stones were lifted from their sockets and the cavities were carefully backfilled. Excavation of these Q and R Holes in 1954 showed that earth and dirty chalk had tumbled back into the pits as the stones were dragged out. This rubble had been rammed down before clean white chalk was packed firmly on top of the holes and in the middle section of the 'dumb-bells'. Then new holes to receive the sarsens were dug. The fact that one of these, for circle-sarsen 3, cut into the edge of the pit where Q4 had stood proved that the bluestone rings had preceded the huge circle of Stonehenge III. Radiocarbon dates from antlers in an unfinished R Hole (1620 ± 110 bc, c. 2000 BC) and from the ramp down which the colossal sarsen 56 had been manoeuvred into its socket (1720 ± 150 bc, c. 2100 BC) suggested that the transformation from the bluestone to the sarsen phase had taken place in the decades before 2000 BC at the beginning of the Early Bronze Age (Fig. 11).

Thirty sarsens were erected in a perfect circle rather bigger than the outer bluestone ring. Thirty lintel-stones were placed along their tops to form a structure three times taller than a man. Inside it were five settings of two uprights with a lintel across them like constricted archways, first called 'trilithons' (three-stones) by William Stukeley. These were arranged in a horseshoe shape that rose in height towards the south-west. Of the bluestones perhaps only the Altar Stone was left standing upright near the centre of the new ring in front of the tallest trilithon. Outside the circle the Four Stations remained, their untooled roughness in contrast to the smoothed and ground faces of the sarsen ring. At the entrance to the surrounding earthwork there were certainly two, perhaps even four, sarsen portal-stones and beyond them, isolated, was the Heel Stone, 'corroded like worm-eaten wood', as Stukeley remarked of the outlying pillar at the Rollright Stones in Oxfordshire, 'by the harsh jaws of time'.

Described so casually, one might think that there was nothing exceptional about Stonehenge, but reconsideration demonstrates how remarkable an achievement this monument was. The transportation of the stones over 20 miles of uneven countryside, the provisioning and shelter of the workers miles out on the exposed plain, the shaping of the stones, the pre-planning of the design so that only stones of the right length, width and shape were selected, the manufacture of ropes and sledges, the lifting 13 feet (4 m) into the air of lintels six or more tons in weight, all these and many more problems leave one in astonishment and admiration that people with only primitive equipment could ever have completed their task.

The crux of their difficulty and their triumph was the length of the circle-stones, for it was intended that despite the sloping site on which the ring was to stand the tops of its lintels were to be exactly level. Because of the 6 inch (15 cm) fall of the land from south to north, and 1 foot 3 inches (37 cm) from west to east, some sarsen uprights had to be over a foot (30 cm) longer than stones on the other side of the circle. And the thirty stones were to be of similar width. All this had to be calculated and checked before

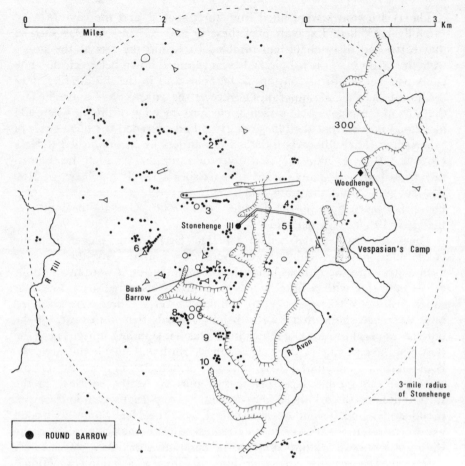

Fig. 11. The Stonehenge Region 2000 – 500 BC. Stonehenge IIIa-IV.
Important barrow cemeteries: (1) Rollestone; (2) Durrington
Downs; (3) The Cursus group; (4) Old King; (5) New King; (6)
Winterbourne Stoke; (7) Normanton; (8) Lake; (9) Wilsford; (10)
Lake Down.

the pillars could be chosen. The solutions lay in the working-practices of
earlier generations.

It was a society of skilled carpenters. One imagines a timber mock-up
on the site. Two adjacent posts, where stones would stand, may have
been erected with a wooden ring-beam across them. Observation over the
centuries of how liquid dribbled over the rim of a filled pot if the vessel
were not level would have shown how a trough of water could be used as
a levelling-device. With the vessel placed on top of the ring-beam, water
would probably have spilled from one of its ends. To overcome this, one
of the supporting posts could have been raised or lowered until the beam

was horizontal and the water was still. Then a third post could have been set up near the second and the process repeated around the entire circumference, meticulously establishing the required heights of the posts. These were to be the templates for the stones as they arrived on site.

The source of the sarsens has seldom been disputed. Since the 17th century it has been accepted that they came from the Marlborough Downs 17 miles north of Stonehenge. Some sarsens, it is true, must have lain on Salisbury Plain itself and this is probably where the Heel Stone and the Four Stations were found, but there is one simple fact that shows that such erratics were uncommon. There is not one megalithic tomb near Stonehenge. The closest is at Tidcombe and Fosbury 14 miles north-east towards Hungerford and the absence of any other stone-built chamber in the sixty earthen long barrows on Salisbury Plain reveals how scarce large boulders and slabs must have been. Although the small bluestones had been conveniently placed, when taller pillars were wanted for the stone circle men had to go far afield for them.

Enormous blocks of sarsen covered the upper slopes of the Marlborough Downs. People at Avebury close by had used hundreds of them for the construction of their great circles and avenues and for the earlier Neolithic long barrows such as West Kennet and the Devil's Den. Formed by the natural cementing of a bed of quartzite, itself created in a prehistoric sea from deposits of clays, sands and loams 26 or more million years ago, this thick layer of saccharoidal sandstone settled and concreted on the chalk of the sea-bed. When the sea retreated coniferous forests grew on the exposed surface, the tree-roots penetrating the still-soft sand. Their holes can still be seen in some of the stones of Avebury and Stonehenge. Then the freezing millennia of Ice Ages broke and cracked the bed of sarsen into gargantuan slabs ideal for the building of a stone circle.

Sometimes called druid-stones, bridestones and grey-wethers from their similarity at a distance to grazing sheep, the stones are better-known as sarsens, perhaps because they are 'saracens' or 'foreigners' in their chalk landscape. There is an alternative explanation. Some prehistoric burial-grounds on the Chotanagpur Plateau of India, built of big stone slabs, are known as *sasans*[1] and it may be that the 'sazzans', as they were once known in Wiltshire, and the 'sasans' of India have a common derivation from a long-forgotten word in the Indo-European language of the Neolithic western world and Asia.

The stones were excellent for a megalithic ring. 'They are so hard that no toole can touch', wrote John Aubrey, 'and take a good polish'.[2] Lying embedded in turf and earth, they had to be dug out, with wedges driven into the natural fissures, then levered and broken free and manhandled onto hardwood sledges. To lift one end of a 26-ton stone demanded the strength of twenty men heaving down on long timber levers, straining as they shifted the slab inch by inch until it could be lashed down and the long, slow, dragging journey to Stonehenge begun. Oxen may have been used for pulling the load, but the advantage of their strength would often have been discounted by their dulness and their slow reactions in a crisis. Good traction animals when ploughing a level field, they were liabilities on slopes and twisting trails. Rollers were equally unhelpful. Except on prepared tracks or on flat, firm ground, they presented problems on the hillsides and wet patches where they sank almost inextricably to the dismay and anger of their tired handlers.

Sledges were better, dragged by men hauling on thick ropes of plaited thongs, guided round outcrops, tugged along the contours of the downs, slithering over the winter grass when the soil was hardest, moving day by grudging day towards Stonehenge. Such oak-built sleds, capable of supporting a huge sarsen, would have been very heavy and for an average expedition a total payload of thirty or more tons can be assumed. Over six hundred labourers were needed, travelling no more than half a mile a day, a tedious safari of more than a month before they reached Stonehenge.[3]

The route was not a direct one. Immediately to the south of the Marlborough Downs were the marshes of the Vale of Pewsey, whose ill-drained greensands spread over miles of swamp and wasteland, thick with reeds at its edges, willows and birches and alders growing on its islands. It was a wilderness and only the spoonbills and tiny reed-warblers were at home there. Today it is a rich countryside. In 2000 BC it was wild and forbidding.

To its east was Savernake, a primordial forest gloomy with oaks and ashes and thorns, which even now, after centuries of clearance, 16 miles around, is a 'marvellously lovely woodland', but then as much a barrier as a mountain range.

The sarsens had to be taken westwards. First a stone was moved cautiously down the slope of Overton Hill, then on, slowly upwards, towards present-day Bishops Cannings, *Caneganmaerse*, 'Cana's marsh', passing between the ridges and the wetlands, onto Coate, dragged around Etchilhampton hill, along the line of the future Roman Lydeway and on to Foxley Corner and the foot of Salisbury Plain. Fourteen miles had been covered. Weeks had gone by. Daily, helpers had fetched provisions from the locality, had dragged the poles and skins of shelters for the cold nights of the long trek. But now, if Atkinson's proposed route is the correct one, and it is more plausible than many other suggestions,[4] the stone lay below the appalling slope of Redhorn Hill.

There the escarpment climbed 250 feet (76 m) in half a mile, a slope of 1 in 11, steep enough for an unencumbered person and almost impossible for hundreds of men straining and slipping around the dog-leg of the easiest passage, heaving at taut, near-breaking ropes, jamming levers behind the sledge, the burden threatening to slither sideways on the bends, crawling and inching upwards until, days and nights later, the crest was reached. Then, on gentler downslopes, the group dragged past the conspicuous mound of the Ell long barrow where Thurnam was to find skeletons, across

16. 'European' (E) beaker; height about 6 ins (15 cm) (Bristol University)

17. A Wessex/Middle Rhine (W/MR) Beaker burial from Roundway Down, Wiltshire

18. Axe carving on the capstone of the passage-grave chamber, Table des Marchands, Morbihan, Brittany (Aubrey Burl)

19. Outcrops of dolerite (bluestone) on Carn Meini, Preselis, Dyfed, south-west Wales (Aubrey Burl)

20. Salisbury Plain building materials of clay, thatch, wood and flint in houses at Stratford-sub-Castle, 6 miles south of Stonehenge (Aubrey Burl)

21. Worked and shaped sarsen stones at Stonehenge (Aubrey Burl)

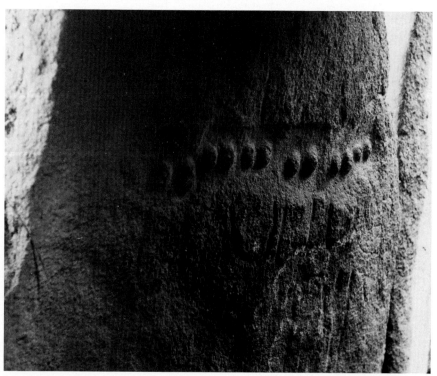

22. 'Breasts' and 'necklaces' carved inside the allée-couverte of Kerguntuil, Côte-du-Nord, Brittany (Aubrey Burl)

23. 'Figurine' carved inside the passage-grave of Les Pierres-Plates, Morbihan, Brittany (Aubrey Burl)

24. Bronze daggers and axe, and the mace from Bush Barrow, Wiltshire (Devizes Museum)

25. Goldwork from Bush Barrow (Devizes Museum)

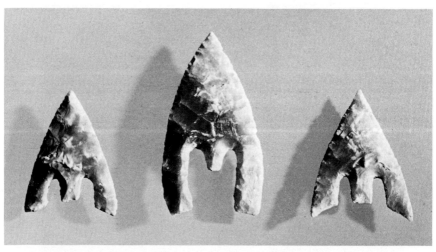

26. Barbed-and-tanged flint arrowheads from Wimborne St Giles 9 round barrow, Dorset (University of Bristol)

27. The 'astronomical window' between Trilithon 51–52 showing an arc
about 8 degrees wide and not at all precise (Aubrey Burl)

28. The shaped and curved sarsen lintels of Stonehenge III (Aubrey Burl)

29. The last round barrow: Amesbury 11 near Stonehenge (Aubrey Burl)

the plain where the Bustard Inn now stands and finally to Stonehenge, the weary weeks over, the trial of fatigue, accident, even death concluded.

The exact route may never be known. Perhaps the perils of Redhorn Hill were shunned and a shallower but miles-longer way was preferred, moving from Etchilhampton south-westwards towards Lavington, then turning sharply to the left up a long, steady valley towards Tilshead and Rollestone and Stonehenge. Whatever the chosen path, it was an undertaking to be remembered and told and retold.

It may have been decades after the first that the last, huge, exhausting sarsen was sledged past the Cursus to Stonehenge. During those years each stone had been fashioned as though it was a block of wood, battered into an unlikely shape to suit the design of the carpenters who had planned the new ring. The result was a masterpiece of woodworking, timber transformed into stone, decaying oak changed into enduring sarsen, a wooden house of the dead turned by the skills of men into an everlasting temple of the gods.

The tools used for this architectural metamorphosis were recognised in 1901 during a limited excavation around Stone 56. This survivor of the tallest trilithon had been tilting forward ever more dangerously for centuries and when Stone 22 of the outer circle and its lintel fell on 31 December, 1900, it was decided to straighten Stone 56 before it too collapsed. The work was entrusted to Professor William Gowland. Following his meticulous investigation of the surrounding ground, a wooden frame was fitted round the sarsen and over eight anxious days it was winched upright and set in concrete so that 'the hitherto leaning stone has been made safe for all time'.[5]

This was the first of the stones to be stabilised and the use of artificial cementing material had a touch of humour about it. In his *Britannia Depicta* of 1763 John Owen had described Stonehenge as 'a strange structure of a vast bigness. . . . Camden and others are of Opinion that these Stones were not Hewn out of the Rock, but Artificially made of pure Sand and by some glutinous matter cemented together.' Nonsensical though such a belief was, by 1964 it did contain a little truth. Twenty years after Gowland's consolidation of Stone 56 Hawley set six stones upright in concrete. Trilithon 57–58 was re-erected in 1958. In 1963 Stone 23 blew over in a gale and in 1964 it and Stones 4, 5, 28, 53, 54, 57, 58 and 60 were bedded in concrete. Indeed, Stonehenge and concrete are almost as intimately connected as the fullscale American model erected on the edge of the Columbia Gorge in the United States 150 miles south-east of Seattle. Two million pounds of reinforced concrete went into this replica which was built as a memorial after the First World War. There was an ironical coincidence about this patriotic gesture. Centuries earlier Geoffrey of Monmouth had claimed that the real Stonehenge also had been built as a cenotaph to commemorate British noblemen treacherously killed by their Saxon enemies.

During the 1901 excavations Gowland recovered over a hundred rounded mauls of sarsen, some no bigger than a tennis-ball but others as large as a pumpkin and weighing up to 64 lbs (29 kg), more than most men could lift easily. It was with this repertoire of rough stones that people had shaped the pillars and lintels of Stonehenge. Jagged projections had probably been heated and then suddenly chilled with cold water before the largest mauls, encased in a network of leather and perhaps fitted with long handles 'in order that they might be used by two or more men', were crashed down on the sarsen time after time, pulverising away uneven lumps, slowly smoothing the surface. Similar 'hammers' were found near the unfinished obelisk at Aswan in Egypt, their sides patchily flattened from the pounding. 'A more economical or efficient tool can hardly be imagined.'[6]

Once the worst bits had been removed, gangs of workers lined up, four or five on either side of the stone, and with smaller mauls rubbed backwards and forwards on it as though it were a prehistoric washboard, sandy dust trickling away, scraping and scouring the surface into fluted ridges that would later be polished flat by a similar process. The effect of this broad tooling can still be seen on the fallen Stone 59 whose ripples were left untouched.

It was tiring, it was boring and it must have seemed everlasting. Calculations suggest that in an hour of continuous rubbing no more than 6 cubic inches (98 cm³) of dust would be removed.[7] If some 2 inches (5 cm) of stone had to be levelled from the face of an average upright, 13 feet 6 inches long, 7 feet wide and 3 and a half feet thick ($4.1 \times 2.1 \times 1.1$ m) the task would have taken 378 man-hours. Assuming eight people working ten hours daily on the stone, they would have spent four or five tediously long days before the sarsen could be turned over for its side to be dressed, then over again and its outer face smoothed, then over again for its second side to be polished, a fortnight or more of aching, day-long toil.

In the turmoil of those years Stonehenge must have been a bustling, dirty, rowdy place with the crashes of the hammerstones, the rhythmical scrape and screech of the grinding mauls, the chatter, the bellowing of orders over the noise as the stones were levered upright, cries of warning, the distant shouting of a team dragging yet another sarsen across the last mile of the Plain. It will never be known how many people were involved but it has been estimated that one and three-quarter million working-hours were needed to build this sarsen phase of Stonehenge. Around 2000 BC the entire population of Wessex, from north Wiltshire to the south coast of Dorset, may have been about 50,000 men, women and children. With a thousand labourers, perhaps one in twenty of the inhabitants of Salisbury Plain, working ten hours every day, hauling, shaping and erecting the stones, the project, theoretically, could have been completed in six months.[8] It is most unlikely that any prehistoric community would have persisted so unceasingly and the work of preparing the stones alone is quite likely to have taken far longer than a few months. Years, and quite probably generations, are more convincing. No sarsen probably had its surfaces battered and ground and smoothed in a few weeks. When one realises that there were to be thirty pillars, thirty lintels, two or more portal stones and fifteen massive sarsens for the trilithons, the mere slog and drive required for the smoothing of the stones amazes the modern reader. And this was the beginning.

Woodworking techniques demanded more than planed surfaces. The stones had to be connected together as though dowelled by a megalithic carpenter. The tops of the uprights had to be bashed and scoured into two tenons or bulbous pegs to hold the lintels securely. The circle-lintels had to be delicately curved to follow the long line of the circle. They had to be chamfered, with bevelled edges, to fit firmly on their uprights and they had to have two deep mortise-holes pounded and pestled out of their undersides, the spacing neatly measured so that they could receive the tenons of the two pillars across which they would lie. The ends of these incredible lintels were also beaten into toggle-joints, with the V-shaped 'beak' of one end to be inserted into the V-shaped groove of the adjoining lintel like pieces of a geometrical jigsaw, socketed together, stone by stone, in a huge, immovable ring high above the ground. In a timber building the result would have been an achievement for any prehistoric architect. In sarsen it was almost a miracle.

The workers had to be fed and they had to be sheltered if they came from far away. There is the chance that the base of a skin-covered hut 'for at least one skilled stone-worker' was discovered in 1980. During an excavation a stone 'floor' was found in a shallow dip just outside Stonehenge to the west of the Heel Stone.[9] In the debris were the signs of occupation, flint implements, knapped stones, animal bones and what may have been a hearth whose charcoal provided a date of 1450 ± 150 bc (c. 1780 BC), late but not impossible to reconcile with the time when the sarsen ring was under construction. Men who could fashion the almost intractable sarsen were essential if the stones were to be turned into replicas of wooden beams. As rather similar floors had been noticed by Hawley, there may have been a temporary camp of expert masons dwelling on site during the warmer months of the year. It may have been these men who supervised the methods and decided on the order by which the uprights and the lintels were set in place.

Centuries of moving huge stones for megalithic tombs and circles and of lifting cumbersome oak trunks for buildings such as Woodhenge told the Stonehenge people how the sarsens of the ring and the trilithons were to be erected. There was a straightforward technique for raising the uprights. With the use of rollers on the even ground, the stone was pushed forward until it was balanced at the edge of its hole. This boxlike pit had one sloping side down which the lower end of the stone was slid until its base butted up against four or five thick poles standing protectively against the back of the stonehole. Stripped of their bark, these posts were sticky with sap that lubricated the movement of the stone's heel as the sarsen was levered and pulled up. Ropes fixed around its top were attached to great sheer-legs of seasoned timber that afforded extra leverage to the rope-handlers. Behind the stone other men jammed posts against it, preventing it from toppling backwards.[10]

The method was simple but demanding of man-power. Oxen could not be used and a stone three-quarters of the way to the vertical required a pull of a fifth of its dead weight to haul it the last few feet upwards. A hundred men, each exercising a strenuous and short-lasting pull of 100 lbs, would have been needed to move a 26-ton pillar of the outer circle. Stone 56 of the Great Trilithon, 50 tons of awkward sarsen, required twice that number, straining at a spread fan of ropes as the stone crunched and quivered slowly, apprehensively, into its deep hole.

Then, having checked with a plumb-line that the pillar was perfectly erect, men crammed chalk blocks, stones, bits of sarsen and bluestone into the sides of the hole, wedging the rubble around the stone, holding it securely. There is a minor mystery. In the packing were pieces of fine rock from Chilmark, 11 miles away. They may have been imported because there was insufficient local stone. But their presence may have been the result of some magical belief irrecoverable today.

Getting the lintels into position would have been the responsibility of carpenters knowledgeable in the problems of lifting heavy ring-beams and fitting them onto the heads of wall-posts. Stone-masons lacked this experience. Other than Stonehenge there is no stone circle in the British Isles with lintels, and the capstones of the passages and chambers of megalithic tombs were almost certainly dragged up the sides of the barrow mounds. No remains of such ramps have been detected at Stonehenge and other means must have been employed for positioning its lintels.

There have been many theories. The most plausible is that of building a platform or crib of squared logs under the stone, layer by 6 inch (15 cm) layer, levering one end of the lintel up, inserting a beam under it, levering the other end, putting more logs beneath it for a floor, then commencing the stage above with the timbers at right-angles to those below. It was a practice observed in modern Pakistan where a 60-ton metal cylinder, many times the weight of any lintel, was elevated by this stage-by-stage process with no danger as long as the platform was kept long enough to accommodate the workers. Although a mile of heavy timbers would have been needed at Stonehenge, the method had the advantage that the crib could quickly be dismantled and its joists re-used time after time.[11] Archaeologically it would be undetectable.

As long as the spacing of the tenons and mortises agreed with each other and as long as the heights of the sarsens were level, the lintels could be moved forward onto their uprights. Any error, however, would have been disastrous and today one can still see how the ends of some pillars and lintels were shaped into shoulders and steps to overcome the setback of a sarsen that was too short or a lintel that was too thick. Megalithic nuances such as these increase one's respect for the engineers of Stonehenge.

Commonsense suggests that it was the trilithons that were set up first. Gaps in the outer circle were too narrow for any large stone to have been passed safely through them, but it is just possible that the erection of the circle and its internal archways went on together, with the uprights of the five trilithons rising above the stones of the ring.

The inner faces of the sarsen ring follow the line of an almost perfect circle. It is difficult to understand how this could have been achieved if the trilithons had stood in the way of a marker-rope being swung from a focal point. It is feasible, therefore, that the ring was laid out and built with one gap left by Stone 11 at the south and another at the north-west where Stone 21 stands slightly outside the circumference. The huge pillars of the trilithons could have been dragged through these, erected, and once they were perpendicular, the gaps closed. This might explain why the ramp for Stone 56 came in unexpectedly from the west,[12] avoiding the circle-stones standing to north and east. It was here that Hawley found the axe of chalk. It would also explain why Stone 21, unlike the other stones in the ring, had its ramp inside the circle, because it could not have been pulled up from inside once the stones of trilithon 57–58 were erect.

For a megalithic ring that was constructed four thousand years ago with only the simplest of tools, the layout is surprisingly symmetrical. Thirty stones, on average 26 tons in weight and measuring 13 feet 4 inches high, 7 feet wide and 3 to 4 feet thick (4.1 × 2.1 × 1.1 m), were surmounted by thirty 6–7 ton lintels whose tops were never more than 4 inches (10 cm) from the horizontal, despite the skewed nature of the site. Petrie, in his precise survey of 1877, calculated that the mean error from the level was only 1.9 inches (48 mm), an astonishing accuracy attained by pre-planning, so that Stone 30 by the entrance was nearly a foot shorter than Stone 10 at the south where the land was lower.

The regularity of the spacing also is remarkable. The builders tried to have the stones twice as broad as the gaps alongside them so that the 7 foot (2.1 m) wide sarsens had 3 foot 6 inch (1.1 m) spaces on either side. How well the planners succeeded can be demonstrated by simple arithmetic. One stone plus one gap (7 + 3½ feet) = 10 feet 6 inches (3.2 m). Thirty such combinations would produce a circumference of 315 feet (96 m). The actual perimeter is 306 feet (93.3 m), a deviation of no more than 4 inches (10 cm) for each stone and the gap by it.

There were two exceptions. Stone 11 at the south was shorter and more slender than the others. The reasons for this will be considered. And the gap at the north-east between Stones 30 and 1, facing the causeway to the henge, was a foot wider than the rest, whereas the adjacent gaps between Stones 29–30 and 1–2 were narrower, producing an optical illusion of a big and impressive entrance. Even the lintel above it, Stone 101, was heavier. Stukeley noticed this: 'That impost which lies over the grand entrance, we said, was deeper and longer than the rest. Abraham Sturges, an architect, and myself measured it, in presence of Lord Winchelsea.'[13]

He also noticed the better finish to the interior of the ring: 'They set the best face of the stones inward . . . the stones of the inside both of the outward circle and of the cell [the horseshoe of trilithons], are the smoothest, best wrought, and have the handsomest appearance. . . . I find they took care to set those stones that had the best outward face, toward the front or entrance.'[14]

Stukeley was the first of many investigators to grasp at that will o'the wisp, the question of whether the builders had used a standardised unit of measurement. He decided that they had. He was convinced that the unit was not French, Roman or Greek. Instead, being certain that the people had come to Britain after the Flood, he decided it was related to Hebrew and Egyptian measures, 'most probably deriv'd from Noah and Adam', and was a 'Druid's Cubit' of 20.8 inches (53 cm). This could be multiplied by six to make a measuring staff 10 feet 4¾ inches (3.2 m) in length, the rod used in setting out the ring.[15]

Although Stukeley recognised that the hardness of the sarsens hindered their 'being chizel'd and squar'd to such preciseness as Roman works are', yet he believed there was a mathematical neatness to the ring, with the outer circle having a radius of 30 Druid's Cubits (DC) and each of its thirty stones being 4 DC in breadth, twice the width of the gaps between them. In this he anticipated the almost identical conclusions of Alexander Thom two hundred and fifty years later.

Sadly, despite his enthusiasm, Stukeley's surveys were not always accurate and did not impress John Wood, an asthmatic architect who visited Stonehenge twice in 1740. Scoffing at Stukeley's 'architect' as a 'jobing Bricklayer and Mason' from Amesbury, Wood was pleased to hear from 'Gaffer' Hunt, the old man who kept a drinks stall under Stone 60, that 'no regular survey had been taken of Stonehenge'.[16] Hardly had Wood begun his own planning when a storm blew up causing the locals to think that he had raised the Devil, a reflection of the widespread superstition that to interfere with ancient stones would result in thunder and lightning. It was a fear that preserved many megalithic sites from destruction.

Within a few days Wood had finished. His estimate of 97 feet (29.6 m) for the diameter of the circle was close to the 97 feet 4 inches (29.7 m) established by Petrie in the following century. Perhaps by good fortune, when he made a survey for Charles II in 1666 John Aubrey stated that 'the Diameter of the great circle is 32 yards ½',[17] or 97 feet 6 inches, even closer to Petrie's figure.

Flinders Petrie began his planning in 1874 but, dissatisfied with the results, he returned to Stonehenge in 1877 with newly-patterned chains which, he said, made the survey precise within a few tenths of an inch. The work was carried out in detail, stone by stone, and checked constantly.[18] From the final data Petrie concluded that the sarsen circle had an inner diameter of 97 feet 4 inches ± 1.7 inches (43 mm), and this has been accepted ever since. So have his dimensions for the sarsens and bluestones. He also discussed the possibility of a unit of length having been used. Stukeley had proposed his Druid's Cubit. Petrie believed in two separate units, a 'Phoenician Foot' of 22.51 ± 0.2 inches (57 cm) for the henge and a 'Roman Foot' of 11.68 inches (30 cm) for the stone circle. In 1930 Ludovic Mann claimed there had been two prehistoric units, an α Foot of 14.85 inches (38 cm) and a β Foot of 13.28 inches (34 cm), with a longer unit of 20.425 feet (6.3 m) for laying out large sites.[19] Interestingly, although deduced by Mann long before the analyses of Alexander Thom, this last measure is exactly three times the length of Thom's Megalithic Rod of 6.8 feet (2.1 m).

In 1974 Thom himself suggested that the stones of the sarsen circle had been contained inside two concentric circles whose respective circumferences measured 48 and 45 Megalithic Rods (326.4 and 306 feet; 99.5 and 93.3 m). Then, strangely like Stukeley of whose work he was apparently unaware, he wrote that the stones were twice as wide as their adjoining spaces, the widths being not of Stukeley's 4 and 2 Druid Cubits but of 1 and ½ of his own Megalithic Rods.[20]

To recover the measures used by prehistoric communities which, if ever they existed, were probably never standardised is an almost hopeless quest. At Stonehenge the only certainty is that the circle had an inner radius of 48 feet 8 inches (14.8 m) and if any unit of length was employed it was presumably a division of this. Petrie, with his 100 Roman Feet, may have been right in assuming that people had been using a counting-base of 5. There is a repetition of 5s in the 30 of the sarsen uprights and the 5 trilithons, a choice of number imposed by no obvious alternative. If the radius of the circle had been computed in multiples of 5 a possible unit is 2 feet 5¼ inches (74 cm) or a 'Foot' of 1 foot 2⅝ inches (32 cm). But in matters of prehistoric mensuration there are so many variables that a statistician could offer several plausible possibilities.

The trilithons offer different problems. Inigo Jones, believing Stonehenge to be a temple built by the Romans on principles of classical design, thought that originally there had been six arches arranged in a hexagonal figure, the one missing at the north-east having been lost through the 'Violence of Time, and injury of Weather' as well as by the 'Rage of Men likewise',[21] but John Aubrey disagreed: 'The Ruines of it doe cleerly enough show (without further demonstration) that it could neither be a Hexagon, or heptagon'.[22] Stukeley was less restrained about Jones: 'But this trilithon in dispute', he wrote sarcastically, 'must needs have been spirited away by nothing less than Merlin's magic'.[23] Nor did Hawley find any vestige of this imaginary setting.

There were never more than five incredible trilithons standing around a U-shaped space about 43 feet (13.11 m) long by 46 feet (14 m) wide. Alexander Thom suggested that the outer and inner faces of the uprights had been planned to lie between two concentric ellipses measuring 30 × 20 and 27 × 17 of his Megalithic Yard of 2.72 feet (0.83 m), and it is true that several of the stones do fit quite neatly. The centre of the hypothetical ellipses, though, is a full 4 feet (1.2 m) from the centre of the sarsen circle and Stone 56 of the Great Trilithon is a similar distance inside the south-west of the inner ellipse. That stone, observed Thom, 'has been re-erected and we cannot be certain of its exact original position',[24] but Gowland's meticulously recorded excavation proved that the pillar could not have been more than a few inches to the south of its present position and never near to Thom's hypothetical elliptical design.[25]

By another arithmetical coincidence William Stukeley anticipated Thom here also. He too believed that the trilithons lay between two concentric ellipses but his were formed from the intersection of two circles whose centres were 21 feet 8 inches (6.6 m) apart. The rings were each 52 feet (15.9 m) across, all the dimensions based on Stukeley's Druid Cubit. The ellipses were laid out using a string 60 cubits long, 'turn'd round upon two centers, according to the gardiners method'.[26] Like Thom, Stukeley was wrong. The stones do not fit the plan.

The five trilithons, whose purpose will be considered in the next chapter, were obviously meant to create an imposing, inner sanctum. Their inner faces were carefully smoothed and although the arches were spaced 10 feet 6 inches (3.2 m) apart, the gaps between their uprights were no more than 13 inches (33 cm) wide, like arrowslits in a tall, dark wall. Yet near their tops they widened abruptly into inverted triangles, neatly tooled and finished.

Occasionally there were botches. The lintel-stone 156, lying across the prostrate Altar Stone, has two deep mortise-holes on its former underside, but there are also two shallower depressions on what had been its upper surface, showing that for some unknown reason, or simple blunder, people had started to pound out the holes on the wrong side. Such mistakes did not detract from the overall effect.

It is noticeable that the five arches rise in height towards the Great Trilithon at the south-west. The trilithons opposite each other nearest the entrance, numbers 51–52 and 59–60, are some 20 feet (6.1 m) high. The intermediate pairs, 53–54 and 57–58, slightly angled inwards, stand about 21 feet 4 inches (6.5 m) tall. The ruined Great Trilithon, 55–56, at the flattened head of the horseshoe, once rose more than 2 feet (60 cm) above them, 24 feet (7.3 m) high and a full 8 feet (2.4 m) above the lintels of the surrounding circle.[27] Such grading of heights was deliberate. Had the stones all been of the same height a continuous horseshoe of lintels could have been arranged along their tops, an architrave that was impossible with trilithons rising at angles of 7° and 15°. The effect was to draw the eye towards the massive Great Trilithon. Only its very top could be seen from outside the ring, its bulk concealed from all those forbidden to enter the circle.

There was an insistence on visual effect. Indeed, more concern was shown over the heights of the stones than over their safety, and in several instances the builders' experimental solutions, sacrificing stability for spectacle, ultimately failed. When Stone 60 of the northernmost trilithon was being put up a huge fragment, half a ton in weight, broke from its base leaving the pillar too short by 2½ feet (76 cm). Not content to lower the intended trilithon by so much, perhaps because its counterpart, 51–52, at the east was already standing, the workers rolled boulders into the stonehole and balanced the truncated sarsen precariously upon them.[28] Its partner, Stone 59, fell and shattered before AD 1575. By 1959 Stone 60 was leaning and shifting so badly that it was straightened and set in concrete.

To the south-west both the uprights of trilithon 57–58 were erected in extremely shallow holes, presumably so that the stones would be of the same height as trilithon 53–54 opposite. Both fell outwards on 3 January 1797 'with a considerable concussion', 58 lying flat but 57 tilted at a convenient angle for Victorian boys to slide down its inner face on their hobnailed boots. The stones were re-erected by a 60-ton crane in 1958.

The erection of the Great Trilithon was a similar compromise between dramatic effect and architectural prudence. When two stones of exactly the right length could not be found, the workers dug an 8 foot 3 inches (2.5 m) deep hole for Stone 56, reducing its height above ground to about 22 feet (6.7 m). As its partner, Stone 55, was much shorter, but probably the longest suitable sarsen available, its pit could not be so deep. In an attempt to avert its collapse the masons battered the base of the stone into a broad and ugly club-foot. They were not successful. At some time the stone fell, bringing its lintel, 156, down with it and knocking over the Altar Stone. Stone 55 broke. Today its clumsy foot pokes out anatomically close to the Friars Heel of the fallen circle-stone 14.

Despite the errors and the compromises, when the five trilithons and the circle were at last erect they must have awed any prehistoric visitor. There was nothing so overbearing anywhere else and in the colossal ring the past dominated the present. It was a place where imagery, the transformation of tradition into new but recognisable forms, was more important than technical considerations of safety. The whole purpose of Stonehenge was to preserve antiquity and absorb it into a new form, the sarsen pillars and lintels being the ancient mortuary house made everlasting, a temple for the whole of society whose customs and beliefs were as old as the ancestors and the ghosts and the gods of the past. This is the answer to the ninth and tenth questions about Stonehenge. The stones were brought to a stoneless region because wood was mortal and stone was immortal, and the lintels were there because the first mortuary-house had timber lintels, the ring-beams of a house of mortality now given eternity by the genius and piety of people whose Neolithic forefathers had brought their dead there.

It was dark, claustrophobic, godlike. Stukeley was aware of the enclosing atmosphere: 'The stones that compose it, are really stupendous, their height, breadths and thickness are enormous, and to see so many of them plac'd together, in a nice and critical figure, with exactness; to consider, as it were, not a pillar of one stone, but a whole wall, a side, an end of a temple of one stone, to view them curiously, creates such a motion in the mind, which words can't express.'[29]

He was so impressed by the trilithons that he climbed onto the top of 53–54: 'My Lord Winchelsea and myself took a considerable walk on the top of it, but it was a frightful situation.' His feat was emulated in the 19th century by two young men who used a rope ladder and 'found the situation anything but frightful, for the lintel itself measures 15 ft 3 inches in length, and is 5 ft wide, so that one has space enough . . . to move about freely, and with no fear of toppling over'. In 1900 two Canadian cyclists were photographed on the same trilithon – with their bicycles![30]

It was on a stone of this trilithon that carvings were noticed in 1953. The engraved name IOH: LUD: DEFERRE had long been known, sharply etched at eye level on the inner face of Stone 53. Below, however, weathered and blurred, were carvings of a dagger and several axe-heads, all of them prehistoric.[31] Other carvings of axes were discovered on the outer surfaces of Stones 3, 4 and 5 of the circle. A rectangular carving on the inner face of Stone 57, almost erased by children sliding down the stone before its re-erection, had been considered to be modern, but keen eyesight showed it to be akin to the anthropomorphic 'figurines' known in the chambered tombs of Brittany. An even smaller, even more worn version can be seen below it. In 1958 yet another was found on the fallen lintel, 120. 'In its original position it would have been on the underside of the lintel, framed between the two supporting uprights, and would have been difficult to discern against the glare of the sky above it.'[32]

In 1934 Ludovic Mann thought he had detected a sickle-shaped carving and nine cupmarks on the underside of the prostrate lintel 156 from the Great Trilithon. The Bronze Age artist, he asserted, had made them using Mann's prehistoric 'β Foot' of 13.28 inches (35 cm). He was mistaken. Seventy years earlier John Thurnam told the Wiltshire Archaeological Society that Joseph Spreadbury, a hedger, remembered seeing the marks chiselled on the stone by a 'mechanic' around 1828. A similar mason's mark can be seen inside the lovely church at Edington in west Wiltshire where a Bishop of Salisbury, William Ayscough, was stoned to death in 1450 by a mob of Jack Cade's followers.[33]

The sickle can be ignored like other modern graffiti on the sarsens. The prehistoric markings, however, are important. They are significant not only for their symbolism as evidence of the axe-cult at Stonehenge and their links with a 'goddess' of the dead but also for the stones chosen to receive them. Pattern and purpose were closely linked in the prehistoric mind, as the grooved ware deposits proved earlier. The carvings show the same awareness of the connection between the object and its situation. Without exception they occupy cardinal positions. Stone 53 is due south of the centre of the circle, Stone 4, framed by Stones 3 and 5, is due east, and Stone 57 is due west, with lintel-stone 20 of the sarsen circle directly behind it. Only at the north, the place in the sky where the sun and moon never appeared, is there no carving. Over a thousand years after Neolithic people had laid out the henge with entrances both at the north-east and at the south, their Bronze Age descendants continued the tradition by carving their cult-symbols only on the stones at the east, west and south. One of the circle-stones also emphasises how important positioning was to the builders of Stonehenge.

Stone 11 is an oddity. It huddles like a wizened dwarf amongst the giant sarsens of the circle. Only 8 feet high and 3½ feet wide (2.4 × 1.1 m) it is over 5 feet (1.5 m) lower than Stone 10 to its east. Yet that pillar has a tenon to hold the lintel that was to span the gap between it and Stone 11. Various explanations have been offered for this anomaly: the stone, being soft, weathered badly; it was the last stone to be put up and there was room enough only for a thin pillar; it had been struck by lightning or smashed by stone-robbers; the builders ran out of big stones.

None of this is convincing. Either there had been a change of plan or the lintel had been removed years after its erection and Stone 11 pushed over and removed, being replaced by a lower, slighter stone. It is unlikely that the original stone was simply shortened, for it would have been very difficult to reduce the width of the stone in the same way. Instead, it is arguable that the slender stone had been chosen, like the carvings, to occupy and stress a specific location. Being so thin, it would widen the gaps on either side of it just as the gap was wider at the north-east entrance to the circle. Stone 11 also is at an entrance. It stands at the due south of the ring, exactly in line with the southern causeway. Quite possibly it was selected in the first place as the slimmest possible pillar to stand there and it was only later that men decided to draw even more attention to it by removing its lintel and shortening Stone 11 to make it more conspicuous.

The old and rough Station Stones may also have received some dressing to improve their appearance just as the portal-stones were shaped at the north-east causeway. Today their one survivor, Stone 95, popularly known as the Slaughter Stone, lies half-buried just inside the eastern terminal of the bank. About the same size as the uprights of the circle the sarsen seems to have been given its gruesome name late in the 18th century. Aubrey, Stukeley, Wood and Smith all refer to it merely as a stone by the entrance, but in Edward King's *Munimenta Antiqua, I* of 1799 it is called the 'slaughtering-stone', the slab to which the druids had dragged their human offerings.

> It is the sacrificial altar, fed
> With living men – how deep the groans! the view
> Of those that crowd the giant wicker thrills
> The monumental hillocks.
> William Wordsworth. *The Prelude, XIII*

It is all fantasy and 'the visitor will listen in vain for the ghostly shrieks of expiring victims spreadeagled on its bloodstained surface'.[34] Prostrate now, the stone once stood erect alongside a partner that was removed late in the 17th century.

In 1620 Inigo Jones dug around the Slaughter Stone to see if there was any connection between it and the sarsen circle but found nothing.[35] In 1801 Hoare and Cunnington investigated the fallen pillar and discovered it was not a rough sarsen block. It had been pounded and worked into shape like the circle-stones but, proving that it had once been perpendicular, its base had been left 'in its rude state, and unhewn. This we proved, by digging so completely under it as to be able to examine the undermost side of the stone, where we found fragments of stag's horns.' In a letter to a friend Cunnington reported that he had 'dug around it, and also into the excavation where it originally stood when erect'.[36]

What he did not mention was that he had put a bottle of port under the stone before filling in the cavity. Over a century later Hawley recovered the gift. Years before Hoare's and Cunnington's time the Slaughter Stone had been pushed over into a pit that was not quite long enough for it, its end resting on the pit's sloping sides, leaving a hollow under its centre which Cunnington backfilled with the spoil of his excavation. 'There could be little doubt about this', wrote Hawley, 'as we found a bottle of port left under the stone, presumably by him out of consideration for future excavators. The seal was intact, but the cork had decayed and let out nearly all of the contents.' The relic of this vinicultural tragedy is now displayed in Salisbury Museum.[37]

In the same season, 1920, Hawley found the large hole where a stone had been set some 8 feet (2.4 m) to the north-west of Stone 95. Together the pair would have stood symmetrically across the axis of Stonehenge and there can be little doubt that they had been portal-stones. What is questionable is whether they had stood alone or were the inner two of a four-sided setting with two more just outside the earthwork. Inigo Jones showed four stones in his formalised plan but his conviction that there had been three entrances to the henge makes his evidence unreliable. His nephew John Webb, however, using Jones' posthumous notes, made a sketch of Stonehenge 'from the North-East' with one entrance only. There, calling the stones 'pyramids', he drew 'the two Pyramids thereof on the outside of the Trench' and 'the two others on the inside'. Nearly fifty years after Jones' visit John Aubrey saw the two inner stones, but one of the outer pair had gone. All were standing. By Stukeley's time only the Slaughter Stone remained, 'at present flat on the ground'.[38]

Equivocal though the evidence is, it would not have been unusual for four great stones to stand at the entrance. Many other henges and circles had impressive portals: Long Meg & Her Daughters, Swinside and Mayburgh in Cumbria; perhaps Arbor Low in the Peak District; and, nearer to Stonehenge, Maumbury Rings in Dorset and Gorsey Bigbury and

Priddy South in the Mendips. There is an imaginative sketch by Stukeley in the Bodleian Library, Oxford, with an avenue of stones leading up to Stonehenge where a lintelled portico rises gracefully at the entrance. It is elegant but incorrect. The absence of a tenon on the Slaughter Stone shows it could never have held a lintel. It was a tall, shapely pillar standing with its partners at the gateway to the henge, the rough bulk of the Heel Stone looming behind them.

As though indifferent to the ancient alignments, the people positioned the Slaughter Stone so that from the centre of the ring the Heel Stone was half-hidden by it. 'If so placed', noted Barclay, 'it would hide the Sun-stone from an observer standing on the axis',[39] and this leads to the question of whether there were any intended sightlines in this sarsen phase of Stonehenge. There has been no shortage of astronomical vigour in the search for them.

Although the Heel Stone, the causeway postholes and the Four Stations have been subjected to almost constant astronomical analysis, the grossness of the sarsen circle and the trilithons have discouraged researchers. No refined sightline seemed possible amongst such heavy, close-set blocks and it has generally been agreed that in its sarsen phase Stonehenge was not an observatory. There was an ingenious notion that some hollows in the upper surfaces of the lintels over the entrance at the north-east had been sockets for poles which served as solar and lunar foresights for an observer standing on a lintel at the far side of the ring. This precarious priest must have been disconcerted to find that the Great Trilithon blocked his view, a planning blunder which suggests a lack of foresight rather than the opposite.[40] The hollows are, of course, the results of primordial tree-roots and later weathering and can be seen on the sides as well as the tops of many stones.

There have been more persuasive ideas. 'Peter' Newham suggested that the 29 sarsens of the circle and the diminutive Stone 11 were representations of 'the 29.5 days of the lunar month'.[41] This is worth consideration. Stonehenge did have associations with the moon, and prehistoric people did make symbols of their world. Their art reveals this. Passage-grave carvings have been seen as numerical records of the lunar month. Spiral patterns, carved on rocks and standing stones, may have represented the shadows cast by the sun.[42] The pillar-and-lozenge-shapes of the stones of the Kennet Avenue at Avebury have been interpreted as sexual symbols of fertility and death. That Stone 11 at Stonehenge had a combined role as a portal and as an image of a lunar half-day is quite possible. The sarsen circle may have been devised not only as the symbolic framework of a house. Its stones may also have been regarded as the moon's journey made into unmoving stone.

This could not be true of the five trilithons. John Smith, who explored Stonehenge in 1770, believed they were tokens of the four brightest planets then known, the 'telescopic' planets of Uranus, Neptune and Pluto only being detected many years afterwards. Trilithon 51–52 was Venus, 53–54 was Jupiter, 57–58 was Saturn and 59–60 was Mars. The Great Trilithon, 55–56, was the sun. To accommodate Mercury and the Moon, Smith invoked two bluestones, no. 48, 'much injured by ignorant people, who pay no regard to this venerable piece of antiquity', and no. 150, a bluestone lintel which Smith saw as the remains of a lunar archway. As will be seen, these two stones were not part of the first sarsen design. The bluestones were returned to Stonehenge many years later, perhaps not before 1500 BC, and were erected in an imperfect circle inside the sarsen ring with nineteen well-smoothed bluestones arranged in a horseshoe inside the U-shape of the trilithons.

Smith explained everything. The thirty sarsens of the circle when multiplied by the twelve signs of the zodiac portrayed the 360 days of the druidical year. Other stones were emblems of the harvest and hunter's moon. Every stone had meaning. The inner circle of bluestones was 'the lunar month: Between it and the great ellipsis [the trilithon horseshoe] you see the phase of the moon when she is six days old; the Druids then began to reckon her days, till she put on the same appearance again: which were 29 days and 12 hours: Herein they had an opportunity of comparing the lunar months, with the solar year'.[43] His book, *Choir Gaur . . .* , had a triumphant sub-title: Stonehenge, it proclaimed, was the Grand Orrery of the Ancient Druids, and was now 'Astronomically explained, and Mathematically proved to be a TEMPLE . . . for observing the Motions of the HEAVENLY BODIES'. Unfortunately, many of his calculations were faulty and his work is now only of historical interest as the first detailed attempt to examine Stonehenge astronomically.

The trilithons with their extraordinarily narrow gaps remained a problem for the archaeoastronomer. Even Sir Norman Lockyer in his studious investigation of Stonehenge could only suggest that they had acted as the walls of a dark, observing place like the passage of a chambered tomb.[44] It was not until 1963 that a scholarly explanation was put forward by Gerald Hawkins.[45] The gaps were for observing the extreme positions of the sun and moon. One had to peer through them towards the wider gaps in the sarsen circle. 'If you stand in that horseshoe, as I did, and try to look through the trilithon archways down viewing lines other than those . . . you will find, as I did, that you cannot. Your view is constricted by the narrowness of the archways. You cannot look down lines which point to no meaningful sun or moon position; you are forced to look through paired archways towards the inevitable sun-moon extreme positions.'

Hawkins was right about the limited views afforded by the circle and the trilithons. When all the stones were standing, it would have been impossible to see into the centre of Stonehenge except from the north-east. It was almost equally impossible to see out. Hawkins' statement, therefore, was quite correct. The lines did exist. The questions were whether they had been intended and how accurate they were.

**TABLE 15. Suggested sightlines for the trilithons**

| From Trilithon | To Circle Gap | Azimuth | Celestial Event |
|---|---|---|---|
| 51 – 52 | 6 – 7 | 131°.6 | Midwinter Sunrise |
| 53 – 54 | 8 – 9 | 120°.6 | Midsummer Moonrise (Minor) |
| 53 – 54 | 9 – 10 | 139°.4 | Midsummer Moonrise (Major) |
| 55 – 56 | 15 – 16 | 231°.4 | Midwinter Sunset |
| 57 – 58 | 20 – 21 | 292°.0 | Midwinter Moonset (Minor) |
| 57 – 58 | 21 – 22 | 315°.2 | Midwinter Moonset (Major) |
| 59 – 60 | 23 – 24 | 304°.7 | Midsummer Sunset |

There are problems. Several stones, as Hawkins noted, are missing or fallen or have been replaced, so that where they once stood within a few inches is unsure. Moreover, as Hoyle remarked, if all the trilithon gaps had been as narrow as that between 51 and 52 an observer at 53–54 and 57–58 would have found it exceptionally difficult to sight through more than one gap in the sarsen ring. Gaps in that ring were also very wide, offering a range of as much as 10° of the skyline. This meant that instead of seeing the midwinter sunrise neatly framed between Stones 6 and 7 for the three or four days of its 'standstill', an observer would have been able to see sunrises for three weeks before and after the winter solstice. Nevertheless, concluded Hoyle, 'The fact that each of these five directions happens to "agree" with an astronomical alignment seems to indicate that the trilithon positions were deliberately chosen in terms of those alignments'.[46]

If so, the lines were ritualistic rather than observational. The baselines were far too short, never more than 25 feet (8 m) long, for any well-defined astronomical sighting,[47] and the errors, up to 8° from what might have been expected,[48] militated against any observer using them for lunar or solar predictions. Hawkins did not claim that they had. To the contrary, he thought the lines 'helped to create and maintain priestly power, by enabling the priest to call out the multitude to see the spectacular risings and settings of the sun and moon, most especially the midsummer sunrise over the heel stone and midwinter sunset through the great trilithon'.[49]

In 1953 R.S. Newall, who had often helped Hawley on his excavations, made a similar suggestion. To him Stonehenge was sepulchral and had a connection with the world of the dead. 'This connection is symbolically represented by the Winter Solstice sunset, the sun passing as it were through the great trilithon representing the door of a tomb to the Netherworld.'[50] As always, it was the dead who controlled the living at Stonehenge.

# 10

## To the bleak midwinter
## Stonehenge IIIc: 1650 – 1250 BC

*Death hath so many doors to let out life.*

John Fletcher, *The Custom of the Country*

For more than a thousand years, farther back in time than the earliest Viking invasions are from today, Stonehenge had been changing. Yet through all those brief lifetimes, all those deaths, there had been a constancy within it like a landscape through the seasons, different in the leaves and mists and snows but, underneath them, the same, unchanging.

After the early Neolithic long barrows and the mortuary stockades and after the cursuses there had been the first Late Neolithic native mortuary house, round and heavy with bodies of humans and skulls of oxen inside it. There had been the earthwork of the henge, erected around the charnel-house, with moonlit posts at its entrance, with an axe of chalk buried at its heart and with a human burial across its axis. Centuries later, at the time of grooved ware domination, there had been great rings of posts and the digging of the Aubrey Holes with their cremations and long bone pins, and other cremations near the bank, one of them a child with whose ashes a macehead had been laid. There was always the axe, the sun and moon, and there was always death. With the emergence of beakers there had been the unfinished circles of bluestones, one inside the other reproducing the walls of the mortuary house but now facing the rising sun at midsummer.

Then there was the resurgence of native customs and the sarsens of the Early Bronze Age, their lintels like the husk of the mortuary house with the cold winds of the plain whispering through its empty walls. There were carvings and trilithons whose meaning becomes clearer as the centuries before them are understood better. Stonehenge was still to change. But the final changes make its understanding even clearer. It was, and would be, for the dead. Death was familiar here, in the moonlight and the sunrise and then, as Stonehenge grew older, in the dark setting of the sun.

So be my passing . . .
Let me be gathered to the quiet west,
The sundown splendid and serene,
Death.
      W. E. Henley. *Margaritae Sororis*

It is not only the dead that can be seen. Settlements are known at this time on Salisbury Plain, groups of huts for petty landowners living comfortably with their families and workers inside the protection of ditched and banked enclosures. The farmsteads were quite small, perhaps for no more than twenty people, and they lay amongst a pattern of square and rectangular fields with droveways keeping the herds and flocks away from the wheat and barley. Near the enclosures postholes of vanished stockades show where cattle were sheltered during the hard winter months. Dunghills by the huts were convenient dumps for rubbish such as broken pots, and scattered sherds recovered from fields reveal how manure had been spread there in early attempts to enrich the soil.

There must have been scores of such tiny settlements crowding together in the landscape. A deep V-shaped boundary-ditch at Snail Down just north of Stonehenge was over a quarter of a mile long, dividing one land-holding from another. An enclosure near Woodhenge had a droveway leading to it. There was another on Boscombe Down to the east. Several circular huts near the Winterbourne Stoke crossroads were associated with enclosures and boundary-ditches and the presence of others at Rox Hill and Fargo Plantation suggest that much of the Plain was now under intensive cultivation.

Husbandry and domesticity meant increasing comfort, but it did not mean that the old beliefs had been abandoned. To the contrary, at Thorny Down, 7 miles south-east of Stonehenge, a mixture of the mundane and the magical was discovered.[1]

Inside an enclosure high on the downs and covering nearly half an acre the postholes of nine round huts were found, some with porches and hearths and probably thatched. Around the huts were cooking-places, hollows for parching grain, and pairs of posts that had served as corn-drying racks and granaries for the seed-corn. A few of the huts were small and may have been storehouses, but the majority were about 20 feet (6 m) across, large enough for a family of five or six people eating and working near the middle, sleeping alongside the walls, warm under soft skins, farm-dogs drowsing by the hearth.

Built of timber, the huts had to be repaired. Some posts were replaced, but it is unlikely that any building was occupied for more than fifty years and this is in keeping with what is suspected about the semi-permanent agricultural practices of those centuries.

Although dark and smoky, the interiors of the huts were clean. Far from living in squalor the inhabitants had been tidy and it was only in the darkest recesses that litter remained. Sherds of poorly-fired domestic pots lay there, vessels known as Deverel-Rimbury ware, in barrel and bucket shapes, badly fired, 'extremely coarse . . . [with] a rough, rasping sensation to the touch'. There were flint scrapers showing that most people still wore leather clothing, although two loom-weights were evidence of weaving for the privileged. There were querns for grinding flour, stone pounders, pot-boilers, a bone needle, bones of ox and pig and sheep, all very ordinary except for a fragment of a bronze bracelet and a bronze spearhead, signs of luxury beyond the thoughts of the majority.

With virtually no bones of wild animals anywhere, there could have been little hunting and the spearhead hints at continuing violence and warfare amongst Bronze Age society. Brutality was common. The skeletons of two young men dumped in a ditch or pit on West Littleton Down near Tormarton in Gloucestershire had been murdered. One had a spearwound in his pelvis. The other had been savagely cut on the head and then, as he fell, two spears had been driven into his spine so fiercely that their heads broke off and were embedded in his bones. The thrusts deliberately paralysed the man. Another skeleton at Queensford Farm in Oxfordshire also had a spearhead in its pelvis, and a segment of spine in Lillau museum in France has a similar wound. Most tellingly, a rock-carving in the Camonica Valley of Italy shows a man being pierced through the lower part of his body by a spearsman. The carving alongside is of a man without legs, apparently signifying the fate of the stricken person. Bronze Age warriors quite ruthlessly incapacitated their foes.[2]

The inhabitants of the Thorny Down settlement may have been protected on earth by the spear but they were safeguarded spiritually from the dead and the Other-World by the axe. In the posthole of one hut was the broken part of a Cornish greenstone axe, hundreds of years old but deliberately buried there before the post was erected. Even as late as the 19th century AD such stone axes, known as 'thunderstones', were placed in the walls or doorways of peasants' cottages, and in the Neolithic settlement of Trøldeb-jerg in Denmark a pit inside a longhouse contained a complete pot and a stone axe with its cutting edge facing upwards. An axe-cult, somewhat akin to that in Britain, is known to have existed in Denmark and will be referred to again in this chapter. Here it is sufficient to remark that the Thorny Down axe, a survivor from Neolithic times, shows not only how an axe-cult persisted into the Bronze Age but how strongly the relics of previous ages were revered.

Stone, however, was outmoded for weaponry. Stone axe-hammers were still used for heavy work but it was the bronze axe that was fashionable, skilfully manufactured in a two-piece mould. These axes of the Arreton Down industry, with slender bodies, flaring cutting edges and flanged sides, are masterpieces of the bronzesmith's craft. They were polished so smoothly that every trace of a casting-seam was removed and their surfaces were decorated with fine incisions in triangles and bars of exquisite design. It was the shapes of native axes like these, from about 1600 BC, that were carved on the sarsens of Stonehenge.

There were other splendid articles. As well as spearheads there were bronze daggers with ogival sides that tapered gracefully inwards, and the blades had thick midribs and three rivet-holes to attach the daggers to their handles. They were very similar to others from Brittany and are sometimes called Armorico-British B from their Breton counterparts, or Camerton-Snowshill after the places in which they were first recognised in southern England. The dagger carving at Stonehenge is a representation of one of them.

There were bone tweezers and there were tiny bronze razors with an oval blade 'sharp enough to mend a pen', wrote a contemporary of Sir Richard Colt Hoare. These were all luxuries and they were the luxuries of the well-to-do on Salisbury Plain whose temple was Stonehenge and whose burial-places were the great cemeteries that gathered and grew along the skyline around the circle. With the dead were objects of amber, copper and tin, shale, bone and jet. There were miniature halberds and axes, bronze pins, necklaces of black jet, and there were exotic faience beads. These had been formed from quartz and alkali fired together to make a glassy material coloured blue-green with copper salts. Attractive jewellery was manufactured from this in segmented or star or quoit shapes, perforated for beading into necklaces. The technique probably originated in Egypt and although some pieces may later have been produced in Scotland, these seem to have been imitations of their southern predecessors in Wessex that had been placed with the ashes and urns of the wealthy dead.

Only excavation could have recovered these articles. There has been no shortage of excavations on Salisbury Plain but the sadness is that much of it has been unrecorded plundering. Stukeley, to his credit, did describe the finds from the ten or more barrows he dug into and noted how bluestone chippings from Stonehenge lay in Amesbury 4, a fine bowl later explored by Cunnington who discovered a cremation with a bronze dagger and awl beneath another large fragment of bluestone. This, like Stukeley's pieces, had presumably been placed in the barrow at a time when the discarded bluestones of Stonehenge II were being reshaped before their return to Stonehenge. They may have been deposited as talismen and, if so, it would not be the only example of 'foreign' material being left with the dead. At Winterbourne 9, a small bowl on Thorny Down, 145 flint flakes and cores, none of them local, had been heaped over a cremation. At another bowl, Bulford Down 9, tons of wood ash covered an urned cremation in a layer so thick that during the excavation, one of Hawley's earliest, 'the ash collapsed and buried a man nearly to his shoulders'.[3]

Disc-barrows, those attractive mini-mounds inside encircling ditches, have provided much information about this later period of the Early Bronze

Age. Of the forty-six investigated no fewer than forty-three contained cremations in pits, some, like Winterbourne Stoke 67, of a corpse burnt on a
distant pyre before its ashes were carried in a cloth bag to the grave. The
frequent occurrence of beads, small bronze knives rather than daggers and
sharp bronze awls for leather-working suggests that these elegantly-
designed barrows were the burial-places of highly-ranked women. At
Winterbourne Stoke 67 the low mound covered a bronze awl, five shale
rings, a shale bead, another of amber and more of faience, all of them
beautiful ornaments of female attire.

It has sometimes been possible to reconstruct the funerary rites. Collingbourne Kingston 8, a small bell barrow in the Snail Down cemetery, was
dug into by Cunnington, who found an urn, now lost, and human ashes.
By 1955 the mound was being so badly damaged by army tanks that it
was re-excavated. Beneath it an alignment of stakeholes arranged WSW-
ENE towards sunrise in early May suggests that people may have begun
preparing the burial-place after a death in Springtime. A circular furrow
was scribed out whose focal point, 'a small post-hole, 2–3 inches in diameter, was found at the geometrical centre of the [later] barrow'.[4] Its diameter
was 115 feet (35.1 m), of no relevance to the Megalithic Yard but, interestingly, exactly 48 of the 'Beaker Yards' theorised for Woodhenge 7 miles
away. A corpse of an adult male may have been exposed in this precinct
or temporarily buried in a pit to the north.

As in so many of these protracted funerary rites, it was not until months
later in the autumn, when acorns lay on the ground, that a pyre of heavy
timbers was erected at the centre of the ring and the bones were burned.
When the ashes had cooled, an untidy pit was dug through the reddened
earth and charcoal. The charred bones, in an urn, were placed in it. Over
the burial the mourners heaped a stack of turves. Then, using the furrowed
circle as a guideline, they trenched out a ditch and carried basketloads of
turf, earth and chalk to dump over the stack, heaping up a round barrow
7 feet high and 60 feet across (2.1 × 18.3 m).

More gruesome was the fate of another corpse nearby, exposed on a
raised platform at Collingbourne Kingston 11. Its slow corruption attracted
the slow, wheeling buzzards, carrion birds with broad, tattered wings like
the torn cloaks of wind-blown witches. Hunched on the platform they fed
on the putrescent flesh, tearing at the body. Their droppings were scattered
like pellets all around the scaffold.

> The rain has washed and cleansed us,
> And the sun dried and blackened us,
> Magpies and crows have hollowed out our eyes
> And torn away our beards and eyebrows.
> Never, never are we at rest. . . .
> François Villon. *Epitaph* (trans. A. Bonner)

Later the bones were burned and the ashes buried in an urn. Next to the grave-pit three smaller holes were dug, one holding splinters of cremated bone, a second with charcoal from the pyre, and the third neatly packed with tiny sherds from an urn,[5] replicas of the process by which the dead person had moved into the Other-World. An almost identical funerary microcosm came from the recumbent stone circle of Loanhead of Daviot in Aberdeenshire. Everything was a symbol, an essence of reality.

Sphagnum moss from the New Forest 15 miles away lay in the bell barrow of Amesbury 85 on Boscombe Down. The man in it had not been cremated but buried with his dagger in a wood-lined grave. Elderly, with some rheumatism of the spine, he had 'lived under conditions when food was abundant and well-cooked', for his teeth were not worn down. Nevertheless, he had had painful pyorrhoea.[6] So had the 30-year old man under the bowl barrow of Figheldean 16. Of poor physique, his hide-wrapped corpse showed an unpleasant infection of the mouth with mortification of the left jaw, with several teeth missing and many others in a bad state of decay.[7]

As with the youths at Todmarton, it was assault rather than illness that caused the death of a man in a barrow near the Snail Down group. Before the cremation of his body his head had been removed. 'Perhaps the skull, which had evident marks of a contusion, and which very probably occasioned the Briton's death, was reserved on purpose to denote to posterity the cause of it.'[8] Another aspect of the fearful treatment of the dead appeared in the barrows around Durrington, nos 34, 45, 49 and 50, where the cremated bones had been put right at the bottom of deep pits and covered with masses of ash from the pyres. Even stranger, at Kingston Deverill 2b only 'very black ashes, and charred wood' were found. There was no trace of human remains.

The cremations of the later Early Bronze Age, the Wessex II period, were interred in large, collared urns. Frequently these were accompanied by a small 'accessory' vessel. These pots, no bigger than a breakfast cup and without handles, have been given different names according to their appearance: grape cups, incense cups, pygmy cups, Aldbourne cups, the last with motifs of impressed triangles and horizontal lines and with outward-flaring lips like the vase-supports of Brittany. Frequently the sides of these miniature vessels have perforations in opposing pairs or fours, near the bottom as well as the top, making it very unlikely that the holes were for suspension. The pots rarely show signs of having been burnt with the cremation and it is arguable that they were ritual containers for the ceremonial flame with which the pyre would be ignited, the holes made in them for ventilation. In 19th century India pieces of sandalwood were lit in the dead man's house, placed in a bronze vessel and carried solemnly to the pyre as a sacred flame.[9]

It may have been at night that the last rites were performed, with burning torches lighting the way to the pyre and then, when the cremation was done, illuminating the raking of the ashes and the placing of the urn in its pit, sometimes with the accessory vessel inside it on top of the burnt bones. Grave-goods were left, a lovely necklace of forty-eight beads of shale, red amber and segmented faience at Upton Lovell 1 'such as a British female would not in these modern days of good taste and elegance disdain to wear', wrote Colt Hoare.[10] A similar necklace was buried with one of seven cremations under a phallic-shaped cairn of flints, Winterslow 21, on Easton Down.[11]

When the funeral was done, the mourners may have circled the barrow night by night for weeks, walking or dancing, chanting threnodies as silent now as the ancient skies. At a disc barrow on Snail Down, Collingbourne Kingston 18, in spite of the weather the surrounding ditch had been kept clean for months. It was 'sufficiently flat-floored and wide to have been intended for the movement of people'. Sir Cyril Fox noticed the same at Pond Cairn in Glamorgan: 'The trodden floor of the interspace suggests a ceremonial movement (of men, or both sexes) round the stack.'[12] Grieving for the dead and fear of the dead went together, the living and the dead never far apart in the animistic world of prehistory.

It was during these years that it was decided to return the bluestones to Stonehenge. Twenty-two of the largest may have been picked out and smoothed before being arranged in an ellipse inside the trilithon horseshoe. The evidence is ambiguous, but whether there was such an ellipse or not it was not satisfactory. The stones were taken away and some unknown leader decided that sixty bluestones should stand in two concentric circles around the sarsen ring.

In 1923 Hawley discovered the pits that had been dug for them, calling them the Y and Z Holes, an inner ring (Z) roughly 126 feet (38.4 m) in diameter and an outer (Y) 174 feet (53 m) across. In a very irregular layout, each was intended to have thirty stones corresponding to the thirty sarsens of the ring. Hawley excavated twenty-three of them and two more were investigated in 1953.[13] Like the sarsens, they were numbered from the north-east, Y1 and Z1 in a clockwise direction up to Y30 and Z30.

They were not well planned. For some reason not apparent today, the prehistoric workers seem to have started at the SSE, opposite Stone 9, digging one hole, Z9, 12 feet (3.7 m) from it, and another, Y9, 24 feet (7.3 m) further out so that Stone 9, Z9 and Y9 stood in a straight, radiating line 36 feet (11 m) long. These distances correspond exactly to 5, 10 and 15 'Beaker Yards', but the undertaking was not carried out by skilled or even careful surveyors. It was casually done. With the sarsen ring and the trilithons in the way it was impossible to use a marking-out rope from the centre of Stonehenge and the positions of the holes had to be decided by eye in offsets from the sarsens. As the work progressed, the 'circles' of the Y and Z Holes became more and more out of true until, finally, almost as the diggers reached the end, they realised how erratic their line had been. They gave up. The last hole of the outer ring, Y7, was only half dug. Z8 was not even started.

Three good pieces of evidence prove that the holes were made long after the erection of the sarsens. The hole for Z7 cut through the filled-in ramp of Stone 7. In the Y and Z Holes there were sherds of Deverel-Rimbury pottery like that from Thorny Down, a type of pottery not in existence when the sarsens were being raised.[14] And an antler from the bottom of Y30 gave a date of 1240 ± 105 bc, about 1550 BC, centuries after the building of the great ring.

The intention had been to put the bluestones in these holes but, yet again, the project was unfulfilled as though men could not decide what to do with these strange and perhaps dangerous foreign stones. Not one hole had the impression of a stone in its base. Instead, the pits were left open, ugly cavities that slowly filled with blown soil in the dry, windy conditions of the age. Yet, as in all things connected with Stonehenge, there were rituals. The holes nearest the north-east entrance, Y30 and Z30, were treated specially. Y30 had five antlers propped in it and Z30 was given a small stone disc like the funerary tokens of earlier times. Z29 also had antlers. Significantly, a fragment of human skull was found in Y6 alongside an antler. Fertility and death were still companions, even in a design that had been forsaken.

Perhaps, being outside the sarsens, the holes were deemed too close to the profane world to receive stones. The closeted interior of the circle was better. It is noticeable that while bits of Deverel-Rimbury ware, that wretchedly-made domestic pottery, were found in the Y and Z Holes, not a single piece was recovered inside the ring of sarsens. Only beaker and urn sherds were found there, funerary vessels used in the ceremonies for which Stonehenge had been built. Yet, even as they denied the Y and Z Holes the stones for which they had been prepared, men took care not to offend the spirits of the Other-World. In the holes bits of bluestone were dropped, mostly of rhyolite, fine-grained, mottled, distinctive, easily recognised, symbolising the pillars that should have stood there, image and reality becoming one. 'These fragments seem to be deliberate deposits . . . substitutes for the stones themselves, to ward off any evil consequences that might result . . . from depriving the gaping holes of their rightful and expected contents.'[15]

At last, one and a half thousand years after people had first come there, Stonehenge was to take its final form. Sarsens and bluestones were joined together in a harmony of shape and stone that would endure for a few centuries before neglect, the weather and greedy farmers wrecked it. A circle of bluestones was put up inside the sarsen ring. A horseshoe of bluestones was arranged inside the horseshoe of trilithons. The Altar Stone was erected halfway between the circle-centre and the Great Trilithon. Stonehenge was complete.

There could hardly have been a greater difference between the treatment of the horseshoe bluestones and those in the ring, the first being elegantly composed, its selected stones meticulously shaped, polished and neatly positioned, the circle leftovers hastily and carelessly put up as though the construction of the ring had been no more than a method of using up the stones.

Nineteen bluestones, all of them dolerite, were chosen for the U-shaped setting that was to stand inside the trilithons. Its open end was in line with the two lower trilithons at the north-east and its closed arc swung within two paces of the Great Trilithon. All the stones had been skilfully dressed into tall, conical pillars, likened by some to phallic effigies, and they were graded in height with the lowest at the north-east a full 3 feet (1 m) shorter than the tallest, Stone 67, at the apex of the horseshoe, its top 9 feet 3 inches (2.8 m) above ground. In this grading the bluestone horseshoe repeated the rising heights of the trilithons as they climbed steadfastly towards the south-west.

Two of the stones had been used before. Stone 68, leaning near the gigantic Stone 56 of the Great Trilithon, has a long, deep groove down its side. Stone 66, now broken and concealed beneath the huge fragment of Stone 55, has a projecting tongue. Atkinson has persuasively suggested that, in an earlier phase, the two stones were fitted together, their combined width matching that of a broad stone on the other side of the axis in a setting that served 'as a backsight for the observation of the midsummer sunrise'.[16]

It has been suggested that just as the 29½ stones of the sarsen circle may have represented the moon it its monthly course, so the 19 stones of the new horseshoe stood for the time it took the moon to complete its 18.6 year cycle back to its extremes. It is possible. It was probably during this phase at Stonehenge that Stone 11 was replaced by a sarsen half its size and a similar lunar symbolism could well have been intended by the erectors of the bluestone horseshoe, men wishing to restore the moon to its old temple.

Within the horseshoe and some 10 feet (3 m) south-west of the circle-centre men raised the Altar Stone, a name given to it by Inigo Jones because it lay flat beneath the shattered Stone 55 in a situation ideal for a sacrificial slab. It had, however, stood upright. Cunnington almost certainly discovered its massive stonehole, 6 feet (1.8 m) deep on the axis of the monument. Now 15 feet 9 inches (4.8 m) long, this block of Cosheston sandstone once rose 10 feet (3 m) high, blocking most of the narrow gap through the Great Trilithon. Its north-west end has been chipped and battered by souvenir-hunters, but its base still shows signs of having been bevelled to make its erection easier, confirming that this imposing stone was once upright, smoothed and regular, a major feature of Stonehenge.

Days, weeks must have passed as the stones were wearily prepared. Bits from them have been found inside the circle, in the area of the adjacent car-park, by the Cursus, even in round barrows where they may have been placed because of their magical powers. Geoffrey of Monmouth wrote that the circle-stones were famous for their healing powers and even two hundred years ago people were removing pieces as talismans, maybe in the vaguest of folk memories of how the stones had once been both venerated and feared. But however much care was taken over the horseshoe and the Altar Stone, this was not true of the stones in the bluestone ring.

Almost as indifferently as they had set out the Y and Z Holes, men dragged some sixty stones into Stonehenge and, without shaping them, set them close together in a haphazard circle inside the sarsen ring. They did it badly. In diameter the 'circle' varied from 75 to 78 feet (23–24 m) and even with the obstructive trilithons and the bluestone horseshoe preventing the swinging of a laying-out rope, a more symmetrical result could have been attained if the workers had been concerned about it. The resultant shoddy shape suggests that astronomer-priests and meticulous surveyors did not dominate Bronze Age society as has sometimes been supposed, and may not even have existed. Mathematics mattered less than imagery. It was not geometry but mortality that moved the minds of men.

So irregular is this ring that its diameter has been variously calculated as 78 feet (23.8 m) by John Wood, 78 feet 9 inches (24 m) by Flinders Petrie and 77 feet 11 inches (23.8 m) by Alexander Thom. Some stones like 31, 37 and 49 were placed inside the circumference, others were outside it. Stone 33 was nearly 2 feet (60 cm) off the line. Such gross errors could have been avoided if people had used the perfect circle of the sarsens as a base from which to measure inwards. If the diameter of the bluestone ring was meant to be 78 feet (23.8 m), its perimeter would have been no more than a short 9 feet 8 inches (2.9 m) from the inner faces of the sarsens. A yardstick could have determined this within a few inches. Whether the distance was measured as 5.6 Druid's Cubits of Stukeley or 9.9 Roman Feet of Petrie or 3.6 of Thom's Megalithic Yards or 4.0 'Beaker Yards', the method would have resulted in only the most minor of deviations from a true circle.

The erratic positioning of the bluestones shows that nothing systematic was undertaken. It also shows carelessness and perhaps impatience to get the job done. It certainly creates scepticism about the belief that many British stone circles were planned neatly by eye alone.[17]

It is hard today to visualise what the ring once looked like. Only six stones remain erect, five lean and the rest are fallen, are smashed stumps or no longer exist. Because of this chaos Petrie was restricted to numbering the identifiable stones from no. 31 at the north-east round to 49, its partner, at the other side of the entrance. Yet if the poorness of the circle-shape itself is ignored it can be seen that this new setting of bluestones had properties in common with what had gone before.

Even in the ravaged state of the ring it is possible to discern patterns. There is a wider gap between Stone 49 and 31 at the entrance, reproducing the broader space between Stone 30 and 1 of the sarsen ring. Despite being unshaped the bluestones were arranged alternately as thin pillars and squatter blocks like the 'male' and 'female' stones of Avebury's avenue.

This is most obvious at the entrance where the slender Stone 49 is 4 inches (10 cm) higher than its broad partner, 31, male on the right, female on the left, like the arrangement of the men's and women's beds inside the Neolithic village of Skara Brae in the Orkneys. For a circle like Stonehenge, deeply concerned with death and fertility, such sexual impressionism is quite feasible.

Some attempt also was made to pair opposite stones, particularly those of rhyolite, the type of bluestone deposited in the Y and Z Holes, In the ring Stone 36 faced Stone 46 and Stone 40 looked across the circle to Stone 48. Again, it seems it was necessary to 'bond' materials together in combinations inexplicable to us today. Most remarkable of all, a gap was left between Stones 35 and 36, a space at the south that was in line with the timber-walled passageway of the first Stonehenge, in line with the southern causeway of the succeeding henge and in line with the diminutive Stone 11 of the sarsen circle, the perpetuation of an alignment through three distinct structural phases separated by a millennium and a half. Traditions changed but were never obliterated.

Some traditions, indeed, may have survived into modern times, diluted and christianised but with recognisably pagan elements. For over a thousand years on the feast-days of local saints in Brittany there have been annual *pardons*, gatherings of devout Christians for the forgiveness of sins and for the taking and fulfilling of vows. The greatest is at Ste-Anne-d'Auray, 10 miles north-east of Carnac-Ville, where a torchlit procession on the evening of 25 July is followed next day by a religious service conducted by the priest in his most splendid vestments. This is followed by a magnificent procession from the church, with people in ceremonial costumes carrying candles, banners and statues of the saint. When the long parade has passed through the crowded streets the onlookers move happily to the restaurants that line the route and, having fed and wined well, turn to the enjoyment of what has become a fun-fair but which was once a medley of market-stalls, wrestling matches, races and general festivity, not all of it christian.

Another *pardon*, at St-Jean-du-Doigt 9 miles north of Morlaix, is as marvellous. There, during the time of the summer solstice, on the night of 23 June sacred relics are carried through the streets, after which the statue of an angel is lowered by machinery from the church tower. She holds a burning torch with which a bonfire is lit, 'The Passion of the Fire', in a ritual manifestly descended from prehistoric rites of sympathetic magic in which the flames of the setting midsummer sun were imitated.

It is noteworthy that these *pardons* begin at night-time just as Celtic festivals did. Then, the next day at St-Jean-du-Doigt there is the same mingling of devotions and profane feasting, the meeting of friends, and entertainments that linger on into the night. It is just such a mélange of the devout and the worldly, the mingling of the rulers of society and the commoners, the mixture of mysteries and the mundane that may be imagined for Stonehenge on the great occasions of the year. One can visualise a comparable procession moving, jostling, along the stone rows of Carnac up the slopes towards the huge stone circles, burning torches flaring in the night air, priests or shamans leading the throng of celebrants.

A question that is rarely asked is how, in a pre-literate and semi-numerate age, people, some many miles away from Stonehenge, would know the time of a festival. It is unlikely that ordinary men and women kept tallies, scrutinising and recording the sun and moon on their courses. Someone, however, must have done so and recent analogies suggest who this may have been. Several American Indian tribes, the Hopi amongst them, had sun-watchers whose duty it was, using natural features or man-made structures as foresights, to follow the movement of the sun and recognise when the solstices had arrived or when the time for planting had come. They were not all highly competent. 'We think the sun-watcher is not a very good man. He missed some places, he was wrong last year. . . . All the people think this is why we had so much cold this winter and no snow.'[18] At Stonehenge an 'astronomer-priest', perhaps no more efficient than his transatlantic counterpart, may have performed a similar function.

The megalithic mechanism for a 'calendar' to be used by a sun-watcher existed at Stonehenge, although there was nothing delicate about it. It was clumsy and perhaps not even intended but it could be used. All that was required was for an observer standing on the NE-SW axis to place himself on the line between the gaps of trilithons 51–52 and 59–60 (Fig. 12). From that position, about 20 feet (6 m) in front of the Altar Stone, eight solar and lunar settings would be apparent over the year. The major southern moon would set just behind the left-hand side of Stone 55. Sunsets in early February, the festival of Imbolc, and November, Samain, would have been seen a little to the right of Stone 56. West was defined between the stones of trilithon 57–58. The sunsets of early May, Beltane, and August, Lughnasa, occurred close to the left edge of Stone 59, and the major northern moon would have set through trilithon 59–60.

The midwinter sunset was even more dramatic. Each evening, as the winter days shortened, the sun set more and more towards the south-west. Eventually, by mid-November, it would be hidden behind the bulk of Stone 56. From that evening onwards it would set behind the sarsen for a fortnight or more until it reappeared near the beginning of December in the gap of the Great Trilithon. To see it the sun-watcher would have had to move to the far side of the obscuring Altar Stone. From there the space between the trilithon stones was over 5° wide and it would have been a simple matter to note the succeeding sunsets until the solstitial sun reached its southern extreme.

There can be no proof that the sarsens of Stonehenge were actually employed in this way as a megalithic calendar that would indicate the times of the festivals. Not only are the stones silent but the ruinous condition of the circle in the critical south-west sector adds to the uncertainty. One

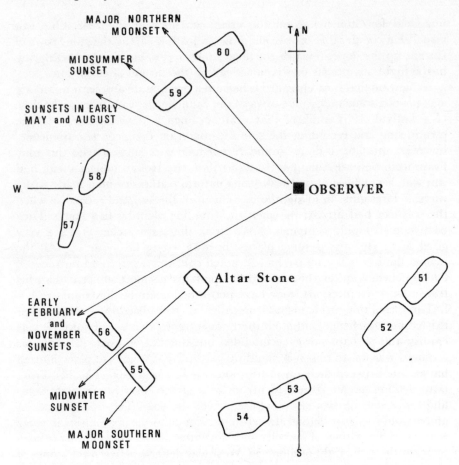

MAJOR NORTHERN
MOONSET

MIDSUMMER
SUNSET

SUNSETS IN EARLY
MAY and AUGUST

W ─────

OBSERVER

Altar Stone

EARLY
FEBRUARY
and
NOVEMBER
SUNSETS

MIDWINTER
SUNSET

MAJOR SOUTHERN
MOONSET

Fig. 12. The Possible Trilithon 'Calendar'.

can say only that it is a possible method, uncomplicated, inexact, accurate not to a day but in some alignments only to a week or so. Yet it may have been sufficient. By word, passed outwards to the farthest farmsteads, the message would be given and the people would gather, coming in their hundreds, thousands, the elderly dragged on fur-softened travois sleds, cattle and sheep herded by dogs, children running, playing in and out of the tents and lean-tos and ramshackle shelters that spread over the downland for the days and nights of the assembly.

The people would see the stones, but not as we see them. They would see them with ordinary eyes but in their minds the circle would become almost translucent, dimly revealing ancient figures through the sarsens, the men who raised the pillars, the heroes and half-gods of the times before the stones, and, concealed in the dark heart of the ring, the spirit whose home it was, never to be seen, nor heard, but always there and always to be dreaded.

Whether watching a funeral cortège wailing and dirging its path along the avenue, or awed by the brilliant richness of the inauguration of a new ruler, whether welcoming leaders from other regions, or celebrating the harvest or the cold turning-point of the year, on none of these occasions would the commoners enter Stonehenge or even be able to see the rituals at its centre.

Unlike the first henge, the circle was not big enough for more than a few people and was never intended to be. For those outside it the barricading sarsens and bluestones overlapped and blocked the views to the middle. From the inside one could see out. But like net curtaining at a window it was almost impossible to see in. Only at the south-west and north-east were there clear lines of sight and at the former the Altar Stone obscured the centre of the ring. At the north-east the banks of the avenue barred all but the privileged from entry. One could look but one could not see. The circle had become a secret place.

For the élite it was different. Approaching uphill, the faded lines of the Cursus behind them, the avenue marking their way, they would be led towards the ditch-circled Heel Stone and then across the causeway flanked by its tall portal-stones. In front of the group, across a stretch of grass, was the circle of sarsens. As they moved towards it they could see sharply-cut carvings of axes on its eastern stones.

They were on Stones 3, 4 and 5, Stone 4 at the precise east of the ring having at least a dozen. Low down on Stone 3 there was also a trellis or lattice pattern resembling a grooved ware motif as though that cult still lingered, feeble but not entirely dead. All the carvings are weathered today and barely distinguishable except in very favourable light, but for three reasons they are important.

They are the only carvings on the outside of the circle and it seems significant that they are at the east facing that part of the horizon where the sun would rise twice each year at the vernal and autumnal equinoxes. Like a cross standing outside a cathedral, the axe-carvings signified a meaning to all who saw them.

They also signified death. It is easy to write of guardians of the tomb and protectresses of the dead and it is only too easy to make superficial interpretations of the symbols inside the chambered tombs of Brittany. Yet it is incontestable that in those rare instances where axe-carvings have been found in the British Isles they have always, without exception, been associated with death, fastidiously fashioned, neatly pecked and ground out on prepared slabs.

In the attractive line of cairns in the Kilmartin cemetery of Argyll there are two which contain such carvings. One, Ri Cruin, was opened in 1870 and three stone-lined graves were uncovered. The central cist had a thin, upright stone in its north-east corner. On it there was a carved pattern like the teeth of a garden rake. It was similar to carvings of hafted axes in some later Breton tombs,[19] and the 'teeth' of the Ri Cruin axe may have portrayed pennants flying from its long handle like those on the halberds of Ireland. The western slab of the cist had carvings of eight flare-headed axes on it. No bones of any kind were found, but the clay that lined the grave was dark and sticky and gave off a 'very close unpleasant smell'.[20]

At the far end of the cemetery the cairn of Nether Largie North also covered a cist in which a body had decomposed. All that was left of it was a human molar tooth which 'fell to pieces when it was lifted'. There were two large axe-carvings on the end-slab and the underside of the capstone was covered in cupmarks and impressions of flat, bronze axes.[21] Here, as elsewhere, the axe was a cult symbol. In a bowl barrow near Coombe Hill in Sussex four flanged axes of the same style as those carved at Stonehenge had been deliberately broken and set with their cutting-edges upwards like those at Nether Largie. Similar axes arranged in a similar way were found under a barrow at Willerby Wold in Yorkshire.

The most telling evidence for a funerary axe-cult came from the Shapwick 6a round barrow near Badbury in Dorset. Before it was finally ploughed away in 1845 a hasty and poorly-recorded rescue excavation revealed how elaborate its construction had been. Under a thick capping of chalk there was a massive sandstone wall which, in turn, surrounded a wide ring of sharp, dark flints. This covered a central cairn of sandstone. Comparable structures which show the fascination different colours and materials had for the prehistoric mind have been remarked on in other parts of Britain.[22]

Inside the cairn was a sandstone slab weighing over half a ton. On it were carvings of five cupmarks, two bronze daggers and two flat, triangular axes of early Breton type. 'The Badbury stone therefore represents an art-style, presumably of magico-religious significance, which has undoubted connexions with, and probably originated in, megalithic carvings such as those from the Breton passage-graves.'[23]

This makes the third point about the art on the Stonehenge sarsens. It is Breton, doubtlessly executed by British artists or priests but inspired by traditions from Brittany. Of all the hundreds of stone circles known to the writer in western Europe there is only one, other than Stonehenge, that bears definite axe-carvings and that is Er-Lannic in southern Brittany. It is a huge ring, partly submerged in the Gulf of Morbihan, and it stands alongside an enormous horseshoe of stones now hidden beneath the sea. Three of the circle-stones, two at the north-west, one at the ENE, have carvings on their inner faces. Four of them, on the pillars in line with midsummer sunset, are of stone axes. A cupmarked packing-stone was also found by a fallen pillar nearby, such artificial depressions perhaps being images of the sun or moon.[24]

One possible companion to the 'axe-circles' of Stonehenge and Er-Lannic is Drombeg, a ring with a central cremation, in Co. Cork. The recumbent stone there, on the midwinter sunset alignment, has a debatable outline of a stone axe around a deep cupmark on its upper surface.[25] Another cupmark is nearby. It can hardly be coincidence that these axe-carvings occur so consistently in important solar positions and as Drombeg lies in the same area as many Irish wedge-graves, believed to be derived from the allées-couvertes of Brittany, its inclusion does nothing to diminish the idea that the axe-cult at Stonehenge, associated with the sun and with death, was also associated with funerary traditions emanating from western France.

The axe-carvings at Stonehenge will not have been unknown or ignored by the people coming to the circle. Just as crossed-swords printed on a map are recognised as showing where a battle was fought, so the axe was accepted as an abstraction for the guardian of the ring, a statement that she was present. Evidence from many other sites suggests that the Altar Stone, once standing alone near the centre of Stonehenge, may have been her personification.

It dominated the ring. Anyone approaching was faced by it. Groups would pass under the heavy sarsen lintel at the entrance. They would move between the tall 'male' and broader 'female' bluestones, aware of them but always confronted by the high, isolated pillar. Surrounded by bluestones and trilithons it stood near the centre of the circle like a waiting figure and this, perhaps, was how the people saw it, the focus and the purpose of their rites.

This rectangular column of pale-green sandstone may have occupied an equally spectacular position in the second phase of Stonehenge when the concentric rings of bluestones were being erected. South-west of the centre there was a deep stonehole and it was conjectured that the Altar Stone may once have been placed there, directly opposite the entrance, dwarfing the stones on either side of it. If it had been considered the *persona* of a weapon-carrying guardian of the dead, then the worn-down Cornish stone axe discovered in its pit becomes explicable. On 14 September 1802 Cunnington probably dug into the other hole, where the stone finally stood some 15 feet (4.6 m) in front of the Great Trilithon. It was about 6 feet (1.8 m) deep, suggesting that the top of the Altar Stone was 10 feet (3.1 m) above ground. Near the bottom of its pit Cunnington came upon charred wood, animal bones, antlers and sherds of urns dropped there when the stone was lifted to the perpendicular.[26]

It is not over-fanciful to consider this pillar, standing free near the middle of the ring, as the representation of a fearsome protectress of the dead. There are other stones, free-standing in stone circles like the Stripple Stones in Cornwall or in chambered tombs such as Ty-ar-Boudiquet in Brittany, and they have good antecedents in earlier pillars that are recognisably both female and warlike.

On the islet of Île Guennoc off Brittany's west coast, 120 miles south of Land's End, three passage-graves each have a stone standing at the entrance to the burial-chamber. Crude heads and shoulders were battered out on these blocks of local granite, turning them into figures watching over the dead. At Barnenez, the famous collection of passage-graves under a cairn in northern Brittany, a similar stone was put up by the chamber of one of the tombs. There are also menhirs, individual standing stones, that were carved into female forms. At Kermené and at Laniscar the pillars were finely shaped with domed heads, tiny breasts and shrunken arms. Closer to Britain there are almost identical 'anthropomorphs' on Guernsey at Catel and in the churchyard of St Martins.

They are female, they are isolated and they are connected with death. At Razet, 40 miles south of Reims, images of females and axes were carved on the walls of the chalk-cut subterranean chambers. In prehistory, it seems, shaped pillars or carved slabs were equally acceptable to the community. The 'statues' were more lifelike but difficult to work in awkward granite, the slabs were easier to carve. Belief in such interchange-ability is supported by two chambered tombs on Anglesey, one with art, the other with a free-standing pillar. Barclodiad-y-Gawres on the west coast of the island has smooth stones covered with geometrical patterns that are generally accepted as being anthropomorphic. Bryn Celli Ddu, 11 miles to the east, has a tall stone standing by itself in the chamber.

Most impressive of all for anyone trying to understand the meaning of these decorated stones is the example in northern Brittany of Crech-Quillé near Lannion. The short passage of this allée-couverte leads to a long burial-chamber at right-angles to it and divided into a small eastern cell and a far longer western compartment. It was always the west that was more important. At the junction of these chambers, facing down the passage to the entrance just as the Altar Stone does at Stonehenge, is a slab of gross granite on which shoulders, arms, a necklace and shrunken breasts have been fashioned. Buried in front of 'her' was an offering of five complete pots and a pendant.

Such representational art never became widely popular in Britain, prob-ably because influence from Brittany diminished rapidly as the distance increased. It is noticeable that the majority of British stone circles with central pillars are in the south of these islands, as might be expected if they were the result of a funerary cult in western France that had gradually affected customs in Britain as contacts grew with the expansion of copper prospecting and the visits of powerful chieftains.

There are a few rings like Glenquickan in south-west Scotland that possess internal pillars, but most centre-stone circles are near the south coast.[27] Some are in Cornwall inside great rings such as Boscawen-Un, whose central stone leans like a shuffling hag. There are several amongst the recumbent stone circles of Co. Cork, at Gortanimill, Dunbeacon and others in a region known to be in touch with Brittany. And there were more in the Wiltshire rings, at the outer limits of Breton traditions, the smashed Obelisk at Avebury and a 12 foot (3.7 m) greensand pillar at Tisbury, now anonymously built into a grotto at Old Wardour Castle. Only the Altar Stone survives, half-buried beneath a broken trilithon pillar.

Inigo Jones, who believed that the bank of the henge was a barrier 'into which it was unlawful for any profane Person to enter', speculated on the purpose of the prostrate Altar Stone: 'Within the Cell an . . . Altar was placed. . . . And, that there hath been the Heads of Bulls, or Oxen, and Harts, and other such Beasts digged up, or in, or near this *Antiquity* is not to be omitted; for who can imagine but these were the Heads of such as anciently there offered in Sacrifice.'[28]

Inside the circle, in the confined area of the bluestone horseshoe, no bigger than one side of a tennis-court and reduced further by the presence of the Altar Stone, perhaps no more than twenty people could comfortably have watched the rites. Offerings, inaugurations, funerary rituals, sacrifices of animals and of human beings, they are all possible, performed in mystery in front of the great stone while, outside, the people waited, 'the promiscuous, common Multitude', Jones called them, attending 'the Ceremonies of their solemn though superstitious Sacrifices'.

At Stonehenge even more credence is given to the belief in a guardian of the dead by the presence of her carvings inside the ring itself. Standing by the Altar Stone the onlookers would see them, her weapons to their left, the 'death-goddess' herself to the right on the western trilithon. The dagger- and axe-carvings are on Stone 53 at the south and only a few paces from the bystanders. Weapons had been associated with the protectress since early Neolithic times when men had raised statue-menhirs of her in southern France. At Collorgues near Nîmes the chamber of a long passage-grave contained fifteen skeletons. Above them two capstones, once standing separately in the open countryside before being re-used in a megalithic tomb, had been shaped into her form with face, owl-like eyes, small breasts, a necklace and, near her arms, a stone axe.[29]

These first female statues were relatively realistic, but over the centuries the portrayals became more formalised, more abstract, ending in simple rectangles carved on side-slabs, with circles for breasts, arcs for arms, a tiny dome for the head and a 'U' for the necklace. With the coming of copper her stone axe was replaced by metal types or by daggers and these can be seen in late allées-couvertes in northern Brittany such as Mougau-Bihan. At Stonehenge the imagery was plain. There was a bronze dagger, perhaps two, and there were flanged bronze axes on the inner face of trilithon 53–54 by the Altar Stone in the deepest, most obscured part of Stonehenge.

Facing the weapons was the fourth trilithon, re-erected in 1958 after its fall in 1797. On its west pillar, Stone 57, there is a rectangle about halfway up on the left-hand side of its inner face. The carving is quite large, about 3 feet 6 inches (1 m) square, but it is shallow and almost indistinguishable from the rest of the sarsen except with the eye of faith. A brown stain spreading from its lower right-hand corner is the result of rain dribbling down the stone when it was leaning heavily towards the ground after its collapse. During this time it was used as a slide by children whose boots and bottoms wore a polished area down it but luckily did not obliterate the rectangle.

Examination of the carving, which is just above eye-level, shows that it is man-made. Its interior has been smoothed and pecked into delicate dimples in contrast to the rougher sarsen surface around it. It is regular in shape and the upper parts of its sides angle sharply inwards to join a flat top like a child's drawing of a house. A semicircle rises from the centre of the 'roof', so that the carving might be likened to a handled attaché case seen in profile.

The existence of this figurine had been known long before 1953 when the dagger and axes were first detected, but no one, until Richard Atkinson, mentioned it in print, probably because nobody else realised its significance. In a letter to the author of February, 1987, Professor Atkinson wrote: 'It was only in 1953, when [R.S.] Newall made a rubbing for the first time (with heel-ball on tissue paper) that he discovered the faint traces of the projection on top, thus leading to identification with the Breton *mère-déesse* carvings.' A photograph of Stone 57, before its re-erection, in Atkinson's *Stonehenge* shows this rectangular carving very clearly.

It has no parallel in the British Isles but there are rectangles like it in northern Brittany. At the west end of the allée-couverte of Prajou-Menhir there are two side by side in a strangely cramped and blocked-off cell. They have inner borders of little cupmarks and between the rectangles there is a metal dagger or spearhead with another outside them. There is a third rectangle and another 'dagger' on the adjacent stones, the dagger near two minuscule breasts and necklace. In the Paris Basin there was a similarly decorated side-slab in the oddly-named Mississippi gallery-grave near St Germain, a megalithic tomb covering the remains of many adults and children. The cupmarked rectangle there, in a Neolithic burial-place, was associated with a hafted stone axe.

More and more often over the centuries these 'figurines' were carved at the western end of a monument where the dead lay, set down towards the setting sun. Such a tradition made it inevitable that the Stonehenge figure should be added to Stone 57 in the only position where the west would be emphasised. Below it, as though to stress the sanctity of the stone, there is a smaller, even more worn-away version of the figurine. In 1958 a very weathered third rectangle was recognised on a broken lintel, Stone 120, that had once capped sarsens 19 and 20. These had stood at the west of the circle behind trilithon 57–58. The carving had been on the underside of the lintel and anyone passing between the pillars would have had the figurine above him, almost invisible but always there, reminding the living that the west was the domain of the dead and their guardian.

The two larger rectangular figures, the axes and dagger, the Altar Stone, were closeted inside the U-shaped settings of the bluestones and the immense sarsen trilithons. This raises the eleventh of the questions about Stonehenge, why the five great archways were arranged in a horseshoe inside the circle. If there was symbolism inherent in the carvings, in the focal pillar, in the numbers of stones and the lintelled circle it is reasonable to suppose that the 'horseshoe' also symbolised something.

It was not an imitation of a real horseshoe. Horses were not shod in those days. It has been suggested that it was a good-luck token derived 'from its resemblance to the upcurved horns of the bull'.[30] This is an idea all the more attractive because of the bull-cults elsewhere in the European Bronze Age and because of the ox-skulls found with the dead in the British long barrows and inside Stonehenge itself. The trilithon 'horseshoe', however, is the wrong shape. Bulls' horns curve outwards at their tips, as artists and architects well knew. The sculpted horns of stone in the Cretan palace of Knossos demonstrate this. At Stonehenge the ends bend inwards. Nor has the setting any close similarity to the shallow crescent of the moon, despite the lunar alignments that existed in the circle. If there was symbolism in the arrangement of the trilithons then it was symbolism with a different origin.

Stonehenge was not unique. Something which is not well-known is that there are many other U-shaped settings in the prehistoric British Isles and Brittany, some Neolithic, some built in later periods. There are horseshoes of stones inside circles such as Croft Moraig and Loanhead of Daviot in Scotland and Dun Ruadh in Northern Ireland. There were horseshoes of paired posts, probably lintelled, inside the earthwork of Lugg near Dublin and in the Norfolk henge of Arminghall dated to about 3100 BC. There are even free-standing horseshoes. As well as Achavanich and others, hundreds of miles to the north of Stonehenge in Caithness, there are enormous U-settings, known as cromlechs, in Brittany. Mainly in the south there is at least one northern site, Tossen-Keler, near Lannion.

These unconsidered structures of western Europe share many features in common with Stonehenge. The shapes, the orientations, the graded heights of stones, the occasional art, all reveal affinities that help to explain the beliefs behind the erection of the trilithons. Death also is a part of their background. Many of them, especially in the British Isles, are associated with burials. So was Tossen-Keler. And it is noteworthy that the nickname for Kergonan, 'Er-Anké', means 'affliction' or 'mourning'.

The origins of the Breton cromlechs are unclear but it is noticeable that some like Kerlescan and Crucuno are near passage-graves the shape of whose chambers is reflected in the later, larger open-air settings. It may be that such circles and horseshoes were simple, unroofed enlargements of the earlier enclosed cells of chambered tombs and were put up to accommodate a greater number of participants within the familiar shape of the traditional funerary monument.

A similar process occurred in the British Isles where some Neolithic long burial-mounds had deep, crescentic forecourts added to them to provide more room for the mourners. Standing stones, fires and ritual deposits are sometimes discovered in these claw-like settings. These, at cairns such as Carn Ban on Arran or Cashtal yn Ard on the Isle of Man, are like the

Stonehenge horseshoe in miniature, U-shaped and rising in height towards the head of the crescent and the entrance to the tomb, drawing attention to it. There are many forecourts like these amongst the court-cairns of northern Ireland. There is even one in Brittany, at the tide-covered allée-couverte of Kernic on the north coast.

Indeed, sometimes, as at Street House in Cleveland, the forecourt was more ostentatious than the low mound that covered the burials. At its entrance tall posts lined three sides of a spacious courtyard. Such settings, whether of timber or stone, gradually replaced the cramped chambers of tombs as the focus of funerary rites.[31] In time, with the end of long barrow building, only a symbolic component of a megalithic tomb was constructed. Occasionally, as at Avebury, this took the form of an empty chamber, a 'Cove' of three great stones like a roofless sentry-box. Elsewhere, men raised 'horseshoes' of posts or stones, the vestigial memories of forecourts where mourners had assembled for their rituals. Even in transformation the spirit of the tomb survived, although the great mound had gone.

A horseshoe has a property not possessed by a circle. It has an axis. It faces a particular direction and this is defined by a line from the apex to the midpoint of the open end. Because of this, unlike circles, horseshoes could be used as devices to 'catch' the sun or moon. Analysis of their orientations seems to bear this out, for most of them do look towards significant celestial positions. For a foresight a circle required an outlying pillar such as the Heel Stone. A horseshoe was complete in itself.

The U-shaped setting inside Stonehenge, looking towards the midsummer sunrise, similarly acted as a trap to 'catch' the sun. Here it was no different from those in Brittany. The open jaws of Kergonan were aligned on midwinter sunrise. The settings of St Pierre-Quiberon and Er-Lannic South faced the equinoctial sunrise. So did Tossen-Keler. Here there was a great granite block at the west and two large boulders at the eastern terminals. The art there, moreover, provides yet another link with Stonehenge and the protective powers of the Other-World. Several decorated pillars were re-used in the construction of this slightly lobster-clawed monument. A slab at the SSE had a carving of a hafted axe, chevrons had been worked on the stone at the south, and there was a 'figurine' on a pillar at the north-west in line with the midsummer sunset. At Kergonan the Breton archaeologist, Zacharie le Rouzic, recorded an axe-carving but, perhaps because the dense vegetation prevented an accurate compass-bearing being taken, he did not specify which stone it was.[32]

It is tempting to see these megaliths, particularly the British forecourts, as prototypes for the great setting at Stonehenge. Their direct connection with funerary practices and their 'doorway' leading into the tomb accord perfectly with the suspected rites in the sarsen ring. Most of these enhanced 'courtyards' are to be found in south-west Scotland and northern Ireland where they were a late and local response to the needs of a growing population. Elsewhere in these islands a different solution created the open-air henges and stone circles. In Brittany rings and 'forecourts' were constructed, vast and free-standing, in areas of passage-graves such as the complexes of Kerlescan and Er-Lannic. The same was true at Broubster in Caithness where the now ruined horseshoe was put up in a cult-centre of chambered tombs, menhirs, rows and a stone circle. Fourteen miles to the south-east the heather-spread horseshoe at Achavanich, between a lane and a tiny loch, remains the most impressive of the free-standing settings in the British Isles.

Many miles to the south of Achavanich a stone circle in Perthshire almost explains Stonehenge. In its beginnings as a timber structure, in its later henge, in its megalithic horseshoe inside a ring of stones, in its orientation and its art, Croft Moraig is a microcosm of the Wessex monument.[33] Standing by the lovely waters of Loch Tay not far from Aberfeldy, the site started as a wooden building, perhaps roofed, of head-high posts arranged in a horseshoe open to the south. A low boulder rested by a possible hearth inside it. Two slender posts, one at the entrance, another 25 feet (7.6 m) outside it, marked this southern alignment which is very reminiscent of the orientation of the causeway and post-lined avenue leading to the mortuary house of Stonehenge's earliest phase.

Some of the posts were renewed but eventually all of them were replaced by stones just as the timbers had been at Stonehenge. At Croft Moraig the pillars were arranged in a horseshoe and, again like Stonehenge, the axis was subtly changed, here from N-S to NNE-SSW on a lunar alignment. A stony bank, the equivalent of the earthwork at Stonehenge, surrounded this new setting and on it, opposite the mouth of the horseshoe, men laid a long slab on which over a score of cupmarks had been carved on the upper surface.

Finally a circle of stones rising in height towards the NNW was put up around the horseshoe with two extra pillars just outside the ring at the east to form a portalled entrance. This, and the circle, the internal horseshoe and the carvings make Croft Moraig almost a scaled-down version of Stonehenge, lacking only the lintels of that great site. It is particularly significant, remembering the situations of the dagger-, axe- and figurine-carvings at Stonehenge, that the cupmarked slab at Croft Moraig was set down directly in line with the major southern moonset, the moon often being the focus of rituals in the stone circles of central and north-eastern Scotland.[34] Sometimes cupmarks were carved on lunar-oriented stones.[35]

Stonehenge, with its carvings and its north-east orientation, with its highest sarsens at the south-west, can be included amongst this group of U-shaped settings, open to the sun, associated with an axe-cult, acting like a doorway to the Other-World. This would explain the twelfth and last question about the monument. The five trilithons rose in height towards the south-west because this was the direction of the midwinter sunset and the dark, cold end of the year.

'The faces of the celebrants', wrote Abercromby, 'would be turned in the direction of sunset at the winter solstice. It may be supposed, then, that Stonehenge was erected after enormous labour to commemorate annually at midwinter the death of some great divinity.'[36] Equally, the sarsens may have been put up to be the everlasting house of such a deity whose role it was to safeguard the dead.

From Swedish rock-carvings, contemporary with this phase of Stonehenge, at Västergötland and Bohuslän one can imagine suppliants holding axes aloft, the other hand raised with fingers outstretched, saluting the sun. There are similar scenes carved in the Camonica Valley of Italy suggesting that the custom of brandishing axes and lifting hands high in honour of some powerful spirit was widespread amongst Bronze Age societies in Europe.[37]

What the rites were at Stonehenge will never be known in detail. Words, gestures, dances, processions, all are gone. There would have been funerary rituals, for this was how Stonehenge began. There would have been offerings, celebrations on the great feast-days, acts of propitiation in times of hardship, there would have been ceremonies of soothsaying when priests or shamans looked into the future or tried to discover the cause of a disaster. What should not be rejected from these considerations is the probability of sacrifices, both animal and human, taking place inside the circle.

Just as some historians have attempted to change the rapacious Vikings into gentle traders peacefully bartering at monasteries and towns like early members of a European Market so some prehistorians have tried to purify the Iron Age druids of their blood-drenched reputation, describing them instead as Platonic philosophers more concerned with calendars and reincarnation than with divination and death. It is an arid exercise. The writings of Caesar and Tacitus, of Pliny and Strabo repeatedly condemn the atrocities of the druids and it should not be forgotten that these Roman authors were themselves members of a society that was prepared both to strangle enemies of the State such as Jugurtha and to watch gladiatorial bloodbaths. If such writers considered the druids barbaric in their treatment of men and women it may be presumed that the druids were indeed so.

Caesar claimed that it was the druids who officiated at those sacrificial rites that were concerned with prophecy and who burned human beings alive to appease the gods. Tacitus described altars covered with blood, the druids communing with the Other-World 'through human entrails'. Diodorus Siculus added that druids would foretell the future by stabbing a man in the stomach and then watching his writhings, 'a form of divination in which they have full confidence, *as it is of old tradition*'.[38]

Such barbarity might have nothing whatsoever to do with Stonehenge were it not that druidical practices appear to have been founded in age-old customs. Men and women were ritually slaughtered by priests who used methods that had been known a thousand years before the Iron Age.[39]

Whether killing people as offerings to the gods or slaughtering them in order that prognostications might be made from their dying convulsions, the customs were cruel, useless and a savage reminder that the prehistoric world was not ours. The question is not whether the druids and their adherents engaged in human sacrifice but whether those practices extended back to the Bronze Age and the time of Stonehenge. Some evidence hints that they did.

Sacrificed bodies, dating back to Neolithic and Bronze Age times, have been recovered from Danish bogs. Some, like those from Bolkilde and Stenstrup, had been killed by hanging or strangulation and occasionally the rope around their necks has been preserved. 'They must . . . be regarded as offerings, placed in watery places to assuage the powers there.'[40] Early prehistoric people in Britain may just as willingly have offered human beings to their own gods.

The Woodhenge sacrifice, the murdered man in the Stonehenge ditch, the young men killed by spears, reveal a way of life more callous, more emotional than our own. There are other indications that offerings, of objects, beasts and human beings, were made to the Other-World. Only a mile south-west of Stonehenge a shaft almost 100 feet (30 m) deep was found at Wilsford. It may have been no more than a well, as the discovery of waterlogged rope and broken wooden tubs suggests, but the presence in it of an ox-skull, organic remains and sherds of Deverel-Rimbury pottery offers the possibility that this was a votive pit for gifts to spirits dwelling far below the ground. A radiocarbon determination of 1380 ± 90 bc, about 1700 BC, shows that the shaft had been dug when the sarsen circle was being constructed nearby.

If this were all, then the Wilsford Shaft would be little more than a curiosity. But near Fareham in Hampshire another shaft at Swanwick, although not so deep, was more informative about Bronze Age beliefs. Deverel-Rimbury loom-weights in it proved its age. At the bottom a wooden stake had been set upright and around it were traces of flesh or dried blood. Sacrificial pits such as this, with a human being lashed to the post, are known on the continent and perhaps the rites of the Iron Age druids, repulsive and inexplicable to our minds, may have begun long before in the Neolithic and Bronze Ages.

Indirect confirmation that this was so comes from another classical source. The widely-read Greek geographer, Strabo, writing at the time of Christ, mentioned the druids in Book IV of his *Geographica*. He described their repugnant attempts to see into the future by stabbing and impaling: 'We are told of still other kinds of sacrifices; for example, they would shoot victims to death with arrows. . . .'[41] Such a form of execution could hardly have been introduced by Iron Age druids. Archery was almost unknown in Britain and France at that time and if priests did use bows and arrows in sacrificial rites they must have been perpetuating a centuries-old tradition from times when those weapons were commonplace. The killing by arrowshot of the Beaker man at Stonehenge may have been the forerunner of later, more ritualised offerings to the gods instituted by shamans or priests who were themselves the Bronze Age precursors of the druids.

'The antiquity of Druidism . . . has been stressed more than once, and all recent discoveries confirm this thesis. And with the British parallels for henges and long enclosures and ritual shafts long centuries before the Druids, may we not have to reconsider Caesar's statement that their doctrine was in fact of British origin?'[42]

Stonehenge was not an academy for research into the stars and the nature of the universe. It was a place of death, built by people whose needs and fears were very different from our own. They safeguarded their lives through the dead, honouring them but imprisoning their ghosts, using the ancestral spirits to communicate with the greater forces of nature. Their methods were not processes based on scientific knowledge. Theirs were traditionally performed rituals that were believed to be effective because they had worked before, through magic and imitation, through propitiation of capricious but controllable spirits. The worse the crisis the greater the offering.

In 1964, a year before his country became independent, Dr Hastings Banda of Malawi said, 'I wish I could bring Stonehenge to Nyasaland to show there was a time when Britain had a culture that was savage'.

# 11

## Eternal rings of light
## Stonehenge IV: 1250 – 500 BC

*I saw Eternity the other night*
*Like a great Ring of pure and endless Light,*
*All calm, as it was bright,*
*And round beneath it, Time in hours, days, years*
*Driv'n by the spheres*
*Like a vast shadow mov'd.*

Henry Vaughan, *The World*

It did not last. Just as the chambered tombs had been blocked up, just as Avebury had flourished and declined, so the power and dominance of Stonehenge dwindled into desolation. Changing beliefs, a deterioration in the climate, the increasing wealth of other regions, poor harvests, famine, outbreaks of plague, all contributed to the decay of Wessex. By the end of the second millennium Stonehenge was almost deserted, its stones cold and grey in the creeping winds of the Plain. A half-hearted attempt was made to extend its avenue down to the River Avon but this too was abandoned. By the Iron Age the circle was a relic.

The only obvious Iron Age structure near the ring is the tree-covered hillfort of Vespasian's Camp a mile and a half to the east. This sprawling earthwork overlooks the place where the destroyed long barrow, Amesbury 104, once stretched with a 'cist' that some people have thought might have been a megalithic chamber but which was probably a simple pit like those discovered by Hoare and Cunnington alongside Neolithic skeletons.

John Aubrey called the hillfort 'The Walles' and believed it 'without doubt the Camp of the Emperor *Vespasian* for it is a perfect Roman fortification'.[1] To Stukeley it was 'a fine and ancient camp', but it was not Roman. It belonged to the Iron Age, built around the middle of the first millennium BC and later refortified just before the Roman conquest. Its ditched-and-banked rampart enclosed a triangle of 37 acres (15 ha) that today lies like a wizard's pointed hat just north of Amesbury. In the 18th century the interior was romantically landscaped with ornamental paths and with a 'druidical' grotto, 'Gay's Cave', on its eastern side where visitors could sit and contemplate the Gothic past. Now it is congested with beeches and its walks are deterringly overgrown.

Hoare understood its purpose: 'This was originally the stronghold of those numerous Britons who inhabited the plains around STONEHENGE, an asylum in times of danger, for their wives, children and cattle . . .'[2] No recorded excavation is known, but the widening of the Stonehenge Road from Amesbury chanced upon fragments of early and late Iron Age vessels showing that the hillfort was begun around 500 BC and continued in use for many centuries.

Similar Iron Age pottery was found by Hawley in the upper levels of the Y and Z Holes, dropped there long after the abandonment of those gaping and crumbling pits. None, however, has come from the centre of Stonehenge and the Y and Z sherds look like the rubbish of squatters and curious passers-by wandering around the deserted stones but not lingering for long inside the ring. Roman litter suggests the same story of later tourists casually visiting an ancient monument.

It is unlikely, therefore, that Stonehenge was used by the occupants of the nearby hillfort. Nor was it despoiled by the Romans whose army ruthlessly destroyed centres of resistance, as the razed temple of Sarmizegetusa proves. Had Stonehenge been a sanctuary of the druids and a focal point of British defiance, its sarsen circle would have been dismantled, the bluestones smashed, the whole monument devastated. There is no sign of such destruction. Stonehenge has been pillaged rather than demolished, and it was the weather and the avarice of men that created the ruin. Long before the Romans and long before the Iron Age the ring was in neglect, left in disuse some time between 1250 and 500 BC.

This was a period very different in southern England from what had gone before. With a climatic deterioration that left the weather by 1000 BC very much as it is today, limiting cultivation, and with a growing population there came a need for more land. Marginal areas of thin, difficult soils were settled. Homesteads of peasant farmers cluttered the landscape and a duller, less exotic way of life replaced the previous dominance of the élite.

Rich burials became rare. In those Knighton Heath, Taunton and Penard phases of British prehistory, the Middle and Late Bronze Ages, people on their dispersed holdings often buried their dead in existing round barrows or in new flat cemeteries, but no longer with beakers or collared urns or food-vessels.[3] Instead, there were ugly Deverel-Rimbury bucket-and barrel-urns with finger-tipped ribs decorating their uneven, emery-rough sides.

It was an age of violence. Rapiers of bronze were manufactured for roving bands of young warriors eager for plunder. In turn, these weapons were supplanted by leaf-shaped swords, round shields and studded leather helmets. Ditched-and-banked fortifications with palisades and heavy, timber gates were built around the tops of hills where people could retreat with their flocks and herds when their lands were threatened by marauders. Buried caches of metal axes, broken daggers and ingots for resmelting, gold bracelets and torcs, tell of tinkers and merchants concealing the bulk of their wares before taking a few objects to trade locally. The unrecovered hoards show grimly that their owners never came back.

Sudden death was frequent. In 1901 a skeleton was dug up at Queensford Farm near Dorchester in Oxfordshire. Embedded in its pelvis was the snapped-off end of a bronze spearhead. The man, brutally murdered, may have been buried by his kinsfolk, for with his body was a perforated stone, 'used as a charm', perhaps a Bronze Age funerary disc like those so often found with Neolithic burials.[4]

It was a time of disruption and change. Links between Wessex and Brittany weakened as other, more powerful centres developed in the lower Thames Valley and East Anglia, prospering from contacts with the Low Countries and northern France. Metalworking industries in North Wales and Ireland by-passed the once-dominant areas of southern England, and Wessex became a backwater, its customs no more than feeble imitations of the past, recognisable but sometimes bizarre.

At Winterslow, near the choked shafts of the Easton Down flint-mines, a bell-barrow contained a skeleton, head to the north, with a beaker, dagger, wristguard and two flint arrowheads. Generations later a cremation was inserted in the mound. With it was a pin and a fluted razor of bronze. The burnt bones had been wrapped in cloth and placed with a tiny accessory vessel in a large urn of Cornish design. By the bones were snippings of human hair, ¼ – ⅜ inches (6–9 mm) long. They had 'the characteristics of hair from the eyebrow' and had come from more than one person, presumably shaven from the foreheads of grieving men and women in acts of mourning. The practice was known elsewhere. Two large coils of hair discovered in a cist at Soussons Common on Dartmoor may have been the result of a similar rite. Other hair with a burial was found close by at Lydford.[5]

The Stonehenge region was no longer sacrosanct. Round barrows were put up inside the Cursus, one of them, Winterbourne Stoke 30, with a long, phallic-shaped nodule of flint near the skull of a child.[6] Hardly half a mile south-west of Stonehenge a small barrow, Amesbury 3, 'produced the largest sepulchral urn we have ever found, it measures 15 inches in diameter at the top and is 22½ inches high' (38 × 57 cm), wrote Hoare, and there is a delightful sketch of William Cunnington in his horsedrawn trap, whip in hand, driving home with his little daughter happily clutching the giant urn. Despite its size it contained only a few burnt bones with a big triangular stone across its mouth. It is now in Devizes Museum.[7]

Even closer to Stonehenge, barely 100 yards (90 m) east of the ring and against the road, the bell-barrow of Amesbury 11 was raised, roped-off and whiskery with grass today but still elegant, the nearest of all the burial places to the circle. Cunnington's first excavation failed to recover anything except bluestone chippings in its mound but on his return he found he had stopped within inches of a large urn, upside down over a pile of cremated bones in which a pair of bone tweezers, like an old-fashioned peg, had been left. The urn has been lost but the tweezers survive and, like the Stonehenge urn, are on display in Devizes Museum.[8] The existence of this barrow, fine though it is, so close to Stonehenge demonstrates more vividly than anything else how the sarsen circle was slowly but inexorably losing its aura of secrecy and dread.

In place of the old gods and spirits water-cults were developing, maybe because the ancient sanctuaries no longer seemed effective. Valuable articles of bronze were thrown into rivers, over three-quarters 'of all the dirks and rapiers of Britain and Ireland having been recovered from water'.[9] Shields were dropped into swamps, sometimes with human skulls. Amongst a maze of waterlogged poles and piles in the River Trent there were skulls, spearheads and rapiers. These were offerings to new, emergent deities with human features and with names. *Sulis*, at Bath, was one of several water-goddesses or nymphs whose Celtic shrine was later taken over by the Romans. The deep pits at Wilsford and Swanwick may have been Bronze Age manifestations of this belief that water and the Under-World were the homes of the gods, gods who demanded gifts not only of luxuries but of human life also. Stonehenge was not exempt from this transformation.

In its last years of use the circle was given a closer association with water. Geoffrey of Monmouth wrote of the curative powers of the stones when drenched with water, and in his *Travels over England* of 1707 the Rev. James Brome remarked that 'if the stones be rubbed, or scraped, and water thrown upon the scrapings, they will (some say) heal any green wound, or old sore'. It may have been to strengthen this link with water that men began to extend the avenue towards the River Avon.

The original avenue, over a third of a mile (520 m) long and 40 feet (12 m) wide, had led downhill, exactly straight, pointing towards the eastern gap in the Cursus. Now it was changed. Its western ditch was lengthened and redirected, swinging abruptly eastwards and continuing in a gradual curve for over a mile and a quarter (2 km) almost down to the river. It was roughly-cut, V-shaped, but its partner on the other side of the avenue was never dug. Instead, the project was forsaken and the first ditch was backfilled.[10] Antlers from it provided two radiocarbon determinations, one from near the Amesbury by-pass of 800 ± 100 bc (c. 975 BC), the other, by a lane in West Amesbury, of 1070 ± 180 bc (c. 1345 BC), showing that the work was undertaken during the centuries when the prestige of Wessex was dying and when Stonehenge was no longer the paramount centre of ceremony and ritual. The fate of its avenue is paralleled by the single bank at Arbor Low in the Peak District, another region in decline, and by the unfinished rows at Callanish in the Outer Hebrides. In times of crisis men turned to the gods. But when the gods proved false or without power they were relinquished.

So great had the social disruption been, so startling the change in customs and beliefs, that it has been suggested that there may have been an outbreak of plague, possibly widespread across Europe where there are other signs of collapse and disturbance as far away as Greece and the Aegean. 'The population of Britain, after reaching a maximum around 1300 BC, perhaps as high as the Domesday figure [around 1½ million people] collapsed during the next century or two, and by the end of the millennium had been halved. Recovery in the ensuing centuries was slow at first. . . .'[11]

Through the indifference of men Stonehenge mouldered, year by year becoming frailer in the snows and rains. Freezing earth loosened the holes in which the sarsens stood. Winds blowing in from the south-west imperceptibly but steadily shifted some uprights from the perpendicular. Even a breeze of 20 miles an hour would have exerted a push of 2 lbs on each square foot of an exposed surface and a sudden winter gust, howling across the plain at 100 miles an hour, would have smashed against a pillar of the Great Trilithon as heavily as a 3-ton hammer-blow. It was man's neglect and God's effect that toppled many of the sarsens.

Yet even in ruin Stonehenge may not have been completely deserted. A metal tablet was dug up in or near the circle in the reign of Henry VIII. Reading about this in the 1637 edition of Camden's *Britannia* John Aubrey guessed that 'The Inscription on Lead found at Stonehenge, w^ch Mr Lilly the Schoolmaster, and Sir Tho. Eliot could not read, might be made by the Druides'. Stukeley added his own regrets: 'Eternally to be lamented is the loss of that tablet of tin, which was found at this place . . . inscrib'd with many letters.'[12]

This enigmatic object has disappeared with no record of the writing on it, but it may have been a 'curse' like those offered in Roman times to the goddess Sulis and other deities. Known as *defixiones* and written on imperishable lead, such curse-tablets were intended to punish a wrongdoer, the suppliant demanding vengeance from the gods against an enemy. It would have been fitting if in the dying ages of Stonehenge someone had come to the silent circle begging for revenge from the almost forgotten spirits of the place.

Today, all that is left is the wreckage, changing with every colour of the day, shadows of clouds drifting darkly across the stones like wraiths of the people who once walked there. In summer wild flowers grow inside the ring and the sarsens glitter and glow goldenly as though eternity had its home there, caught in an everlasting circle of sunlight.

Then death returns. 'To my mind the magic of Stonehenge is never more powerfully felt than during the wild tempestuous autumnal gales that usually sweep across the Plain in October. . . . Thoughts rise suddenly of the many tragedies, feasts, sacrifices, mysterious rites that must have been enacted here in far-off, bygone days.'[13]

The days are finished. The people have gone. Now the ring is like a broken cage around which sightseers wander as in an empty zoo, disappointedly hoping to understand, to see something, sense some presence inside in the vacant circle. But there is nothing to be seen. If there were some invisible power it may have escaped between the fallen bars into its own Other-World. Or. . . .

Or, quite possibly, it has never wished to leave.

# Further reading

There has been no shortage of books about Stonehenge, serious, speculative, foolish, technical, astronomical, fictitious, escapist, poetical. In a rather unreliable Bibliography published in 1901 Jerome Harrison listed hundreds of references and since then the number has almost doubled. Much, however, is either superficial or repetitious. The present Bibliography and Notes cite everything I have found worthwhile.

The authoritative work on the archaeology of Stonehenge is Professor Richard Atkinson's *Stonehenge* (Hamish Hamilton, 1956), slightly expanded in 1979 in a paperback version by Penguin Books. For readers interested in the historical background to Stonehenge from medieval times onwards there is nothing better than Christopher Chippindale's thorough and delightful *Stonehenge Complete* (Thames & Hudson, 1983). It describes every foible of Stonehenge fanatics, including one stating Stonehenge was 'the first accurate sex-machine and it still works', a claim which should alarm half its unsuspecting visitors.

For those wanting to read the actual words of ancient writers there is a fascinating collection of excerpts about Stonehenge, including the full text of the rare *A Fool's Bolt soon Shott at Stonage*, in *Stonehenge Antiquaries*, edited by Rodney Legg, Dorset Publishing Co., 1986.

For the prehistory of the period the essential book is *The Age of Stonehenge* by Colin Burgess (Dent, 1980), a masterly review of current knowledge about the Late Neolithic and Bronze Ages. For those wishing to know more about the excavations of Cunnington and Hoare there is a facsimile version of the two volumes of *Ancient Wiltshire* issued by EP Publishing Ltd in 1975.

A limited range of literature, including a guidebook in various languages, is available from the sales counter at the entrance to Stonehenge, but for many books it is safer to order copies through a bookseller. There are four inexpensive, sensible and readable paperbacks about aspects of Stonehenge. Leslie Grinsell has written three: *The Legendary History and Folklore of Stonehenge* (1975) and *The Druids and Stonehenge* (1978), both published by the Toucan Press, Guernsey; and *The Stonehenge Barrow Groups* (Salisbury, 1978), available from the splendid museum by Salisbury cathedral in whose north transept there is a statue of Sir Richard Colt Hoare. The museum itself has an outstanding display of Stonehenge material. More artefacts, including replicas from the Bush Barrow burial, can be seen in the equally entrancing Devizes Museum.

The fourth booklet, *Beyond Stonehenge* (1985) by Julian Richards, should not be confused with the 1973 book of the same title by Gerald Hawkins. Richards' is a well-illustrated short introduction to Stonehenge and the surrounding landscape. It provides descriptions of the sites and contains a map showing the roads and footpaths by which the barrow cemeteries, the Cursus, Woodhenge and other local places of interest can be visited. Any reader who has reached this page in the present book will surely wish to go to them. They are the last memorials of the Stonehenge people.

# Abbreviations

| | |
|---|---|
| Ant J | *Antiquaries' Journal* |
| Arch J | *Archaeological Journal* |
| Bull. Inst. Arch | *Bulletin of the Institute of Archaeology* |
| CBA | *Council for British Archaeology* |
| J. Anthr. Inst | *Journal of the Anthropological Institute* |
| JCHAS | *Journal of the Cork Historical & Archaeological Society* |
| JHA | *Journal for the History of Astronomy* |
| JRSAI | *Journal of the Royal Society of Antiquaries of Ireland* |
| PPS | *Proceedings of the Prehistoric Society* |
| PRIA | *Proceedings of the Royal Irish Academy* |
| PSAL | *Proceedings of the Society of Antiquaries of London* |
| PSAS | *Proceedings of the Society of Antiquaries of Scotland* |
| WAM | *Wiltshire Archaeological Magazine* |

# Select bibliography

Atkinson R. J. C. (1979). *Stonehenge*. Harmondsworth (revised edition).

Aubrey J. (1980–2). *Monumenta Britannica, I, II*. Sherborne.

Barclay E. (1895). *Stonehenge and its Earth-works*. London.

Bradley R. (1984). *The Social Foundations of Prehistoric Britain*. London.

Bradley R. & Gardiner J. (eds). (1984). *Neolithic Studies. A Review of Some Current Research*. Oxford.

Burgess C. (1980). *The Age of Stonehenge*. London.

Burl A. (1976). *The Stone Circles of the British Isles*. London.

Charleton W. (1725). *Chorea Gigantum*. London.

Chippindale C. (1983). *Stonehenge Complete*. London.

Clarke D. V., Cowie T. G. & Foxon A. (1985). *Symbols of Power*. Edinburgh.

Cunnington M. E. (1914). 'List of the long barrows of Wiltshire', *WAM* 38, 378–414.

Cunnington R. H. (1935). *Stonehenge and its Date*. London.

Duke E. (1846). *The Druidical Temples of the County of Wilts*. London.

Grinsell L. V. (1957). 'Archaeological Gazetteer', in: (eds) Pugh R. B. & Crittall E. *A History of Wiltshire, I (1)*. London, 21–279.

——(1978). *The Stonehenge Barrow Groups*. Salisbury.

Harrison W. J. (1901). 'A bibliography of the great stone monuments of Wiltshire – Stonehenge and Avebury. *WAM 32*, 1–169.

Hawley W. (1921). 'Stonehenge: Interim report on the exploration', *Ant J 1*, 17–41.

——(1922). 'Second report on the excavations at Stonehenge', *Ant J 2*, 36–52.

——(1923). 'Third report on the excavations at Stonehenge', *Ant J 3*, 13–20.

——(1924). 'Fourth report on the excavations at Stonehenge', *Ant J 4*, 30–39.

——(1925). 'Report on the excavations at Stonehenge during the season of 1923', *Ant J 5*, 21–50.

——(1926). 'Report on the excavations at Stonehenge during the season of 1926', *Ant J 6*, 1–25.

——(1928). 'Report on the excavations at Stonehenge during 1925 and 1926', *Ant J 8*, 149–76.

Heggie D. (1981). *Megalithic Science*. London.

Hoare, Sir Richard Colt (1812). *The Ancient History of Wiltshire, I*. London.

Jones I. (1725). *The Most Notable Antiquity of Great Britain, Vulgarly Called Stone-Heng*. London.

Legg R. (1986). *Stonehenge Antiquaries*. Milborne Port.

Lockyer, Sir Norman (1909). *Stonehenge and Other British Stone Monuments Astronomically Considered*. London.

Long W. (1876). *Stonehenge and its Barrows*. Devizes.

Niel, F. (1975). *The Mysteries of Stonehenge*. New York.

Petrie W. M. F. (1880). *Stonehenge: Plans, Descriptions and Theories*. London.

Piggott S. (1954). *The Neolithic Cultures of the British Isles*. Cambridge.

Pitts M. W. (1982). 'On the road to Stonehenge: report on the investigations beside the A344 – 1968, 1979 and 1980', *PPS 48*, 75–132.

RCAHM-England (1979). *Stonehenge and Its Environs*. Edinburgh.

Smith J. (1771). *Choir Gaur: the Grand Orrery of the Ancient Druids, Commonly Called Stonehenge*. London.

Stone E. H. (1924). *The Stones of Stonehenge*. London.

Stukeley W. (1723). 'The history of the temples and religion of the antient Celts', MS 4.253, Cardiff Public Library.

——(1740). *Stonehenge a Temple Restor'd to the British Druids*. London.

Thom A. (1967). *Megalithic Sites in Britain*. Oxford.

——A. & A. S. (1978). *Megalithic Remains in Britain and Brittany*. Oxford.

Thurnam J. (1869). 'On ancient British barrows, especially those of Wiltshire and the adjoining counties (Part I. Long barrows)', *Archaeologia* 42, 161–244.

Wood J. (1747). *Choir Gaure, Vulgarly called Stonehenge*. Oxford.

Wood J. E. (1978). *Sun, Moon and Standing Stones*. Oxford.

# Notes and references

## Introduction

1. Hoare I, 165 (Amesbury 56).
2. Aubrey II, 785.
3. Hoare I, 124 (Winterbourne Stoke 13).
4. Hoare I, 125 (Winterbourne Stoke 10).
5. *WAM 36*, 1914, 616–17 (Bulford 27).
6. *Proc Dorset Arch Soc 78*, 1956, 84.

## Chapter 1: Tombs in an empty land: 4200 – 3500 BC

1. Simmons. I. & Tooley M. (eds). *The Environment in British Prehistory*. New York, 1981.
2. Hutchinson W. *The History of the County of Cumberland, I*. Carlisle, 1794. 7.
3. O'Nuallain S. *JRSAI 102*, 1972, 49–57.
4. Keillar A. & Piggott S. *PPS 6*, 1938, plates 31–2.
5. Hoare I, 86 (Knook 5).
6. Hedges J. W. *Scottish Arch. Review 1*, 1982, 5–20, 144–8.
7. *Catalogue of Antiquities in the Museum . . . at Devizes, II*. 1934, 8–10.
8. Grinsell, 1957.
9. Ashbee P. *Archaeologia 100*, 1966, 1–80.
10. Thurnam, 1869, 184.
11. Renfrew C. (ed). *The Explanation of Culture Change: Models in Prehistory*, London, 1973. 539–58.
12. Thorpe I. J. in: Bradley & Gardiner, 1984. 41–60.
13. Cunnington, 1914, 390.
14. Hoare, I, 100.
15. Hoare, I, 87–8.
16. Lukis W. C. *WAM 8*, 1864, 155.
17. Willis. *Archaeologia 8*, 1787, 88–99.

18 Hoare, I, 45 (Mere 13a); *WAM 26*, 1892, 319.
19 Vatcher F. *PPS 27*, 1961, 160–73.
20 Hoare, I, 206.
21 Vatcher F. *PPS 25*, 1959, 15–51.
22 Thurnam, 1869, 184.
23 Hoare, I, 66; *WAM 52*, 1948, 216–17.
24 *WAM 24*, 107; *ibid*, 116.
25 Thurnam, 1869, 184.
26 Hoare, I, 21.
27 Hoare, I, 123; Thurnam, 1869, 181.
28 Cunnington M. *WAM 45*, 1930, 83.
29 Hoare, I, 21.
30 Ashbee P. *The Earthen Long Barrow in Britain*. London, 1970. 80.
31 Note 12, Thorpe I. J., 49.
32 Marsden B. *The Early Barrow Diggers*. Princes Risborough, 1974. 58.
33 Thurnam, 1869, 194.

## Chapter 2: Homes for the living and the dead: 3500 – 3200 BC

1 Abercromby, Hon. J. A. *A Study of the Bronze Age Pottery of Great Britain and Ireland, I, II*. Oxford, 1912. I, 68.
2 Burgess, 1980, 37.
3 Cunnington M., 1914, 401.
4 Radiocarbon dates for Durrington Walls: 2634±80 bc; 2625±50 bc; 2450±50 bc; 2320±125 bc.
5 Chapman A. 'Neolithic Geometry', 1984. Unpublished typescript.
6 Drewett P. *PPS 43*, 1977, 223.
7 Mercer R. *Hambledon Hill. A Neolithic Landscape*. Edinburgh, 1980.
8 Note 7, 63.
9 Note 5, 21.
10 Thomas N. *WAM 59*, 1964, 1–27.
11 Cunnington M., 1914, 390–1.
12 Pryor F. *Fengate*. Princes Risborough, 1982. 22.
13 Dixon P. *CBA Calendar of Excavations*, 1978. 109.
14 Featherstone D. *The Bowmen of England*. London, 1967. 66.
15 *Antiquity 48*, 1974, 56–8; *PPS 29*, 1963, 50–98. For prehistoric warfare, see: Green H. S. *The Flint Arrowheads of the British Isles*. Oxford, 1980, 132ff.
16 Connell E. S. *Son of the Morning Star*. London, 1985. 310, 348.
17 Note 7, 51.
18 *Popular Archaeology*, October, 1980, 27.
19 Clough T. McK. & Cummins W. (eds) *Stone Axe Studies*. London, 1979.
20 Bradley, 1984, 57.
21 *Antiquity 48*, 1974, 220.
22 Barnatt J. *Prehistoric Cornwall. The Ceremonial Monuments*. Wellingborough, 1982. 51.
23 Note 20, 20.
24 Stukeley, 1723, 75; Stukeley, 1740, 4.
25 Grigson C. *Archaeologia 100*, 1966, 69.
26 Lockyer, 1909, 155.
27 *The Place-Names of Wiltshire*. Cambridge, 1970. 365.
28 Stukeley, 1740, 41.
29 Hoare, I, 165 (Amesbury 56).
30 Stukeley, 1740, 41; Hoare, I, 158.
31 Cunnington M., 1914, 383–4.
32 *Springfield Cursus and the Cursus Problem*. Westcliff-on-Sea, 1981.

33  Stukeley, 1740, 42.
34  Chambers R. A. *PPS 49*, 1983, 394.
35  Note 33, 5.
36  Stone J. F. S. *Arch J 104*, 1948, 7–19.
37  Loveday R. 'Cursuses and related monuments of Great Britain, I, II'.
    Unpublished PhD thesis, Leicester University, 1985. (Un-numbered pages.)
38  Bradley R. *The Dorset Cursus. The Archaeology of the Enigmatic.* Salisbury, 1986. 3.
39  Burl A. *Megalithic Brittany: a Guide.* London, 1985. 157.
40  Megaw J. V. S. & Simpson D. D. A. *Introduction to British Prehistory.* Leicester, 1979. 94–5.
41  Thurnam, 1869, 195.
42  *WAM 31*, 1901, 331.
43  Hoare, I, 54.
44  *WAM 47*, 1935, 267.

## Chapter 3: The first Stonehenge: Stonehenge Ia: 3200 – 2700 BC

1   Petrie, 1880.
2   Hawley, 1923, 20.
3   Hawley, 1924, 35.
4   Hawley, 1926, 3.
5   Musson C. in: (eds) Wainwright G. J. & Longworth I. H. *Durrington Walls: Excavations, 1966–68.* London, 1971. 365, note 1.
6   Note 4, 2.
7   Hawley, 1925, 31.
8   Note 4, 8.
9   Hawley, 1928, 172.
10  Note 4, 15.
11  Kilbride-Jones H. E. *PRIA 53C*, 1950, 311–32.
12  Note 5.
13  Note 5, 366.
14  Coles J. M. & B. J. *From Sweet Track to Glastonbury.* London, 1986. 110.
15  *PPS 37 (1)*, 1971, 124.
16  Atkinson, 1979, 72, 170–1.
17  Note 9, 170.
18  Camden W. *Britannia.* London, 1695. 96.
19  Note 3, 35.
20  Aubrey, I, 93.
21  Stukeley, 1740, 32.
22  *ibid.* 13.
23  Smith, 1771, 58.
24  Note 9, 159.
25  Hoare, I, 14.
26  *ibid*, 150.
27  Long, 1876, 86–7.
28  Webb J. *A Vindication of Stone-Heng Restored.* London, 1725. 11.
29  Jones, 1725, 66.
30  *ibid*, 69.
31  Note 28, 123.
32  Stukeley, 1740, 32.
33  Note 9, 167.
34  Hawley, 1922, 50; Note 3, 31.
35  Note 9, 163.
36  Charrière G. 'Stonehenge: Rythmes Architecturaux et Orientation', *Bull. Soc. Préhistoire Francais*, 1961, 276–9.

37  Newham C. A. *Yorkshire Post*, March, 1963; Hawkins G. S. *Nature 200*, October, 1963, 306–8.
38  Hawkins G. S. *Stonehenge Decoded*. London, 1966. 155.
39  Atkinson R. J. C. 'The Stonehenge Stations', *JHA 7*, 1976, 142–4.

**Chapter 4: Moonlight on Stonehenge: Stonehenge Ia continued**

1  Stukeley, 1740, 75.
2  Hoare, I, 170, and map opposite.
3  Burl A. *Prehistoric Astronomy and Ritual*. Princes Risborough, 1983. 16–20.
4  Brennan M. *The Stars and the Stones*. London, 1983. 134–57.
5  Penny A. & Wood J. E. *Arch J 130*, 1973, 66, 69, 72.
6  Hawley, 1924, 35; *ibid*, 1925, 31.
7  Newham C. A. *The Astronomical Significance of Stonehenge*. Leeds, 1972. 15–17.
8  Heggie, 1981, 202; Atkinson R. J. C. 'Aspects of the astronomy of Stonehenge', in: (ed) Heggie D. C. *Archaeoastronomy in the Old World*. Cambridge, 1982. 107–16, 111; Wood, 1978, 101.
9  *WAM 33*, 1904, 188.
10  Hawley, 1925, 24–5.
11  Atkinson, 1979, 66.
12  Note 10. Wood, 162–3.
13  Burl A. *Antiquity 54*, 1980, 191–200.
14  Stukeley W. *Abury*. London, 1743. 20.
15  *Lindow Man. The Body in the Bog*. London, 1986. 131–3, 167–8, 180.
16  Jones, 1725, 37.
17  Aubrey, I, 74.
18  Hawley, 1923, 18.
19  Note 6, 32–3.
20  Burl A. *Prehistoric Avebury*. London, 1979. 226.
21  Hawley, 1926, 5.
22  Note 3, 32. For plans and descriptions of these splendid circles, see: Thom A., A. S. & Burl A. *Megalithic Rings: Plans and Data for 229 Sites*. Oxford, 1980.
23  Thom A., A. S. & A. S. 'Stonehenge as a possible lunar observatory', *JHA 6*, 1975, 19–30.
24  Ramsay, Sir J. H. *Foundations of England, I*. London, 1898. 34–8; Hutchinson W. *History of the County of Cumberland, I*. Carlisle, 1794. I, 244.
25  Aubrey, I, 95.
26  *WAM 35*, 1908, 317.
27  Smith J., 1771, v.
28  Stukeley, 1723, 112; *ibid*, 1740, 56.
29  Hawkins G. S. *Stonehenge Decoded*. London, 1966. 110; Hoyle F. *On Stonehenge*. London, 1977. 57.
30  Pitts M. W. *Nature 290*, 1981a, 40–1; (*ibid.*) *Archaeoastronomy IV (2)*, 1981b, 16–21; (*ibid.*) *PPS 48*, 1982, 75–132.
31  Aubrey, I, 76.
32  Lukis W. C. *PSAL 7*, 1877, 268–71.
33  Note 30, 1982, 90–3.
34  Note 30, 1981b, 19.
35  Note 8, Wood, 163.
36  Note 7, 16.
37  Burl, 1976, 122.
38  Hoare, I, 143.
39  Hoare, I, 65.
40  Burl A. *Megalithic Brittany: a Guide*. London, 1985. 15.
41  *Gentleman's Library, Archaeology, Part II*. London, 1886. 72.

## Chapter 5: Prestige, pottery and pitfalls: Stonehenge Ib: 2700 – 2200 BC

1 Smith I. F. in: (ed) Renfrew C. *British Prehistory*. London, 1974. 113–14; Burgess, 1980, 37–9.
2 *WAM 46*, 1934, 447.
3 Bradley R. *et al*, in: Bradley & Gardiner, 1984. 98–9.
4 Clarke D. V. *et al*, 1985. 37.
5 Aubrey, I, 76. The suggestion that in 1666 the 'cavities' were untidy pits from which the stones of an outer stone circle had recently been removed is unlikely because Inigo Jones, 40 years before Aubrey, never mentioned such stones.
6 Stukeley, 1723, 94.
7 Hawley, 1921, 30.
8 *Ant J 32*, 1952, 14–20.
9 *Antiquity 3*, 1929, 82.
10 Stone circles: Pitts M. W. *Archaeoastronomy IV (2)*, 1981, 21; timber ring: Cunnington R. H., 1935, 26; smoke: Ivimy J. *The Sphinx and the Megaliths*. London, 1974. 143; ritual pits: Atkinson, 1979, 171–2; eclipses: Hawkins G. S. *Nature 202*, 1964, 1258–61.
11 Stevens F. *Stonehenge Today and Yesterday*. London, 1936. 69–70.
12 Waters F. *The Earp Brothers of Tombstone*. London, 1978. 171; *Tombstone Epitaph*, October 27, 1881.
13 Note 10, Hawkins; Hoyle F. *On Stonehenge*. London, 1977. 79–90.
14 Note 10, Hawkins, 1259.
15 Hawkins G. S. *Stonehenge Decoded*. London, 1966. 140.
16 Brown P. L. *Megaliths, Myths and Man*. London, 1976. 125.
17 Cairnpapple, *PSAS 82*, 1950, 68–123; Llandegai, *Antiquity 62*, 1968, 216–18; Maxey, *Current Archaeology 1*, 1967, 2–4, *Popular Archaeology 3*, 1981, 36–7; Dorchester, *Excavations at Dorchester, Oxon, I*. Oxford, 1951; Maumbury Rings, *Arch J 105*, 1976, 1–97; Stonehenge, Atkinson, 1979.
18 Hoare, I, 83.
19 Burl A. *Prehistoric Avebury*. London, 1979. 126, 196.
20 Hawley, 1928, 170; Atkinson, 1979, 62, fig. 3a.
21 Thom A., A. S. & A. S. 'Stonehenge', *JHA 5 (2)*, 1974, 83.
22 Note 21, 83.
23 Atkinson, 1979, 171.
24 Hawley, 1923, 14.
25 Evans J. *Land Snails in Archaeology*. London, 1972. 103.
26 *WAM 78*, 1983, 13.
27 Note 4, 54–5.
28 Brennan M. *The Stars and the Stones*. London, 1983.
29 Richards C. & Thomas J. in: Bradley & Gardiner, 1984. 189–218.
30 *WAM 52*, 1948, 287–306.
31 *Antiquity 43*, 1969, 310–11.
32 Cleal R. in: Bradley & Gardiner, 1984. 150.
33 Bradley R. in: Bradley & Gardiner, 1984. 65. See also, Thomas J. in the same volume, 169.
34 *Antiquity 10*, 1936, 221. Hawley did not mention their discovery in 'Crater 2'. See: Hawley, 1926, 4.
35 Note 17, Dorchester, 9.
36 Note 17, Dorchester, 126–7.
37 Hawley, 1924, 37.
38 Note 17, Dorchester, 142–4.
39 Hoare, I, 145.
40 Note 24, 17.

41 Note 7, 33; Chippindale, 1983, 193.
42 Note 37, 33; Hawley, 1926, 45.
43 Note 20, 157.
44 Hawley, 1925, 34.
45 Manby T. *Grooved Ware Sites in the North of England.* Oxford, 1974. 98.
46 Hoare, I, 124.
47 Note 44, 33.
48 Hawley, 1926, 2.
49 Note 24, 18.
50 Burl A. *Rites of the Gods.* London, 1981. 77–8.

## Chapter 6: Beakers, burials and bluestones: 2500 – 2200 BC

1 Childe V. G. *Prehistoric Communities of the British Isles.* London, 1940. 91.
2 Hawkes J. & C. *Prehistoric Britain.* London, 1949. 54.
3 *Antiquity 40*, 1966, 180.
4 Lethbridge T. *The Legend of the Sons of God.* London, 1973. 110.
5 Clarke D. *Beaker Pottery of the British Isles, I, II.* Cambridge, 1970. I, 107.
6 Burgess C. & Shennan S. in: (eds) Burgess C. & Miket R. *Settlement and Economy in the Third and Second Millennium BC.* Oxford, 1976. 12.
7 Scott B. G. 'Dancing, Drink or Drugs? Comments on the "Beaker-Cult Package" Hypothesis'. *Irish Archaeological Forum IV (2)*, 1977, 29–34.
8 Bruce M. G. 'The skeletons from the cists', in: Shepherd I. A. G. *Powerful Pots.* Aberdeen, 1986. 17–22. For the Upavon Flying School, see: *WAM 40*, 1917, 8.
9 Wellman P. *Death on the Prairie.* London, 1958. 105–9.
10 Harrison R. *The Beaker Folk.* London, 1980. 154.
11 Fehrenbach T. R. *The Comanches.* London, 1974. 95–6.
12 Greenwell W. *British Barrows.* Oxford, 1877. 227; Shepherd, Note 8, 13; Mortimer J. *Forty Years' Researches. . . .* London, 1905. 164.
13 Burl A. 'Intimations of numeracy in the Neolithic and Bronze Age societies of the British Isles', *Arch J 133*, 1976, 9–32.
14 *WAM 78*, 1983, 7–30.
15 New Statistical Account of Scotland, IV. Edinburgh, 1845. 332.
16 Note 5. I, 84–107.
17 Barton K. G. *Pottery in England from 3500 BC to AD 1700.* Newton Abbot, 1975. 63–7.
18 Downton – *WAM 58*, 1962, 127; Easton Down – *WAM 46*, 1933, 225–42; Snail Down – *WAM 57*, 1958, 6.
19 Stone J. F. S. *Wessex Before the Celts.* London, 1958. 42.
20 *WAM 46*, 1933, 320; *ibid 47*, 1935, 76; Hodges H. *Artifacts.* London, 1964. 148–50.
21 *WAM 46*, 1934, 563–7; *ibid 48*, 1938, 181.
22 *PPS 4*, 1938, 219.
23 *WAM 70/71*, 1978, 28.
24 Hoare, I, 163.
25 Wells C. *Bones, Bodies and Disease.* London, 1964. 148.
26 Note 5, II, 453.
27 Note 10, 40–1, 50, 61, 68.
28 Ucko P. *World Archaeology I (2)*, 1969, 272.
29 *WAM 52*, 1948, 270–1.
30 Taylor J. *Bronze Age Goldwork of the British Isles.* Cambridge, 1980. 23–4, 131.
31 Note 5, I, 95.
32 *Bull. Hist. Metallurgy 7*, 1973, 20.
33 Cannon H. L. 'Botanical prospecting for ore deposits', *Science 132*, 1960, 591–8.
34 Cunnington M. *Woodhenge.* Devizes, 1929; *Antiquity 1*, 1927, 92–5.

35  Thom A., A. S. & Burl A. *Megalithic Rings, Plans & Data for 229 Sites.* Oxford, 1980. 130–1.
36  Note 34, 6.
37  Note 13, 29.
38  Thom, 1967, 73.
39  Burl A. 'Stone circles: the Welsh problem', *CBA Report 35*, 1985, 72–82.
40  Note 34, 9–13; Note 35, 130–1.
41  Thomas N. 'A Neolithic chalk cup from Wilsford . . .' *WAM 54*, 1952, 452–63.
42  *PPS 38*, 1962, 231.
43  Thomas J. in: Bradley & Gardiner, 1984. 168.

## Chapter 7: 'Not far from Naas . . .': 2200 – 2000 BC

1  Wainwright G. J. *Mount Pleasant, Dorset: Excavations, 1970–1.* London, 1979. 224–47.
2  Atkinson, 1979, 176.
3  Jones, 1725, 23.
4  Stukeley, 1740, 30.
5  Thomas H. H. *Ant J 23*, 1923, 236–60.
6  Geoffrey of Monmouth [AD 1138] *The History of the Kings of Britain.* Harmondsworth, 1966. Book VIII, 12; Burl A. 'Geoffrey of Monmouth and the Stonehenge bluestones', *WAM 79*, 1985, 178–83.
7  Stone, 1924, 65.
8  *Antiquity 15*, 1941, 319.
9  Howard H. *PPS 48*, 1982, 104–24; G. A. Kellaway, 'Glaciation and the stones of Stonehenge', *Nature 233*, 1971, 30–5, suggested that glaciation had brought the bluestones and sarsens to the Stonehenge area.
10  Judd W. *WAM 33*, 1903, 47–64.
11  Burl, 1976, 408.
12  Hoare, I, 129; Gerald of Wales [AD 1187] *The History and Topography of Ireland.* Harmondsworth, 1982. Part II, 51.
13  Note 6, Geoffrey of Monmouth, 198.
14  Note 9. Howard, 117.
15  Daniel G, *Antiquity 56*, 1982, 64.
16  Note 9. Kellaway, 33.
17  *WAM 21*, 1884, 142.
18  Stukeley, 1740, 12.
19  Atkinson R. J. C. 'Aspects of the astronomy of Stonehenge', in: (ed) Heggie D. C. *Archaeoastronomy in the Old World.* Cambridge, 1982. 107–16.
20  Note 2, 113.
21  Pitts M. *PPS 48*, 1982, 126–9.
22  Mercer R. *PSAS 111*, 1981, 63–171.
23  Hawley, 1928, 172–3; Atkinson, 1979, 204–6.
24  Note 2, 205.
25  Note 11, 309–10.
26  Wood, 1747, 40, 57; Stukeley, 1740, 5.
27  Aubrey, I, 95; *WAM 11*, 1869, 395; Aubrey, I, 93; *WAM 46*, 1933, 395–7.
28  Hawley, 1924, 30.
29  Thom A., A. S. & A. S. 'Stonehenge', *JHA 5 (2)*, 1974, 84.
30  Note 19, 112. See also: Atkinson R. J. C. 'Some new measurements at Stonehenge', *Nature 275*, 1978, 50–2.
31  Note 18, 56.
32  Stukeley, 1723, 59; Note 18, 35.
33  Gale, in: *PSAL 7*, 1877, 268–71; Note 21, 90–1.
34  Jones, 1725, 37; Aubrey, I, 76, 96.

35   Note 11, 262–3.
36   Hoare, I, 157.
37   Stone E. H. 'Stonehenge: Concerning the Four Stations'. *Nature*, 1923, 220.
38   Note 30. Atkinson, 51.
39   Hawley, 1923, 14–15.
40   Stukeley, 1740, 14; Wood, 1747, 44; Smith, 1771, 52.
41   Note 29, 84; Note 2, 80.
42   Duke, 1846, 142–6.
43   Petrie, 1880, 21.
44   Lockyer, 1909, 93; Trotter A. P. 'Stonehenge as an astronomical instrument', *Antiquity 1*, 1927, 53.
45   Newham C. A. *The Astronomical Significance of Stonehenge*. Leeds, 1972; Vatcher L. & F. 'Excavation of three post-holes in Stonehenge car park', *WAM 68*, 1973, 57–63; Burl A. *Rings of Stone*. London, 1979. 65.
46   Hawkins G. S. *Stonehenge Decoded*. London, 1966. 108, 111, 172.
47   Dibble W. E. *JHA 7*, 1976, 141–2.
48   Note 30. Atkinson, 50–2.
49   Thatcher A. R. 'The Station Stones at Stonehenge', *Antiquity 50*, 1976, 144–5.
50   Grinsell L. V. *The Archaeology of Exmoor*. Newton Abbot, 1970. 44–5.
51   Whybrow C. *Antiquary's Exmoor*. Dulverton, 1970. 13.
52   Lewis A. L. *J. Anthr. Inst. 25*, 1886, 13.
53   *Current Anthropology 14*, 1973, 450–4.
54   Burl A. *Megalithic Brittany: a Guide*. London, 1985. 133.
55   Matthiessen P. *Indian Country*. London, 1985.

## Chapter 8: Early chieftains in a landscape: 2000 – 1500 BC

1   Clarke D. *Beaker Pottery of Great Britain & Ireland, I, II*. Cambridge, 1970. I, 227.
2   Ashbee P. *The Earthen Long Barrow in Britain*. London, 1970. 101–3.
3   Stukeley, 1723, 89.
4   Smith, 1771, 20.
5   Hoare, I, 205.
6   Note 3, 89.
7   *WAM 10*, 1867, 86.
8   Note 5, 202–5.
9   Cunnington R. H. *From Antiquary to Archaeologist*. Princes Risborough, 1975. 130.
10   *Antiquity 45*, 1971, 12.
11   Taylor J. *Bronze Age Goldwork of the British Isles*. Cambridge, 1980. 45–50.
12   Note 5, 202.
13   Clarke *et al*, 1985, 128–40.
14   Briard J. in: *France Before the Romans*. London, 1974. 136. See also: *Protohistoire de la Bretagne*. Rennes, 1972. Ch. 2. 'Les Temps des Tumulus', 59–107.
15   Note 11, 25.
16   de Valera R. & O'Nuallain S. *Survey of the Chambered Tombs of Ireland, IV*. Dublin, 1982. 119 and Fig. 43.
17   Ucko P. *World Archaeology 1*, 1969, 262–80.
18   Grinsell, 1978, 18–23.
19   Roe F. in (eds) Coles J. M. & Simpson D. D. A. *Studies in Ancient Europe*. Leicester, 1968. 168.
20   Grinsell L. V. 'Disc-barrows', *PPS 40*, 1974, 79–93.
21   Hoare, I, 164.
22   Bakker J. A. *Antiquity 53*, 1979, 107–11; Atkinson, 1979, 43–4; Chippindale, 1983, 33–5.
23   Stukeley, 1723, 165.
24   Grimes W. F. *Bull. Inst. Arch. 4*, 1964, 89–121.

25 Hoare, I, 239.
26 Johnston D. E. *WAM 72/3*, 1978, 29–50.
27 Antlers – Amesbury 4 and 15, Lake, Wilsford S 1, Winterbourne Stoke 56, all in Hoare, I, 127, 205–6, 211, 206, 115; Fovant I – *WAM 44*, 1928, 102. Chaldon Herring 6d, 6e – Grinsell L. V. *Dorset Barrows*. Dorchester, 1959. 98.
28 Amesbury 22 – Hoare, I, 199; Huish Idmiston 25e – *WAM 33*, 1904, 410–4.
29 Bulford 27 – *WAM 36*, 1910, 616–17; Litton Cheney 3 – Note 27, Grinsell, 117; Collingbourne Ducis 9 – *WAM 10*, 1867, 85–103; Boyton Down – Hoare, I, 101.
30 Zulu huts – Binns C. T. *The Warrior People*. London, 1975. 146; Morris D. R. *The Washing of the Spears*. London, 1966. 31. Zulu sanitation. Ritter E. A. *Shaka Zulu*. Harmondsworth, 1978. 239–40.
31 Ashbee P. & ApSimon A. *WAM 55*, 1954, 326–9.
32 Hoare, I, 113–14.
33 Glob P. *The Mound People*. London, 1974. See also: Burgess, 1980, 180–92.
34 Stukeley, 1740, 46.
35 Megaw J. V. S. 'Penny whistles and prehistory', *Antiquity 34*, 1960, 9–10.
36 Hoare, I, 42.
37 Note 30. Binns, 149.
38 Hoare, I, 76.
39 Piggott S. *WAM 58*, 1962, 96.
40 Kendrick T. D. *The Druids*. London, 1927. 125.
41 Gristhorpe – Williamson W. C. *Description of the Tumulus opened at Gristhorpe near Scarborough*. Scarborough, 1872. 15; Oban – *PSAS 13*, 1879, 336; Winterbourne Stoke – Hoare, I, 122.
42 Hoare, I, 212.
43 Amesbury 101 – *WAM 49*, 1940, 238; Hunter's Barrow – Hoare, I, 184.
44 Cunnington. 'A Bronze Age barrow at Manton . . .' *WAM 35*, 1908, 1–20.
45 Hoare, I, 201; Stukeley, 1740, 44–5 and Tab. XXXII.
46 Note 11, 46.

## Chapter 9: House of the Dead: Stonehenge IIIa: 2000 – 1600 BC

1 Sarsens – Brentnall H. C. *WAM 51*, 1946, 419–39; Barron R. S. *The Geology of Wiltshire*, Bradford-on-Avon, 1976. Sasans – Singh P. *Burial Practices in Ancient India*. Varanasi, 1970. 104, 153–4.
2 Aubrey, I, 91.
3 Atkinson, 1979, 114–15, 116–22; Coles J. *Archaeology by Experiment*. London, 1973. 88.
4 Note 3, Atkinson, 118; Garfitt J. E. 'Moving the stones to Stonehenge', *Antiquity 53*, 1979, 190–4.
5 Gowland W. 'Recent Excavations at Stonehenge', *WAM 33*, 1903, 1–62. 3.
6 *WAM 42*, 1924, 593–4.
7 Stone, 1924, 4–7, 87; Note 3, Atkinson, 122–9.
8 Startin W. & Bradley R in: *Astronomy and Society in Britain during the Period 4000–1500 BC*. Oxford, 1981. 292–4.
9 Pitts M. W. *PPS 48*, 1982, 97–104.
10 Stone, 1924, 104–8; Atkinson R. J. C. 'Neolithic engineering', *Antiquity 35*, 1961, 298.
11 Pakistan – *Antiquity 53*, 1977, 143–4; Note 3, Atkinson, 134–9.
12 Atkinson, 1979, 207.
13 Stukeley, 1740, 17.
14 *Ibid*, 15.
15 *Ibid*, 6, 15.
16 Wood, 1747, 35.
17 Note 2, 75.

18  Petrie, 1880.
19  Mann L. *Craftsmen's Measures in Prehistoric Times*. London, 1930; 'A forgotten researcher: Ludovic McClellan Mann'. *Institute of Geomantic Research. Occasional Paper 7*, 1977. 4.
20  Thom A., A. S. & A. S. 'Stonehenge', *JHA 5*, 1974, 179–80.
21  Jones, 1725, 37, 42.
22  Note 2, 75.
23  Note 13, 22.
24  Note 20, 80–1.
25  Note 5, figs. 5 and 7.
26  Note 13, Tab XI, pp 20, 24.
27  Note 18, 6, 12.
28  Atkinson R. J. C. *Stonehenge Viewpoint*, June, 1986. 2.
29  Note 13, 25.
30  Note 13, 28; Long, 1876, 62; Harrison, 1901, 17.
31  Note 12, 43–7.
32  Note 12, 31–2.
33  *WAM 47*, 1936, 530–1; *WAM 9*, 1866, 268–74; Edington – *WAM 51*, 1946, 379.
34  Note 12, 31–2.
35  Webb, 1725, 16.
36  Hoare, I, 144; Long, 1876, 56–7.
37  Hawley, 1921, 34.
38  Jones, 1725, 38; Webb, 1725, 141; Aubrey, I, 80; Stukeley, 1740, 33.
39  Barclay, 1895, 75.
40  *Nature 263*, 1976, 465–9.
41  Newham C. A. *The Astronomical Significance of Stonehenge*. Leeds, 1972. 29.
42  Brennan M. *The Stars and the Stones*. London, 1983. 144, 190.
43  Smith, 1771, 65.
44  Lockyer, 1909, 41.
45  Hawkins G. S. 'Stonehenge decoded', *Nature 200*, 1963, 306–8; *Stonehenge Decoded*. London, 1966. 110, 116.
46  Hoyle F. *On Stonehenge*. London, 1977. 74–6.
47  Wood, E. S., 1978, 174.
48  Heggie, 1981, 200.
49  Note 45, 117.
50  Newall R. S. *Stonehenge*. London, 1955 (2nd edition). 15.

## Chapter 10: To the bleak midwinter: Stonehenge IIIc: 1650 – 1250 BC

1  *PPS 7*, 1941, 114–33.
2  *Trans. Bristol & Gloucs Arch Soc 91*, 1972, 14–17.
3  Stukeley, 1740, 46; Hoare, I, 127; Grinsell, 1957, 200; *WAM 36*, 1910, 618–20.
4  *WAM 56*, 1955, 137–9; Hoare, I, 183.
5  *WAM 58*, 1958, 7; Hoare, I, 183.
6  *WAM 45*, 1932, 432–58.
7  *WAM 36*, 1910, 621–2.
8  Hoare, I, 181–2.
9  Greenwell W. *British Barrows*. Oxford, 1877. 93.
10  Note 8, 76–7.
11  *WAM 46*, 1933, 218–24.
12  *WAM 56*, 1955, 134; Sir Cyril Fox. *Life and Death in the Bronze Age*. London, 1959. 122.
13  Hawley, 1925, 26f, 38–50; Atkinson, 1979, 33–6, 80–4.
14  I am grateful to Peter Berridge for the information about the pottery in the Y and Z Holes and in the centre of Stonehenge.

15 Atkinson, 1979, 84.
16 Note 15, 212.
17 *PPS 50*, 1984, 197–216.
18 (Ed. Aveni A.) *Archaeoastronomy in the New World*. Cambridge, 1982. 38.
19 Chambered tombs with kindred motifs include Gavr'inis where they occupy the top of the sixth stone on the left of the passage; Mané Kerioned East; Mané Lud; Mougau-Bihan, and Poulguen.
20 *PSAS 8*, 1870, 380.
21 *PSAS 65*, 1931, 269–75.
22 Burl A. *Rites of the Gods*. London, 1981. 164–5.
23 *Ant J 19*, 1939, 291–9.
24 le Rouzic Z. *Les Cromlechs de Er-Lannic*. Vannes, 1931. 12.
25 Fahy E. *JCHAS 64*, 1959, 1–27, 4–5.
26 Note 15, 206; Hoare, I, 150; Cunnington R.H. *From Antiquary to Archaeologist*, Princes Risborough, 1975. 39.
27 Burl, 1976, 124–5, 205–8.
28 Jones, 1725, 49–50.
29 Daniel G. *The Prehistoric Chamber Tombs of France*. London, 1960. 167; Cles-Reden S. *The Realm of the Great Goddess*. London, 1961. 222–3.
30 Stover L. E. & Kraig B. *Stonehenge: the Indo-European Heritage*. Chicago, 1978. 174.
31 *PPS 50*, 1984, 151–96.
32 Tossen-Keler – *L'Anthropologie 72*, 1968, 5–40; Kergonan – Minot R. S. *Les Monuments Mégalithiques de l'île aux Moines*. Le Havre, n.d. 26–7. For Breton 'horseshoes', see: Burl A. *Megalithic Brittany: a Guide*, London, 1985.
33 *PPS 37*, 1971, 1–15.
34 Burl A. *Prehistoric Astronomy and Ritual*. Princes Risborough, 1983. 42–3.
35 Ruggles C. L. N. & Burl H. A. W. *JHA 16*, 1985, 25–59. 52–56.
36 Abercromby, Hon. J. *A Study of the Bronze Age Pottery of Great Britain and Ireland, II*. Oxford, 1912. 95.
37 Gelling P. & Davidson H. *The Chariot of the Sun*. London, 1969. 28, 30, 57; Anati E. *Camonica Valley*. London, 1965. 32ff.
38 Kendrick, T. *The Druids*. London, 1927. 82.
39 Green, Miranda. *The Gods of the Celts*. Gloucester, 1986. 20, 27–8.
40 *Antiquity 60*, 1986, 199–208.
41 Note 38, 84.
42 Piggott S. *Ancient Europe*. Edinburgh, 1965. 234–5.

## Chapter 11: Eternal rings of light: Stonehenge IV: 1250 – 500 BC

1 Aubrey, I, 293.
2 Hoare, I, 160.
3 Burgess, 1980, 131.
4 *Berks, Bucks & Oxon Arch J 8*, 1902, 31.
5 *WAM 52*, 1957, 126–7; *Trans Devon Arch Soc 36*, 1978, 104.
6 *WAM 58*, 1963, 378.
7 Hoare, I, 126.
8 Hoare, I, 128.
9 Note 3, 131, 351.
10 *WAM 68*, 1973, 42–56.
11 Burgess C. 'Population, Climate and Upland Settlement', in: *British Archaeological Reports, no. 143*, Oxford, 1985. 213.
12 Aubrey, I, 92; Stukeley, 1740, 31.
13 Antrobus, Lady. *A Sentimental and Practical Guide to Amesbury and Stonehenge*. Amesbury, 1900. 19.

# Index

Main entries appear in **Bold**. *Illustrations are Italicised.*